The Power of Pride

The POWER of

Stylemakers and Rulebreakers of the Harlem Renaissance

CAROLE MARKS

AND

DIANA EDKINS

CROWN PUBLISHERS, INC.
NEW YORK

PRIDE

Josephine Baker

Walter White

Zora Neale Hurston

A'Lelia Walker

James Weldon Johnson

Ethel Waters

Louis Armstrong

Bessie Smith

Alberta Hunter

Jessie Fauset

Nella Larsen

Florence Mills

Duke Ellington

Bill "Bojangles" Robinson

Carl Van Vechten

Langston Hughes

Dorothy West

Endpapers: Night-Club Map of Harlem by E. Simms Campbell, 1932

Published by Crown Publishers, Inc., 201 East 50th Street, New York, New York 10022. Member of the Crown Publishing Group.

Random House, Inc. New York, Toronto, London, Sydney, Auckland
www.randomhouse.com

CROWN is a trademark and the Crown colophon is a registered trademark of Random House, Inc.

Printed in China

Design by Lauren Dong

Library of Congress Cataloging-in-Publication Data
Marks, Carole.
  The power of pride : stylemakers and rule breakers of the Harlem Renaissance / Carole Marks and Diana Edkins. — 1st ed.   Includes index.
    1. Afro-Americans—Intellectual life—20th century—Sources. 2. Harlem Renaissance.
3. Afro-American arts—History—20th century—Sources. 4. Afro-American intellectuals—Biography. 5. Afro-American artists—Biography. 6. Afro-American authors—Biography.
7. Harlem (New York, N.Y.)—Intellectual life—Sources. 8. New York (N.Y.)—Intellectual life—Sources. I. Edkins, Diana. II. Title.
E185.6.M35   1999
947.7'100496073'00922—dc21   98-31259
                                                              CIP

ISBN 0-609-60096-6

10 9 8 7 6 5 4 3 2 1

First Edition

Cris Albertson   James Allen   Jervis Anderson   Houston Baker   Jean-Claude Baker   Junius Banks   Amiri Baraka   Sandra Baynes   Sidney Bechet   Lerone Bennett   Eubie Blake   Charles Blockson   Donald Bogle   Robert Bone   Florence Bonner   Arna Bontemps   Tamara Bracker Bricktop   Sterling Brown   A'Lelia Bundles   Hazel Carby   James Collier   Matthew Countryman Edmund David Cronon   Harold Cruse   Nancy Cunard   Thadious Davis   James DeJongh   Ann Douglas   Frank Driggs   Martin Duberman   Gerald Early   Robert Fleming   Kenneth Gains Henry Louis Gates   Paula Giddings   Lynn Haney   Sharon Harley   Daphne Duval Harrison James Haskins   Robert Hemenway   Michele Hilmes   Darlene Clark Hine   Anne Hollander bell hooks   Nathan Huggins   Gloria Hull   Fannie Hurst   George Hutchinson   Derek Jewell Bruce Kellner   Amy Kirschke   Charles Larson   Eugene Levy   David Levering Lewis

THIS BOOK IS DEDICATED TO THE SCHOLARS, WRITERS, RESEARCHERS, AND IMPORTANT PEOPLE WHO KEPT THE RENAISSANCE ALIVE. SPECIAL THANKS AND APPRECIATION GO TO OUR AGENT, JANIS A. DONNAUD.

Alan Lomax   Manning Marable   René Marks   Angie Marsh   Helen Marvill   Deborah McDowell   Nallie McKay   Nickolas Muray   Charles Nichols   Gilbert Osofsky   Margaret Perry   Ruth Perry   Claudia Roth Pierpoint   Mike Pinfold   Richard Powell   Betty Prashker Arnold Rampersad   Ruth Elizabeth Randolph   Renate and Tjark Reiss   Philip Richardson Elizabeth Campbell Rollins   Phyllis Rose   Loraine Elena Roses   Mabel Rowland   Addison Scurlock   David Singer   Amritjit Singh   Monica Smith   Morgan and Marvin Smith   Allan Spear   Hortense J. Spillers   Robert Stepto   Grace Sullivan   Leon Sullivan   Carolyn Sylvander Wilbert Tatum   Frank Taylor   Rosalyn Terborg-Penn   Joe Trotter   William Tuttle   Bruce Tyler   Doris Ulmann   Donna Mussenden VanDerZee   Eleonore van Notten   Edward Waldron Alice Walker   Cheryl Wall   Mary Helen Washington   Steven Watson   Dorothy West   Joel Williamson   Deborah Willis   Oprah Winfrey   Cary Winz

CONTENTS

ACKNOWLEDGMENTS

Margaret Andersen, University of Delaware; Don Bowden, Wide World Photos; Beverly Brannon, Library of Congress; Ole Brask; Gail Brittingham, University of Delaware; Brian L. Bruening, Department of Special Collections, Boston University; A'Lelia Bundles; Henri Bureau, Roger-Viollet; Robert E. Colely, Special Collections Library, Millersville University; Mary Corliss, Film Stills Department, the Museum of Modern Art; Betsy Corsiglia, *The Vineyard Times;* Maria Elena Rico Covarrubias; Paul Crater, Robert W. Woodruff Library, Atlanta University; Norman Curry, Corbis-Bettmann; Liza Daum, Département des Photographies, Bibliothèque de Nationale de la Ville de Paris; Keith de Lellis; Joyce Dewsbury, Department of Special Collections, University of Florida Libraries; Janis A. Donnaud; Frank Driggs; Jo Ellen Elbaschir, Moorland-Spingarn Research Center, Howard University; Elaine Engst, Rare Book and Manuscript Collections, Cornell University; Kevin Glick, the Beinecke Rare Book and Manuscript Library, Yale University Library; Marie Helène Gold, the Arthur and Elizabeth Schlesinger Library on the History of Women in America, Radcliffe College; Kevin Grogan, Fisk University; Jennifer Gyn; Homer Hall, Westfield Historical Society; Elizabeth Higginbotham, University of Delaware; Chester Higgins; Carol Johnson, Library of Congress; Howard Johnson, University of Delaware; Bruce Kellner; Janis Madhu, the George Eastman House; Terence Pepper, National Portrait Gallery, London; Ford Petrus, Library of Congress; Richard Pitkin, *Illustrated London News;* Renate and Tjark Reiss; Allen Rueben, Culver Pictures; Elizabeth Campbell Rollins; Scott Schwartz, the Duke Ellington Archive, the Smithsonian Institution; Dolores Sheen, the Sheenway School; Lynn Slawson; Esther Smith, Institute of Jazz Studies, Rutgers University, Newark; Monica Smith; Brenda Square, the Amistad Research Center; Carla M. Summers, Department of Special Collections, University of Florida Libraries; Lynn Surry, Margo Feiden Galleries, Ltd.; Cathy Cesario Tardosky, Sygma; Antony M. Toussaint, Schomburg Center for Research in Black Culture; Donna Mussenden VanDerZee; Donna Wells, Moorland-Spingarn Research Center, Howard University; Alma D. Williams, Hogan Jazz Archive; S. J. Williams, Agence France-Presse.

FOREWORD

In jazz, art, literature, or even boxing the men and women who can reinvent their identity right before your eyes—compel you to see them differently, in a new and better light—are the geniuses. So it is with a race of people as they emerge from oppression and seek to reinvent their image by rekindling their crushed humanity.

In the early twentieth century large numbers of African Americans with genius began to express their spirit, their songs, their stories, their sexuality, anger, and joy, forcing a new view of their American experience. It was a renaissance of the human spirit that crystallized as black Americans moved away from the rural plantations of the south to the big cities—especially those to the north—and found white and black audiences fascinated by a new view of American life from the black perspective. This amazing experience is called the Harlem Renaissance.

In *The Power of Pride*, Carole Marks and Diana Edkins take readers inside the artists at the heart of the Renaissance. Here are the people who made the music, the dance, and the stories. Their art stands as a landmark in American life. But their lives were as interesting as their art. Lacking any role model, and absent any wealth to supply them the time or the canvas necessary for art, these artists had to find patrons and psychic space in which to express themselves. And they had to defy all of the cultural stereotypes that weighed on them as children of slaves, people put down in the official U.S. culture of the period as lacking in intellect, beauty, glamor, or sense of art.

Most often the story of this dynamic period is told only through the works of its prominent artists—a Langston Hughes or a Josephine Baker. But in *The Power of Pride*, Marks and Edkins bring the whole era to life by telling the stories of more than a dozen key figures in the Renaissance.

Those lives are works of art as fascinating as any of their staged or written performances. Readers will be fascinated to learn about the power of creating yourself as it was done by these young black people nearly a hundred years ago. This book serves as a wonderful introduction and context for the works of Renaissance artists. And from the historical perspective, it goes beyond the art to supply the political and racial pressures, in both the black and white worlds, that led to this moment of critical mass of artistic expression.

Here is the map for all who dare enjoy the cultural explosion that comes when a formerly enslaved people dance, sing, and write in a new fashion—when they begin to express their humanity.

JUAN WILLIAMS

INTRODUCTION

A T THE AGE OF FIFTEEN, BLUES singer Alberta Hunter left her home in Memphis, Tennessee, and journeyed to foreign territory on the South Side of Chicago. She had hoped to find greater economic opportunity, but like so many migrants, she found herself, and her roots, instead. It was 1910 and the Great Migration, the first mass exodus of blacks from the South, was beginning. By the end of the teens over 450,000 would move north. Many, like Alberta Hunter, were awakened to a new understanding of the meaning of being black in America.

From these modest beginnings the New Negro Renaissance was born. Mainly based in the 1920s, this artistic and literary movement used African-American culture as its subject matter. Alain Locke, Howard University philosophy professor and a Renaissance figure, explained that "for generations, in the mind of America, the Negro had been more of a formula than a human being—a *something* to be argued about, condemned, or defended." That was about to change as the Renaissance figures forced America to confront the central question: What place does race have in the formation of American identity? The artists, writers, poets, and musicians of the movement found diverse answers, but their work shared a common thread. Their intent, as writer Ralph Elli-

son had articulated it, was "to arouse the troubling suspicion that whatever else the true American is, he is also somehow black."

The Power of Pride features seventeen (sixteen black and one white) of the most prominent men and women of the New Negro Renaissance, artist-migrants who hungered to "arouse the troubling suspicion." Alternately irreverent, racy, and painfully honest, they were unique: risk-takers in dangerous times, sophisticated *salonières* in an age of bourgeois provincialism, and experimenters who briefly managed to transcend race by immersing themselves in it. They wrote and sang and played about "race matters," attempting to discover, examine, and explore the subject—within themselves, between black and white, everywhere and anywhere.

Of primary significance is their attempt to reveal to a white audience the experience of being black in this time and place, an effort that required them, first, to understand it themselves. For years, negative images of black people were depicted in every aspect of American life. Polite, restrained protests about these images were made by older black leaders. After the First World War, the young increasingly challenged both the portraits and the method of response.

Theirs was an awesome task attempted at a

time when an overwhelming majority of white Americans believed that blacks were sub-human, when a black man could be lynched for merely looking at a white woman, and when the only occupational choice for most black women was work in someone else's kitchen. The seventeen men and women in this book were not timid or complacent; at times they were positively heroic. Walter White, assistant secretary of the fledgling National Association for the Advancement of Colored People, traveled through the South passing as white to investigate lynchings. Louis Armstrong, the great jazz trumpeter, transformed an Andy Razaf and Fats Waller song about skin color into what was hailed as the first protest lament: "My only sin is in my skin. Why am I so black and blue?" And hair-care heiress A'Lelia Walker marched into the Cotton Club in Harlem and dared the mob-dominated managers to enforce their white-patrons-only policy. They did not.

But though sometimes serious, our Renaissance figures were rarely strident. Life had much to offer them, they felt, and there was little time for anger or despair. "Lightly, slightly and politely" was their mantra. "It was characteristic of the Jazz Age," F. Scott Fitzgerald remarked, "that it had no interest in politics at all." Gaiety and good feeling were recurring themes that seemed to mark both their travels and the age. "It was a period when every season there was at least one hit play on Broadway acted by a Negro cast," recalled Langston Hughes. "And when books by Negro authors were being published with much greater frequency and much more publicity than ever before or since."

Migration was a significant backdrop to the Renaissance. The physical movement out of the familiar was the catalyst that sparked the journey toward self-discovery. Throngs of country folk left rural backwaters and a significant number of educated middle-class blacks sought greater opportunity in the less segregated North. Their passage out of the South inspired them to give voice to complex emotions and strategies. "It was a *decision* Negroes made to leave the South," asserts contemporary poet Imamu Amiri Baraka (Leroi Jones), "not an historical imperative."

The migration created a critical mass—a cadre of young, innocent, eager, in some cases well-educated, and in many cases extraordinarily talented black Americans descending on an urban white America that had never seen anything like them before. Blacks migrated out of Florida and Georgia and Louisiana and Missouri and even Utah. They strutted and danced and sang the blues and insisted they knew the way. The white intelligentsia, tired of war, tired of provincialism, tired of conventionality, welcomed them with open arms. As Carl Van Doren, editor of *Century Magazine*, observed in 1924, "What American literature decidedly needs at this moment is color, music, gusto, the free expression of gay or desperate moods. If the Negroes are not in a position to contribute these items, I do not know what Americans are."

Most of the Renaissance figures came of age during the 1920s and were instantly drawn into a New York literary scene that was also searching for its roots and its identity. America was "a country settled by the people of all nations," wrote Van Wyck Brooks in *America Coming of Age*. The weakness of American literature, he said, was its reliance on "hegemonic Puritan and pioneer traditions" to the exclusion of all the rest. Others argued that a society that ruled the world economically must surely have made some unique cultural contribution, if only it could be found. "Do you suppose Christopher Columbus would have taken all that trouble just to go to the opera with the Selfridge Merrys," a character in Edith Wharton's 1920 novel, *The Age of Innocence*, asked. Searching for the authentic America was a favorite pastime. Creating an atmosphere of invention was a major result. Cultural critic Ann Douglas, author of *Terrible Honesty*, lists some of those firsts.

> *This generation was the first in American history to make, buy, and fit into ready-made, exact-sized (rather than "stock-sized") clothing. Its members patented Victrolas, cameras, microphones, radios, and talking pictures and initiated IQ tests, sex education, birth control clinics, opinion polls, consumer organizations, and syndicated gossip columns. Aiming to leave little to the imagination, they found out more about themselves, how they looked, how they sounded, what they wore, what they said and did, with whom, where, and why, than any previous generation had ever done, and they made of self-knowledge a fad and an industry.*

The gravitation toward the African-American community was logical but not planned. The death and destruction of the First World War inspired a search for new beginnings and new meanings. A sensibility emerged among the intelligentsia that rejected the traditional, the classic, and the familiar. Turn everything on its head, they reasoned. Black is better than white. Primitives are superior to the civilized. Blacks are passionate and delightful primitives. Even before the war, Freud, who was fashionable in the United States, had contributed to this perception. "Civilized and hypocritical camouflages come and go," he wrote. "But the primitive mind they seek to disguise is imperishable." Some years later James Baldwin would expand upon this major Renaissance theme when he wrote, "The only way [the white man] can be released from the Negro's tyrannical power over him is to consent, in effect, to become black himself, to become a part of that suffering and dancing country that he now watches wistfully from the heights of his lonely power and, armed with spiritual traveler's checks, visits surreptitiously after dark."

Though they did not orchestrate it, the educated elite and the truly talented tenth of the African-American population were eager to seize the moment. For years they had been hoping for a place, for recognition. Some, like Harvard-trained W. E. B. Du Bois and Alain Locke, thought the future of the race depended on the doctors, lawyers, scientists, writers, poets, and actors, whose example would break down the barriers for others. The traditional elite, historian Nathan Huggins believed, saw "art and letters as a bridge across the chasm between the races." Locke and Du Bois opened the door, and the New Negro rushed past them.

The newcomers' stories are more compelling than most biographies. Renaissance writer Arna Bontemps recalled that "suddenly stars started falling on a part of Manhattan that white residents had begun abandoning to black newcomers." They left an enduring legacy.

The women in our collection were especially interested in finding a new place. Because of the discrimination of the broader society and convention within their own communities, they had been forced to live "half in shadow." During the Renaissance, they operated from key positions of power. Jessie Fauset was the literary editor of *Crisis*, the movement's most influential journal. Zora Neale Hurston, who somehow managed to grow ten years younger as she traveled north, was considered one of the important leaders of the younger group. Nella Larsen wrote two of the most acclaimed novels of the era and was the first African-American woman to receive a Guggenheim Fellowship. Even before the jazzmen took center stage, the female blues singers were the most popular and highly paid black entertainers.

But the women's private lives confounded their public successes. All were married at least once—but few happily. All were childless and saw that fact as a great weakness. Four—Bessie Smith, Ethel Waters, A'Lelia Walker, and Josephine Baker—attempted to compensate by adopting children, three with disastrous results. Almost all loved other women but refused to admit it for fear, it would appear, not of what others thought but of what it said about them. "There's two things got me puzzled, there's two things I don't understand; that's a mannish-acting woman, and a skipping, twistin' woman-acting man," complained Bessie Smith.

Their songs about the troubles in their lives were often met with polite dismissal or, at worst, with charges of disloyalty to the race. The "colored" woman "is confronted by both a woman question and a race problem," writer Anna Julia Cooper pointed out as early as 1904. Instead of improving during the Renaissance, the position of the "colored woman" became more difficult as racial politics overshadowed feminist concerns. Richard Wright, the foremost African-American writer of the 1930s, wrote in reviewing Hurston's novel *Their Eyes Were Watching God:* "no theme, no message, no thought." Jessie Fauset observed in her 1928 novel, *Plum Bun,* "Men had a better time of it than women, white men than white women, colored men than colored women."

Still, the question remains, why write another book about one of the most studied periods of modern literary history? We do not offer a scholarly book about the epoch. There have been many brilliant ones: *The Harlem Renaissance* by Nathan Huggins, David Levering Lewis's *When Harlem Was in Vogue,* Ann Douglas's *Terrible Honesty,* and *The Life of Langston Hughes* by Arnold Rampersad, to name but a few. We have relied extensively on them and encourage readers hungry for more to consider the sources. We have also worked in an extended framework beginning nearly a decade before *Opportunity* magazine's awards dinner, when many people say the Renaissance began,

and ending in the late thirties, some years after the death of hair-care heiress A'Lelia Walker (Langston Hughes's end) or the death of writer Wallace Thurman (Dorothy West's end). We have virtually ignored, for different reasons, three of the bright lights of the Renaissance: Jean Toomer, Countee Cullen, and Alain Locke. We mention Toomer, whose novel *Cane* is arguably the finest literary piece of the period, only in passing because Toomer viewed the Renaissance as "something that had no special meaning for me." We discuss but do not provide a center stage for Cullen and Locke ("eloquent and elegant booster") because we believe theirs were best supporting parts and not starring roles.

Why pick the seventeen we did? We could say simply that the women and men of our collection were something special; they were the strivers—the dicty—who could not be categorized. The writers like Langston Hughes, Jessie Fauset, and Zora Neale Hurston published in the finest literary journals: the *American Mercury,* the *Century,* the *Saturday Review of Literature.* The statesmen, like James Weldon Johnson and Walter White, consulted with presidents, senators, congressmen, and occasionally foreign heads of state. Performers like Louis Armstrong, Duke Ellington, and Josephine Baker were even more acclaimed in Europe than in their homeland. And nobody sang the blues like Bessie Smith, Alberta Hunter, and Ethel Waters. They were part of what Ann Douglas has termed "a dazzling array of black talent and ambition."

But something else caught our attention. These dazzlingly talented people shared three obsessions, which were woven in various configurations into all of their tales: a passion for learning that was never satisfied, a fascination with the theme of passing—as in "passing for white"—that raised questions of authenticity, and a fixation on skin color that weakened but did not destroy their faith in their own dark selves. These obsessions tied them intimately with the African-American community they championed and made their stories familiar to rich and poor alike. Such examinations of the self would have immobilized lesser spirits ("to be not afraid of anything, not even of truth"), but for these seventeen they became the major source of pride.

The importance of rising above the crowd at the bottom was a cherished value of the aspiring black middle class in the first decades of the twentieth century. As W. E. B. Du Bois's mother told him, "The secret of life and the losing of the color bar lay in excellence, in accomplishment. If others of my family, of my colored kin, had stayed in school instead of quitting early for small jobs, they could have risen to equal whites." That the reality never quite matched the promise, as Du Bois's own academic career would reveal, did not seem to matter. Education could keep a woman out of someone else's kitchen, a man from the factory's dirty work.

To learn became the special goal of the privileged few. James Weldon Johnson, teacher and school superintendent, spoke three languages and wrote poetry and prose and popular song lyrics. Jessie Fauset, a graduate of Cornell University, was rarely pictured without her Phi Beta Kappa key, which she received before the end of the first decade of the twentieth century. She earned a master's degree in French literature from the University of Pennsylvania before the First World War. Walter White, a graduate of Atlanta University, wrote two novels, two investigative studies, and numerous articles, which appeared in mainstream literary journals. Beyond elite institutional credentials, Langston Hughes spoke Spanish and French, Nella Larsen worked difficult crosswords and other puzzles, and Zora Neale Hurston measured heads in Harlem under the tutelage of white anthropologist Franz Boas.

Their love of learning flourished in the 1920s in a society that admired the trappings of erudition, from crossword puzzles and reading societies to book-of-the month clubs and radio contests, and that valued scientists' attempts to measure things like intelligence and the number of calories in certain foods. But more significant in the African-American community, this love of learning was tied to a yearning for something constantly valued and long denied. It had been illegal to teach slaves to read. Frederick Douglass, recalling a school he set up for fellow slaves in 1845, wrote, "They came because they wished to learn. Their minds had been starved by their cruel masters. They had been shut up in darkness. I taught them because it was the delight of my soul to be doing something that looked like bettering the condition of the race." In 1865, during Reconstruction, Booker T. Washington commented on what appeared to him to be "a whole race trying to go to school."

Although the formal education of Josephine Baker, Bill Robinson, Madam C. J. Walker, Alberta Hunter, Louis Armstrong, and Bessie Smith ended early, they too were eager to learn. Baker and Robinson were, as adults, unable to sign their names, but as their fame and fortune increased, they went about the business of teaching themselves. Josephine Baker learned French and how to walk and talk and dress. Madam C. J. Walker hired tutors who helped her and her daughter, A'Lelia, with public speaking, and Bill Robinson, who married three educated women, visited a Harlem school every year to donate a cash prize to the brightest student and to give a one-sentence graduation speech: "Boys and girls, go as high as you can!"

Passing for white was the second obsession. The definition of "white" was not consistent, however; it varied by colony, by time period, and by political system. In 1705 in colonial Virginia, for example, one had to be at least seven-eighths white to be considered legally white, but in South Carolina "known and visible mulattoes could by behavior and reputation be white." South Carolina never prohibited interracial marriage during slavery and "refused to relegate free mulattoes to the status of blacks, slave or free." New Orleans, according to historian John Blassingame, was characterized in the antebellum period by "the pervasiveness of miscegenation."

After the Civil War, however, a universal "one drop" rule was introduced, which meant that any known black ancestry—even one drop of African blood—made one black. Walter White's designation, one sixty-fourth black, was unusual but not unique. The lack of a mulatto classification made racial identities more fixed in the United States but not more clear. Was passing good or bad and for whom? "My love for my children makes me glad that I am what I am," James Weldon Johnson's protagonist concludes in *The Autobiography of an Ex-Colored Man*, "and keeps me from desiring to be otherwise; and yet, when I sometimes open a little box in which I still keep my fast-yellowing manuscripts, the only tangible remnants of a vanished dream, a dead ambition, a sacrificed talent, I cannot repress the thought that, after all, I have chosen the lesser part, that I have sold my birthright for a mess of pottage."

Passing for white was the surest route to upward mobility for light-skinned African-Americans, although not one chosen by all who could have. Historians can only guess at how many did. Historian Joel Williamson estimates that some 25,000 light-skinned blacks passed into white society each year between the end of Reconstruction and the 1920s. Anthropologists estimate that as much as one-quarter of the American white population may have some black ancestry. Satirical novelist George Schuyler dedicated his book *Black No More* "to all Caucasians who can . . . confidently assert that there are no Black leaves,

twigs, limbs, or branches on their family trees."

For those who stayed within the race, a light-skinned privilege prevailed. "Throughout the twentieth century," researchers Kathy Russell, Midge Wilson, and Ronald Hall found in *The Color Complex*, "most of the leaders of the Black community have been extraordinarily light-skinned." Some critics regard the Renaissance itself as a glorification of the mulatto elite.

The theme of passing dominated the fiction of Jessie Fauset, Nella Larsen, James Weldon Johnson, Walter White, and Dorothy West and the lives of all. The fascination with passing generated a number of story lines, from Larsen's tragic mulatto who cannot find a home in either world (*Passing*), to Fauset's tale of a light-skinned mother who despises and destroys her own darker-skinned child because he exposes the family shame (*Comedy: American Style*). There were hundred of permutations.

But we suggest a related theme of "passing in their lives" that is more complex than racial escape. "Passing in their lives" involves adopting a disguise for the purpose of knowing an "other" and ultimately discovering a hidden part of yourself. Race was the simplest disguise, wandering through a white world so that a black one comes into sharper relief. All sixteen engaged in this act of passing. Bert Williams, a black comic in blackface who imitated whites imitating blacks, is the best example. And they adopted other disguises as well. Zora Neale Hurston was in high school, a happy fourteen-year-old, except that she was twenty-four. Josephine Baker, attired in couturier gowns or men's formal evening wear, altered people's perception of race, class, and gender. Louis Armstrong, who invented a sophisticated art form, performed it onstage in a clown's mask.

The preference for light skin was the third obsession and the most difficult. It weighed like a millstone upon a community longing to be free. Ironically, it was not their invention. It was not African-Americans who first demanded quadroon balls in Charleston and New Orleans where light-skinned women were auctioned off, nor was the "high yaller" chorus line at the Cotton Club their idea. Skin color could influence even menial employment, mainly because many whites developed a "taste for light skin." Many African-Americans bought into the notion that light-skinned people were somehow better. "Wouldn't they be surprised," Maya Angelou wrote in *I Know Why the Caged Bird Sings*, "when one day I woke out of my black ugly dream, and my real hair, which was long and blond, would take the place of the kinky mass that Momma wouldn't let me straighten?" Frequently, dark-skinned blacks were denied admission to Negro schools and colleges even though they were academically qualified. "Whiter and whiter, every generation," Wallace Thurman wrote in *The Blacker the Berry*. "The nearer white you are the more white people will respect you. Therefore all light Negroes marry light Negroes."

Skin color obsessions also leaped into the Renaissance community in explosive ways. So A'Lelia Walker, the richest and most successful African-American businesswoman in the country, was ridiculed by a "light-skinned" crew of ne'er-do-wells and hangers-on within black society. So Jessie Fauset was outraged by a white artist's suggestion that black teachers would have dark skin and nappy hair. So Dorothy West was affectionately known as "little black Dorothy." So Josephine Baker was shunned by her birth family for being too light and by the chorus line for being too dark. So Ethel Waters adopted a light-skinned child and chose a light-skinned husband in the hope of finding acceptance. She met instead with the humiliation of being cast as the maid.

Rather than being consumed by them, most Renaissance figures used their obsessions as springboards for their discoveries. Much of their success arose from the fact that they never stopped learning. It was said that the most fascinating piece of music for Duke Ellington "was the one he was writing at a given moment." Jessie Fauset, unmasked, never wavered in her desire to present an "undisguisedly beautiful presentation of Negro ability." And Langston Hughes proclaimed that younger artists "intend to express our dark-skinned selves without fear or shame."

"Pride and vanity are different things," Mary Bennet, "the only plain one in the family," observes in Jane Austen's novel *Pride and Prejudice*. "Pride relates more to our opinion of ourselves. Vanity is what we would have others think of us." In the early decades of the twentieth century, these seventeen artists led the movement that gave black America its first opportunity to form an opinion of itself. Slowly at first and then with ever greater persistence, from their efforts a pride emerged. "Up you mighty race," Marcus Garvey was counseling at this same moment. "You can accomplish what you will!" This they all believed.

But even more than their education, talent, and courage, these seventeen possessed a modern arrogance and self-consciousness that made them powerful. "It is a rare and intriguing moment," Nathan Huggins wrote, "when a people decide that they are the instrument of history making and race building. It is common enough to think of oneself as part of some larger meaning in the sweep of history. But to presume to be an actor and creator in the special occurrence of a people's birth (or rebirth) requires a singular self-consciousness." And the goal of all consciousness, W. E. B. Du Bois has observed, is "to enjoy that anarchy of the spirit" that it produces.

The Power of Pride is about seventeen people who possessed this singular self-consciousness and anarchy of spirit. In little more than two decades they changed forever the African-American experience and left an indelible mark on the American character. They had few outright victories. Many of their poems, plays, and novels and some of their music did not survive for even one decade. Some of their masterpieces, like Zora Neale Hurston's novel *Their Eyes Were Watching God,* had to wait fifty years for recognition. But their contribution was not about their product. The movement represented "a conscious, organized, and insistent access of power to those whom America had robbed and dismissed," writes Ann Douglas.

In 1917, James Weldon Johnson, Renaissance songwriter, poet, and secretary of the NAACP, organized a silent march in Harlem to protest lynchings in the South. The Great Migration, which had started as a trickle, was reaching a peak in that year. If we use 1917 as the starting point and 1938, when three of our seventeen had already died, as an end, we find crowded into a relatively short time frame a great explosion of artistic expression. The figures fed on each other—for inspiration, support, and sometimes destruction. "Flaming, burning, searing, and penetrating far beneath the superficial items of the flesh to boil the sluggish blood," wrote Wallace Thurman. Johnson hired Walter White at the NAACP. Jessie Fauset, literary editor of the journal *Crisis,* published unknown writers such as Hurston, Thurman, and Langston Hughes, and after 1932 Carl Van Vechten photographed all of them. Their efforts set the stage for the later literary achievements of Ralph Ellison, Richard Wright, and James Baldwin, and for the continued success of jazz musicians, blues singers, and photographers. Though their time on the stage was brief, their impact survives.

We examine race and migration in the Renaissance from the perspective not only of Harlem but also of Washington, D.C., Chicago, and Paris, migration points all, where new Negro societies sprang up and became fashionable. "The New Negro is not to me a group of writers centered in Harlem during the second half of the twenties," said Sterling Brown, a Renaissance writer and poet. "Most of the writers were not Harlemites: much of the best writing was not about Harlem, which was the show-window, the cashier's till but no more Negro American than New York is America." Washington, D.C., home of Howard University, was important because it served as a scholarly center—and figures like Hurston, Hughes, and Ellington spent time there. Chicago was the music center. As historian David Levering Lewis has pointed out, jazz in New York was "derivative, polished, commercialized," but the real jazz was on the South Side. Louis Armstrong, Bessie Smith, and Alberta Hunter traveled first to Chicago, not to New York. And Paris was for many—Josephine Baker, Alberta Hunter, Florence Mills, Langston Hughes, and Jessie Fauset—the home away from home where race consciousness could be explored without regret.

Migrants shifted the center of black life in America northward to the great urban centers. For Renaissance participants in particular, cities became places where they "could be themselves, as they saw fit." With a new self-confidence, they marveled at the simplicity and the power of their discoveries. It was a time when being black itself was in vogue.

Strange,
That in this nigger place
I should meet Life face to face;
When for years, I had been seeking
Life in places gentler speaking,
Until I came to this vile street
And found Life stepping on my feet!

LANGSTON HUGHES

OUT OF THE SOUTH

THE FIRST TWO DECADES OF THE TWENTIETH CENTURY WERE DIFFICULT ONES FOR AFRICAN-AMERICANS, MOST OF WHOM LIVED IN THE SOUTH. JIM CROW AND CASTE RESTRICTIONS SEVERELY LIMITED ECONOMIC OPPORTUNITIES AND THE CHANCE FOR UPWARD MOBILITY. DIGNITY AND SELF-RESPECT WERE ALMOST NONEXISTENT IN A LAND WHERE EVEN OLD BLACK MEN WERE CALLED BOY. BEGINNING SLOWLY AT THE TURN OF THE CENTURY AND REACHING A CRESCENDO BY 1917, BLACKS BARGAINED, SCHEMED, AND CAJOLED THEIR WAY OUT OF THE SOUTH, AND YET THEIR SOUTHERN ROOTS HAD SPECIAL MEANING FOR THESE RENAISSANCE FIGURES.

COLORED WAIF'S HOME BRASS BAND, 1910. LOUIS ARMSTRONG IS IN THE CENTER. IT WAS HIS FIRST INSTRUMENTAL GROUP.

JOSEPHINE BAKER AT
THE CASINO DE PARIS,
1927, HOME OF
FRENCH SUPERSTAR
AND BAKER RIVAL
MISTINGUETT.
IT WAS CONSIDERED
A HIGHER CLASS OF
ENTERTAINMENT THAN

1

JOSEPHINE BAKER

$\mathcal{I}$N MAY 1927, CHARLES A. LINDBERGH, a handsome young man from the Midwest, readied his plane, the *Spirit of Saint Louis*, for takeoff. He was preparing to be the first individual to fly nonstop from New York to Paris. In 1919 a prize of $25,000 had been offered for the feat by Raymond Orteig, owner of the Brevoort and Lafayette Hotels in New York. Lindbergh was not the only contestant, but the press had been following this daring but modest young man with particular pleasure. His plane took off a little before eight o'clock on the morning of May 20. As the story hit the wires, the nation was gripped by the drama. That night 40,000 boxing fans in Yankee Stadium bowed their heads in silent prayer for Lindbergh. "The next day came the successive reports of Lindbergh's success—he had reached the Irish coast, he was crossing over England, he was over the Channel," wrote journalist Frederick Lewis Allen. When Lindbergh landed at Le Bourget in Paris, he was mobbed. President Coolidge sent a navy cruiser to bring him and his plane home. He received a commission, the Distinguished Flying Cross, and the Congressional Medal of Honor. America was in love. Lindbergh, said the *New York Evening World*, had "performed the greatest feat of a solitary man in the records of the human race." Oddly, Lindbergh believed that his race had something to do with it.

"UNTERMENSCH!"—SUBHUMAN—the Berlin audience called out in the early spring of 1928 as Josephine Baker of the Folies-Bergère, scheduled to appear for six months, opened at the Theater des Westens. A beautiful blond singer, Lea Seidl, also appeared on the program. She recalled the "hoots and catcalls" for Josephine on that first night. Outrage was expressed at the pairing, an Aryan lovely and an African beast. "They denounced me as the black devil," Josephine later told biographers. "She had a very elegant chinchilla coat," Lea Seidl added, and three weeks into the run "I saw her in her coat with a big sack on her back and she whispered, 'Don't say anything, I run away.' And she did." Hitler and the National Socialists had not yet come into power in Germany. They had not yet put through a law banning blacks and Jews from the stage and jazz from German radio. But Josephine Baker's 1928 tour was a harbinger of things to come.

Lindbergh was the toast of the Continent in 1928. Even Josephine was drawn into the whirlwind that surrounded him, and thought herself a poor substitute. "He was a real hero," she said. "What was a dancer draped in bananas beside him?" But somewhere along the way, the notion surfaced that Lindbergh's feat was proof of the superiority of the "master race." Lindbergh, who espoused isolationism in the 1930s ("western civilization should not commit racial suicide by internal conflict") and was rumored to be a Nazi sympathizer, thought "aviation one of those priceless possessions which permits the White race to live at all in a pressing sea of Yellow, Black, and Brown." Lindbergh believed that the white race was in danger from the "pressing sea," but he was also convinced of the "sensate superiority of the black race," and visited the Folies often.

Josephine Baker was a collector: she collected children, animals, and lovers with almost equal enthusiasm. Josephine Baker was a heroine; she fought in the French resistance during World War II and was awarded the Legion of Honor, the Rosette of the Resistance, and the Medallion of the City of Paris by the French government. Josephine Baker was a humanitarian; she gave benefit performances for orphanages, for the sick, and for the poor. Josephine Baker was also a predator. Born into abject poverty, a victim of abuse and neglect, she learned to survive by devouring friends and foes alike. As Jean-Claude Baker, one of her "adopted" children, once said, "Everyone who came too close to Josephine got burned." But Baker's contribution to the Renaissance lies not in her good deeds or bad ones, not in her songs or her performances, but in her uncanny ability to plunge successfully into uncharted waters without first considering how to get back. She was the modern's modern.

"How can I convey the spontaneity, the vitality, the gentleness, the simplicity of Josephine Baker?" Jean Guyon-Gesbron, a reporter for *Européen*, asked in 1931. It was a question many would pose over the years in covering this larger-than-life Paris creation. Josephine, an original, gave many answers. "I had no talent when I started, and I still have none," she once explained. "What I did on stage, the music told me to do. My personality was created by press agents. They gave me their brains." Chroniclers soon learned that any attempt to capture, understand, or pay tribute to Josephine Baker inevitably ran afoul of her endless capacity for invention. "I don't lie," she said, "I improve on life."

⁎

JOSEPHINE BAKER WAS BORN Freda Josephine McDonald in Saint Louis, Missouri, on June 3, 1906, the daughter of Carrie McDonald, who was "coal black, pretty, tall, slender, and full of life," and an unknown father, who was thought to be white. Carrie, who had been adopted and cared for by four adults—her mother, Elvira; her father, Richard; her father's sister, Caroline; and Caroline's husband, Charles—was spoiled and a bit wild. She was twenty when she had Josephine. After a difficult delivery she came home from the hospital and left the baby, so much lighter-skinned than she, with her aunt Caroline. Carrie's family had been heartbroken at the news of her pregnancy, hoping for better things for this adored child. Carrie had other ideas. A year later she had a second child, a boy she named Richard. Richard's father, whom Carrie did not marry, was a black man. The two children, only a year apart in age, were very different in appearance. Josephine was "light brown, the color of café au lait." Said Josephine, "He had black skin . . . he was the welcome one."

Eight months after Richard was born, Carrie married Arthur Martin. The Martins had two children of their own, all resembling Richard in skin color. "Josephine's brown skin continued to be a tacit reproach to her black mother," Jean-Claude Baker reported. Being rejected by her mother was traumatic for Josephine, as it would be for any child, and being rejected because she was too light was confusing. Dancer Harry Watkins claimed that Josephine "wanted at any price to become white. She would fill her bath-

JOSEPHINE IN SATIN FOR HER ROLE IN
CHOCOLATE DANDIES (FORMERLY *IN BAMVILLE*),
WITH FLOURNEY MILLER AND JOHNNY HUDGINS,
AT THE COLONIAL THEATRE, NEW YORK, 1924.

tub with goat's milk, Eau de Javel [a bleach, like Clorox], lemon, honey, and hot water, then plunge into it. In the process, she would burn her pussy." Said another friend, "She hated the color of her skin so much it made me feel terrible for her."

Tumpy, as she was called, lived with Aunt Caroline until she was five, when Carrie, who needed help caring for the other children, took her back. Josephine lived in her mother's house for only two years before she was sent away again to work as a maid for a Mrs. Kaiser, who lived in the country. Baker worked and went to school there until one day, as punishment for leaving a pot too long on the stove, Mrs. Kaiser dunked her hands in boiling water. Baker ran from the house screaming and had to be taken to the hospital. Carrie was forced to take the child back.

Baker was soon hired out again, in the house of a white couple named Mason. Mr. Mason was fond of giving Josephine "wet kisses" and began visiting her room at night. Once again Tumpy was sent home. At the age of ten she was given food and clothing in exchange for working for the Joneses, a family of traveling musicians. Josephine at last had found a degree of happiness: she was now in show business.

She continued her life as a hired girl, leaving the Joneses but finding other work until December 1919 when, at the age of thirteen,

THE ARRIVAL OF *LA REVUE NÈGRE* PERFORMERS FROM THE COTTON CLUB IN PARIS AT THE SAINT-LAZARE RAILROAD STATION ON THE MORNING OF SEPTEMBER 22, 1925.

she married Willie Wells. At first Josephine and Willie lived on their own in a furnished room, with Willie holding a menial job, but Josephine spent all the money he earned on clothes and soon they could not afford to pay the rent. To avoid a fight, Josephine announced that she was pregnant. When Willie discovered that she was not, they argued and "Josephine cut his head open with a beer bottle," according to her biographer Jean-Claude Baker. The marriage ended.

Age thirteen also marks the last mention of formal schooling for Josephine, who had constantly played hooky even before her marriage. Ada "Bricktop" Smith remembered that when Josephine arrived in Paris ten years later she "could hardly write her name." After the success of La Revue Nègre, Bricktop gave Josephine a rubber stamp bearing her signa-

ture to avoid the embarrassment of signing autographs in the slow, deliberate manner of a semiliterate.

For entertainment, Josephine frequented the Booker Theater in Saint Louis, home of "mirth, music, and merriment." The theater brought in vaudeville acts from the Theater Owners Booking Association, called TOBA. Many suggested that the letters stood for Tough on Black Asses. It was there that Josephine first saw Bessie Smith. But it was another Smith who took notice of Josephine, the great blues singer Clara Smith. Her voice, wrote Carl Van Vechten, was so powerful it "tears the blood from one's heart." Clara, who was twenty-six and something of a big sister to the fourteen-year-old Josephine, got her a job in her touring company. They also became lovers. Josephine described her as "very black, fat, and short." When the company left Saint Louis, Josephine went along. When Carrie discovered that Josephine had run away, she said simply, "She has chosen her path. Let her be." Josephine, improving on life, wrote that she left her mother a long note: "I'm sorry it has to be this way; but it's the only way for me to get away." In this invention, Josephine leaves not with Clara but with Bessie Smith.

Baker's journey out of Saint Louis was not north, like that of the other migrants, but south. Josephine savored her first train ride, journeying with the touring company to Memphis, the blues capital. She worked there as a dresser, taking care of costumes and props, but she was also given time on the stage in bit parts. More than anything, she loved to perform and be noticed.

After winding through the South, the company arrived in the North in 1921. In Philadelphia, they played at the Standard Theater where Ethel Waters had also played. They had left Clara Smith, who always preferred the South, behind. In Philadelphia, Josephine met her second husband: Billy Baker, "a pretty boy with fair skin," the son of a restaurant owner. Josephine Baker was fifteen. The younger Bakers, apparently happy and in love, lived over the restaurant with the older Bakers, who took Josephine in as one of their own. It was her first real home. She would sleep during the day, perform at the theater at night, and return faithfully after each show. But she dreamed of a better life. When Noble Sissle and Eubie Blake began auditions for *Shuffle Along*, Josephine went to New York and tried out. But Sissle, she said, thought she was "too young, too small, too thin, too ugly. And too dark." Bitterly disappointed, Josephine returned to Philadelphia.

Shuffle Along was such a hit in New York that other cities clamored for the show, so a tour was planned. Again Josephine Baker tried out in New York. This time she made it. She packed her bags and bought a one-way ticket, and Billy Baker became yet another ex-husband of a soon-to-be-famous wife.

Members of the *Shuffle Along* touring company were very competitive because there were many more willing aspirants than places on the line. Spats and petty feuds erupted, many of which centered on Baker, who was perceived as too uneducated and constantly seeking attention. Fredi Washington, who was in the chorus, remembered one occasion when the other performers put all of Josephine's things out in the hotel hallway, refusing to room with her. "All those girls . . . looked down on Josephine, who was so much darker," Washington recalled. It was difficult for Baker, who had labored most of her young life under the cloud of being too light, suddenly to be burdened with the "shame" of being too dark. She responded by creating a unique persona that was increasingly less ethnic and more eccentric. Chorus line member Mildred Hudgins, wife of comedian Johnny, remembered one version: "She'd wear big picture hats with evening dresses, and . . . everybody made fun of her. But Josephine just went about her business. She didn't humble to nobody."

One of the cities that *Shuffle Along* visited was Saint Louis. Josephine, without explanation, left the show during that period. Carrie, knowing that Josephine was in the company, went to the theater to see her daughter. Standing backstage as the performers were leaving, she shyly asked for Josephine. Most ignored her. Adelaide Hall did not. She remembered telling a very dark woman, who identified herself as Josephine's mother, that Josephine was "doing fine and just didn't come with us." It was never clear to the other chorus girls why she took this absence, but avoiding her past was something at which Baker learned to excel.

Several months later, the tour returned to Saint Louis, and this time Baker was there. She met with other members of her family, but not with her mother, and began sending them monthly checks. She did not visit them again for fourteen years.

In 1924 Sissle and Blake wrote a special part for Josephine in their new musical, *In Bamville*. The show tried out in Rochester and Pittsburgh and, after many revisions, opened in New York as *Chocolate Dandies*. Compared to *Shuffle Along*, it was a lavish production. The show starred Johnny Hudgins. The audiences loved it. The critics did not, except for Hudgins's part.

With rumors flying that the show was in trouble, nightclub promoter Lew Leslie invited her to perform at the Plantation where Florence Mills, the most popular black performer in New York in the 1920s, had reigned. With Florence on tour, Ethel Waters was the star. Baker was in the chorus, but every night she stepped out to do a speciality dance. She claimed that one night she actually replaced an ailing Waters, got rave reviews, and forced Waters to hurry back from her sickbed. Ethel remembered nothing of the incident, but in an uncharacteristically kind review, she said, "Josephine was a mugger with a great comic sense, and she had a beautiful form. She could dance and she could clown joy into you. She could also play the trombone."

Fate plucked Baker out of the chorus. Caroline Dudley Reagan, "one of a trio of sisters said to be bright, rich, and daffy" from Chicago, was married to a foreign service officer about to be transferred to Paris. Caroline's ambition was to take an all-black revue to Paris. In pursuing this dream she sought aid from the directors of the big halls in Paris, all of whom turned her down, until finally she contacted Rolf de Maré, who had a vacant theater. De Maré gave Reagan the necessary fund-

ing and the name of Will Marion Cook, who she was told would help her find talent for the show. Cook obliged. Reagan wanted Florence Mills as the star but could not afford her. She wanted Ethel Waters, but Waters was not keen to leave the country. Against Cook's advice, Reagan went after Josephine, the chorus girl she had seen at the Plantation. Josephine was almost as reluctant as Waters. She was finally persuaded by the promise of designer clothes, pearls, and $200 a week. Along the way Reagan also got bandleader Claude Hopkins and clarinet player Sidney Bechet. On September 15, the *Berengaria* sailed for France with two dozen black singers, dancers, and musicians.

"My dear, don't ever do that to me again," André Daven the manager of the Théâtre des Champs-Élysées said to Rolf de Maré. "Why, those people actually had pieces of iron on the bottom of their shoes. All they did was tap! What a racket!" Daven had just auditioned some of the performers recently arrived from New York to perform in *La Revue Nègre*, including Josephine Baker. De Maré instead returned to the Théâtre des Champs-Élysées and asked the dancers to do some of their numbers again. He too was deafened by the noise of the taps, but he kept noticing "the little one on the end of the line." Realizing that she was noticed, Josephine went into her act, "hips swaying, eyes crossed, pigeon-toed."

La Revue Nègre, which consisted of six vaudeville acts and lasted less than an hour, was the second half of a two-part show. The first half featured Japanese acrobats, a trapeze act, and a strongman who balanced six men on a merry-go-round on his head. The second half began slowly but poignantly. Louis Douglas, a Harlequin in blackface and tailcoat, sang of his love for Columbine. Then Josephine did a frantic Charleston and Bechet played his clarinet. The final number was "Danse de Sauvage." Josephine, wearing a feathered costume, was carried onstage upside down by Joe Alex, who "swung and lowered his birdlike burden to the floor." Josephine's hair was plastered against her head. She slithered down the length of Alex's torso and then, "to the accompaniment of clarinet and drums, she wove and coiled around the great planted trunks of her partner's legs in a ritual of serpentine coupling." As the beat became frenzied, Josephine shook, some would later say, "like a hummingbird." Her performance was primitive and erotic and, to many, pornographic. Said Essie Robeson, wife of singer Paul: "The 'Danse de Sauvage' was fine until the star did this ridiculously vulgar wiggling." Paris was shocked and delighted. Janet Flanner, on her first assignment for the *New Yorker*, wrote, "Her magnifi-

cent dark body, a new model to the French, proved for the first time that black was beautiful."

Josephine's instinct for survival told her that Paris would soon lose interest in the revue, which was hastily constructed and thin in content. She also realized that a star who was "too dark, too thin, too ugly" would not last long. Unknown to the rest of the company, she was approached by Paul Derval of the Folies-Bergère and had begun negotiations with them. Caroline Reagan and the remaining cast, however, dreamed of taking the show to the rest of Europe when the Paris light faded. They got only as far as Berlin. *La Revue Nègre* opened there on New Year's Eve 1925.

Berlin, devastated by the First World War,

A GREAT COLOURED STAR!

—GOLFING—

MISS JOSEPHINE BAKER AFLOAT—

Miss Josephine Baker, who is one of the world's greatest coloured stars, is at present in Berlin after an extensive tour of the Continent. She is intending to open a cabaret in the capital of Germany on the same lines as the one she has opened in Paris. These intriguing studies of the famous dark lady were taken on an estate at Grunewald, near Berlin, where it is said she combines business with pleasure. Besides being a world's wonder at high-speed dancing, Miss Josephine Baker must be a marvellous shot, if that is a rook-rifle she has, and with which, presumably, she is downing duck or teal. Miss Josephine Baker has had big successes in Vienna and Paris

—AND SHOOTING

"A GREAT COLOURED STAR," FEATURED IN THE *TATLER*, OCTOBER 17, 1928.

FRENCH POSTCARD FEATURING JOSEPHINE IN FEATHERS, PHOTOGRAPHED BY WALERY IN PARIS, 1920S.

JOSEPHINE (ABOVE) IMITATING JOHNNY HUDGINS (RIGHT) BY DRESSING IN CLOWN OUTFIT AND BLACKFACE, FOLIES-BERGÈRE, PARIS, 1927.

MANNEQUIN OF THE TRADEMARK SIEGEL IN WAX WITH SCULPTED HAIR, AS THE IMAGE OF JOSEPHINE BAKER, CIRCA 1926.

JOSEPHINE WITH HER "JOSEPHINE" DOLL BY HER SIDE, PARIS, 1928.

had high unemployment, memories of ruinous inflation, starving people, and a level of despair unmatched in the rest of Europe. But much of Berlin, one of the most decadent cities in the world, loved Josephine. "I was given rings with fire as big as an egg; I was given a pair of ancient earrings which belonged to a duchess 150 years ago; I was given pearls like teeth; flowers that came in one day from Italy in moss and baskets. . . . Perfume in a glass horse. One fur, two furs, three furs, four furs. Bracelets with red stones for my arms, my wrists, my legs." Not everyone approved of her. When *La Revue* opened, an antiblack demonstration was held outside the theater. Pamphlets were distributed by Brownshirts describing Josephine as subhuman. She took little notice at the time, celebrated as she was, only commenting, "I'm not immoral; I'm only natural."

Caroline Dudley Reagan heard rumors that Josephine was next to appear with the Folies, but she wrote off the stories as idle gossip. Unknown to her, the great German director Max Reinhardt was also trying to persuade Josephine to stay in Berlin, proposing to make her an actress. Derval took the fickle nature of his star more seriously and sent an envoy to Berlin to offer Josephine more money. Baker accepted. Caroline realized her mistake at last, but too late. Josephine gave three days' notice. Caroline, though furious, said simply, "Josephine had flown, she had been stolen from me. It was the end of the beautiful Revue Nègre. It didn't breathe anymore." Josephine's version, again improving on life, was slightly different. She said she was offered a job as a solo dancer paying her the equivalent of ten dollars a day when the revue closed and the rest of the cast was stranded. Broke, she happily accepted.

But in an interview done at another time, her explanation was more honest. "I *had* to succeed. I would never stop trying, never. A violinist had his violin, a painter his palette. All I had was myself. *I* was the instrument I must care for. . . . That's why I spent thirty minutes every morning rubbing my body with half a lemon to lighten my skin and just as long preparing a mixture for my hair. I couldn't afford to take chances." Josephine was very cognizant of the precariousness of her situation and of her limited set of choices. Caroline herself had warned Josephine of simply becoming a mannequin with feathers.

For Baker's premier performance with the Folies-Bergère, the costume designers presented numerous sketches to Derval, all of which he rejected. Baker in a stupendous gown was to him uninteresting. What was created instead was a costume made of bananas on a string. It became the rage of two continents.

Josephine added one other touch. She noticed that when it was cold outside, her breasts became very firm and pointed. In her dressing room that night, she held two bowls of cracked ice to them in preparation for her entrance. The next night, every chorus girl in France did the same.

Opening night for Baker was hardly a minor affair. Derval invited the Rothschilds, Maurice Chevalier, Charles de Gaulle, Ernest Hemingway, Edith Piaf, René Clair, and Igor Stravinsky. Some were friends to whom he had promised something special. Also in the audience was the crown prince of Sweden, who would later become King Gustav VI. Josephine would later say of him, "When he spoke, it was like you poured warm honey into some hot butter."

Baker's performance began slowly. The stage was set as a Hawaiian scene at sunrise with mountains, grass, blue water, and sand. Baker was in the water, surrounded by dancers and dressed in a muumuu. Suddenly, as she was lifted high in the air, she cast aside her robe and was clad only in the banana costume. She

JOSEPHINE IN HER NIGHTCLUB, CHEZ JOSEPHINE, 40 RUE FONTAINE IN THE 9TH ARRONDISSEMENT, WHICH OPENED ON DECEMBER 19, 1926.

was then tossed "like a fabulous flying swan" into the dancers' arms, and the Hawaiian set receded to be replaced with mirrors where "a thousand banana-clad Josephines" appeared. The audience, according to Stephen Papich, a Baker friend and biographer, "exploded in a frenzy." At the end of the scene, Baker rushed to the center of the stage and, in an unrehearsed move, leaped and landed on top of the one banana tree that remained. "Slowly she spread back the leaves to reveal herself. She was squatting down, and like a little monkey she started crossing her eyes, tilting her head, and waving to the audience." Baker had created something that was mad and wild, and Paris loved it.

Baker's star rose immediately. She was praised by the press and showered with gowns from the couturiers. Paul Poiret, the premier designer of the time, loved to dress her. Baker loved the attention but never paid her bills, eventually sending Poiret into bankruptcy. But she wore the clothes well and developed similar nonpaying arrangements with Dior, Balenciaga, and Worth. Bricktop observed that "her reputation for performing nude too often overshadowed the fact that she was born to wear couturier styles."

Langston Hughes visited her when she was at the Folies and was dazzled by her success. He recalled: "Just as the show was about to start, Miss Baker arrived in a chauffeur-driven car. Her man in livery opened the car door for her. A theater attendant flung open the stage door. Miss Baker swept into the backstage corridor of the Folies-Bergère. Just inside the entrance a French maid received her cloak. As she walked down the hall, another maid took her gloves, her purse, and anything else she wished to discard. Before I got around to the entrance of the theater and into my seat, Josephine Baker was coming on stage, dressed to the nines by some great designer, tall, glittering, brownskin and beautiful, the music rising in a flood of melody, and the audience applauding madly. Here indeed was a star treated as no star I have ever seen, white, black, green, grizzly or grey, treated in America."

THE APPEAL OF BAKER —exotic, primitive, and available—to Frenchmen was obvious, and her exploits were legendary. Hemingway remembered dancing one hot night with a fur-clad Josephine who revealed that she was naked under the coat. Much later there were several stories about Bubu, a gorilla that she dressed like a man, paraded down Paris streets, and used to make her fourth husband jealous. Banning the husband from the bedroom, she said: "I don't need you anymore."

JOSEPHINE AT LAKE COMO, ITALY, 1933.

Her appeal to Frenchwomen was more complex. Women had taken on major employment during the First World War, only to be shackled again at war's end. They could not vote. They could not enter the professions or politics. They could not even open a bank account. Considering a defiant sexual display their only weapon, many young women boldly made up their faces, drank cocktails, smoked cigarettes, and cropped their hair. They were in revolt, and they saw Josephine as their heroine. And Josephine remained on the cutting edge. In an age when women had only recently shed corsets and ankle-length dresses, her appearance in the nude, in gowns with no backs and no fronts, and in top hats and tails broke all the rules. The lines that divided men and women, that dictated what a nice young woman could do and should wear, were irrevocably changed. "Thin bodies, flat chests, and impulsive movements once thought to be lacking in any hope of style became the elements of extreme chic," wrote historian Anne Hollander. By the fall of 1926, "there were Josephine Baker dolls, costumes, perfumes, and pomades." The women of Paris wanted her look.

The Baker style went beyond bold and striking dress. It helped to solidify an emerging attitude of recklessness. Hollander described it as "a naughty schoolboy ready for any kind of perverse experience, especially sexual; independent, adventurous, and daring, but still very much played off against men—rather like a thirteen-year-old male hustler." The hustler image was called up in Josephine's imitation (complete with trousers and tails) of comic Johnny Hudgins.

But Josephine was not the only Paris attraction of 1926. Two months after she opened at the Folies, Florence Mills and Johnny Hudgins stormed into town in Lew Leslie's *Blackbirds of 1926*. It was a moment of challenge for Josephine, the new celebrity. She arrived at opening night in a floor-length ermine coat over a black velvet evening gown with a hood. She was accompanied by eight white men in tails. "We had to hold the curtain for her," Johnny Hudgins recalled. *Blackbirds* did well in Paris, but Florence had London still to conquer.

Always a bit lonely among all her friends and admirers, Josephine welcomed most people from home. She said she loved Florence Mills, and both Bessie de Saussure and Bricktop were early companions and confidantes. Bricktop, called "small, pale and absolutely unique" by Langston Hughes, ran a nightclub in Montmartre and introduced Josephine to the beautiful people, Scott and Zelda Fitzgerald, the Cole Porters, John Steinbeck, and Ernest Hemingway. Bessie and "Joe" would also go to clubs together, and it was at one that they met Pepito, a Sicilian gigolo who spoke Italian, French, German, and English. Bricktop described him as good-looking, in his late thirties, and too poor to buy a bottle of beer. He reminded Josephine of her screen idol, Adolphe Menjou. Now twenty, she was in love—again.

After the couple appeared everywhere together, Pepito took a short, calculated absence

JOSEPHINE WITH HER HUSBAND AND PROMOTER,
COUNT PEPITO ABATINO, PARIS, 1926.
HE WAS A STONEMASON FROM PALERMO WHO
BRICKTOP CALLED THE "NO-ACCOUNT COUNT."

that drove Josephine wild. He soon returned, announced that he couldn't live without her, and declared that he was becoming her manager. Baker was delighted. Pepito's first task was to provide her with an education. Said Bricktop: "He practically put her through school. He saw that she learned to read and write and speak proper French. He educated her in music and art and the social graces."

But Bricktop, like most of Josephine's friends, was not an admirer of Pepito. "Josephine was a smart kid," she said. "She could have picked a lot of that up on her own, or from someone else who wasn't so interested in using her."

Pepito told Baker that she should have nothing more to do with Bricktop. He was aware, no doubt, of the many rumors circling around Paris that Josephine and Bricktop were lovers. Bricktop privately confirmed those stories to Jean-Claude Baker, who concluded that "in Josephine's scheme of things, men were more important, or at least more necessary, than women. Not so much for sex as for power. Still, once in a while there would be a lady lover in Josephine's life." In this case, she did as she was told by Pepito.

Baker's acquiescence was not blind faith. She did everything with such a calculated intensity that many people were frightened of her. In the early days of her career, she put in eighteen-hour days, working two or three jobs. Once introduced to learning, she never stopped, and by the time of her death she was well schooled in art with more than a passing knowledge of literature. She hired private tutors for all of her adopted children, trying to provide for them what she had not been given. "Josephine was a life force," said Jo Bouillon, her fourth husband, "and living meant growth and change."

By October, *Blackbirds* had gone to London, and Baker was again the biggest black star in Paris. Pepito, skilled in both financial affairs and public relations, "manipulated her back into stardom." He decided she should go into business for herself, and thereafter the hair straightener that Josephine used was sold under the name Baker-Fix. Pepito also helped her open a nightclub, Chez Josephine. Open twenty-four hours a day, it was a place where the rich and not yet famous could mix and relax. "I want people to shake off their worries the way a dog shakes off his fleas," Josephine remarked. The club made a lot of money.

Ever anxious to stay in the limelight, Baker announced that in June 1927 she had married Pepito, who was a count, and that she was now a countess. Harlem was elated. Interviewed by the *Amsterdam News*, the countess "admitted that she had made a fortune," but was looking to the future. "The Count is going to devote the rest of his life to perfecting me." Hungry for details, the press pursued the story, only to discover that none of it was true.

As if that was not enough, Baker's memoirs were published that summer, written by Marcel Sauvage. In them she observed: "I've heard a lot of talk about the war. What a funny story. I swear I don't understand it at all, but it disgusts me. I have a horror of men with only one arm, one leg, one eye. I sympathize with them with all my heart, but I have a physical repulsion from everything unhealthy."

The press pounced on Josephine's insult to wounded veterans. Becoming frightened of the bad publicity, she claimed: "That book? I don't know anything about my book. I never wrote nor read a line of it." She then threatened to sue Sauvage. He replied, "I don't know whether Josephine Baker will be so ill-advised as to sue me on the score that I wrote her book without her, but if she does, I shall take delight in publishing additional and very spicy details. I shall tell brutally what I learned about Miss Baker's private life from her own lips." Josephine decided not to sue after all and gave a benefit performance for crippled war veterans. The book sold well, and Sauvage and Baker remained friends. But Pepito decided it was time to give Paris a rest.

In January 1928 Josephine, Pepito, Pepito's mother, his cousin Zito, a secretary, a maid, two dogs, 196 pairs of shoes, and assorted dresses, furs, and face powders set off by train for Vienna. They were met by armed guards at the Vienna station because petitions had been circulating from right-wing student groups to "ban Josephine's brazen-faced heathen dances." The theater she was scheduled to appear in was shut down by the City Council on a technicality. A smaller theater was found, next to a Catholic church. Father Frey, a Jesuit priest, announced that he would hold services for three days "in atonement for outrages on morality committed by Josephine Baker and other performers." There for a month, every performance was sold out. She went to Prague next and was greeted by a mob wanting to catch just a glimpse of the "black devil." In Budapest "they tore my dress apart, they wanted to see me naked," she wrote. She went to Holland, to Norway and Sweden, and finally to Germany.

Her Berlin engagement was cut short, and she went on to Dresden: "The citizens of Dresden were scandalized to see Germany's national dances parodied in the convulsions of the coloured girl." Munich prohibited her performance: "It would have been disagreeable . . . to have to protect from the public fury this Negress who has already been booed everywhere." French reporters, covering the Central European tour, treated the events with "lighthearted irony." This was a fight between the violin and the sax, they said. "The sax was going to win." Baker left the Continent for South America.

She returned to Paris in April 1929, telling the press: "I don't want to live without Paris. It's my country." Her tantrums had preceded her, however, and no big theaters wanted to engage this temperamental star who brought her animals to the theater, was always late, and went through many mood swings. At that time producers Henri Varna ("a dapper vaudevillian and opera star") and Oscar Dufrenne ("a former music hall comic") were preparing a new revue, *Paris Qui Remue* (Paris Which Bustles), built around the forthcoming

JOSEPHINE WITH HER PET LEOPARD, CHIQUITA, PRESENTED TO HER BY PRODUCER HENRI VARNA, DEAUVILLE, FRANCE, SEPTEMBER 1930.

Exposition Coloniale, a celebration of the French Empire. The exposition had little to do with Paris or France, focused as it was on the colonies—Martinique, Algeria, Indochina, Equatorial Africa, and Madagascar—and the show followed suit. Who better than Baker to represent those possessions? A song for her was written in that show, "J'ai Deux Amours," that

moved a nation to tears and became her signature. "I have two loves," she sang, "my country and Paris." Opening night was September 26, 1930. Paris, formerly enchanted, was now deeply in love. Organizers of the Colonial Exposition were so taken with Josephine that they selected her in 1931 as the queen of the exposition, only to rescind the title when reminded that she did not come from any colony of France and was not a native speaker.

INCREASINGLY through the twenties, Josephine was transformed from *l'enfant sauvage* to a sophisticated lady. The change was slow at first and very subtle. This woman who had made her mark by appearing naked on the stage with a feather between her legs and a string of bananas around her waist, could not afford to proceed hastily. Poet e. e. cummings noted the metamorphosis: "In *Chocolate Dandies* she resembled some tall, vital, incomparable fluid nightmare, which crossed its eyes and warped its limbs in a purely unearthly manner. It may seem preposterous that this terrifying nightmare should have become the most beautiful star of the Parisian stage. Yet such is the case." Josephine knew that failure to change would surely doom her career. Pepito arranged acting, singing, and dancing lessons for her. Varna taught her how to walk regally down a flight of stairs. She also took ballet lessons.

In 1929 Josephine and Pepito had purchased a large châteaulike suburban house in Le Vésinet, outside of Paris. The house stood on several acres and had plenty of room for the menagerie she had collected over the years. Baker had thirteen dogs as well as cats, rabbits, and a leopard. Baker's private life was, of course, highly visible. "At home she dressed simply in skirts and blouses. She seemed much younger, almost like a little girl. She loved nature. The most cynical interviewers who saw her in this setting were charmed," wrote biographer Phyllis Rose. A new Josephine Baker, the protector of abandoned animals and lover of the simple life, emerged. She was often photographed in domestic pursuits. By 1931 the Baker who sang "J'ai Deux Amours" was fully accepted. "She left us a negresse, droll and primitive, she comes back a great artist," reporters said.

In the early thirties, Baker began a successful recording career and starred in several forgettable motion pictures. She had one world left to conquer, the country of her origin. "She wanted to come home," said Langston Hughes. Pepito and Baker sailed for New York on the French liner *Normandie* in September 1935. It had been ten years since she had been in New York. She had high expectations. Pepito had arranged for her to star in a lavish production, reminiscent of the Folies. Vernon Duke, the composer of "April in Paris," wrote the music, Ira Gershwin the lyrics, Vincente Minnelli designed the sets and costumes, and the ballet master was George Balanchine. In addition to Josephine, the show starred Fanny Brice, Eve Arden, and Bob Hope. The Josephine Baker who appeared in this 1936 Ziegfeld Follies was not appreciated. The reviews were disastrous. The worst was a strangely bitter piece that appeared in *Time:* "Josephine Baker is a Saint Louis washerwoman's daughter who stepped out of a Negro burlesque show into a life of adulation and luxury in Paris during the booming 1920s. In sex appeal to jaded Europeans of the jazz-loving type, a Negro wench always has a head start. The particular tawny hue of tall and stringy Josephine Baker's bare skin stirred French pulses. But to Manhattan theatregoers last week she was just a slightly buck-toothed young Negro woman whose figure might be matched in any night-club show, and whose dancing and singing might be topped practically anywhere outside of Paris."

Stunned, Baker blamed Pepito for making a poor contract and not overseeing the production. Feeling put upon just one time too many by his famous companion, he left for Paris without her. They never saw each other again. Diagnosed with cancer, Pepito died months later in the spring of 1936. He left everything to her, with the ominous statement, "She'll need it."

On her own, Baker returned to France. All too soon she was drawn into a world war and faced financial ruin as a result of her adoption of "a family of man," twelve children of various races and nationalities. Friends had to rescue her more than once. But Josephine always had an amazing ability to create and re-create herself. So after each fall, she would return anew as *Josephine Baker, Star.* In 1973 she at last made triumphal visits to Carnegie Hall and to Harlem. In 1975 she appeared in a revue in Paris that celebrated her fifty years in show business. She told reporters they would find four Josephines at the show: "One of four years, one of twelve, one of twenty, and of course me. They don't look very much alike," she said, "but in the theater, illusion is what counts." She died four days later.

THE FUNERAL PROCESSION FOR JOSEPHINE BAKER ON APRIL 15, 1975, BEGAN AT THE SALPÊTRIÈRE HOSPITAL, PASSED IN FRONT OF THE BOBINO THEATRE, AND PROCEEDED TO THE MADELEINE, WHERE THOUSANDS CAME TO PAY THEIR LAST RESPECTS. ON THE FOLLOWING SATURDAY, A SECOND FUNERAL SERVICE WAS HELD IN MONTE CARLO.

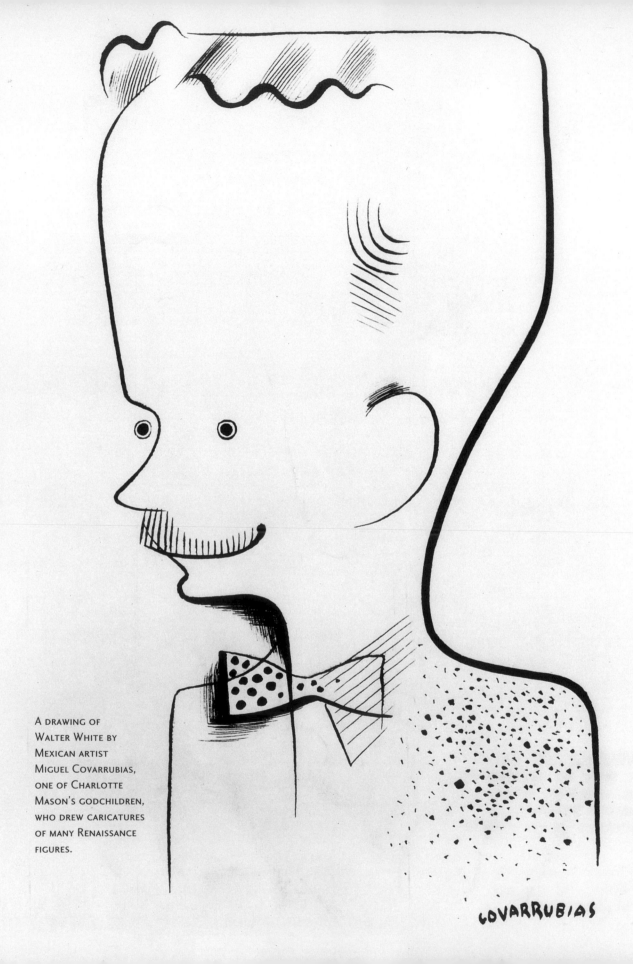

A DRAWING OF
WALTER WHITE BY
MEXICAN ARTIST
MIGUEL COVARRUBIAS,
ONE OF CHARLOTTE
MASON'S GODCHILDREN,
WHO DREW CARICATURES
OF MANY RENAISSANCE
FIGURES.

COVARRUBIAS

2
WALTER WHITE

Thirteen-year-old Walter White, so light-skinned he could easily have passed for white, vividly remembered the moment in 1906 when he became black. Atlanta, his hometown, was the scene of a race riot brought on by newspaper stories of brutal attacks on white women by black men, by a bitter political campaign that played the race card, and by an unbearably hot summer. A torch-bearing mob was advancing toward the house of the "nigger mail carrier," Walter's father. "In the flickering light the mob swayed, paused, and began to flow toward us," he wrote in his autobiography, *A Man Called White*. "In that instant there opened up within me a great awareness; I knew who I was. I was a Negro, a human being with an invisible pigmentation which marked me a person to be hunted, hanged, abused, discriminated against, kept in poverty and ignorance, in order that those whose skin was white would have readily at hand a proof patent and conclusive, accessible to the moron and the idiot as well as the wiseman and the genius." The house did not burn. Black friends who lived nearby fired shots, and the mob turned back in fear. White later said that he was at that moment "gripped by the knowledge of my identity, and in the depths of my soul I was vaguely aware that I was glad of it."

GOING TO NEW YORK IN 1918 was not Walter White's idea: he had been recruited by James Weldon Johnson to work as his assistant at the NAACP. At first reluctant to leave a career in actuarial insurance, White came to see that an opportunity to assume the mantle of a national race leader fit in well with his life's mission of service. He would during the course of his long career in civil rights take it as his special task to explain the meaning of race to white audiences. An inveterate letter writer and dilettante novelist—Carl Van Vechten called his work good propaganda and bad fiction—he lobbied constantly during the 1920s on behalf of himself and others, successfully arranging funding, book contracts, and fellowships. His congenial personality was much commented upon in the letters, biographies, and diaries of other Renaissance figures. He rarely got angry, preferring instead to disagree with a disarming politeness.

Yet there was something about Walter White that made people both admire and distrust him. W. E. B. Du Bois, with whom he often quarreled, wrote, "White could be one of the most charming of men. He was small in stature, appealing in approach, with a ready smile and a sense of humor. Also he was an indefatigable worker, who seemed never to tire. On the other hand, he was one of the most selfish men I have ever known." Van Vechten, whom White considered a friend, wrote simply, "I was never completely sold on Walter. He wasn't all there, really."

◆

WALTER WHITE WAS BORN on July 1, 1893, in Atlanta, Georgia, the second of five children. His parents, George and Madeline White, were members of Atlanta's small black middle class, a class defined as much by sensibility as by income and occupation. His father, a mail carrier who had attended college for one year before his parents died, was a religious man who taught his children to value education and service above all. Walter's mother, a former teacher, kept a spotless house (Walter considered himself a victim of his mother's "passion for neatness") and supported her husband in his goals for their children. Both were light-skinned. "His mother was one-sixteenth Negro and his father, one-fourth," a 1948 *New Yorker* profile pointed out. Their son, Walter, had blue eyes, thin lips, and blond hair. "It seems altogether fantastic that whites in the South should call him a 'nigger' and whites in the North, a Negro," poet Claude McKay wrote. "White is whiter than many Europeans—even biologically." Indeed, Harvard anthropologist Walter Hooton would later calculate that on the basis of physical features like skin color, hair structure, nose, and jaw shape, White was 63/64 white.

Over the years the race pride of the thirteen-year-old evolved into a kind of pride with a vengeance. "I decided that I would infinitely rather be *what I was* than be one of the race which had forced the decision upon me," he explained. Unlike the other older Renaissance figures who spoke of racial identity in apologetic language—blacks are as good as whites—White was more militant, often pointing out the evils of white race pride. "No matter how low a white man fell," White wrote, "he could always hold fast to the smug conviction that he was superior to two-thirds of the world's population, for those two-thirds were not white." White was particularly critical of southern whites, writing on one occasion, "The South has so dehumanized and brutalized itself by its policy of repression of the Negro that my white characters [in novels] are true to life. They are ineffectual. They are depraved. They are rotten."

Walter began his secondary education at Atlanta University in 1908 and advanced from there to the college program, graduating in 1916. The university attracted light-skinned blacks from all over the South. Historian David Levering Lewis has observed that "so many of the students straddled the South's vigilant categories of black and white that a curious term, 'no-nation,' came into common use—denoting people who in time would face the wrenching choice of either falling back into Afro-America or exiting from it into troubled whiteness." Many chose to pass. "Every year approximately twelve thousand white-skinned Negroes disappear," White wrote. He was not one of them. Upon graduation he got a job preparing actuarial tables at the black-owned Standard Life Insurance Company.

White's commitment to service quickly got him involved in local educational controversies. The expense of maintaining a "separate but equal" school system, the law of the South, led the school board in Atlanta to abolish the eighth grade for black students in 1914 as a cost-cutting measure. The strategy worked so well that in 1916 the board proposed abolishing the seventh grade for black children. White along with several other community leaders decided to appeal to the NAACP in New York for help. He was elected to write the letter. Fearing the potential power of the black leaders, the school board withdrew its proposal. The leaders, fresh from their victory, formed an Atlanta branch of the NAACP and elected White secretary. To show-

WALTER WHITE (FRONT RIGHT) WAS A MEMBER OF ATLANTA UNIVERSITY'S VARSITY DEBATING TEAM, 1916.

case their efforts, they invited James Weldon Johnson to speak. At a mass meeting held for Johnson, White gave an impromptu "impassioned, rabble rousing" introduction that impressed Johnson and led to his recommendation that White be brought to New York.

The job at the New York office paid $1,200 a year, less than he had earned at Standard Life. At that time, James Weldon Johnson had worked for the association for less than two years, its total membership was under nine thousand, and the office staff was small. "We never knew from payday to payday whether salaries, rent, postage, and printing bills could be paid," Johnson would later write. With so much at risk, White weighed his decision carefully, seeking advice from a number of people. Edgar Weber, a former professor at Atlanta University, strongly advised against taking the job, warning him that "the only independent man is a businessman." White's mother thought New York City unsafe. His father, on the other hand, favored the move, suggesting to Walter that he could do much good. "It is your duty," he said, "to pass on what you have been given by helping others less fortunate to get a chance in life."

⚜

WALTER WHITE ARRIVED at the NAACP offices in New York on January 31, 1918. The work involved handling complaints of discrimination from across the country and lobbying legislators for antidiscrimination and anti-lynching laws. White participated in all these efforts but was most drawn to undercover work. On one of his first trips to the South, he posed as a "white man interested in buying cotton land" and befriended local whites, who confided to him the details of an event involving a black sharecropper who had been slowly burned to death for defending himself from a beating. Walter's light skin gave him an effective camouflage to investigate conditions in the South, a task he took on with zeal and at great personal risk.

In 1922, White married Leah Gladys Powell, who was a staff member of the NAACP. Born in Philadelphia and reared in Ithaca, New York, Gladys was the daughter of a concert baritone. Though light-skinned, she was not as fair as Walter, and she remembered, when they began courting, people "whispering about them when they walked into restaurants together. Usually it was someone shocked at a Negro woman with a white lover." They responded to such situations by speaking French, a ploy that lifted Gladys out of the African-American category.

She was mentioned fondly by a number of Renaissance figures. "Walter White and his glamorous Gladys used to have me over and feed me on good fried chicken in my student days for no other reason than that they just wanted to," Zora Neale Hurston recalled.

Russian movie director Sergei Eisenstein is said to have called her one of the most beautiful women he had ever seen. Essie Robeson "never saw anything quite so funny as the attempts of poet Witter Bynner, tall and clumsy, to do the tango with her." But Gladys White was not portrayed in any detail; she was assigned the accepted role of woman behind the successful man and was made more obscure by their eventual highly publicized divorce.

The divorce became the subject of national headlines because Walter's second marriage, to Poppy Cannon, was across the color line. Poppy was a white South African and a well-known cookbook writer. They had met at a party in 1929 but did not marry until 1949. At the 1929 party, Poppy remembered: "More vividly than Walter himself, I can repicture his wife, Gladys, and her twin sister. All eyes were on them. They were the most beautiful women I had ever seen—identical twins with glorious deep bronze complexions and both of them wearing white satin evening dresses."

Poppy and Walter met again in 1931, and their secret affair began at that point. It was not clear what finally propelled them into marriage, although by 1949 White's health was failing. ("Hanging like a cloud over me was the chilling fear that possibly I haven't as many years left as we dream of," Walter wrote Poppy a year and a half before they were married.) Walter said his marriage to Gladys had ended

PORTRAIT OF WALTER WHITE INSCRIBED TO JAMES WELDON JOHNSON, HIS BOSS, MENTOR, AND FRIEND, 1924.

years before. Nonetheless Walter and Poppy took a great risk; interracial marriages were rare and frowned upon. Both had children from previous marriages, whom they wanted to protect. ("Along with these fears, Darling," he continued, "is the thing which has haunted and plagued me with increasing devastation these recent weeks—what our marriage will do to the children.")

Walter submitted his resignation to the NAACP board. "After a highly emotional session" it was rejected. "About almost every reaction, public and private, we miscalculated," Poppy Cannon recalled. The white press, which they thought would crucify Walter, reported the event as fact. The black press, however, was outraged. "Newspapers rose in a storm of condemnation," Poppy reported. They described her as "a large white woman with grey eyes and long hair." She was furious at the characterization. Walter asked if she wanted to sue. He was nothing if not a survivor.

One glimpse of Walter's private life with Gladys, his wife of twenty-seven years, is provided by daughter Jane, who in 1948 gave an interview to *Ebony* magazine. Speaking of the twenties she said, "We lived in a wonderful apartment, with five enormous rooms. There were wonderful floors in our building, hardwood floors. There were moldings and panels on the walls." The Whites lived at 409 Edgecombe Avenue, in Sugar Hill, the most fashionable section of Harlem, and in its most sought-after building. "Indisputably, the most splendid; it has a doorman, an elevator with an operator, and a fine view of the Bronx," Jane White recalled. "The parties in Daddy's and Mother's apartment were formidable."

Of Gladys it is said that in 1923 she made an appearance in *Deep River*, an operetta that ran for six weeks on Broadway. Apparently those weeks were among the most thrilling of her life. "Since that time I have led a rather se-

cluded life," she told the *Ebony* reporter. Referring to the present, the article claimed: "The Whites belong to few organizations, are seldom seen in nightclubs. Mrs. White has not seen the interior of a nightclub in ten years." When in 1949 Walter finally told her of his love for Poppy, Gladys responded, "In all my married life there has never been anyone but you. I have lived a very lonely life. The children were all I've ever had with me when you were away." She did not, however, contest the divorce. Walter told Poppy he felt like "a heel."

WHITE REVEALED IN HIS 1942 autobiography that two significant events occurred in 1922. The first was his marriage to Gladys. The second was his meeting with H. L. Mencken, then editor of the *Smart Set*. That encounter marked the beginning of White's literary career.

After their meeting, White "received one of Mencken's characteristically terse and salty notes, asking, "Why don't you do the right kind of novel? You could do it, and it would create a sensation." Mencken's suggestion appealed to White, whose travels through the South on behalf of the association had given him a mine of rich material. NAACP board member Mary White Ovington lent Walter and Gladys her vacation home in Great Barrington, Massachusetts, and the Whites spent part of that summer there.

Writing "feverishly and incessantly for twelve days and parts of twelve nights, stopping only when fatigue made it physically and mentally impossible to write another word," White completed the first draft of his novel, *The Fire in the Flint*, a title taken from the English proverb "The fire in the flint never shows until it is struck." The story dealt openly with race hatred and lynchings in the South. On September 12, 1922, he wrote to Johnson: "By the time I come back, I hope to have a corrected draft ready for the caustic and devastating criticisms of yours and the two Spingarns and Mencken et al. Ora pro nobis."

As it turned out, White got many people to read the manuscript over the next two years. Joel Spingarn, an NAACP board member, felt that the novel, for all its power, simply was not well written. White was not discouraged by criticism and took every opportunity to promote the book, regardless of the critic or the nature of the critique. If the first approach failed, he would simply try someone else.

A chance encounter with John Farrar, editor of the *Bookman*, published by George H. Doran and Company, led White to show his manuscript to Farrar, who passed it on to Doran. Eugene Saxon, an associate editor, rejected it with the explanation that "the Negro characters of the novel are not what the readers expect." Doran's most profitable author at that time was Irvin S. Cobb, a champion of the South who wrote "happy darky" stories. While the manuscript was still under review, White sent the publisher a list of people he thought would write endorsements. The list included H. G. Wells (whom he had met in London in 1921); Carl Van Doren, editor of the journal *Century;* and H. L. Mencken.

Still the editors rejected it, writing that "the verdict, I am sorry to say, is against the book. No one here, I can assure you, lacks sympathy for the thesis underlying your work but it is the method of presentation to which we take exception." Saxon felt that White's treatment of race "would only result in putting off into the future a decent settlement such as we all desire."

White's response was three pages. To the specific charge of one-sidedness he asked, "Is it not about time that the prosecution should be heard? For fifty years or more the argument has been all on one side, i.e., for the defense. Thomas Nelson Page, George W. Cable,

Thomas Dixon, Irvin Cobb . . . all have painted the Negro as a brute, a rapist, a 'good old nigger,' or as a happy-go-lucky, irresponsible and shiftless type."

Again Saxon answered: "I have no quarrel —or practically none—with what you say in your book. It is what you don't say that I find fault with. Personally I should be entirely willing to have ninety-five percent of all you say remain in the book if there were some moderately fair presentation of the white man's case."

White once again responded, suggesting that the book be published with a preface containing their correspondence, "thus giving the publishers an opportunity to express disagreement with the novel's thesis." White also wrote Joel Spingarn, sending copies of the correspondence. Spingarn was not encouraging; he expressed the hope that the book would be turned down for White's own good.

On October 8, Saxon sent a third and final rejection notice. "I am sorry to say that the chance for your book here is definitely closed." He offered to help place the book elsewhere, though, and he and White remained friends through the years. At the same time, White wrote to Mencken "to see if he would submit it to Knopf."

Mencken was more helpful. His willingness to promote White's book was in part based on his campaign at that moment to bash the South, a region he saw as filled with "yokels, hillbillies and peasants." When White sent him a copy of the manuscript, Mencken wrote back, "I can't imagine why any sane man should object to anything in the novel. It is admittedly a Tendenz piece. But it is certainly fair and accurate enough. The Southern crackers, if anything, are worse than you make them."

Mencken was at first skeptical about taking the book to Knopf, however, writing that it might be wiser to send to it a Negro publisher. "Aren't there some colored publishing firms

WALTER WHITE WITH HIS BEAUTIFUL FIRST WIFE, GLADYS, AND THEIR CHILDREN, JANE AND WALTER JR.

WHITE AT ATLANTA UNIVERSITY. JAMAICAN POET CLAUDE MCKAY ALWAYS WONDERED HOW AMERICA COULD HAVE THOUGHT OF WHITE AS BLACK.

WITH POPPY CANNON, HIS SECOND WIFE, IN TOKYO, AUGUST 1949, JUST AFTER THEIR MARRIAGE. THIS WAS THEIR CHRISTMAS CARD THAT YEAR.

WHITE, GRACE NAIL JOHNSON, AND JAMES WELDON JOHNSON AT THE JOHNSONS' SUMMER HOUSE, FIVE ACRES, IN GREAT BARRINGTON, MASSACHUSETTS.

already in existence? If not, wouldn't it be possible to induce somebody to organize one?" he asked. Mencken felt that such an outlet would provide White and other black writers the freedom to write what they pleased without the sort of criticism made by Doran.

White rejected this suggestion, arguing that "colored people know everything in my book—they live and suffer the same things every day of their lives. It is not the colored reader at whom I am shooting but the white men and women who do not know the thing that you and I know." Aware that both promotion and profit would be lacking in a black press, White was determined to obtain the most conservative and respectable white publisher he could find.

Careful not to offend, White once again wrote to Mencken: "You wrote me recently you doubted whether Knopf would be interested in my novel. Would you object to my talking the matter over with him?" Mencken did not object. White immediately contacted Blanche Knopf, wife of publisher Alfred, asking her to read a novel "that I know has many gaucheries, many inept and crude phrases, but one that could be improved with expert editing." He also persuaded her to have his friend Carl Van Doren read the novel and give an opinion of it. Blanche was more receptive, relying heavily on Van Vechten's opinion as well as Van Doren's, and agreed to publish it.

WALTER WHITE'S
New Novel

FLIGHT

The Story of a Girl who "Passes"

Mr. White's chief character is perhaps more significant and representative than is commonly realized—a colored girl of Creole descent, she successfully goes white and marries a millionaire.
Her life apart from her own people, however, becomes gradually unsatisfactory and through a series of experiences which lead her to discover the true genius of her race, she returns to it.
Those who know Mr. White's work need not be told that this novel is not only important but keenly interesting throughout.

$2.50 Everywhere

THE WEARY BLUES

THE WEARY BLUES
by LANGSTON HUGHES
With an introduction by Carl Van Vechten.

This young poet has been recognized by the *New York Times* as "the most startlingly human of all this advance guard from Parnassus. . . . We sincerely hope that Langston Hughes will receive the wide reading he deserves".

$2.00 Everywhere

ALFRED A. KNOPF

730 Fifth Ave   BORZOI BOOKS   NEW YORK

WHITE'S SECOND BOOK, *FLIGHT*, ABOUT THE RENAISSANCE THEME OF PASSING, ADVERTISED IN THE JOURNAL *MESSENGER* WITH LANGSTON HUGHES'S FIRST BOOK OF POETRY, *THE WEARY BLUES*.

Not wishing to alienate Joel Spingarn, who had been so insistently negative, White confided to him, "I realize my story is far from being what it should be. But some day I can perhaps tell you the reason why it is necessary for me to try my hardest to get it published now. I am sorry I cannot divulge it now, but when I can you will see the situation." White's reason was never revealed. He may have had financial problems, as he did ask Knopf for a $250 advance. However, it seems more likely that this was simply a sympathy ploy. It was W. E. B. Du Bois's opinion that White "was often absolutely unscrupulous" in pursuing his objectives.

Once published, White encouraged both friends and acquaintances to write reviews. Carl Van Vechten called the novel "a bitter and sensational arraignment of a pseudo-civilization, written by a Negro, [which] would arouse the latent sense of injustice even in the soul of a U.S. senator." White sent an autographed copy to NAACP board member Oswald Garrison Villard, stating, "I shall not feel bad if after reading it you do not feel disposed to review it in the *Nation*. If, however, you should find anything of merit in it which would cause you to want to review it, I need not tell you how happy I would be." As a result of his efforts, *Fire in the Flint* was given a large number of flattering reviews by prominent literary figures.

For all of White's efforts, the book was only a moderate success, selling about 700 pre-release copies out of the 3,000 printed but gaining in popularity after its release. He wrote James Weldon Johnson at one point, "Knopf tells me that sales are going along pretty well, though nothing to boast of as yet." Published in August, it was in its third edition by November. White suggested in December 1924 that it had sold between five and ten thousand copies. Given his penchant for self-promotion, the lower figure is probably closer.

Spurred on by the notoriety of his first book, White began work on a second novel in the fall of 1924. With Van Vechten's help, he sought to improve his style. *Flight* was a novel about passing, the favorite Renaissance theme. "It is a pleasure to be able to state that Mr. White's second novel is much better than his first," Van Vechten wrote. "It is written with a calm detachment of which *The Fire in the Flint* contains no hint." Unfortunately, *Flight* did not sell as well as *Fire*. The novelty and the hard-hitting story evident in the first book were missing from the second. Wallace Thurman gave it a stinging review in the *Messenger:* "a novel must, to earn the name, be more than mere social service report." Frank Horne, a black writer, wrote an even more negative review in the black journal *Opportunity:* "Mr. White's style suffers mainly from a woeful lack of clarity. Such elementary matters as faulty sentence structure often rise to affront one."

Negative reviews in the black press angered White. Horne's review in *Opportunity* particularly infuriated him, and he wrote a protest to the editor, Charles Johnson, "solely for private consumption." White said it was not the adverse criticism he objected to but the inexperience and lack of comprehension of the reviewer. "Mr. Horne's strictures on *Flight* would be more bearable, too, if there were fewer split infinitives in his piece," he added.

Not wishing White's ire to be elevated into controversy within the civil rights ranks, Charles Johnson arranged for Nella Larsen, White's friend, to write a response to Horne's negative review. Larsen's piece was a spirited rebuttal, indicating she felt "surprise, anger and pity" upon reading the review, and suggesting that "Horne fails to realize the heart of the tale." White appreciated Larsen's review and turned his considerable lobbying efforts in the direction of her writing projects as a result.

White published no more novels, but he did use his personal and professional influence to promote the work of other writers. On January 4, 1925, for example, he wrote to Blanche Knopf, thanking her for sending him the proofs of Langston Hughes's first book, *The Weary Blues*. "I have followed Mr. Hughes' writing since he was first published in the *Crisis* and I look forward eagerly to reading these poems." To Hughes he wrote, "I hasten to extend to you my warmest congratulations on the acceptance of your book of poems by Knopf. It is certainly great to have a foreword by Van Vechten and have Covarrubias to do the jacket."

White had a somewhat more convoluted relationship with poet Claude McKay. In his autobiography, McKay describes White as "ingratiating as Y.M.C.A. secretary." Their correspondence ran along two tracks—discussions of art and propaganda and McKay's dire appeals for money and contacts. McKay, less naive than Hughes, understood the nature and extent of White's support. A few months later White wrote to Langston Hughes: "Claude had sent me a number of poems and one short story, and I don't like to say it, but they are almost uniformly third rate. The story is too long to go into here, but I will tell you all about him when I see you."

For Countee Cullen, White reserved the greatest largesse. He was instrumental in

Cullen's publication of four volumes of verse and individual poems in the *American Mercury*, *Century*, *Harper's*, the *Bookman*, and an anthology of black American poetry. In addition, White tried unsuccessfully to arrange a Rhodes scholarship for the Harvard student and to persuade the committee by publishing a volume of poems. Toward this end, he collected a bunch of poems and sent them to Carl Van Doren at *Century*. Van Doren replied, "I hardly think Countee Cullen has enough verse here for a volume that would be quite worthy of him. Perhaps ten of his poems are excellent; the rest are below his best."

White continued to promote other writers well into the thirties and forties. But as the twenties drew to a close, he concentrated on what would be his major avocation: championing civil rights for black citizens. He increasingly took on the duties and the burdens of the NAACP. It was a fortuitous decision, because by the thirties, literary Harlem was no longer in vogue.

ON NOVEMBER 20, 1931, Walter White received a telegram from his brother George, saying that their father was dying. George White Sr., who had retired from the post office in 1921 after forty-three years, had been walking home one night when he stepped off a curb and into the path of a passing car. The driver, "Dr. Henry Grady, a white physician from the municipal hospital, placed the victim in his car and sped to the 'modern, sanitary, beautifully equipped medical facility for white Atlantans.'" He was placed in intensive care. Hearing of the accident, one of his brown-skinned sons-in-law went in search of George senior, looking first in the colored hospitals and ending up at the white facility. When the staff realized that George senior was black—"Have we put a nig-

ger in the white ward?"—they ceased caring for him and sent him in a driving rain to the "dilapidated building reserved for Afro-Americans."

Walter immediately went to Atlanta and sat with his father for the seventeen days that he lived. His descriptions of the hospital were appalling. He wrote that "Dinginess, misery, and poverty pressed so hard on one from every side that even a well person could not avoid feeling a little sick in those surroundings." Huge cockroaches scampered about the wards and corridors, and "the pattern of nocturnal nausea they made was occasionally varied by the appearance of a rat." A band of white missionaries "screeching hymns about Jesus's love" at the moment of his father's death brought out all the strain and bitterness that Walter felt. "I suspect my own voice was as harsh as theirs," he wrote, "and I told them to go away and at least let my father die in peace."

After his father's funeral, as Walter White returned to New York by train in a Jim Crow car, his wallet was stolen. This man of charm, good humor, and dedication did not go directly home. He went to the apartment of Poppy Cannon and wept in her arms. This was the beginning of an affair that would last for many years and end in the breakup of his marriage.

It was also in 1931 that James Weldon Johnson left New York for Fisk University and was succeeded at the NAACP by Walter White. White requested—and was granted by the board, over the strong objections of W. E. B. Du Bois—a twelve-hundred-dollar raise. According to Du Bois, "White's assumption of office was to set off an explosion within a year. His attitudes and actions were unbearable." Du Bois hinted that Johnson had left in part because Walter was out of control. Certainly after so many years in Johnson's shadow, White was determined to make his own mark. Even Du Bois was eventually no match for the methodical White, who was a superb orator and fund-

PORTRAIT OF WALTER WHITE BY PHOTOGRAPHER CARL VAN VECHTEN,
AUGUST 17, 1932. VAN VECHTEN ARRANGED TO MEET WHITE THROUGH
ALFRED KNOPF, THEIR MUTUAL PUBLISHER. WHITE WAS VAN VECHTEN'S FIRST
GUIDE TO THE UPTOWN CROWD.

manded that Du Bois recant, accept censorship, or leave. Du Bois resigned, writing, "In 35 years of public service . . . I have not always been right, but I have been sincere, and I am unwilling at this late day to be limited in the expression of my honest opinions in the way in which the Board proposes."

Du Bois resigned, and Walter White was left alone to run the NAACP on his own terms. Unlike James Weldon Johnson, who was a behind-the-scenes power broker, White loved to be in front of the camera, reported upon in the press, feared, admired, and respected. A superb lobbyist, by the 1940s he was considered the most powerful black man in America. His sister Madeline, an Atlanta social worker, wrote him once, "You have no idea, Walter, how many of these homes [in the backwoods] have your picture, often cut out of a newspaper and tacked to a beam. Or pasted on a little cracked mirror. They depend on you. For many of them you are all they have." His prominence, however, also brought him criticism from all sides. Many whites feared his program to end segregation in America. Many blacks distrusted his approach. Said Lerone Bennett Jr.,

raiser. With the journal *Crisis* no longer self-supporting and dependent on the association's contribution, Du Bois was forced to choose between accepting White's board-approved direction or resigning. What touched off the furor was an essay Du Bois wrote on the advantages of segregation, a curious position for one who had so long opposed Booker T. Washington's notions of separation. White de-

editor of *Ebony:* "He was a gregarious man who loved good food, old wine, and the company of important white people." But White left an important legacy. As Bruce Kellner, biographer of Carl Van Vechten, observed: "Walter White forced the issue of race relations to national attention and stripped racists of their most prized resource, public indifference." It was an important contribution for a black man called White.

3

ZORA NEALE HURSTON

IN 1925 LEONARD "KIP" RHINELANDER—white, highly educated, and heir to the fortune of a wealthy New York family—married Alice Jones, who was passing for white. Kip learned of his wife's race early in their marriage, and in 1926 he sought an annulment, claiming that Alice had seduced and duped him. During the trial, she was forced to strip to the waist in the courtroom to determine if he could have known that she was black. The sensational trial lasted ten days and was covered extensively in the New York press. At stake, according to the *Inter-State Tattler* was settling, "for the time being at least, the claim by members of the Ku Klux Klan and other bodies of white people that the white race is superior to all others." The court eventually granted the divorce, and Alice Jones Rhinelander was paid a settlement. The *Tattler* reported that the bride was paid up to one million dollars to "soothe her wounded feelings" and not disclose certain letters "alleged to be very damaging to the Rhinelander family." Asking a woman to bare her breasts in public was unthinkable in the 1920s. "A'n't I a woman?" abolitionist and former slave Sojourner Truth reportedly asked in a speech at a women's rights convention in 1851. The New York court in 1927 was not so sure.

PORTRAIT OF ZORA NEALE HURSTON BY CARL VAN VECHTEN, NOVEMBER 9, 1934. MANY SCHOLARS NOW SUGGEST THAT HURSTON WAS THIRTY-FOUR BUT PASSING FOR TWENTY-FOUR AT THIS TIME.

SOMEWHERE ALONG THE SOUTHeastern seaboard in 1914, Zora Neale Hurston was making her way north to Baltimore, hiring herself out as a domestic and dreaming of another life. We do not know if this witty and eccentric young woman from Eatonville, Florida, had hopes of being called the foremost woman writer of the New Negro Renaissance or if she suspected that the world war just beginning would propel her into the national limelight. We do know that when she was a child, she climbed "to the top of one of the huge chinaberry trees which guarded her family's front gate, and looked out over the world." What she saw was the horizon.

Like all the migrants of this era, Hurston wanted a better life. Unlike some, who wished to dig up the bones of their ancestors and carry them North, she never lost her fondness for the South. She returned many times to gather research and finally resettled there in the early 1950s to live "the kind of life for which I was made, strenuous and close to the soil." But it was the northward journey in 1914 to the end of the world, as she called it, that propelled Zora into the Renaissance.

Zora Neale Hurston, always viewing the world from the perspective of that chinaberry tree in her parents' yard, was off-key, the word she used to explain how she came to write her first novel, *Jonah's Gourd Vine*. Hurston wanted to write about the moment in the day when the sun and the "bossman" were gone and the community, feeling powerful and human, was

HURSTON AT HOWARD UNIVERSITY, WASHINGTON, D.C., CIRCA 1920.

left to its own devices. Although some have suggested that by so doing she created a black world "with no white folks to command them," her view was more complex. Those who sat on the porch, she explains, were "tongueless, earless, eyeless" all day long, but at sundown "they became lords of sounds and lesser things. They passed nations through their mouths. They sat in judgment."

One understands Zora Neale Hurston best when one realizes that she was almost always in debt. Her constant search for money produced an unpleasant side to this woman already in disguise, who was noted for her humor. "She was full of sidesplitting anecdotes, humorous tales and tragicomic stories," Langston Hughes wrote in his autobiography. "She would make you laugh one minute and cry the next." As an artist, she struggled with an insatiable desire to be left alone to create. "I shall wrassle me up a future or die trying," she once wrote her patron, Charlotte Mason. What these opposing desires—to survive and to create—produced was a character that was often unsympathetic. "There is something about poverty that smells like death," she wrote. "Dead leaves dropping off the heart like leaves in a dry season and rolling around the feet; impulses smothered too large in the fetid air of underground caves."

The contrast between Zora Neale Hurston and James Weldon Johnson (see chapter 5) could not be more striking. Born in Notasulga, Alabama, and raised in Eatonville, Florida, an all-black incorporated town, she had few of the middle-class supports that were the mainstays of Johnson's upbringing. Eatonville was but five miles from Orlando and was economically dependent on that urban center. Yet it was also a world unto itself. Hurston's father was the town's three-term mayor, a position that offered high status but low pay. He was also a carpenter and a traveling Baptist preacher, two other low-paying positions in the rural South. Nevertheless, he provided well for his family. "There were plenty of oranges, grapefruit, tangerines, guavas, and other fruits in our yard," Zora wrote. Her mother, who like her father possessed only a primary school education, insisted that her children work hard in school. While she "exhorted all at every opportunity to jump at de sun," Zora was her special child.

In her youth, Zora spent hours on the front porch of Joe Clark's General Store, "the heart and spring of the town." It was here that she was introduced to the rich oral tradition that would be the foundation of her work. Hurston wrote that "there were no discrete nuances of life on Joe Clark's porch . . . all emotions were naked and nakedly arrived at."

WHEN HURSTON WAS NINE, her mother died, and her world exploded. "That hour began my wanderings," she wrote. "Not so much in geography, but in time. Then not so much in time as in spirit." Often at odds with her father, she got along even less well with her stepmother. As a consequence she was sent away to live with relatives, and by the age of fourteen she was left to fend for herself. She found work as a maid and at one point served as a maid and wardrobe assistant for a touring Gilbert and Sullivan troupe.

Hurston seems to have reinvented her persona at various points along the way. In her au-

tobiography, she calls her life a combination of "sham and tinsel, honest metal and sincerity." Even her date of birth was a matter of some dispute. It is now suspected that at the age of twenty-six she graduated from Morgan Academy (now Morgan State University) in Baltimore. She was passing for sixteen. As a character in *Their Eyes Were Watching God* explains: "The worst thing Ah ever knowed how to do was taking a few years offa her age and dat ain't never harmed nobody." Owning a single dress, one change of underwear, and a pair of tan oxfords, she got along well with her more privileged classmates. Her abilities were noticed by her teachers, who on several occasions left Hurston in charge of their classes. Though an erratic student, doing well in classes she liked and less well in those she did not, she next enrolled at Howard University in Washington, D.C. It was there that she met Alain Locke, a philosophy professor and Renaissance leader, and became a part of his campus literary society. Through Locke, she also met poet Georgia Douglas Johnson and attended her Saturday night literary sessions.

"Although Locke rarely saw promise in young women," according to Steven Watson, he made an exception of Zora Neale. Her first short story, "John Redding Goes to Sea," was published in *Stylus*, the literary society's magazine. In the fall of 1924, Locke recommended her to Charles S. Johnson, editor of the journal *Opportunity*, who was collecting material for a competition. She sent him several short stories and a play titled *Color Struck*. Johnson urged her to come to New York and to submit some of her work to the *Opportunity* competition. She arrived there with a single bag containing her manuscripts, her clothes, and $1.50. "No job, no friends and a lot of hope" was how she put it.

In May 1925 she won second prize for drama (*Color Struck*), second prize for fiction ("Spunk"), and honorable mention for two other works. Drawing attention to herself by striding up to the lectern, her scarf flung dramatically over her shoulder, she shouted, "ColorRR Struck!" for effect. Many years later Alice Walker would comment that Zora was apparently "not humbled by second place."

At the awards dinner she met best-selling novelist Fannie Hurst and Annie Nathan Meyer, founder of Barnard College. Fannie Hurst hired Hurston as a secretary and chauffeur. Hurst's remembrance of Hurston's job interview reveals much of Zora's character. Hurst wrote:

> She walked into my study one day by telephone appointment, carelessly, a big-boned, good-boned young woman, handsome and light yellow, with no show of desire for the position of secretary for which she was applying. Her dialect was as deep as the Deep South, her voice and laughter the kind I used to hear on the levees of St. Louis when I was growing up in that city. As Zora expressed it, we "took a shine" to one another and I engaged her on the spot as my live-in secretary.

Hurst soon fired Zora because her typing was abysmal, her handwriting illegible, and her patience for her work sporadic, but retained her as a chauffeur and companion.

Annie Nathan Meyer arranged for Hurston to attend Barnard on scholarship. Zora began her studies in 1925. She was by then thirty-four years old, passing for twenty-four. As the only black student on campus, she collected "no lurid tales of race discrimination," and she called herself "a sacred black cow." Her correspondence suggests, however, that she was ordered not to attend the Barnard prom, held at the Ritz, because Annie Nathan Meyer thought it unseemly.

Hurston made friends at Barnard, as she had everywhere else. One particular friend, Elizabeth Beer, and her mother schooled Hurston on good manners, etiquette being a national craze at that time. "I found out about forks, who entered a room first, sat down first, and who offered to shake hands," Zora revealed. Skills, no doubt, that lent a degree of charm to her outrageous behavior. Her friends complained constantly to each other about her and forgave most of her acts of rudeness and unreliability. "You made all the girl's faults seem to be her virtues," her friend Carl Van Vechten wrote in response to a piece Fannie Hurst did about Zora. "As a matter of fact, they were not faults, they were characteristics. There is quite a difference," he added.

Also as a result of the awards dinner, Hurston became a frequent guest at the parties of Carl Van Vechten and his wife, Fania Marinoff. "When Zora was there, she was the party," poet Sterling Brown once commented. Van Vechten described one occasion on which she "appeared attired in a wide Seminole Indian skirt, contrived of a thousand patches" and "still another time in a Norwegian skiing outfit," complete with flaps over her ears. Once, when she came into a room, he said, she "tossed a huge straw hat (as big as a cart wheel) on the floor and yelled, 'I am the queen of the niggerati.'" On another occasion Zora recalled being taken to a "swanky" hotel by Fannie Hurst, "dressed up as an Asiatic person of royal blood and keeping a straight face while the attendants goggled at me and bowed low." These exaggerated instances of Uncle Tomming led Langston Hughes to characterize her as the perfect darky for her white acquaintances—"naive, childlike, sweet, humorous, and highly colored Negro." Yet even to him it seemed to be one of her great disguises. "Miss Hurston was clever, too," he wrote, "a student who didn't let college give her a broad *a* and who had great scorn for all pretensions, academic and otherwise."

Whatever her disguise, she was "a highly reserved and serious writer," critic Mary Helen Washington suggests, and an accomplished storyteller. Langston Hughes said that Hurston was the only individual he knew who could walk up to strangers on the street in Harlem and ask, as part of her anthropological work at Columbia, to measure their heads. She would not be refused.

Like all writers, Hurston and Hughes required a steady income so that they could create. Their choices were limited. Educated blacks could teach or go into business for themselves. Women could also go into nursing. That was it. During the Renaissance, support was offered, for the first time, by wealthy white patrons. Hurston and Hughes jumped at the opportunity. They soon learned it carried a price.

JESSIE FAUSET, LANGSTON HUGHES, AND ZORA NEALE HURSTON AT THE GRAVE OF BOOKER T. WASHINGTON, TUSKEGEE INSTITUTE, IN THE SUMMER OF 1927, ON THE SOUTHERN CAR TRIP THAT SPAWNED *MULE BONE*.

IN SEPTEMBER 1927, Hurston visited Charlotte Mason for the first time. Mason, born Charlotte van der Veer Quick, was of an old New York family who considered the Vanderbilts new money. At the death of her husband in 1908 she became increasingly interested in spiritualism and formed the opinion that through association with "primitives" she could recover something important that had been lost in Western civilization in general, American culture in particular. A cult of primitivism growing out of the disillusionment at the death and destruction of World War I appealed not only to Mason but to many wealthy Americans at this time. She wrote on one occasion to Alain Locke, "We have trampled every primitive instinct in the heart of man to dust, and today there is no recognition of vision or divine will among us."

With Locke's help, Mason focused her attention and her wealth on the New Negro in the twenties. Mason told Locke she wanted her "Negro protégés to slough off white culture and be their savage selves." Mason is said to have paid between $50,000 and $75,000 to Aaron Douglas, Miguel Covarrubias, Langston Hughes, Alain Locke, and Zora.

Among her protégés Mason counted Langston Hughes—"a golden star in the Firmament of Primitive Peoples." Mason dressed him in evening clothes and had him escort her to concerts and dinners and public occasions. She also supported him so he could write. Yet it was Hurston who was more often accused, in the words of Mary Helen Washington, of "playing the obsequious role of the swinging, happy darkie" for Mason. Mason asked her "children" never to reveal her name publicly as a patron, and only Hurston did. Langston held Mrs. Mason in such reverence that he even refused to give her name in his autobiography, written years after their breakup, speaking of her only as "a distinguished and quite elderly white lady who lived on Park Avenue." Hurston was more open in her assessment: "sometimes I would feel like a rabbit at a dog convention."

Mason drew up a contract with Hurston, as she had not done with Hughes, so that Zora could collect folklore and write. Hurston was paid $200 a month and was given money to purchase a car and a movie camera, but Mason was to control everything Hurston published. The contract stipulated that Zora was "faithfully to perform her task and to retain and lay before Mrs. Mason all of said information, data, transcripts of music, etc., which she shall have obtained." The arrangement continued from December 1927 to March 30, 1931, and then irregularly until September 1932. It was Hurston's major source of income during the heart of the Depression and one explanation for Mason's peculiar power over her. Hurston referred to her as the "guard mother who sits in the twelfth heaven and shapes the destinies of the primitives."

At the time of her meeting with Mason, Zora and Langston were very close friends. Hughes, then in his junior year at Lincoln University, received a note from her: "I went to see Mrs. Mason and I think we got on famously. God, I hope so!" The plan was that Hurston and Hughes were to write a folk opera together. Zora left for Mobile in December 1927 to begin the research. She wrote Hughes, urging him to follow her when school let out. During the winter of 1928, Hurston and Hughes spent time together in Westfield, New Jersey, working on their collaboration, titled *Mule Bone*. Louise Thompson—called attractive and brilliant by historian David Levering Lewis, called "a little bitty thing with a great big Momma who wanted her to marry someone in the arts" by writer Dorothy West—was hired by Mason as the typist. The three of them lived in a modest rooming house in the colored section of West-

field, and several versions of what transpired there have surfaced. Hughes suggested that Zora, who felt seriously hemmed in "in village-like Westfield," was restless and moody. Alain Locke, Mason's "precious brown boy," whom Hurston would later call "a malicious, spiteful little snot," visited the trio and reported that "too much horseplay and too little play" was being done. Mason, relying on Locke's snooping, decided to withdraw her funding. Only a long, contrite letter from Hughes restored them to her good graces and deep pockets. Though Thompson and Hughes remained good friends, Zora spoke in increasingly bitter terms of that "vile" Louise Thompson. Acting like a woman scorned, Hurston, who had always been attracted to younger men, finally left Westfield in May, saying, "I just went off to myself and tried to resolve to have no more friendships. Tears unceasing have poured down inside me."

Hurston and Hughes went their separate ways after Westfield. Hughes broke off his relationship with Mason over issues of censorship and control. Locke told Mason that it was Thompson's radical influence that steered him away from Park Avenue. The breakup was difficult for him. Becoming physically ill over the loss of mentor and money, Hughes left New York for Cleveland to recover with his family. There he learned that a local theater group was about to perform Hurston's play, *Mule Bone*. Obtaining a copy of the script, Hughes realized that "except for a few minor revisions of the first and third acts, this was their collaboration." He demanded recognition. The controversy enveloped many of the Harlem literati. Arthur Spingarn heard the details of the dispute from both sides at least twice and warned that "litigation is the last thing either of you should think of." Years later Van Vechten told Hughes that Zora "had a tantrum in my library . . . and threw herself on the floor and screamed and yelled! Bit the dust, in fact. You

ZORA WITH UKULELE IN HAND, POSSIBLY IN HER COLLEGE DAYS.

A YOUNG ZORA NEALE HURSTON.

ZORA, CIRCA 1925.
"ZORA IS PICTURESQUE, WITTY, ELECTRIC, INDISCREET, AND UNRELIABLE,"
SAID CARL VAN VECHTEN.

*To Carl Van Vechten —
Who plays lead trumpet in God's gold throne band —
Zora Neale Hurston*

A NOTE TO VAN VECHTEN WITH A COPY OF *THEIR EYES WERE WATCHING GOD.* HURSTON WAS A CLOSE FRIEND. SHE CALLED HIM A "NEGROTARIAN," HER TERM FOR RICH AND INFLUENTIAL WHITES WHO SUPPORTED THE NEW NEGRO MOVEMENT.

ORIGINAL DUST JACKET FOR ZORA'S MASTERPIECE, PUBLISHED IN 1937. "NO THEME, NO MESSAGE, NO THOUGHT," WROTE REVIEWER RICHARD WRIGHT.

ZORA WITH FRIENDS.

A FLAPPER OUTFIT, FLORIDA.

FANNIE HURST PHOTOGRAPHED BY CARL VAN VECHTEN, NOVEMBER 29, 1932. HURSTON WAS BRIEFLY HER SECRETARY AND ASSISTANT. HURST'S *IMITATION OF LIFE* (1934) BECAME A HIT MOVIE STARRING FREDI WASHINGTON.

woulda loved it, had it not concerned you."

Hurston claimed that she had never sent the play to Cleveland, that she had merely passed it on to Carl Van Vechten. Van Vechten supported her in this, although Hurston told him that the work was hers alone. "Langston and I started out together on the idea of the story," she wrote. "But being so much apart from rush of business, I started all over again . . . and this is the result of my work alone."

Hughes tried to contact Hurston by telephone, wire, and letter but got no answer. Finally she wrote to him to say she was coming to Cleveland to view the rehearsals. She agreed at first, according to Hughes, that the production could go forward with his name on it. But then, learning that Louise Thompson had been there, went into a rage "in his mother's living room" and said "that never, under any circumstances, would she permit any of her work to be linked" with his. Hurston made the claim that "it was my story from beginning to end, my dialogue, my situations." She left Cleveland for New York the next day, and Hughes reports in his autobiography that he "never heard from Miss Hurston again."

Apart from the issues of ego and jealousy, it is clear that the financial vulnerability of both Hughes and Hurston was at stake in this controversy. Neither writer was producing the results that "Godmother" Charlotte Mason had

ZORA IN EATONVILLE, FLORIDA, ON A FOLKLORE COLLECTING TRIP, 1935. SHE SAID SHE LEARNED TO "MAKE AND BREAK MARRIAGES, KILL BY REMOTE CONTROL, AND OTHER THINGS."

envisioned and that were the basis of her support, but neither could afford to be dismissed. Proof of authorship was the real issue, rather like "publish or perish." Hurston was still on Mason's payroll and Hughes, once off, spent some time and effort trying to get back on. Mason, however, was strict in her notions of the limits of largesse. When her "godchildren" strayed, her punishment was swift. Discipline and sacrifice were the lessons she sought to bestow on her primitives.

Once out of favor, Mason's children had to be very, very good to receive support. On one occasion in 1932, shortly before her money was cut off, Hurston wrote to beg "Godmother" for a pair of shoes: "I really need a pair of shoes. You remember that we discussed the matter in the fall and agreed that I should own only one pair at a time. I bought a pair in mid-December and they have held up until now. My big toe is about to burst out of my right shoe and so I must do something about it."

Hurston's notions of dignity and self-respect fall victim to these tales about Mason's fanatical control. There were more. Zora, for example, sometimes addressed letters to Mason, "little mother of the primitive world," and signed them, "Your pickaninny, Zora." Alice Walker, one of Hurston's strongest defenders, finding her alternately "winning and appalling," concluded in a classic understatement that "she was quite capable of saying, writing, or doing things *different* from what one might have wished." Hurston had her own explanation. "Born so widely apart in every way, the key to certain phases of my life had been placed in [Mason's] hands. I had been sent to her to get it. I owe her and owe her and owe her. Not only for material held, but for spiritual guidance."

HER "PERFECT DARKY ROLE," as labeled by Hughes, has left doubts in the minds of some about Hurston's racial politics. Her attitudes have troubled a number of black scholars who claim that she "did not write fiction in the protest tradition" and that she "made black Southern life appear easy going and carefree." In a well-known essay, "How It Feels to Be Colored Me," Hurston argued, "I am not tragically colored. There is no great sorrow dammed up in my soul, nor lurking behind my eyes." The core of Hurston's work does indeed not dwell on her racial sorrow. For example, in 1927 Wallace Thurman, tiring of the conventional Renaissance fare, decided to edit a journal of new, more daring writing, which he called *Fire*. Hurston's contribution was a short story about an unfaithful husband killed by a rattlesnake that he had placed in a hamper. His intent had been to use the snake to kill his wife, but he was done in by his own weapon. The humor and social commentary embedded in this piece are vintage Hurston. Locke complained that she loved to dwell on these tales of "pseudo-primitives" at the expense of the more intellectual protest tradition. To a modern sensibility, it was perhaps Locke who was out of step.

The charge of forsaking more serious subjects was leveled most effectively at her discussions of racism and racial identity. Hurston wrote on one occasion about her book *Jonah's Gourd Vine*, "What I wanted to tell was a story about a man, and from what I had read and heard, Negroes were supposed to write about the Race Problem. I was and am thoroughly sick of the subject." The chapter "My People, My People" in her 1939 autobiography, *Dust Tracks on a Road*, has been seen by critics as a denial of communal ideals of racial solidarity. The chapter begins with a discussion of the black middle-class contempt for poor black folk, people who "groan when they board a bus and find other Negroes there with their shoes off, stuffing themselves with fried fish." It then examines the contradiction found between celebrations of black superiority (inventors of the cotton gin and broom) and the demeaning humor of folktales that emphasize greed, stupidity, and cunning and often use animals as stand-ins. "There was a white engineer who drove a train and had a pet monkey who thought he could run the train just as good," a familiar folk tale begins. The monkey takes the helm, drives too fast, crashes, and dies. It ends with "lovely monkey he was, but a damn poor engineer."

Hurston concluded that there is no such thing as race pride, race consciousness ("only an imposing line of syllables, for no Negro in America is apt to forget his race"), or race solidarity. "It is freely admitted that [solidarity] does not exist among Negroes," she adds. "Our lives are so diversified, internal attitudes so varied, appearances and capabilities so different, that there is no possible classification so catholic that it will cover us all." Challenging the claim of a unified black community, which could act as *one* in matters of race, was bad politics. It was, however, closer to the private position of much of the mulatto elite than most would have cared to admit. Zora was exposing one of their dirty little secrets.

Hurston's ideas about race were also very southern and would no doubt find adherents among many traditionalists today. Her biographer, Robert Hemenway, called her a cross between a Republican conservative and a Black Nationalist. While the middle-class tradition of James Weldon Johnson, W. E. B. Du Bois, Alain Locke, and Jessie Fauset favored a public presentation that proved blacks had the same culture and heritage as whites, Hurston believed they did not. At the same time she dismissed slavery as something that no longer concerned her. "It was sad. But my ancestors who lived and died in it are dead. I have no personal memory of those times and no responsibility for them." One of her fictional characters advanced a slightly different but related point of view when she observed, "Ah was born back due in slavery so it wasn't for me to fulfill my dreams of whut a woman oughta be and to do. Dat's one of de holdbacks of slavery. But nothing can't stop you from wishin."

Still Zora made an uncomfortable leap from not dwelling on the past to denying its impact. Critic Mary Washington suggested that Hurston was "determined to write about black life as it existed apart from racism, injustice, Jim Crow—where black people laughed, celebrated, loved, sorrowed, struggled, unconcerned about white people and completely unaware of being 'a problem.'" In her anthropological study *Tell My Horse*, Hurston explains that an indication of a people's self-respect is the love they have for "their own things, like their songs, their stories and proverbs and dances."

ZORA ON A FOLKLORE COLLECTING TRIP IN THE LATE 1930S. COURTESY OF THE JANE BELO ESTATE.

In 1937, no longer attached to Charlotte Mason, Hurston published what has been called her greatest novel, *Their Eyes Were Watching God*. The work introduces a fictionalized Eatonville complete with the front porch of Joe Stark's country store. It tells the story of a young woman who, over a period of twenty years and three failed marriages, finds herself by finally rejecting community standards of a woman's place. Though the reviews were mixed, later critics, according to *The New Yorker*, granted Janie Crawford "the status of earliest heroic black woman in the Afro-American literary tradition." What has fascinated modern reviewers about the work is the fact that it portrays the separation of the public and private self that feminists often write about. Darlene Clark Hine refers to this as the "dynamics of dissemblance," which involves creating the appearance of disclosure and openness while maintaining a private, healing place that is secret. At a climactic moment in the narrative, heroine Janie Crawford finds she has "an inside and an outside now and suddenly she knew how not to mix them."

Janie has three relationships with men that reflect the range of marital possibilities available to black women at that time. The first, a forced marriage to farmer Logan Killicks, represents the only role available to women like her grandmother, who bitterly urges Janie to accept her fate as "de mule of de world." Her second marriage, to Jody Starks, presents the oppression of middle-class black women, who are expected to function only as symbols of their husband's status and wealth, without any regard for their own needs as human beings. Finally, her relationship with Teacake, despite its passion and seeming equality, is marred by his infidelity and belief in his right to physically abuse Janie. It ends with a liberated Janie, alone in her room, having "pulled [the horizon] from around the waist of the world and draped it over her shoulder. So much of life in its meshes! She called in her soul to come and see."

Although she received support from Charlotte Mason, Alain Locke, and Carl Van Vechten, Hurston never really recovered from her feud with Langston Hughes. Locke, soon after the incident, began bad-mouthing her to Mason, who eventually withdrew her backing. Hurston tried to return to Columbia in 1934 to work on a Ph.D., but she was unsuccessful. Though she wrote folktales and novels during the 1930s, they were not critically well received. Richard Wright declared *Their Eyes Were Watching God* to have "no theme, no message, no thought," and during the thirty years that Wright dominated the black literary scene, Hurston's novel was out of print. She died in 1959, a resident of a Florida welfare home, without funds to provide for her burial.

HURSTON WITH DRUMS AT A VOODOO DANCE, 1937. SHE STUDIED ANTHROPOLOGY WITH DR. FRANZ BOAS AT COLUMBIA UNIVERSITY AND BECAME AN ACCOMPLISHED FOLKLORIST, CONCENTRATING ON THE TRADITIONS AND BELIEFS OF BLACKS IN THE RURAL SOUTH.

The most threatening thing about Hurston to her contemporaries was that she created a world rich in southern rural experience that ignored most of the accepted conventions. This had not been done before and was undoubtedly seen by Locke and Wright as not possible. Hurston's way was not a threat but inspiration to modern writers like Alice Walker and Toni Morrison, however. As Walker observed, "That Hurston held her own, literally against the flood of whiteness and maleness that diluted so much other black art of the period in which she worked, is a testimony to her genius and her faith."

As she prepared to write her autobiography, Zora began thinking and writing about her life. She wrote many pages, some of which, like the following, were excised from the final version "for publishers' reasons," wrote Hurston. It was a fitting end.

I have loved unselfishly with all the ardor of a strong heart, and I have hated with all the power of my soul. What waits for me in the future? I do not know. I cannot even imagine, and I am glad for that. But already I have touched the four corners of the horizon, for from hard searching it seems to me that tears and laughter, love and hate, make up the sum of life.

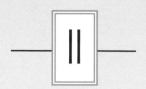

HOME TO HARLEM

HARLEM, THE CAPITAL OF THE BLACK AMERICAN WORLD, WAS HOME TO MANY RENAISSANCE FIGURES. WHILE ORDINARY FOLK YEARNED TO HEAD FOR CHICAGO, THE INTELLECTUAL VANGUARD LONGED FOR HARLEM. "THE NEGRO'S SITUATION IN HARLEM IS WITHOUT PRECEDENT IN ALL HIS HISTORY IN NEW YORK," OBSERVED JAMES WELDON JOHNSON. "NEVER BEFORE HAS HE BEEN SO SECURELY ANCHORED, NEVER BEFORE HAS HE OWNED THE LAND, NEVER BEFORE HAS HE HAD SO WELL ESTABLISHED A COMMUNITY LIFE."

THE SILENT MARCH TO PROTEST LYNCHING HELD IN NEW YORK CITY, JULY 1917.

4

A'LELIA WALKER

O N JUNE 18, 1923, Marcus Mosiah Garvey, "provisional president of Africa," was found guilty of mail fraud. He was sentenced to five years in prison, fined one thousand dollars, billed for court costs, and denied bail during the appeals. Garvey predicted that "hell will be turned loose all over the country" as a result. No disorder occurred, however. Garvey had founded the Universal Negro Improvement Association in New York in 1917 to bring race pride and economic advancement to the black masses. The aristocracy of the blue veins is over, he warned. He established his Black Star Line Steamship Corporation in June, raised almost $200,000 in less than four months, and staged an International Convention of the Negro Peoples of the World in September, with 25,000 delegates in Madison Square Garden. Mary White Ovington wrote that "Garvey was the first Negro in the United States to capture the imagination of the masses." While many of the educated middle class objected to Garvey—W. E. B. Du Bois called him "fat, black and ugly"—by 1919 his organization "seemed to be on the verge of sweeping aside conservative civil rights organizations and absorbing like-minded ones." But in June 1922 Garvey attended a summit meeting of

PORTRAIT OF A'LELIA WALKER INSCRIBED TO HER FRIENDS EDNA AND LLOYD. HAROLD JACKMAN CALLED EDNA ONE OF HER LIGHT-SKINNED LADIES-IN-WAITING.

the Ku Klux Klan in Atlanta and attempted to forge an alliance—consistent with his theme of racial separation but unthinkable to many, including the southern migrant community. "A menace to sound, democratic racial relations, a race baiter and a race traitor, Garvey must go," the *Messenger* wrote that August. Garvey, whose rise to power had first exposed the tension between light- and dark-skinned African-Americans, began to fade.

A'LELIA WALKER WAS THE "JOY-goddess of Harlem's 1920s." Her mother, Madam C. J. Walker, a former washerwoman, invented a process for the "growing out" of kinky hair, the bane of African-American women at the turn of the century. Madam Walker had ambition coupled with business acumen, a combination that netted her over $2 million before the start of World War I. A'Lelia, however, had expensive tastes and a reputation for spending rather than making money, a combination that sent her to the auctioneers in 1930. But along the way she brought glitter, grandeur, and an unmatched style to the Renaissance.

A'Lelia Walker was rich, spoiled, "no judge of character and easily won by flattery," Carl Van Vechten observed in a piece commissioned by the *New Yorker* in 1927 but never finished. Often depicted as the classic poor little rich girl, she was in fact past twenty when the Walker business started and thirty-four in 1919 when her mother died and left her a fortune. She was not a bystander to the family production of wealth. Explained the *Inter-State Tattler:* "A'Lelia comes in for her share of credit. She spent a lot of money in a lot of things her mother thought foolish, but had it not been for A'Lelia the Indianapolis concern might not have become the gold mine it was reputed to be in 1915. It was A'Lelia with her college education, her ideas of system, her ideas of business promotion

and business technique that brought it about."

An imposing figure, she was five feet nine and weighed over 190 pounds. "She was tall and black and extremely handsome in her African manner," Van Vechten wrote. Being wealthy and dark-skinned was a combination that both fascinated and repulsed the New York literati, black and white, in the 1920s. The "princess de-kink," or the "mahogany millionairess," as she was called behind her back, lived in Irvington on the Hudson in a Georgian mansion built in 1917 by her mother for half a million dollars. She also had a double brownstone on 136th Street in Harlem, a place later called Dark Tower, and a lavishly furnished apartment on Edgecombe Avenue. Wherever she went, she was surrounded by "parasites, jesters and well-meaning courtiers." Van Vechten, probably her closest Renaissance friend, once commented that she "looked like a queen and frequently acted like a tyrant." After her mother's death, her lifestyle grew increasingly lavish, her parties infamous, and her time upon the Harlem stage too brief. She died in 1931, during a weekend party near Atlantic City where, ignoring her doctor's warnings about high blood pressure and overeating, she consumed a whole lobster, a chocolate cake, and several glasses of champagne.

Rather than masking her racial identity, as the talented tenth often tried to do, A'Lelia seemed to delight in it, frequently dressing in black, wearing a bejeweled silver turban, and looking, according to Langston Hughes, like a "gorgeous dark Amazon" surrounded by her "light-skinned ladies in waiting." Walker was the ultimate racial modern, a migrant who delighted in creating a setting to "show off her blackness to whites." David Levering Lewis recounted a rumor, never confirmed according to her great-granddaughter, that she once served her white guests pig's feet, chitterlings, and bathtub gin while her black guests, seated in more elegant surroundings, dined on caviar, pheasant, and champagne.

A'LELIA WALKER IN APRIL 1926. SHE LOVED TO DRESS IN TURBANS AND IN RED.

A'LELIA WALKER WAS BORN on June 6, 1885, in Vicksburg, Mississippi, to Sarah Breedlove and Moses McWilliams. Vicksburg was just across the river from Delta, Louisiana, where Sarah had been raised. When her father died in 1887, Lelia, as she was called then, moved with her mother upriver to Missouri. Like many migrants, Sarah had heard that in Saint Louis "gaslights brightened city nights" and "wash-tubs and white folks dirty clothes replaced cotton bolls and the threat of night riders." She worked in Saint Louis as a laundress until 1904, toiling night and day to make a life for herself and her daughter. "As I bent over the washboard and looked at my arms buried in the soapsuds," she later recalled, "I said to myself, 'What are you going to do when you grow old and your back gets stiff?' This set me to thinking, but with all my thinking, I couldn't

see how I, a poor washer-woman, was going to better my condition."

In 1905 she moved to Denver, where she worked briefly as a sales agent for Malone's Wonderful Hair Grower, a Saint Louis company. As a result of stress and poor diet, Sarah, like many poor African-American women, had thin hair that was always falling out. To correct this, she tried many commercial remedies, with mixed results. It is speculated that she decided to work for Malone's because she had better success with their products. But she longed to start her own business and prayed for guidance. Her prayers were answered, according to company literature, one night in a dream. "A big black man appeared to me and told me what to mix up for my hair," she claimed. "Some of the remedy was grown in Africa, but I sent for it, mixed it, put it on my scalp, and in a few weeks my hair was coming in faster than it had ever fallen out."

With $1.50 in savings, thirty-seven-year-old Sarah set out to make hair-care products with her secret formula. By this time, Lelia had been educated in the Saint Louis public schools and had attended Knoxville College in Tennessee, though she didn't graduate and no records of her stay there exist. Now, at age twenty-two, she joined her mother in Denver. Sarah married a newspaper sales agent named Charles Joseph Walker that same year. Adopting the title "Madam," a common practice among black businesswomen in those days, she

TEATIME AT MADAM C. J. WALKER'S BEAUTY SALON, PHOTOGRAPHED BY JAMES VANDERZEE, 1929. THE WALKER COMPANY STRESSED GOOD GROOMING AND ETIQUETTE AS A STANDARD FOR ALL AFRICAN-AMERICAN WOMEN.

called herself Madam C. J. Walker. Lelia also took Walker as her last name.

Madam Walker's husband, C.J., became a business partner, helping her design newspaper advertisements and establishing a mail-order operation. In addition to the hair treatment product, she adapted (some incorrectly suggest that she invented) metal combs and curling irons to make the hair easier to comb. After a shaky start, the business did well as Madam Walker went from door to door selling combs and oils. She soon realized that to make money, she needed to travel beyond Denver. Leaving Lelia to run the mail-order operation, the Walkers began traversing the black South and Southwest, selling their products.

Realizing that the key to success was proper application, Madam Walker decided to open a beauty salon and training school and selected Pittsburgh as the site. In 1908 she opened Lelia College for "Walker hair culturists." Her students learned not only hair-care techniques but also a philosophy of inner and outer beauty meant to create an elegant atmosphere in the salons and to pamper their clients. Selling prod-

ucts that were not available in stores, the agents were given bonuses, trips, and motivational conventions for successful sales records. Madam Walker's business model, extraordinarily innovative for 1908, was something of a prototype for the self-help strategies of modern companies like Mary Kay Cosmetics and Amway. Money flowed into the Walkers' coffers.

They closed the Denver base and installed Lelia in Pittsburgh while Madam Walker and C.J. continued their travels. During one of these trips, Madam Walker visited Indianapolis and saw it as a perfect mail-order center, with the city's access to eight major railway systems. With Lelia still in Pittsburgh, she set up a headquarters in Indianapolis in 1910, purchasing a large home with a factory and a laboratory right next to it, and establishing another training school. Because of business and personal differences, she divorced Charles. As profits in the company grew, Madam Walker hired a talented staff of lawyers and business-people to handle day-to-day operations while she, with Lelia often at her side, crossed the country giving lectures and promoting the business. She had the enviable ability to surround herself with educated people (well paid by her) who could overcome her own shortcomings, and she was said to be a quick study.

What Madam Walker had discovered in her hair-care and cosmetic business (they eventually manufactured twenty-three different products) was a secret ingredient of race pride. She argued strongly that she was not trying to make her customers white but to instill in them pride and self-worth, to make them feel good about being black and about being women. She insisted that Walker agents never use the word "straightener" to describe their product. Hers was a grooming method to heal and condition the scalp. She stressed the importance of helping black American women to find their own unique style, not a derivative one. She also wanted, as a direct result of her own experience, to help them achieve financial independence. "I want to say to every Negro woman present, don't sit down and wait for the opportunities to come," she said in 1913 at the Na-

tional Negro Business League meetings. "Get up and make them." Negro women were the major workers in her factories, the teachers in her schools, the agents in the field. She believed that women were far too reliant on men for survival, and she was determined to change that. In her will, she specified that the president of the Walker Company must always be a woman.

A'Lelia, as she had by then renamed herself, did not cross the country "encouraging women to pursue business opportunities and economic independence" after her mother's death, and indeed the promotional tours ended, but she did live in a manner suggesting that she got the message. Possessing an outgoing personality, A'Lelia was sometimes called stubborn and willful. No one told her what to do, with the result that many of her marriages were stormy and her divorces bitter. A'Lelia married John Robinson, her first husband, around 1910 in Indianapolis, before coming to New York. The *Inter-State Tattler* said of him: "He was dark brownskin, about five feet nine. He had a nice

THE DARK TOWER, PHOTOGRAPHED BY JAMES VANDER-ZEE IN 1928. A'LELIA WALKER DEVOTED A FLOOR OF HER HARLEM MANSION AT 108 WEST 136TH STREET TO A SALON TO WHICH SHE INVITED "YOUNG NEGRO WRITERS, SCULPTORS, PAINTERS, MUSIC ARTISTS, COMPOSERS AND THEIR FRIENDS."

THE WEDDING OF A'LELIA'S ADOPTED DAUGHTER MAE BRYANT, NOVEMBER 28, 1923. "THE WEDDING," SAID THE *AMSTERDAM NEWS*, "IN ALL OF ITS APPOINTMENTS MARKED THE APEX OF ELEGANT SUMPTUOUSNESS."

A'LELIA WALKER'S PRESENT TO THE NEWLYWEDS WAS A MASSIVE MAHOGANY CASE BUILT SPECIALLY BY TIFFANY, CONTAINING A SET OF 126 PIECES OF SOLID SILVER. THE GROOM'S PRESENT TO THE BRIDE WAS A BROOCH SET WITH RARE DIAMONDS.

figure and looked like somebody in his uniform. He was very bossy and I guess he captured Miss Walker's imagination." According to Langston Hughes, Robinson was the only one she ever loved. "Once at one of her parties she began to cry about him. She retired to her boudoir and wept. Some of her friends went to comfort her, and found her clutching a memento of their broken romance." It was a gold shoehorn. As with many of the stories of A'Lelia, we have only Hughes's account of this. She divorced Robinson in 1914.

In 1912 she adopted a thirteen-year-old girl, Mae Bryant of Indianapolis. Initially Mae had run errands for A'Lelia and her mother, and they became fond of her. After getting to know her, they decided that Mae's unusual combination of dark skin and long, thick hair would make excellent advertising for the Walker products, especially their hair grower. Mae's mother, persuaded that A'Lelia and Madam Walker would keep their promise to educate her daughter, consented to their request to adopt her. A'Lelia Bundles, Mae's granddaughter, suggested that Mae never lost contact with her birth family.

A'Lelia treated Mae well, sending her to Spelman College in Atlanta and, in 1923, giving her a "million-dollar wedding," covered in both the black and the white press, and described as "the most elaborate social function ever occurring among the colored citizens of New York City." The *New York Age* in particular took exception to the sarcastic tone adopted by the white dailies about the event. "There was an entire absence of anything approaching gaucherie or lack of culture," the *Age* reported.

Getting married was a relatively easy feat for the Walkers; staying married was another matter. A'Lelia was herself engaged to Dr. James Arthur Kennedy in 1919 with her mother's wholehearted approval. A'Lelia was in Panama with Mae when her mother died. She abruptly broke off her engagement and within months married Wiley Wilson, a physician. Madam Walker had not approved of Dr. Wilson, whom she thought of as a parasite. A'Lelia remained married to him only a short time, and the details of the divorce became front-page news in the December 27, 1922, edition of the *Amsterdam News*. She finally married Dr. Kennedy in May 1926, but the couple lived together only sporadically and were divorced in 1931. Van Vechten observed of all her marriages: "She was too spoiled, too selfish, too used to having her own way to make any kind of compromise."

A'LELIA'S GREAT WEALTH never completely masked her modest origins and lack of entrée into black society. "Quite often, when the matter of her social leadership was mentioned among certain people, there were those who smiled scornfully," the *Amsterdam News* reported in 1931. The source of her wealth was held against her by some, as was the fact that she was not a college graduate. Some of the Harlem elite, like Grace Nail Johnson, simply refused to attend her parties, although the same could not be said of Grace's brother John.

Others made fun of A'Lelia while enjoying her champagne and caviar. Her reasoning powers were said to be slight. "She made no pretense at being intellectual or exclusive," said Langston Hughes. She subscribed to all the leading colored weeklies, the metropolitan dailies, and a score of magazines, she told the *Tattler*; and "had learned the art of reading headlines, and the trick had served [her] well."

One suspects, however, that some of this was part of A'Lelia's disguise. It was she, after all, who persuaded her mother to move to New York, a decision that was very good for the business. It was she who was behind the creation of the Walker Building in Indianapolis, an ambitious plan to bring all services (and presumably most of the dollars) from hair care to doctoring within the black community under one elegant roof. Had the project not begun in 1929, it might well have made another million dollars for the heiress. Yet A'Lelia was not known for her business skills, preferring instead the flighty image. "After seven minutes, conversation went precipitously downhill," it was said.

Unlike her mother who gave much of her fortune to charities and educational institutions, A'Lelia became devoted to manufacturing and molding a unique place for herself. As the *Tattler* explained, she grew tired of toiling and took an extended vacation after her mother's death: "She wore the most expensive clothing and jewelry, acquired from the fashionable shops of New York and Paris." While other blacks were refused service at Harlem's Cotton Club, a table was always available for A'Lelia and her guests. And she loved being surrounded by the literati. "I am to be hostess at the Dark Tower Sunday Night April 21st, and I thought probably you and your friends would like to be present," she wrote to writer and musician Max Ewing in 1929. She never served as a patroness, however. As David Levering Lewis suggests, "to the intellectuals and

Left: The late Madam C. J. Walker.

Center: Madam Walker's palatial residence [...]
Irvington-on-Hudson.

Oval: Mrs. Lelia Walker Wilson, daughter [...]
Madam Walker, and president of the Mme. C. [...]
Walker Manufacturing Company.

Bottom: Cabin where Madam C. J. Walker wi[...]
born.

A'LELIA WALKER PHOTOGRAPHED WITH
HER FRIENDS, THE "LADIES-IN-WAITING."

MADAM WALKER'S LIFE WAS
COVERED IN A FOUR-PAGE STORY IN
THE *MESSENGER*, OCTOBER 1926.

A WEDDING PICTURE.
WALKER WAS MARRIED
THREE TIMES: IN 1910 TO
JOHN ROBINSON
(THAT MARRIAGE WAS
DISSOLVED); IN 1919 TO
DR. WILEY WILSON
(DIVORCED IN 1922);
IN 1926 TO
DR. JAMES KENNEDY
(DIVORCED IN 1931).

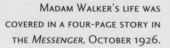

MENU FOR THE DARK TOWER: VEGETABLE SOUP, 25 CENTS; COLD CUTS AND POTATO SALAD, 75 CENTS; A'LELIA WALKER ICED TEA, 25 CENTS. IT WAS NOT A PLACE FOR STARVING ARTISTS.

Prices and Menu subject to change. Attached slip den

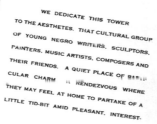

WE DEDICATE THIS TOWER TO THE AESTHETES, THAT CULTURAL GROUP OF YOUNG NEGRO WRITERS, SCULPTORS, PAINTERS, MUSIC ARTISTS, COMPOSERS AND THEIR FRIENDS. A QUIET PLACE OF PARTI-CULAR CHARM A RENDEZVOUS WHERE THEY MAY FEEL AT HOME TO PARTAKE OF A LITTLE TID-BIT AMID PLEASANT, INTEREST-

ING ATMOSPHERE. MEMBERS ONLY AND THOSE WHOM THEY WISH TO BRING WILL BE ACCEPTED. IF YOU CHOOSE TO BECOME ONE OF US YOU MAY REGISTER WHEN YOU FIRST VISIT "THE DARK TOWER." ONE DOLLAR A YEAR. OPEN NINE AT EVE 'TIL TWO IN THE MORN AT THE

WALKER STUDIO
108 WEST 136TH STREET
BRADHURST 0475

P.S.—OUR MEMBERSHIP LIST IS RESTRICTED BECAUSE OUR SPACE IS LIMITED.

MISS LOIS WILSON, HOSTESS

AN INVITATION TO THE DARK TOWER, 1928.

A FEAST OF THE MUSES
Menu
❦
TO-NIGHT

Vegetable Soup....25c   Cream of Tomato or Celery Soup....25c
Olives and Celery.........35c
Pickles.........10c   Mangoes........35c
Oysters on half shell................75c
Chili-Con-Carne....50c   Antipasto........75c
Spaghetti.........50   Waffles and Coffee.......50c
Boston Baked Beans and Brown Bread.........50c
Cream Cheese, Guava Jelly, Toasted Crackers.........75c
Cold Cuts, Lettuce & Tomato Salad 75c   Hot Dogs & Potato Salad....50c
Cold Cuts and Potato Salad ...75c   Asparagus Salad 50c
Cold Cuts and Slaw ....75c   Potato Salad.................50c
Hot Dogs and Slaw.............50c   Lettuce and Tomato Salad.......50c
Pineapple Salad.................50c
Choice of Rye, Whole Wheat, White   Choice of Uneeda, Uneeda Lunch,
    Bread.   Saltines, Water Crackers.
Apple Pie......30c   Chocolate or Cocoanut Cake ... 30c
A'Lelia Walker Iced Tea........25c   Limburger Cheese............35c
Canada Dry Splits.............50c   Edam Cheese................35c
Grape Juice   " ....50c   Muenster Cheese.............35c
White Rock   " ....50c   Camembert Cheese...........35c
Coffee, Bread and Butter........25c   Roquefort Cheese............45c
Tea (pot), Bread and Butter....25c   Cream Cheese..............25c
Chocolate or Cocoa.............25c   Hog's Head Cheese...........30c
Iced Coffee.............35c

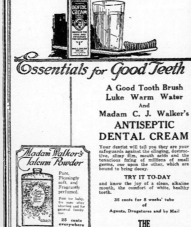

Essentials for Good Teeth
A Good Tooth Brush
Luke Warm Water
And
Madam C. J. Walker's
ANTISEPTIC
DENTAL CREAM

Madam Walker's Talcum Powder
Pure, Pleasingly soft, and Fragrantly perfumed.
Fine for baby, for men after shaving and for general family use.
25 cents everywhere

Your dentist will tell you they are your safeguards against the clinging, destructive, slimy film, mouth acids and the tenacious fixing of millions of small germs, one upon the other, which are bound to bring decay.

TRY IT TO-DAY
and know the joy of a clean, alkaline mouth, the comfort of white, healthy teeth.

35 cents for 8 weeks' tube
of
Agents, Drugstores and by Mail

THE
MME. C. J. WALKER MFG. CO.
640 North West St., Indianapolis, Ind.

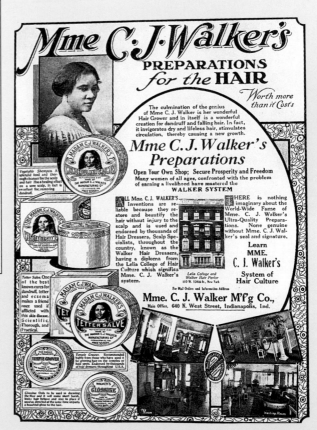

Mme C. J. Walker's
PREPARATIONS for the HAIR
Worth more than it Costs

The culmination of the genius of Mme C. J. Walker is her wonderful Hair Grower and in itself is a wonderful creation for dandruff and falling hair. In fact, it invigorates dry and lifeless hair, stimulates circulation, thereby causing a new growth.

Mme C. J. Walker's Preparations
Open Your Own Shop; Secure Prosperity and Freedom
Many women of all ages, confronted with the problem of earning a livelihood have mastered the
WALKER SYSTEM

ALL Mme. C. J. WALKER'S Inventions are reliable because they restore and beautify the hair without injury to the scalp and is used and endorsed by thousands of Hair Dressers, Scalp Specialists, throughout the country, known as the Walker Hair Dressers, having a diploma from the Lelia College of Hair Culture which significes Mme. C. J. Walker's system.

THERE is nothing imaginary about the World-Wide Fame of Mme. C. J. Walker's Ultra-Quality Preparations. None genuine without Mme. C. J. Walker's seal and signature.

Learn
MME.
C. J. Walker's
System of Hair Culture

For Mail Orders and Information Address
Mme. C. J. Walker M'f'g Co.,
Main Office, 640 N. West Street, Indianapolis, Ind.

THE ESSENTIALS OF GOOD GROOMING FOR THE WALKER COMPANY EXTENDED BEYOND HAIR CARE.

artists of Harlem she opened her houses and almost never her purse."

Still A'Lelia's contribution to the Renaissance was memorable. Annette Tapert and Diana Edkins have said, in *The Power of Style*, that style is "the ultimate expression of character, a way of transforming the vulgarity of existence into a living work of art." And so it was with A'Lelia—except, of course, that like all of the black moderns, she turned the images upside down. "You should have known A'Lelia," Van Vechten wrote to writer Chester Himes. "Nothing in this age is quite as good as *that*." Van Vechten reported that her appearance one night at a box at the opera in Covent Garden "was so spectacular that the singers were put completely out of countenance."

In Van Vechten's controversial best-selling novel *Nigger Heaven*, A'Lelia is Adora Boniface, whose "skin was almost black; her nose broad, her lips thick . . . undeniably warmhearted, amusing, in her outspoken way, and even beautiful, in a queenly African manner that set her apart from the other beauties of her race whose loveliness was more frequently of a Latin than an Ethiopian character." According to Van Vechten, A'Lelia's friends were shocked and offended by his portrayal of her in *Nigger Heaven*, "but she was nicer to me after that, even than before. I miss her. She always treated me to champagne when we had locked ourselves in her boudoir and locked the toadies and sycophants out with a bottle of beer apiece. What a woman!"

Her most lavish parties were held in Irvington at Villa Lewaro, so named by Enrico Caruso for the first letters of her first married name, Lelia Walker Robinson. The house had been designed by Vertner Woodson Tandy, the first African-American licensed architect in New York State. Madam Walker had thought of the house as a symbol: "It is not for me; it is for my people so that they can see what is pos-

sible no matter what their background," she once proclaimed. Lelia furnished the house with a twenty-four-carat-gold-plated piano, a $60,000 Estey pipe organ, Hepplewhite furniture, and Persian carpets, but she was afraid to stay there alone because that was where her mother had died. She held instead ostentatious weekend parties with guest lists that included whites and blacks, royals and racketeers. The black male servants in Irvington wore doublets and hose and white wigs.

She also held successful parties in her town house on 136th Street. "One couldn't help being impressed with the brilliance of the evenings," Harold Jackman recalled. "Literature, politics, painting and music were always discussed. Something interesting was constantly happening." Van Vechten added, "She made no effort to limit society in any strict sense. She invited whom she pleased to her own apartment when she entertained, and frequently they invited whom they pleased." Yet the guest lists were impressive. According to David Levering Lewis, the parties "were attended by English Rothschilds, French princesses, Russian grand dukes, members of New York's social register and the stock exchange, Harlem luminaries, Prohibition and gambling nobility, and a fair number of nattily attired employees of the U.S. Post Office and the Pullman Corporation." Osbert Sitwell recalled on one occasion being ushered into a room decorated in the Parisian style of the Second Empire and then whisked upstairs to the boudoir to witness A'Lelia removing her new shoes, which hurt her feet, complaining of new husbands who had a similar effect, and uncorking several bottles of champagne. A'Lelia in fact often retired to her quarters during her parties, after making only a brief appearance downstairs, so that she could play bridge and poker with her favorites.

A'Lelia entertained on Thursday afternoons at Edgecombe Avenue, with guests treated to the piano music of Carrol Boyd and Joey Coleman, the dancing of Al Moiret and Fredi Washington, and the singing of Alberta Hunter. On Sunday afternoons she held musicales in Irvington. Their purpose was to introduce outstanding musicians who were black, talented, and unknown to audiences that were largely white, rich, and influential. Van Vechten frequently attended.

In the fall of 1927, according to Richard Bruce Nugent, A'Lelia decided to open a place where "artists could meet and discuss their plans and arts, to which they could bring their friends, and at which they could eat for prices within their very limited reach." Aaron Douglas and Nugent were selected to decorate the room. Nugent suggested it be called the Dark Tower, the name of Countee Cullen's column in the journal *Opportunity*. To carry out the idea, A'Lelia organized a group of about fifty artists— a "breed of chiselers," Nugent later called them—who met on several occasions but failed to produce anything that pleased A'Lelia. Losing patience, she hired Manhattan decorator Paul Frankel instead of using Douglas and Nugent to design the room. Frankel papered it with French wallpaper with a gold design and hung framed texts of "The Dark Tower" on one wall, "The Weary Blues" on another. Invitations to the opening of the "salon" were sent in early 1928. They read: "We dedicate this tower to the aesthetes, that cultured group of young Negro writers, sculptors, painters, music artists, composers, and their friends. A quiet place of particular charm." By then, however, A'Lelia had lost interest in establishing a place for struggling artists. Present at the opening were the rich, the prominent, and the striving who had always attended her events, and few others. Nugent wrote: "The great room and hall was a seething picture of well-dressed people. Everyone had worn evening clothes. One of the artists was nearly refused admission because he had come with open collar and wore no cravat, but someone already inside fortunately recognized him and he was rescued." In place of the reasonably priced food were cream cheese, guava jelly, and toasted crackers selling for seventy-five cents and A'Lelia Walker Iced Tea for twenty-five cents—staggering prices for the time.

The Dark Tower remained open for only about one year. In characteristic fashion, A'Lelia sent the following notice upon its closing:

> *Dear Members and Friends:*
>   *Having no talent or gift but a love and keen admiration for art, The Dark Tower was my contribution. But due to the slothfulness on the part of the members to make use of The Dark Tower, it will be closed November 1 as a private institution but available to rent for private parties such as luncheons, teas, card parties and receptions.*
>   *I cannot tell you how sorry I am for this.*
>   *Sincerely,*
>   *A'Lelia Walker*
> *108 West 136th Street*
> *For more information call Bradhurst 0678*

FINANCIAL PROBLEMS BEGAN to plague Walker's once vast holdings. Freeman Ransome, a lawyer who oversaw the operations in Indianapolis, sounded early alarms, but she refused to listen. When circumstances grew worse, she also declined to stop spending money. Marion Perry, the second husband of A'Lelia's adopted daughter, believed that she would literally rather die than give up her way of life. Also, constant gaiety masked a deeply depressed individual who had never stopped grieving over the death of her mother. Walker did make some effort to raise cash, however. In 1930 she tried to find a buyer for Villa Lewaro. She wrote to Van

Vechten: "I have been holding on to this place through sentiment (my mother), but I've arrived at the conclusion it is foolish of me to maintain such a large and expensive home with no family ties and I spend all my time in New York City. It is assessed at $190,000. I'll let it go for $150,000 . . . [and] there isn't a person I'd rather have Villa Lewaro than you."

Van Vechten replied, in part, "But, dear A'Lelia, what would I do with a house? I am always away all summer. And where do you think I'd get all that money? A'Lelia, behave!"

The contents of Villa Lewaro were auctioned off in December 1930 for prices well below what they had cost. "White Buyers Strip Villa of Treasures," one headline read. The entire library of 600 volumes, "many of which had never been opened," was sold for $1,800. It contained a limited-edition boxed set of great operas with an introduction by Giuseppe Verdi that had been purchased for $15,000. "The Flemish oak billiard table went for $225. The ten high-backed armchairs in the same wood brought but $175, and the rugs in that room brought from $25 to $100, less than one third of their original value." Bessye Bearden, mother of the artist Romare Bearden and a member of A'Lelia's circle, was quoted in the *Chicago Defender* as saying, "A few of us who had once enjoyed the hospitalities of the mansion stood with wet eyes and looked on."

Just eight months later A'Lelia attended a birthday party for May Fain, one of her ladies-in-waiting, in Long Branch, New Jersey. Having retired for the evening, she awoke at 4:00 A.M. complaining of not being able to see. She died several hours later. The *New York Times* reported, "Mme. Lelia Walker Robinson, only daughter of the late Mme. Sarah Walker, inventor of a preparation designed to remove kink from Negro hair, died suddenly early today at the home of friends in Lippincott Avenue, Long Branch. Her age was 46 years."

Her funeral was attended by over 10,000 people, according to the *Amsterdam News*. Her casket was silver and bronze and cost over $5,000 dollars. She was laid to rest in "a gown of beige and gold lace over lavender satin, with apple green satin slippers, and an imported necklace of genuine amber Chinese prayer beads." Langston Hughes reported that more invitations had been issued than there was room for. Hundreds of friends stood outside, "waving their white, engraved invitations aloft in the vain hope of entering." Harlem minister the Reverend Adam Clayton Powell Sr., who bore a striking resemblance to the actor who played De Lawd in the Broadway hit *The Green Pastures*, presided over the funeral. The eulogy was read by educator and civil rights leader Mary McLeod Bethune. She spoke in her "great deep voice" of A'Lelia's mother, "who in old clothes, had labored to bring the gift of beauty to Negro womanhood, and a great fortune to the pride and glory of the Negro race—and then had given it all to her daughter, A'Lelia." A nightclub quartet, the Four Bon Bons, who often performed at her parties, sang Noël Coward's "I'll See You Again." Young women from Walker shops across the country came forward to lay flowers on the casket. At the grave site, Herbert Fauntleroy Julian, the celebrated stunt pilot known as the Black Eagle, dropped a floral wreath from his plane.

Walker did not die in embarrassed circumstances. The *Chicago Defender* claimed that she left over $1.2 million and one-sixth of the business to her adopted daughter, Mae Bryant Perry, a sizable sum for the early Depression. Later reports revealed, however, that the estate was worth considerably less. The legacy had been reduced to real estate valued at $500,000, and estate taxes took their toll.

For Langston Hughes, the Renaissance era ended with that funeral. "That was really the end of the gay times of the New Negro era in

A'LELIA WALKER IN 1931. SHE INCREASINGLY TOOK TO DRESSING IN BLACK MONTHS BEFORE HER DEATH.

Harlem," he wrote, "the period that had begun to reach its end when the crash came in 1929 and the white people had much less money to spend on themselves, and practically none to spend on Negroes, for the depression brought everybody down a peg or two. And the Negroes had but few pegs to fall." A'Lelia Walker chose not to be there at this unwelcome end.

5

JAMES WELDON JOHNSON

O N AUGUST 3, 1914, British Foreign Secretary Sir Edward Grey rose in Parliament to rally a reluctant nation to wage world war. In the same month James Weldon Johnson, an African-American poet, lyricist, and diplomat, arrived in New York. These two events, worlds apart, were, in the stream of things, connected. The war would kindle U.S. economic hegemony. It would also spark the first mass migration of blacks from the South. Europe at war's end would, in the words of F. Scott Fitzgerald, "find all Gods dead, all wars fought, all faith in man shaken." America, to this point a culturally derivative society, would be called on to lead the world not only in politics but in the arts. And black America, previously ignored and despised, would be intimately involved in the search for an authentic American art.

JAMES WELDON JOHNSON, A TRUE RENAISSANCE MAN: TEACHER, LYRICIST, LAWYER, DIPLOMAT, WRITER, LOBBYIST, AND SOCIAL ACTIVIST.

JUST ONE YEAR INTO JAMES Weldon Johnson's tenure as field secretary of the NAACP, on July 2, 1917, the worst race riot in American history swept through the industrial city of East Saint Louis, Illinois. Racial tensions in that city were directly attributable to job competition between white and black workers. Many of the blacks were migrants from the South who had come in search of employment and a better life. During the riot, over two hundred blacks were killed and six thousand were burned out of their homes.

Sixteen days later the "conservative" Johnson with "militant" W. E. B. Du Bois at his side staged a silent march of ten thousand in Harlem to protest the riot. "Not one marcher uttered a sound, not even the children clad in white at the head of the silent parade of women in white and men in mourning colors," reported the *New York Times*.

Black Manhattan was familiar with parades and ceremonies. It celebrated lives and deaths, organizational achievements and acts of heroism. But even in Harlem, Johnson's march was unusual. It was social protest and public theater bound into one. In April of that year the United States had entered "a war to make the world safe for democracy." At the silent parade in July, little children—normally difficult to restrain in the hot summer sun—walked solemnly. Black adults carrying banners that read "Why not make America safe for democracy?" followed the children, Johnson, Du Bois, and the mostly white, mostly wealthy NAACP board up Fifth Avenue. The New Negro Renaissance had begun.

James Weldon Johnson was its elder statesman. The product of a Victorian upbringing, he came of age at a time when notions of gentility and the importance of service were characteristic of the tiny upper-middle-class black community of which he was a part. "The ideal constantly held up to us was of education as a means of living, not of making a living. It was impressed upon us that taking a classical course would have an effect of making us better and nobler, and of higher value to those we should have to serve," he wrote. He did so many things well—as novelist, teacher, lawyer, lobbyist—that Zora Neale Hurston described him as "monarch material."

JOHNSON WAS BORN on June 17, 1871, in Jacksonville, Florida, two years before his brother, J. Rosamond. His father was headwaiter at the Saint James, one of the most fashionable hotels in the state. His mother, Helen Louise Johnson, born in the Bahamas and educated in New York, was the first black woman to teach in a public school in Florida. The elder Johnsons were part of the privileged stratum of the black community. She had been too frail after James's birth to nurse him, so a white neighbor took her place. "In a land of black mammies," Johnson wrote, "I had a white one."

A rebel of sorts, Helen Louise refused to sing "America" in church "when the congregation was told of West Point's rejection of a qualified candidate because he was African-American." She instilled in her son the quiet confidence and unbending spirit that he retained throughout his life.

Until he was sixteen, James attended Jacksonville's only school for black children. Then his parents sent him to Atlanta University's preparatory school, a common practice for blacks who were denied local educational alternatives. He journeyed there with a Cuban boy who'd been sent to the United States to learn English and who boarded with the Johnsons. James's father purchased tickets for them in the first-class car of the night train. A state law ordering the separation of the races on trains had

TEACHERS AT STANTON SCHOOL, THE COLORED SCHOOL IN JACKSONVILLE,
FLORIDA, THAT JAMES WELDON JOHNSON ATTENDED. HE LATER BECAME ITS SUPERINTENDENT.

just been passed. The conductor instructed the boys to move to the segregated car. James, unaware of the law, refused, and a heated discussion ensued. His friend, not understanding fully the problem, inquired in Spanish, *"Que dice?"* (What is he saying?). When James replied in Spanish, the conductor withdrew his objection. "As soon as the conductor heard us speaking a foreign language, his attitude changed; he punched our tickets and gave them back, and treated us just as he did the other passengers in the car. We ate our lunch, lay back in our seats, and went to sleep," Johnson wrote. A similar incident fifteen years later led him to conclude that "in such situations any kind of a Negro will do, provided he is not one who is an American citizen."

In 1894, after graduating from Atlanta University, Johnson returned to Jacksonville to become the principal of the Stanton School, a grammar school for black children. Always restless and eager for new challenges, Johnson

also became the owner, publisher, and editor of the *Daily American*, one of the first African-American daily newspapers in the nation. He was one of the first African-American lawyers admitted to the bar in Florida, too, and in his spare time he composed an opera with his brother, J. Rosamond.

When the school year ended in 1899, the Johnson brothers went to New York to try to have their comic opera produced. Though that project failed, they met and were given encouragement by Oscar Hammerstein Sr., a Broadway kingpin. Returning the next summer, they formed a partnership with Bob Cole, a leading black minstrel and lyricist. For nearly seven years, the trio wrote many of the most popular songs on New York's Tin Pan Alley, and Rosamond and Bob Cole performed not only in New York but Europe as well. Cole and Rosamond were booked for six weeks at the Palace Theater in London in 1905. It was a heady experience.

"Great, rumbling London; stupendous, overwhelming," Johnson called it.

Every bus, and there seemed to be thousands of them, carried along its whole length a placard announcing the appearance for the first time at the Palace Theater of "Cole and Johnson, the Great Coloured Comedians." The performers were both thrilled and increasingly anxious about their opening night. A chance meeting on a London street with American actress Marie Dressler eased some of their worry. She talked with us about the opening night, and radiated buoyancy and confidence in a way that made them infectious. She promised to be present to give the boys a hand. Miss Dressler kept her promise; and, more than that, she rounded up every American performer in London she could get hold of and brought them along to help in giving a hand.

The evening was a great success.

Back in New York, James Weldon Johnson studied literature at Columbia, while continuing to write songs. Then, during the presidential campaign, he worked for the new Colored Republican Club. Charles W. Anderson, an ally of Booker T. Washington, was the head of the club and a mentor and key supporter of Johnson. As a political favor, the trio wrote a campaign song, "You're All Right, Teddy." For his efforts, Johnson was appointed to the consular service in Venezuela in 1906.

While sorry to leave his songwriting partners, Johnson eagerly took on the challenge of an exceptional post for an African-American. He spoke Spanish and French fluently, strengths which won him social acceptance in Venezuela. But for Johnson, this victory raised doubts. He worried about his failure to make an impact as a representative of his race rather than an exception to it. So, in 1909, he requested a transfer, having spent a "pleasant two years clearing vessels, greeting Americans, and making reports."

At the age of thirty-eight Johnson married Grace Nail, a member of one of Brooklyn's old and established black families, sister of John Nail, former Tenderloin tavern owner who made a fortune in Harlem real estate. Johnson's marriage to Grace Nail was something of a dynastic merger: a woman of wealth and position and a man of high achievement. They were an interesting couple: he the guardian of a culture, she the guardian of a class. By all accounts, Johnson was deeply in love with his wife. (A Hungarian count spent an evening with them and expressed to the host satisfaction that under certain circumstances racial intermarriage was permitted in the United States, only to be told that Grace Nail was not in fact white.)

The Johnsons lived in Nicaragua, his next diplomatic post, for over three years. While there, James continued his string of extraordinary accomplishments. As David Levering Lewis tells it, he "wrote a novel, directed U.S. marines in aborting a Nicaraguan revolution, and saw his poem commemorating the fiftieth anniversary of the Emancipation Proclamation published on the editorial page of the *New York Times.*" Each achievement gained him personal respect, and all were consistent with his goal of also inspiring respect for the race.

Grace Nail's personality, less forgiving than her husband's, was also revealed during their stay. On one of their trips home, her trunk fell into the water. Johnson wrote:

Grace was heartbroken. We got the trunk and opened it. Everything in it was water-soaked. The hotel proprietor secured us first aid in the shape of a Chinese laundryman, who promised to have everything "back fine" in time for us to catch our train in the morning. He got the things back on time, but Grace declared that their present was worse than their former state.

She and the laundryman had a stiff row. The pidgin Spanish of the Chinese amused me, but the scope, color, warmth, and volubility of Grace's Spanish completely astounded me. Parts of her vocabulary did not come out of any textbook she had studied.

Johnson resigned from the consular service after six years, when the change from a Republican to a Democratic president, plus race prejudice, denied him a promotion to another post. Bitter over his treatment but not discouraged, Johnson left Central America for the fateful journey home to black Manhattan.

Johnson's period of unemployment was brief. His ties with the "colored" Republican Club landed him an editorial position at the *New York Age*, a conservative newspaper controlled by Booker T. Washington. Washington's accommodative, go-slow approach in civil rights was a favorite of wealthy white philanthropists like Andrew Carnegie and of the fledgling black middle class of which James Weldon Johnson and Grace Nail Johnson were a part. W. E. B. Du Bois, a Harvard Ph.D. born in Great Barrington, Massachusetts, was Washington's major opponent. Du Bois championed a more militant strategy and helped found the NAACP in 1910.

Headquartered in New York, the organization was in search of a field secretary. The board, made up of white social activists, wanted to find someone who could bridge this rift within the black community. Joel Spingarn, the board's chairman, saw in Johnson the perfect intermediary. Board member Mary White Ovington, was not convinced, arguing that hiring a conservative "Bookerite" would send the wrong message. Du Bois, also on the board and editor of *Crisis*, the organization's journal, supported Johnson, and in 1916 the offer was made.

UNDER JOHNSON'S LEADERSHIP, the NAACP's membership grew steadily, as did its influence in the field of civil rights. "The central purpose of the National Association," he once observed, "was nothing more or less than to claim for the Negro common equality under the fundamental law of the United States; to proclaim that democracy stultified itself when it barred men from its benefits solely on the grounds of race and color." His major initiative in his first years was a campaign against the most barbarous activity of the day—lynching. While lynchings were not as numerous as they had been, their continued occurrence in a democracy that prided itself on its system of social justice, was a travesty. More than any other practice, it demonstrated the precariousness of African-American life. "In America," wrote poet Claude McKay, "it is much less dangerous to be a Communist than to be a Negro."

During 1920 and 1921 Johnson headed the NAACP's campaign to pass a federal antilynching bill. Advertisements were placed in national newspapers proclaiming lynching "the shame of America." On April 11, 1921, a bill was introduced in the House of Representatives to outlaw it. Lobbying tirelessly for its passage, Johnson "saw and talked with every man in Congress who was interested in the bill or who [he] thought could be won over to it." The bill finally passed the House on January 11, 1921, by a vote of 230 to 119.

The Senate, however, was another matter. The bill was for many months bogged down in committee and then by a southern filibuster. Finally the Republican leadership decided to abandon it and its black constituency, a decision that Johnson saw as an act of betrayal. The antilynching bill never became law.

In September 1921 Johnson went with a delegation of black leaders to visit President Warren Harding (it was later said that he knew personally every president from McKinley to

BRIDAL PICTURE OF MRS. GRACE NAIL JOHNSON, PANAMA, 1910. PHOTOGRAPHED BY JAMES WELDON JOHNSON.

JAMES WELDON JOHNSON IN 1910 AT THE FRONT GATE OF HIS PARENTS' HOME, 138 LEE STREET, JACKSONVILLE, FLORIDA.

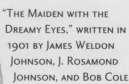

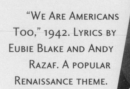

"WE ARE AMERICANS TOO," 1942. LYRICS BY EUBIE BLAKE AND ANDY RAZAF. A POPULAR RENAISSANCE THEME.

"THE MAIDEN WITH THE DREAMY EYES," WRITTEN IN 1901 BY JAMES WELDON JOHNSON, J. ROSAMOND JOHNSON, AND BOB COLE.

JAMES WELDON JOHNSON WITH HIS BROTHER ROSAMOND AND THEIR FRIEND ROBERT COLE. THEY WROTE MUSIC AND LYRICS FOR A NUMBER OF BROADWAY SHOWS AND WERE CALLED THOSE "EBONY OFFENBACHS."

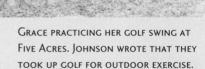

GRACE PRACTICING HER GOLF SWING AT FIVE ACRES. JOHNSON WROTE THAT THEY TOOK UP GOLF FOR OUTDOOR EXERCISE.

THE JOHNSONS ENTERTAINED OFTEN AT FIVE ACRES IN THE BERKSHIRES. JAMES WELDON JOHNSON IS IN THE CAP AND JOHN NAIL IS IN THE DARK COAT.

JAMES WELDON JOHNSON AND WALTER WHITE AT THE NAACP OFFICES IN HARLEM, FEBRUARY 1925.

AN ADVERTISEMENT NOTING THAT NAIL'S SALES GROSSED MORE THAN A MILLION DOLLARS ANNUALLY.

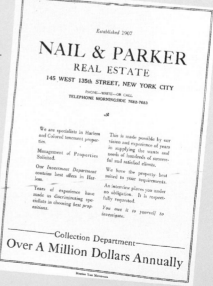

GRACE NAIL'S BROTHER JOHN WAS A REAL ESTATE MOGUL IN HARLEM UNTIL THE DEPRESSION FELLED HIS EMPIRE.

Coolidge) to protest the activities of the Ku Klux Klan and the imprisonment of those involved in the 1917 Houston riots. Alice Nelson Dunbar, ex-wife of the poet Paul Laurence Dunbar, described that meeting in her diary:

We arranged ourselves in a semi-circle around the room, and Johnson began his reading. He was plainly nervous, and had trouble keeping his glasses on. The president remained standing, partly facing Johnson, three quarters away from us. I watched his face closely. It was heavily impassive, as you would expect it to be. His complexion is changed. It is no longer swarthily sallow, but swarthily ruddy, which makes him appear fairer. When Johnson began to read his memorial, the president's lips were slightly parted. Gradually they began to draw together, so slowly that it was almost imperceptible. The rest of his face remained immobile. When Johnson came to that sentence, "The eyes of the colored people will be focused upon whatever action you may choose to take," [Harding] winced perceptibly, and his lips closed in a firm line.

President Harding was noncommittal, promising to look into the matter, but he said that "other things might take precedence." Said Alice Nelson Dunbar of the interview, "We all had the same reaction as to Harding's pronunciamento on the KKK. That lying nigger in the White House." Referring to a rumor that Harding himself was actually black and was passing for white, she added, "Funny how the general disgust at the president among our folks in Washington has resulted in calling him nigger openly." Johnson, ever the diplomat, did not refer to the interview at all in his autobiography. Harding, whose popularity had soared in the beginning of his term, began to lose favor as political scandals rocked his administration. Less than two years later he died on the presidential yacht *Sequoia*

under mysterious circumstances, having ingested "tainted" fish.

From his leadership position, Johnson continued to work to strengthen social justice and also to promote understanding between the races. In this he was uniquely suited by both training and experience. His friendships with Alfred Knopf, Carl Van Vechten, and Julius Rosenwald gave him entrée to wealthy and fashionable circles. As Van Vechten pointed out, "So warm was his humanity, so complete his tact, and so amazing his social skill that he was the master of any situation in which he found himself." Van Vechten, Alfred Knopf Jr., called young Alfred, and Johnson shared a birth date, which they celebrated together each year. At the last of these parties, the year before Johnson died, "on the Van Vechten table there were three cakes, one red, one white, and one blue—the colors of our flag. They honored a Gentile, a Negro, and a Jew—friends and fellow-Americans," Langston Hughes wrote.

Johnson had occasion to meet and strike up a friendship with H. L. Mencken, then editor of the *Smart Set*. Mencken, an influential editor and an iconoclast—he said he was against "all theologians, professors, editorial writers, right thinkers, and reformers"—was a major supporter of writers he liked, including many Harlemites. Their initial meeting occurred, Johnson explained, nearly a decade before "big magazines threw their pages open to Negro writers." Mencken did not offer to publish Johnson's work, but he did provide valuable advice: "Negro writers in writing about their own race made a mistake when they indulged in pleas for justice and mercy, when they prayed indulgence for shortcomings, when they based their protests against unjust treatment on the Christian or moral or ethical code, when they argued to prove that they were as good as anybody else. What they should do is to single out the strong points on the race and emphasize them over and over and over, asserting, at least on these points, that they are better than anybody else." Johnson would later say in praise of Mencken: "He is not afraid of anything, not even of the truth."

While Johnson found great satisfaction in his work with the NAACP, he wrote, "[I] struggled constantly not to permit that part of me which was artist to become entirely submerged." In 1912 he published his first and only novel, *The Autobiography of an Ex–Colored Man*, an examination of the phenomenon of passing. Johnson's treatment of this theme anticipated much of the later Renaissance work. Though largely ignored in 1912, it was reprinted in 1925 by Knopf to much critical acclaim.

In 1921 Johnson began work on an anthology of poetry by African-Americans. He had planned a small volume of thirty to forty poems, starting with Paul Laurence Dunbar and ending with Claude McKay. Dunbar was at that time a familiar figure in literary circles, known especially for his poetry in dialect. McKay, Jamaican born, has been called the first celebrity of the Renaissance.

Early in the project, Johnson decided to write an introduction that would illustrate the contribution African-Americans had made to the arts. His introduction developed into "The Creative Genius of the Negro," a forty-two-page essay. Perhaps mindful of Mencken's advice, he chose to glorify African-American artistic talent. "The final measure of the greatness of all peoples," he wrote, "is the amount and standard of the literature and art they have produced. The world does not know that a people is great until that people produces great literature and art."

The Johnson apartment in Harlem became "a center for literary and theater people," a salon that rivaled the most fashionable in Europe. When Claude McKay, disillusioned and alienated from New York circles in 1922, decided to go to the Soviet Union, the Johnsons threw him a farewell party. "There were present," reports Johnson, "seven or eight white persons prominent in the literary world and a dozen or so colored guests. News about the party leaked out. Harlem was not yet accustomed to social gatherings of the sort, and the local papers referred to it as the 'black and white' party."

The Johnsons entertained often. Langston Hughes recalls one evening in particular when "Clarence Darrow, sitting under the only lighted lamp, read aloud passages from his book, *Farmington*, to an attentive audience that included Ruby Darrow, Carl Van Vechten, and his wife, actress Fania Marinoff. Later that night Paul Robeson held the group spellbound with a reading from Johnson's poem, 'The Creation.'" What Van Vechten remembered most about those evenings was that Johnson was "never in better form than when carving a roast at his own well-laden board while he tossed comments across his shoulder to his Venezuelan friend, Lorita the parrot." Lorita had been presented to the Johnsons while they lived in Nicaragua and was an adored, if aging, member of the family.

Essie Robeson remembered a night in April 1925 when her husband, Paul, gave his first public concert in a Greenwich Village theater. The occasion was arranged by Van Vechten and promoted by Heywood Broun in the *New York World*. By seven-thirty all of "smart New York was there and even standing room had been sold out." The concert was a huge success, with thunderous applause after each piece and sixteen encores. The celebration after the concert included Carl and Fania Van Vechten, the James Weldon Johnsons, the Walter Whites, and "a half dozen other friends." Essie wrote in her diary, "Everybody was wildly hilarious, and we are very, very happy."

Although the Johnsons attended many parties and cabarets, Grace Nail Johnson, called the social dictator of Harlem, refused to attend any of A'Lelia Walker's soirees. "She would as soon have done the Black Bottom on Lenox Avenue," noted David Levering Lewis. Class background and color privilege were rigidly maintained by the elites of which the Johnsons were a part.

Yet within their chosen circle, a very human side of James Weldon emerged. Jane White, daughter of Walter and Gladys, recalled that he "was a close friend of my parents. One thing I shall always remember is going up to Great Barrington to spend a summer weekend with him and his wife in this exquisite house that has always remained as my idea of what a country house should be." Johnson, she revealed, was "always willing to take me on his knee and pore over my [paper doll] dress designs. And I'm sure it was just killing for him, poor thing. But he just endured it, and with such grace. To me, that was a real fellow there— to be able to put up with this annoying little girl and her cutouts."

Johnson's close friendship with Van Vechten was based partly on their shared artistic tastes and whims. "If you are in town please call me up at once," Carl wrote. "Wait till you see our new dining room chairs"—eight stools, the bases of which were blackamoors holding the seats on their heads. Still they were strangely matched. The outrageous Van Vechten toned down some of his commentary for "Jim" and

GRACE AND CARL VAN VECHTEN AT FIVE ACRES, OCTOBER 2, 1927. POSSIBLY PHOTOGRAPHED BY JOHNSON. HE AND VAN VECHTEN NOT ONLY CORRESPONDED OFTEN BUT OCCASIONALLY VACATIONED TOGETHER.

rarely ended letters with demonstrative phrases like "avocados," "peaches," or "black swans," as he did with Langston Hughes. But he did express frequent affection, ending one with "Love to both from us and a special kiss to Grace on Tuesday the 27th when she will be sixteen!" These were very different complimentary closings from Johnson's, whose letters, even to close friends and associates, frequently ended "Yours sincerely." Yet, as Van Vechten explained, "Jim himself was seldom solemn. Nobody ever enjoyed a better sense of humor. Nobody ever was able to laugh more freely."

Writer and critic Heywood Hale Broun recalled the night that Jim sang "Underneath the Bamboo Tree" at a party at his parents' house. His mother, an ardent feminist, "hissed and carried on to the embarrassment of everyone but herself," when Johnson got to the line "I'd like to change your name." But Jim, an old friend, had a "forgiving nature," Broun said, and later sent his mother a copy of his *Book of American Negro Spirituals*, "complete with inscription."

JOHNSON LEFT THE NAACP in 1931 to return to writing. He was given a farewell dinner at the Hotel Pennsylvania attended by three hundred people, including "Supreme Court Justice Benjamin Cardozo, three United States senators, five congressmen, four bishops, two federal judges, three La Follettes, four Van Dorens, and John D. Rockefeller III." Remembered Johnson, "My brother sat at the piano and played over and sang a number of our old Broadway songs. Many of the guests were old enough to join heartily in the choruses of 'The Congo Love Song,' 'The Maiden with Dreamy Eyes' and 'Under the Bamboo Tree.'" Johnson was said to be torn between tears and laughter.

That year he accepted a teaching position at Fisk University and was among the first of the Renaissance writers to leave Harlem. "It was a grateful relief," he wrote, "from the stress and strain that had entered into so considerable a part of my life; and I wondered how I had been able, in such a degree as I had, to make of myself a man of action, when I was always dreaming of the contemplative life." In 1932 he published his autobiography, *Along This Way*.

For the next six years, Johnson taught at Fisk during the school term and summered in western Massachusetts. On June 26, 1938, while vacationing near Wiscasset, Maine, his car was struck by a train at a railroad crossing. He died instantly. Grace Nail, who was driving, was seriously injured but survived. The *New York Times* carried the obituary.

His funeral was held at the Salem Methodist Church in Harlem and was attended by most of the major Renaissance figures. Van Vechten wrote to Grace Nail Johnson, still too sick to attend: "The funeral was beautiful. The day was fine. The church looked lovely with the banks of flowers, and the music was exceptionally good. 'Go Down Death' [one of the sermons from *God's Trombones*] was always my favorite of the sermons. And Juanita Hall's choir gave an extraordinary rendering of this. When they sang 'Since You Went Away', I cried & so did everybody else. With the pall bearers I sat between Arthur Spingarn & Rabbi [Stephen] Wise. Theodore Roosevelt [Jr.] & W.C. Handy were adjacent. Could any one else bring out such a strange combination of people united in love?"

"MONARCH MATERIAL," SAID ZORA NEALE HURSTON. "TRUE NOBILITY OF CHARACTER," SAID CARL VAN VECHTEN OF JAMES WELDON JOHNSON. PHOTOGRAPHED HERE BY DORIS ULMANN.

Johnson was eulogized as "the foremost black man of letters of his time." But black historian Kelly Miller did not share the consensus. Writing in the *New York Age* one month after the funeral, Miller described Johnson as a "literary dilettante, scribbling prose or verse as the mood or the occasion required." His popularity, wrote Miller, "was greater among members of the white race than his own and was based on the fact that he uttered nothing base or offensive to their racial sensibility."

Van Vechten's interpretation was somewhat different. "I don't know anybody who really knew him who didn't love him," he said. "Deep in our hearts we knew this was more than a personal affection: it was also the respect due to dignity and distinction, the appreciation won by true nobility of character. It is because he was like that that Jim can never die."

6

ETHEL WATERS

HOT CHOCOLATES OPENED at the Hudson Theatre on June 20, 1929. It featured two songs destined to become jazz classics, "Ain't Misbehavin'" and "Black and Blue." Lyricist Andy Razaf said that Dutch Schultz, the financial angel of the production, had come to him just before the show's opening demanding that a humorous number be added about "a little colored girl singing about how tough it is to be colored." With only hours to go before opening, Razaf declined and was pinned to the nearest wall at gunpoint. Recognizing the wisdom of the suggestion, he collaborated with Fats Waller on the lines "Browns and yellers all have fellers. Gentlemen prefer them light. Why am I so black and blue?" Schultz was backstage for the song's debut. A hush greeted the closing lines: "My only sin is in my skin. What did I do to be so black and blue." Razaf feared Schultz would finish him off on the spot. The thunderous sound he heard next was not gunfire but applause from the audience, now on its feet. Dutch slapped him on the back and disappeared. A few months later, on September 3, the Dow-Jones average reached the high point of the year. American Telephone and Telegraph closed at $304 and United States Steel at $261.75. Professor Irving Fisher of Yale predicted that the country was entering "a permanently high plateau." Americans were led

A BEAUTIFUL SIREN, PHOTOGRAPHED BY JAMES MARCUS CONNELLY IN CHICAGO.

like lambs to the slaughter, and the crash of October 1929 took almost everyone by surprise. "Stock prices virtually collapsed yesterday, swept downward with gigantic losses in the most disastrous trading day in the stock market's history," the *New York Times* reported. "The crowds about the ticker tape, like friends around the bedside of a stricken friend, reflected in their faces the story the tape was telling. There were no smiles. There were no tears either. Just the camaraderie of fellow-sufferers. Everybody wanted to tell his neighbor how much he had lost. Nobody wanted to listen. It was too repetitious a tale."

ETHEL WATERS WAS NEVER A child. She was born out of wedlock and did not really belong to an identifiable family unit. "I was always an outsider," she said. Her mother, Louise, whom she called Motherweeze, was just twelve years old when she was raped by John Waters, a local youth who hung around her older sisters. John was "dark brown in color though he had white blood." He was the child of Lydia Waters, a white woman who may have had colored blood and was married to a dark brown Negro. "She lived—after her marriage anyway—as a Negro and among Negro people," according to Waters. The Waters family at first denied even the contact, but John eventually confessed, claiming he did not use physical force. Ethel's maternal grandmother was outraged by the arrogance of the Waters family and refused to ask for their help to support the child. She also refused to allow the name to be mentioned in her presence.

Over time, Lydia Waters tried, without much success, to establish contact with her grandchild, who was said to closely resemble certain members of her family. When Ethel was fourteen and working in Wildwood, New Jersey, she received a message that her grandmother wanted to see her. When they met,

Waters recalled, "she took me in her arms. I felt uncomfortable because I couldn't think of her as anything but a stranger whom Mom had regarded as our enemy."

Waters struggled much of her life with these warring visions of self—one black, one white—never comfortably merged. Carl Van Vechten noted upon their first meeting, "She had very good reasons for mistrusting any white person. She had a life of her own, with her own, which she preferred." Yet when she described herself, she often boasted about her "white features" and "mixed blood." In her autobiography she wrote, "I've always thought that I inherited some of the better qualities of both my grandmothers. From little Sally Anderson, who died in defeat and the grimmest poverty, I got my fighting heart. From Lydia Waters, who died rich but heartbroken and quite possibly tortured by a bad conscience, I think I inherited poise, dignity, and whatever intelligence I have."

Waters's bisexuality was strongly hinted at by Alberta Hunter and was said to have been well known in her day, though Waters herself never revealed it. It is evident from her autobiography that her interest in men was sporadic and fleeting and that she had a fondness for physically beating up the girlfriends of her boyfriends. She traveled frequently with male bands. "The boys in the band treated me like a little sister," she said on more than one occasion. In this light, her frequent attempts to create the perfect family, complete with adoring husband and healthy children, appear all the more doomed.

As a cabaret singer and recording star, Ethel Waters introduced such classic songs as "Saint Louis Blues," "Heat Wave," and "Stormy Weather." By the 1930s she was one of the highest-paid black entertainers on Broadway. Yet over time her tremendous contributions in the field of music were eclipsed by "her show biz personality." Biographer Susannah McCorkle wrote, "You don't become a jazz legend by growing old, playing grandmothers, and palling around with Billy Graham and Richard Nixon." Waters managed to stay in the limelight longer than most black women performers by transforming herself from a seductive siren to a happy darky.

SHORTLY AFTER WATERS'S BIRTH, on October 31, 1896, her mother married a man named Norman Howard, but Waters lived only sporadically with her mother. She was more often shuffled among relatives from Chester, Pennsylvania, to Philadelphia to Camden, New Jersey, and back again. Her closest kin was her grandmother, whom she called Mom and who looked after Ethel whenever she could. She worked as a live-in maid, however, and as Waters pointed out, "Her world was really in the kitchen with the white families she worked for." Mom would visit Waters on her day off, but she never had the resources to establish a household for herself and Waters, so much of the time, Waters stayed with Mom's two other daughters, Vi and Ching. They were alcoholics and lived in a series of bug- and vermin-infested shanties that contained few furnishings and inadequate kitchens. Waters ate, in those early years, by stealing. She became very adept at shoplifting, providing not only for her own needs but for those of her aunts as well. Her grandmother's weekly visits were another source of food, since Mom helped herself to her white employers' leftovers by wrapping them up and storing them in pockets she had sewn into her clothing. Her visits were a source of great pleasure to Waters.

Growing up in such disorder, Waters found solace of sorts in education and religion. She loved going to the Catholic school in her neighborhood. She loved the discipline of it, the introduction to worlds never before known, and the attention of her teachers. Waters's gift for memorizing brought her to their attention and gave her an advantage over the other students.

School lasted only a few hours each day, however, and along with her intelligence, Waters had a mean streak. Not only did she steal, but she also fought like a demon and used language that made grown men blush. She also tormented her playmates and managed always to ally herself with the worst group of friends she could find. Waters called it an "education in life in the raw."

At the age of thirteen, she married Merritt "Buddy" Purnsley, a local boy. She had been living with Louise, her mother; Louise's husband; their daughter; and Mom, her grandmother. But her mother's marriage broke up, her half sister was sent to live with her father's family, Mom went to live with her sister, and Louise found a job in Atlantic City. Waters begged to go with her but Louise refused. When Merritt proposed, Mom and Louise encouraged the union as a solution to the problem of what to do about Waters. She was not in love with Buddy and, in fact, didn't even like him, so she felt betrayed. She reasoned that

Buddy wanted to marry her only because he couldn't get her into bed any other way: staying a virgin had been Waters's greatest challenge and proudest accomplishment to date.

According to Waters, the wedding was awful, the wedding night worse, and their financial circumstances as bad as ever. Louise had given them furniture to get them started, along with unpaid installment bills. Buddy had a job with the Pennsylvania Steel Casting Company, but he was not well paid. They lived with his aunt Martha, who did the cooking. Ethel continued in school after she was married, at least until she had completed the sixth grade.

Within months of her marriage her grandmother died, and her aunt Ching passed away several months after that. "With Mom and Ching both gone, things got worse for me," Waters wrote. Buddy turned out to be a jealous type, who beat his wife in frustration and had other women on the side. Waters decided to leave him but had to wait for the right moment. Her opportunity came when Buddy got a job out of town and let her go to Atlantic City to visit Louise. A brief reconciliation, brought on by Buddy's promise to do better, lasted only a few weeks. Waters moved to Philadelphia and, after many pleas from Buddy, wrote: "If you dare set foot on this here soil of Philadelphia I'll have you put in jail for all the bad things you did to me." Waters was fourteen.

She got her first real job working as a maid

ETHEL WATERS AND EUBIE BLAKE SINGING "YOU'RE LUCKY TO ME" IN *BLACKBIRDS*, 1930.

at the Harrod Apartments in Philadelphia. Recommended by Motherweeze and younger than most of the other employees, she scrubbed, mopped, and washed dishes with such enthusiasm that the other workers resented her efforts. But for Waters this job meant more food and security than she had ever had in her life. On October 31, 1917, she sneaked into a Philadelphia saloon that was having a Halloween talent competition. She was prevailed upon to sing when one of the scheduled performers failed to show up. In the audience that night were Braxton and Nugent, a professional vaudeville team. Waters's tearful ballad, "When You're a Long, Long Way from Home," made an impression on them, and they invited her to join them for ten dollars a week. At the Harrod, she was earning only $3.50 a week as a maid, with another $1.50 in tips, so she was tempted by the offer, but she was hesitant to leave her first good job. Finally she made Motherweeze promise "to replace me in my cleaning woman's job and to hold it for me until I got back." With this insurance, a career was launched.

WATERS'S FIRST PROFESSIONAL performance was at the Lincoln Theater in Baltimore. Like many of the other "Negro houses" she would play that season, the theater had no wings, no backstage, and no dressing rooms. The audience was often livelier than the entertainers as they "ran up and down the aisles, yelling greetings to friends and sometimes having fights. And they brought everything to eat, from bananas to yesterday's pork chops. If they liked you, they were very vocal—screaming, shouting and stomping their feet."

Waters wanted to sing a new number in her act that she had once heard performed by Charles Anderson, a female impersonator. The song was restricted, so she had to apply to the copyright owners, Pace and Handy, before she could sing it onstage. She was given permission and became the first woman to sing the classic "Saint Louis Blues." Waters's first performance of that song was met with a shower of coins from the audience. "It fell like rain on the stage," she reported. Receiving a share of the tips as well as $10.00 a week, Waters was soon able to send money home, a practice she continued throughout her life.

Because she was tall and scrawny, the managers of the theater gave her the name Sweet Mama Stringbean, and billed her as "direct from St. Louis and singing 'St. Louis Blues.'" The name Sweet Mama Stringbean stuck. The Baltimore engagement, however, lasted only two weeks. Waters learned at its closing that Braxton and Nugent had been cheating her, and decided to go on without them. As the sister

ETHEL WATERS WAS THE GREATEST BLUES SINGER OF THEM ALL. PHOTOGRAPH INSCRIBED TO CARL VAN VECHTEN, 1920S.

act in the show was also leaving, they invited her to join them and the three became the Hills Sisters.

As the Hills Sisters, the trio traveled throughout the South, performing in saloons much like the one in Baltimore. Working from nine in the morning until midnight, the girls earned between $35.00 and $50.00 a week. Waters soon outshone her partners, though, and the act was billed as "the Hills Sisters, Featuring Sweet Mama Stringbean Singing 'Saint Louis Blues.'" Sweet Mama, for all her newfound acclaim, had modest goals. "I still had only one ambition," she would later write. "That was to become the personal maid of some lady who would take me with her around the world." More immediately, Waters dreamed of things she'd never had—"clean surroundings, a decent, quiet place to sleep, some sense of order, and good meals at regular times of the day."

Realizing the lack of potential for advancement, one of the sisters left the act, leaving only the two. Their next booking was in Atlanta. The city's black section had two vaudeville theaters side by side. They were in number 81, with Bessie Smith booked next door. Ethel got into a misunderstanding with a husband-and-wife act at number 81 and was fired. The sister act was then picked up by the management next door, but with the understanding, demanded by Smith, that only she would sing the blues.

"ETHEL WATERS, EXPERT
AT TONAL EFFECTS," CARL
VAN VECHTEN WROTE IN
VANITY FAIR, 1926.

FREDI WASHINGTON
ON BROADWAY.

A BIRTHDAY PARTY FOR JOE
LOUIS, WITH ETHEL WATERS
AND DUKE ELLINGTON, CIRCA
1938. PHOTOGRAPH BY
MORGAN AND MARVIN SMITH.

GEORGETTE HARVEY,
ETHEL WATERS, AND
FREDI WASHINGTON
(LEFT TO RIGHT) IN
*MAMBA'S DAUGH-
TERS*, 1939—THE
STORY OF A SLOW-
WITTED MOTHER
WHO LOVES HER
FAIR-SKINNED
DAUGHTER AND
KILLS FOR HER SAKE.
PHOTOGRAPH BY
VANDAMM STUDIO.

IN 1935 ETHEL WATERS
INTRODUCED THE HIT SONG
"STORMY WEATHER"
AT A COTTON CLUB REVUE.
YEARS LATER PEOPLE STILL
TALKED OF THE MAGIC OF
THAT PERFORMANCE.

ETHEL WATERS SANG
"HEAT WAVE" IN IRVING
BERLIN'S *AS THOUSANDS
CHEER*, 1935.

Waters described Bessie Smith as "a heavy-set, dark woman and very nice looking." She was the undisputed tops as a blues singer, and was earning $50.00 to $75.00 a week, plus the money thrown to her onstage. She probably took in several hundred dollars a week.

Waters's performance involved shaking and shimmying and singing "I Want to Be Somebody's Baby Doll So I Can Get My Lovin' All the Time." The audience wanted the blues, however, and began shouting for Stringbean to sing them. The manager went to Smith and persuaded her to let Ethel sing "Saint Louis Blues" if the crowd still insisted after she had done her first song. The crowd always insisted. After the engagement, Waters remembered Smith calling her into her dressing room and saying, "You ain't so bad. It's only that I never dreamed that anyone could be able to do this to me in my own territory and with my own people. And you know damn well that you can't sing worth a ———." Waters saw this as the beginning of Bessie Smith's decline. "I've never enjoyed seeing a champ go down, and Bessie was all champ," she wrote. These events were not remembered in the same way or at all by Bessie, however, and as the year was 1917 or 1918, Waters's prediction was certainly premature.

In 1918, on a highway between Anniston, Alabama, and Birmingham, Waters was injured in a car crash and nearly lost her leg. After that, work was sporadic, so she returned to Philadelphia and got a job washing dishes at a Horn and Hardart Automat. She moved in with Motherweeze, her aunt Vi, her half sister, and her sister's baby, Ethel. Barney Gordon, a saloon owner, offered her a job at $15 a week in a place patronized by rowdies and drunks. Waters accepted but World War I soon hurt business so much that Waters was let go. She went back to washing dishes.

Joe Bright, a black actor-producer from New York, rescued Waters this time. He invited her to perform at the Lincoln Theater in Harlem. The year was 1919. "In those days Harlem was anything but an exclusively Negro section," Waters noted. The black belt ran only from 130th to 140th Streets between Fifth and Seventh Avenues. The area was crowded with southern migrants who had come to work in munitions plants. They were crammed in with the folks already living there, creating an uneasy alliance. Blacks were not welcome on 125th Street, which was still a white boulevard. They could not sit on the main floor of B. F. Keith's Alhambra Theater where Bojangles danced, nor were they welcome in any of the white theaters along the street.

Elite blacks were welcomed, however, at Baron Wilkins's nightclub, which also drew white trade from downtown. The baron's brother, Leroy Wilkins, ran a middle-class club at 135th and Fifth. Three blocks north on Fifth was Harry Pyle's place. A little more atmosphere could be found at Connor's Club at 135th between Lenox and Fifth.

According to Waters, "For entertainers, the last stop on the way down in show business was Edmond's Cellar at 132nd Street and Fifth Avenue. After you worked there, there was no place to go except into domestic service." In the same category was Bank's Club on 133rd between Lenox and Fifth.

Waters got a good reception at the Lincoln Theater and was held over for a second week. It was a big step for a performer to move from Philadelphia to New York—the "Big Time." There was also lots of competition, so Waters planned to return to Philadelphia after her engagement ended. A chance encounter with an old acquaintance got her two roommates, a place to live, and a job at Edmond's Cellar. Edmond paid $2.00 a night. The tips the customers gave were thrown into the kitty and divided equally. Edmond's seated 150 to 200 people at tables jammed close together. Waters sang "Shim-Me-She Wabble," "Minor's Blues," and of course her signature song, "Saint Louis Blues."

Waters was the big attraction at Edmond's. People often had to wait upstairs because there just wasn't room on the main floor. With urging both from the owner and the pianist, Lou Henley, she expanded her repertoire to include "Dear Old Pal of Mine" and "My Buddy." Word got around, and "white society folks began to come to hear me," Waters recalled. Money poured in. Sometimes she would take home as much as $30.00 a night. The work was grueling, requiring her to perform until she was exhausted, but she often looked back on that time as the happiest in her life.

Edmond's Cellar was too hot in the summertime, so Edmond had to move his operation to Atlantic City. Ethel was invited to come along, but when she realized that the band was too small for the dance-loving Atlantic City crowds, she quit. She was picked up by Rafe's Paradise, a big club in Atlantic City with mostly white patrons, a new experience for Waters. She developed quite a reputation there. Bert Williams, a star of the Ziegfeld Follies, came three times to see her because friends had told him Waters had his droll quality. Sophie Tucker came several times as well.

When Waters returned to New York that fall, Noble Sissle and Eubie Blake were casting *Shuffle Along*, the hit show that opened in 1921 and launched the career of Florence Mills. Waters tried to get a job, "wanting to get away from smoky nightclub work," but to the producers, she was just a honky-tonk performer. Her family background and lack of education were a constant impediment in her early career.

A talent scout for Black Swan Records, a company on the verge of bankruptcy, had seen Waters's act at Edmond's and persuaded her to make a record for them. She was paid a lump sum of $100. The record—"Down Home Blues" on one side, "Oh Daddy" on the other—was a hit and got Black Swan out of the red. Fletcher Henderson, a recent arrival from Georgia, was Waters's accompanist. She described him, on their first meeting as "sitting behind a desk looking prissy and important." A college chemistry major, Henderson had come to New York to study and was doing music on the side. He was not thrilled with the idea of working with Ethel Waters. "He wasn't sure it would be dignified enough for him . . . to be the piano player for a girl who sang the blues in a cellar," Waters wrote. Eventually, though, Henderson was persuaded, and he and Ethel toured the South plugging their records.

Waters returned to New York after this six-month tour and once again went to work at Edmond's. However, the success of her recordings finally brought her to the attention of Harlem producers Whitney and Tutt, who cast her in their production *Oh! Joy!* It was the first show in which she appeared as a name performer. While it did well in Boston, it closed in New York after a short time. Waters had left it by then, but her career was launched and the opportunities kept coming.

Earl Dancer, a performer and nightclub owner, suggested the next big step for Ethel—"he egg[ed] me into going on the white time." Until now Ethel had resisted performing before white audiences. "No white audience would understand my blues," she explained. "I'd be a complete flop." Her brief engagement at Rafe's Paradise had not changed her mind. But with Dancer's encouragement, she became a vaudeville sensation and traveled from one coast to the other.

In 1925, Waters replaced Florence Mills at the Plantation Club at Broadway and Fiftieth Street. Florence had left the show because she preferred touring. It was there that Waters in-

troduced her hit song "Dinah." She shared her dressing room with a young member of the chorus, who "stepped out of the line to do her speciality once during each show." She was a "mugger with a great comic sense and a beautiful form," Waters recalled. Her name was Josephine Baker. According to Waters, when the show closed, producer Mary Louise Howard invited her to go to Europe and appear in a revue she was planning. Waters refused and Josephine Baker went instead.

Waters appeared in *Africana*, a show produced by Earl Dancer in 1927. It had a good run in New York and then went on the road. Her exposure to "white time" through these productions also introduced her to more and more white people. One night when she was playing at the Lafayette, Carl Van Vechten came backstage and invited her to dinner. "I didn't see any reason for going," Waters said. "White people generally bored me, and we didn't speak the same language." But Carl was insistent and Ethel was talked into attending a "big-time dinner." She hated the food. The first course was "Cold borsch! That is nothing but beet soup and clabber." And "the caviar looked like buckshot."

Convinced that Waters did not like his food, Van Vechten asked her what she ate. She invited him to a dinner she cooked herself and served baked ham and string beans, iced tea, and lemon meringue pie. Carl loved it. "The rich, white historian of my Harlem people reveled in it," Waters said. She recalled suggesting that her "informal way of living" was in some ways superior to his own.

While *Africana* had been a success, not all the performers had been paid. Waters's apartment was picketed, and it so upset her she did not go out. Escaping to Philadelphia, she met and married her second husband, Clyde Edward

ETHEL WATERS IN *AT HOME ABROAD*, BROADWAY, 1935.

"Eddie" Matthews, "who appeared out of nowhere." She also adopted Algretta, the eighteen-month-old child of a friend from Edmond's Cellar. Feeling that important things were missing from her life, Waters threw herself into marriage and motherhood. "Being a mother is what makes a real life for a woman, not applause, your picture in the paper, the roses and the telegrams you get on opening night," she wrote. Yet there was always a surreal quality to this family. Eddie, she said, was "much lighter than I," and Algretta was "almost white and very beautiful. Except for being white, Algretta bore a great resemblance to me, which probably came from association." People "couldn't figure us out," she reported. "I guess they suspected there was a colored gentleman somewhere in the lumberyard."

They sailed first class on the *Ile de France*, with Waters intending to see a specialist in Europe about a throat problem. Waters worked while on her trip, playing the Palladium and the Café de Paris in London to rave reviews. The management of the Café de Paris reserved the same table for her every night. One evening she came in to find the Prince of Wales—later King Edward VIII—seated at her table. When told it was Ethel Waters's table, he came over and apologized. He then came back once a week to hear her performance. Said Waters: "I didn't like it later when he abdicated as King and Emperor and ruler of the Dominions Beyond the Seas and all the rest. After all, he was the only King who had ever apologized to me for anything."

Upon her return to New York, Waters's career took a fateful turn. Hollywood producer King Vidor was looking for a black actress to play the role of Chick, a sexy siren in his movie *Hallelujah*. Ethel was considered but according to her, "the talent man sent East to wave gold bags at me was stalled on the job by colored theatrical people unfriendly to me." He reported that he was unable to find her, and she was passed over. Chosen instead was Nina Mae McKinney, a seventeen-year-old from South Carolina who had been spotted in the chorus line of Lew Leslie's *Blackbirds*. McKinney was a hit in the role. Vidor called her sensational. She was heralded as the first recognized black actress of the silver screen. But her phenomenal success in *Hallelujah* was not the start of an illustrious career. She was given a five-year contract with MGM but soon learned the bitter lesson that there were no leading roles for black actresses and few others of any sort save the sexy siren.

Waters was on the sidelines of this rise and fall but certainly not a disinterested observer. She was thirty-four but passing for thirty and well aware that her own days as a sultry cabaret singer were numbered. Hollywood was beckoning with what film critic Donald Bogle called the "black jester, the high-stepping, highfalutin, crazy as all get out" black male figure, but the female counterpart was less developed. In the meantime, Lew Leslie offered to cast Ethel in his new edition of *Blackbirds*. Leslie had by then lost Bill Robinson, his box-office jester, to *Brown Buddies*, and Adelaide Hall, his other veteran performer, was in Europe. The show opened on Forty-second Street next to a flea circus. The show was a flop, and "the fleas outdrew us at every performance," Waters wrote. The year was 1930.

Despite the Depression, Leslie built a show around Waters called *Rhapsody in Black*. It ran through the earliest and worst days of the Depression but was able, because of Waters's much-heralded performance, to make money. Caught up in a dispute with Leslie over her salary, Waters's lawyer had gotten her a 10 percent share of the gross receipts.

AFTER MANY YEARS AT CENTER STAGE, Ethel Waters was finally invited to the Cotton Club. There she introduced still another hit song, "Stormy Weather." By then her marriage was on the rocks, and Algretta had contracted polio and was sent away because Waters was unable to care for her. The fantasy life of marriage and motherhood had evaporated. "Everything I had is gone. Stormy weather. Keeps raining all the time": the song was a perfect expression of her mood, and she found release in performing it. "I was singing the story of my misery and confusion," she said, "of the misunderstandings in my life that I couldn't straighten out, the story of the wrongs and outrages done to me by people I had loved and trusted."

Irving Berlin came to the Cotton Club, heard her sing, and decided to produce a revue with Waters in it. *As Thousands Cheer* was a smash hit, and that year Ethel became the highest-paid woman performer on Broadway, earning $1,000 a week in the heart of the Depression. "Ethel Waters is having such a delightful present that she doesn't brood over her past," *The New Yorker* reported in December 1933.

Waters's career in films ran curiously parallel to that of Fredi Washington, a celebrated member of the Harlem elite whose sister Isabel married a future congressman, Adam Clayton Powell Jr. Fredi was a striking woman. "Her features were sharply defined, her hair long, dark, and straight, and her eyes a vibrant green." A cabaret singer and dancer in the 1920s, an early friend and supporter of Josephine Baker, she made numerous appearances at the parties of A'Lelia Walker. Washington, called "iridescent" and "sophisticated," was seven years younger than Ethel but twice played her daughter. Fredi was a "tragic mulatto" who embodied the struggle of opposing black and white identities that Renaissance figures like Jessie Fauset and Nella Larsen wrote about. Her first big break came in 1933 when at the age of thirty she was cast as Peola in the movie version of *Imitation of Life*, the Fannie Hurst best-seller. Though hers was a minor part, Washington, like McKinney before her, received both critical acclaim and media attention. In interviews, Washington exploited her tragic mulatto image, complaining that unlike the woman she portrayed in the film, who was passing, her problem was that she was too light. "I wish I was brown-skinned like McKinney," she announced. As Washington would discover, being darker would not have helped. Studios found no role for her other than that of the lovely light-skinned child of the fat, dark-skinned mammy. Actress Louise Beavers introduced in that movie what Bogle called a new, humanized part, "the portrait of the modern black woman, a servant imbued with dignity." It was a character that Waters would later play in the Broadway play *Mamba's Daughters* and in the movies *Pinky* and *The Member of the Wedding*. Fredi Washington soon grew too old to play the daughter and faded from the scene, but Waters settled into the role of the enduring domestic who, like her grandmother, cared for white folks' kids. The *Chicago World* celebrated her transformation, proclaiming that she had traveled from "blues singing to spirituals."

White America found great comfort in the asexual black icon who could wisely counsel, soothe, and protect like a member of the family and yet, unlike a real member, could be let go. "They were blessed with a wonderful colored cook and maid," Langston Hughes wrote in *The Ways of White Folks*, "until she took sick and died in her room in their basement." Ethel Waters became a box office hit playing a role that her grandmother knew well. She had come full circle.

ETHEL WATERS SENSITIVELY PHOTOGRAPHED BY CARL VAN VECHTEN, 1933.

KING OLIVER'S BAND, LOUIS ARMSTRONG'S FIRST BAND IN CHICAGO.

Going to Chicago

In 1910 fewer than 50,000 blacks lived in Chicago. By 1920 their numbers had more than tripled as word spread throughout the South that better opportunities could be found there. Called the promised land by some, it was the first migration stop for many Renaissance figures. The South Side, home of the elite of a thriving black migrant community, was the site of a number of nightspots where "real jazz, with more of the wail of the blues," was played. One of the most famous was the Dreamland Café, a mecca for the moneyed crowd and a showplace for black talent. Al Jolson, Sophie Tucker, and Eddie Cantor were said to drink in every nuance of phrasing and style of Alberta Hunter's performances there and to copy her unabashedly. "Cautious and pragmatic," Louis Armstrong remained in New Orleans until 1922 when his friend Joe Oliver invited him to Chicago to join King Oliver's Creole Jazz Band at the Pekin Inn. Bessie Smith's voice was likened to a "flamethrower licking out across the room."

7
LOUIS ARMSTRONG

O N JANUARY 16, 1920, the Eighteenth Amendment banning the sale and consumption of alcohol in the United States went into effect. It had come before the Senate in 1917 and was passed in a lopsided vote after only thirteen hours of debate. Passage in the House was equally swift. By January 1919 three-quarters of the states had ratified the amendment. It was generally believed that enforced sobriety would do great things for industry, the social order, and the younger generation. The reality was somewhat different. Enforcement for a country with over 18,000 miles of coastline and land borders was almost impossible. Overnight, a host of new industries were created for smugglers, speakeasy employees, and operators of stills. The only debate was whether Prohibition had brought more drinking. By 1931 it was apparent to most that this grand social experiment had failed. The *New York World* published a poem that could be considered the era's epitaph:

> *It's left a trail of graft and slime,*
> *It's filled our land with vice and crime,*
> *It don't prohibit worth a dime . . .*

LOUIS ARMSTRONG WITH HIS MOTHER, MAYANN, AND HIS SISTER, BEATRICE, IN 1922. THE PICTURE, TAKEN JUST BEFORE ARMSTRONG MOVED TO CHICAGO BY VILLARD PADDIO, A LOCAL NEW ORLEANS PHOTOGRAPHER, IS THE ONLY SURVIVING PORTRAIT OF ARMSTRONG'S FAMILY.

In 1920, young Johnny Torrio of Chicago's underworld turned his full attention to the new law's moneymaking possibilities. Torrio soon fled to New York, but his able assistant, Al Capone, stayed on. Capone was a jazz impresario.

THERE IS NO WRITTEN RECORD to prove that Louis Armstrong existed before the age of eighteen—no birth certificate, no school documents, no letters, no diaries, not even a family Bible—but it is fitting that under the circumstances, he chose the Fourth of July, 1900, as his birth date, for the dawn of a new century is the perfect symbol for this American genius, the greatest horn player ever to come out of New Orleans and one of the most important figures in twentieth-century music. According to Duke Ellington, Armstrong "all but invented jazz." Although it was a fitting birth date for him to have chosen, it is also likely that it was untrue.

Armstrong, who resembled the archetypal hayseed in early photographs, brought a sophistication and a discipline to the relatively limited urban honky-tonk music of his youth. Though Louis appeared to be a natural, playful clown onstage, his fame rested on his broad tone, his smooth vibrato, and most of all, his "amazing virtuosity in the highest register." As his biographer James Collier points out, Louis was not an "untutored folk artist." From childhood on, he honed his skills in reading music and playing his instrument.

LOUIS ARMSTRONG WAS BORN in a poor black section of New Orleans, "a city of ancient wealth and deep poverty." Biographers speculate that he was born sometime between 1898 and 1901, in the waning Victorian era. He grew up in a neighborhood where prostitution was everywhere, hard liquor a diet staple, and the contradictions of racial identity played out with a peculiar twist like nowhere else in the South. Turn-of-the-century New Orleans was also saturated with music. Symphony orchestras, three opera companies, and scores of marching bands and dance groups dotted the city. Music was played everywhere: at weddings, birthdays, and funerals, parties, picnics, and parades.

Armstrong had none of the traditional parental supports characteristic of middle-class Renaissance figures like James Weldon Johnson and Jessie Fauset. His father, Willie Armstrong, abandoned his wife and child early in Armstrong's life. He made no effort to see his son for years, and when he did, he gave him nothing. "I was touring Europe when he died," Armstrong recalled. "Didn't go to his funeral and didn't send nothing. Why should I? He never had no time for me or Mayann." Willie Armstrong was described by Louis as "a real sharp man, tall and handsome and well built," who made the ladies swoon. Louis once remarked: "My father did not have time to teach me anything; he was too busy chasing chippies." His mother, Mary Ann—or Mayann, as she was called—was a prostitute and later, after she found religion, a domestic. While she loved her son and the daughter she had two years after Louis, Mayann was not a reliable parent. Armstrong lived at first with his paternal grandmother, Josephine. She earned money by taking in washing and, by Armstrong's account, was very strict.

Sometime when Louis was between the ages of five and seven, Mayann got sick and arranged for him to live with her and help care for his baby sister. Mayann resided in black Storyville, a red-light district established in 1899 by the city fathers to rein in the sin and corruption. Mostly a white area, with white prostitutes and some who were racially mixed, Storyville covered thirty-eight blocks and was centered on Basin Street. Ladies of the evening came from all over the country to this legally sanctioned area of ill repute. Blacks were employed in Storyville only as menials, delivery boys, bouncers, and the like. But the area contained, in keeping with the segregated practices of the day, a small black section of three or four blocks. Here black prostitutes resided and worked, along with black bartenders, gamblers, waiters, and musicians. There were dance halls and honky-tonks on every corner. Louis said that there was not a single decent home in the area. The customers were working men, both black and white, from the levees, cotton mills, cane fields, and railroad gangs. Although they were rough and tough, they were often cheated by the even rougher and tougher denizens of Storyville.

Armstrong was not ashamed of his old neighborhood. Living and learning within five blocks of his house for the first eighteen years of his life, he never lost his attachment for home. "I sure had a ball growing up in New Orleans," he once observed. "We were poor and everything like that, but music was all around you. Music keep you rolling." For all its disorganization, there seems to have been a real sense of community in black Storyville. Louis could always count on the area women to take him in and feed him when Mayann took off for parts unknown. He often referred to "the old sisters of my neighborhood, who had practically raised me."

James Baldwin's father, who grew up to be a minister "chilling in the pulpit," came from the same neighborhood as Armstrong and, though he never revealed why, forbade his children to play Louis Armstrong records in the house. A picture of Louis hung on the wall, however. Said Baldwin: "One of my father's strong willed female relatives had placed it there and forbade my father to take it down. He never did, but he eventually maneuvered her out of the house and when, some years later, she was in trouble and near death, he refused to do anything to help her."

Armstrong's unconventional family life did not translate into a problematic relationship with his mother. She, in fact, allowed him to live as he chose (perhaps the source of Papa Baldwin's disapproval) and was always supportive of him. Once, after he moved to Chicago, rumor reached her that he was doing badly. She took the first train out of New Orleans and arrived while he was performing. Louis looked up from the bandstand that night to see Mayann moving through the crowd, two big paper parcels under her arm. It was the first of several trips she would make to visit him. "I used to take Mama cabareting, and we'd get soused together," Armstrong reported. "Used to have a very nice time."

Mayann was the one who encouraged him, as he said: "to carry on with my cornet blowing because I loved it so much." From an early age, Louis would do odd jobs or fill his pockets with coins from gambling and take his "earnings" home to her. Then, Louis explained, "Mother, sister and I would have enough money to go shopping. Now and then I even bought Mother a new dress, and occasionally I got myself a pair of short pants. . . . Of course I could not get a pair of shoes, but as we went barefoot, that did not matter." When Mayann took up domestic labor, she worked for a white family on Canal Street. That job probably gave her "toting privileges," allowing her to bring food and perhaps clothing home to her children, a common practice in the South. Armstrong always felt his mother did what she could for him. He once said that the only time he wept in his life was when, in 1927, the coffin was closed over Mayann.

Her employment also gave Louis the opportunity to attend the Fisk School, where he learned to read, write, and do arithmetic. We have only Louis's account of the extent of his education because the school burned down and all the records were lost. He said on one occasion, "I did not stay in kindergarten long but was soon in the second grade. I could read the newspaper to the older folk in my neighborhood who helped Mama to raise me."

We do know that in 1912 or 1913, Armstrong attended a New Year's Eve celebration and fired a pistol into the air in retaliation for a shot fired at him by another child. With child welfare a matter of great public concern at that time, Armstrong was arrested and sent to the Colored Waifs' Home for Boys. Run by a black couple who had been caring for homeless children since the turn of the century, it was a two-story building with a dormitory upstairs and a dining hall, chapel, and schoolroom on the first floor. The children were taught reading and writing and were given yard work to do. Twice a week they staged a drill with wooden drums and wooden guns.

Armstrong was at first miserable and homesick in the home, but rather quickly adjusted and warmed to the discipline that had been lacking in his life with Mayann—and more than that, the home had a band. Child advocates believed that music had a civilizing influence on wayward children, and performing bands represented a source of income for orphanages, which were often run on a shoestring. It took six months for Louis to be invited to play in the Colored Waifs' Home band, although he attended their rehearsals almost from the first.

Whether this was due to his great shyness, frequently commented upon by all who knew him well, or to the fact that the bandleader did not like him is not clear. Louis was at first given a tambourine to play and later promoted to the drum and then the alto horn.

Playing in the band gave Armstrong the advantage of at least rudimentary instruction in his instrument, separating him from many of the other musicians of his day. It has been suggested that it was there that he learned his sharp, clean attack. His biographer suggests that Louis's early instruction in brass band techniques, where virtuoso cornet or trumpet soloists stepped forward to play unaccompanied solos, explains a lot about the kind of player he became.

Armstrong spent about a year and a half at the orphanage. His introduction to the horn had taken hold, and upon his return to black Storyville, he was determined to become a musician. Toward that end, he would go around to the honky-tonks and beg cornetists to let him sit in for a few minutes. Known in the neighborhood, he was considered "cute and cheerful with an ingratiating manner"—a little bitty fellow—and so was let in. He started by playing the blues. His talent was soon noticed, and the other musicians encouraged him to keep at it. In 1916, in his midteens, he purchased his first cornet for ten dollars.

Nineteen sixteen was also the year that he met fellow Louisianian Joe Oliver. Oliver, a large man with a voracious appetite who was feared because of his dominating personality, started a band and became known as the cornet king of New Orleans. Though Oliver was an unlikely mentor, he liked Louis and took him under his wing. He got him a better cornet, taught him technique, and got him jobs with better bands. "He was the one who taught me after I left the Home," Armstrong recalled. "I listened to the others, but he gave me the tuition."

KING OLIVER'S CREOLE JAZZ BAND, EARLY 1920S. KING OLIVER IS AT TOP LEFT; LOUIS ARMSTRONG, SEATED CENTER; LIL HARDIN, ARMSTRONG'S FUTURE SECOND WIFE, AT THE PIANO.

That year also marked the start of the Great Migration of blacks from the South, sparked by the labor needs associated with World War I and the employment loss associated with the boll weevil invasion in the South. Between 1916 and 1918, over half a million blacks would move to the North. The migration opened up a world of opportunity never before extended to them. New Orleans musicians discovered, for example, that there was better-paying work elsewhere and eagerly followed the established migration routes to Saint Louis and eventually on to Chicago. In a further stroke of bad luck for New Orleans, the U.S. Navy closed down Storyville, which was considered bad for the war effort. As a result of all these developments there was nearly a total exodus of top players by 1920.

Armstrong at first stayed put, rising in importance with the exit of the others and obtain-ing better and better jobs. In 1918, Joe Oliver left for Chicago and Armstrong replaced him in the top band of that time, the Kid Ory band. "What a thrill that was!" he wrote. "To think I was considered up to taking Joe Oliver's place in the best band in town! I couldn't hardly wait to get to Mayann's to tell her the good news." Then, in 1919, Ory decided to move to Los Angeles. Armstrong was invited along but declined.

Armstrong instead began to play on the latest New Orleans rage, the riverboat. Louis had never been out of New Orleans except for short visits to small Louisiana towns. To meet the riverboat band led by Fate Marable, he had to take his first long train ride to Saint Louis. "I had no idea as to what I should take and my mother did not either," Louis wrote. Mayann brought him a big fish sandwich and a bottle of green olives, and she packed all of his clothes in

Colored Waif's Home Brass Band, New Orleans, 1910. Louis's first instrument was the tambourine.

Louis Armstrong, circa 1931–1932.

"Impossible Interview, Fritz Kreisler versus Louis Armstrong," *Vanity Fair*, February 1926. Drawing by Miguel Covarrubias.

Best wishes To Alberta Hunter. Always a "Great" Entertainer. Louis Armstrong

Lil Hardin Armstrong and Louis at Sebastian's Night Club in Culver City, California, 1931.

Louis inscribed this photograph to his friend Alberta Hunter.

Armstrong's Secret "9" Base Ball Team of New Orleans, LA. 1931

Armstrong with the Armstrong Secret 9, a baseball team he sponsored, New Orleans, 1931.

To my Pal Lee Best Wish form L. the ace Lindsey

a suitcase. It was so crammed that Louis had to carry the olives separately as well as his cornet. The olives never made it through the train changes, the station crowds, and the roaring engines, but Louis somehow did. "I felt pretty bad about those good olives, but when I finally got on the train I was still holding my fish sandwich. Yes, sir, I at least managed to keep that."

Also in 1918, Armstrong married a prostitute named Daisy Parker, "a small, thin, good-looking woman" who was extremely jealous. Above all, she loved to fight and make up with Louis, producing a relationship that was stormy and unsettled. But because he was on the riverboat, and away from New Orleans a lot of the time, the marriage lasted longer than anyone thought it would. It ended unofficially when Armstrong moved to Chicago and officially in 1923, when he married pianist Lil Hardin. But Louis's fourth wife said of Daisy: "She never acknowledged the fact that Louie had divorced her. She considered herself Louie's wife. She would come in the very early days of my marriage to the hotel and see him."

ARMSTRONG WITH LIONEL HAMPTON, 1930. LIONEL'S UNCLE, RICHARD MORGAN, A PROMINENT CHICAGO BOOTLEGGER, WAS A GREAT COMFORT TO BESSIE SMITH AFTER HER BREAKUP WITH HER HUSBAND, JACK GEE.

Armstrong left the riverboat in 1921 and in 1922 was back playing in small clubs in New Orleans. Fletcher Henderson, then a small-time bandleader, went through New Orleans on one occasion on a tour that featured Ethel Waters, and when he heard Armstrong play, he invited him to join his band in New York.

Armstrong declined. Later in the summer, though, Joe Oliver invited him to come to Chicago. This time Louis was ready to leave home.

CHICAGO WAS NOTHING like New Orleans. The Big Easy was no match for Chicago's high energy and great expectations. Situated at the juncture of both railway lines and water routes, it considered itself the center of the country—"hog butcher for the world," as Carl Sandburg had said. Like many migrants before him, Louis boarded an Illinois Central railcar in New Orleans bound for Chicago. He sat next to a woman who had brought her own provisions: "She had a big basket of good old southern fried chicken which she had fixed for the trip. She had enough to last her and her kids not only to Chicago, but clear out to California if she wanted to go that far." It turned out that she knew Mayann, and so she shared her fried chicken with Louis. He recalled, "There was no place for colored people to eat on the trains in those days, especially down in Galilee [the South]. Colored persons going north crammed their baskets full of everything but the kitchen stove."

Joe Oliver had arranged to meet an earlier train, but because Louis played one more set in New Orleans, he had not made it. Arriving in Chicago for the first time in his life—dressed in long underwear because Mayann had heard about the severe northern winters—he had to rely on redcaps and bootblacks to direct him to the South Side, to the Lincoln Gardens where Oliver's band was playing. Preston Jackson, a member of the band, recalled with a mixture of awe and wonder Armstrong's country-boy appearance that first night. "He wore a brown box-back coat, straw hat, and tan shoes," he reported.

Lil Hardin, a pianist at the Dreamland then, would recall "hearing from all the musicians about him—Little Louis, they called him—and what a good player he was. So they brought him in and 'Li'l Louis' was all of 226 pounds!" When she asked why they called him that, they explained that he had been following them around since he was a little boy and the name had never left him. Lil was not impressed at first. "Everything he had on was too small for him. His atrocious tie was dangling down over his protruding stomach, and to top it off, he had a hairdo that called for bangs . . . that jutted over his forehead like a frayed canopy."

But their meeting was one of the more important events of Armstrong's life. Lil was a graduate of Fisk University, a classical pianist, and valedictorian of her class. She had moved to Chicago with her family in 1917, had secretly found work at the Dreamland—telling her parents she worked at a store—and had been introduced to jazz by Delta bandsmen.

LOUIS AND LIL, HOTEL SOMERVILLE, LOS ANGELES, CALIFORNIA, IN THE FALL OF 1930. THEIR PROFESSIONAL COLLABORATION PRODUCED SOME OF ARMSTRONG'S FINEST RECORDINGS.

Two or three months after their meeting, she joined the band at Lincoln Gardens. Louis and Lil were married in 1923. Louis wrote in his autobiography that Lil continued her studies even after they married. They practiced together, sometimes playing classical music. She helped him improve his ability to read music and even taught him to transpose.

Believing in his abilities, Lil pushed Louis forward and attempted to control so much of his life that the band members teased him and called him names. "The guys who called me Henpeck all the time were broke all the time," Louis would later write. "And I always had a pocketful of money. Lots of outside people tried to interfere with Lil and my marriage. . . . We were both young, and Lil with the better education and experience only did what any wife would do. Everything she bought for me were the best, clothes—the very best, and her suggestions were all perfect. I appreciate them all."

John Hammond, a rich jazz devotee who discovered Billie Holiday, said, "One of the most lovable people that ever existed in music, Lil was no match for the vultures who surrounded Louis in the most creative days of his career."

It was Hardin who pressed Armstrong to leave Lincoln Gardens, arguing that the band had room for just one lead horn. Armstrong approached the leading Chicago bandleader Sammy Stewart. Stewart, a light-skinned Negro, turned him down flat. "I wasn't up to his society, as a matter of fact I didn't play a note for him, he just passed me up and within a few years he could have kicked himself into oblivion, but at the time I could have kicked him," Armstrong recalled. According to Earl Hines, it was Louis's "blackness" that prevented him from getting a job with Stewart's "blue vein society." Shortly after that, Armstrong began playing first trumpet with Ollie Powers at the Dreamland, and his fame began to spread. Alberta Hunter was the singer with that band.

Fletcher Henderson, now riding high at New York's Roseland, issued his second invitation to Armstrong. Probably as a result of Lil's urging, Louis accepted. He arrived in New York looking much as he had in Chicago. Henderson's musical director remembered: "He was big and fat and wore high-top shoes with hooks in them and long underwear down to his socks."

Before his arrival, the Henderson band had been very conservative, following their orchestrations closely. Not being familiar with musical terms, Armstrong had problems at first. Henderson later recalled: "We were going through a number which had to be played softly and Louis was giving it full blast. We started all over again but Louis was still blowing high. 'Louis,' I said, 'I've already asked you to play it the way it says on the arrangement.' I then showed him that the score was marked 'pp.' *Pianissimo.* 'Well!' answered Louis, 'I thought it meant *pound plenty!*'"

Armstrong had a stunning effect on the normally staid New York jazz scene. Musicians white and black were said to come running to see who was playing that horn. Louis was also in great demand in the recording studios during his stay in New York, as accompanist to the great blues singers of the day. Recalling his sessions with Bessie Smith, he said, "I remember she just stayed in the studio and wrote the blues there. She finish one, she write another. . . . I'm telling you. She used to just thrill me. . . . Didn't

get to talking to her much, don't think we spoke the same language."

Armstrong's feelings toward New York were not as warm. He thought the Henderson band was too casual and lacked discipline. "When them cats commenced getting careless with their music, fooling around all night, I was dragged, man." He had been away from Chicago for a year and Lil had visited several times, but never for more than a few days, and a pretty young dancer had entered his life. Lil ordered him back to Chicago and Louis went.

Armstrong returned to Chicago in early November to join Lil's Dreamland Syncopators. A short time later he cut the first of the Hot Five sides of OKeh Records, with Johnny Dodds on clarinet, Kid Ory on trombone, Johnny St. Cyr on banjo and guitar, and Lil on piano. This group never played together outside of the recording studio, but their recordings are collector's items.

Life on the South Side of Chicago in 1925 was really jumping. Johnny Torrio ran the drug and alcohol traffic in the neighborhood, ably assisted by his second in command, Al Capone. The crime world in Chicago had been ethnically divided before Prohibition, but the government's restrictions on hooch caused a consolidation of ranks. First Dion O'Banion, boss of the Irish-Jewish North Side, was shot dead at his flower shop. Capone said of this death: "O'Banion's head got away from his hat." In retaliation, Johnny Torrio was shot and wounded near his house by Bugs Moran, an assistant to O'Banion's successor. Torrio fled to New York, leaving his operation to Capone, who slowly merged the rest.

Capone loved jazz. He often visited the clubs to hear the music, and he was known as a big tipper. "Al always showed up surrounded by a gang of triggermen—they sat in a corner, very gay and noisy but gunning the whole situation out of the corners of their eyes," the musician Mezz Mezzrow remembered. "Many stories have been told of gangsters coming into clubs they owned, locking the place and ordering the band to play a favorite number over and over all night long." Not all the musicians delighted in the attention of the bosses, though. Sets were often interrupted by mobsters breaking bottles over each other's heads, and police raids were so common that Earl Hines claimed he "would run to the wagon to get a seat when they came." Armstrong did not seem as upset by the violence as some of the others were. He knew that "danger was dancing all around you back then." But he also knew the rule: "Keep on playing."

Early in 1926 Louis left Lil's band to join Carroll Dickerson at the Sunset Café. Earl Hines was at the piano. Armstrong and the Dickerson band began a musical partnership that produced a number of wonderful recordings. Armstrong always remembered this time in Chicago as the finest of his life. "His salary of seventy-five dollars a week was a considerable amount for any musician at that time," James Collier explained. Hines recalled, "Louis was wild and I was wild, and we were inseparable. He was the most happy-go-lucky guy I ever met." In 1929 Tommy Rockwell of OKeh records suggested that Louis return to New York. Rockwell had meant only Louis, but Armstrong brought the whole band. They drove a number of dilapidated vehicles, made frequent stops during which they played to earn money, and arrived in New York penniless. Rockwell managed, though the Depression was hard upon them, to book the band into a four-month residency at Connie's Inn.

ARMSTRONG HAD A MAGICAL EFFECT on Harlem at this time. "Long before time of opening long lines were seen along Lenox Avenue, eager to get in, but thousands were turned away." His recording of "Ain't Misbehavin'" was placed on the machines of one jukebox company and was so successful that all his recordings were used. Armstrong had done the ultimate—made it in the white world and on his own terms.

Mezz Mezzrow claimed that "Louis's habit of holding a white handkerchief in his hand and clasping his hands in front of himself became a craze in Harlem." Buck Clayton recalled, "When I saw Pops for the first time he was going to a rehearsal at Frank Sebastian's Cotton Club . . . he looked pretty sharp. His hair looked nice and shiny and he had on a pretty gray suit. He wore a tie that looked like an ascot tie with an extra-big knot in it. Soon all the hip cats were wearing big knots in their ties. We called them Louis Armstrong knots."

It was also here that Armstrong met Alpha Smith, a girl of fifteen or sixteen who worked as a domestic, was an avid fan, and became his

ARMSTRONG WITH GIRLFRIEND ALPHA SMITH IN LONDON, 1933. WHEN THEY MET, ARMSTRONG SAID SHE WAS WORKING FOR A WEALTHY WHITE FAMILY IN CHICAGO. SHE BECAME HIS THIRD WIFE.

mistress. Though Louis and Lil had been having troubles, they continued to work together well into the thirties and did not divorce until 1938. Said Lil of Alpha: "Don't know when or how long Louis had an affair with Alpha. I can assure you she was not the only one, so I didn't worry too much about it." Alpha also continued to be a part of Louis's life, although when they finally married in 1938 it was for only a short time. Louis said that as a wife Alpha was not the same as she had been as a mistress. In 1942, having divorced Alpha, Louis married Lucile, his fourth wife, a chorus dancer he had met at the Cotton Club in 1939. This marriage lasted for the rest of his life.

Like others in this collection, Louis had a public and a private side. His quick smile and easygoing manner onstage suggested a man with many friends. But Lucile noted that in private life Louis had few close associates and was often a loner. He developed a habit, as he became fa-

mous, of handing out money to those who were less fortunate. "It reached the point where people would line up outside his dressing room every night—old musicians, casual acquaintances, people looking for a quick fix." It was said that he would set aside several hundred dollars each night just for this purpose. His managers tried to restrain his generous impulses, but Armstrong often prevailed. Over time, he got the reputation among some musicians of being an easy mark. But Armstrong's motives were more complex. "Them characters think I don't know," he once remarked, "but I just give them poor so and so's a few dollars." This shy man believed it was the least he could do. "There is a debt," the *Inter-State Tattler* once observed, "genius inevitably owes humanity." Perhaps Louis Armstrong understood that. He died a wealthy man and one of the best-known musicians in the world. "Way back, I set myself to be a happy man, and made it," Armstrong said.

LOUIS ARMSTRONG'S FUNERAL, NEW ORLEANS, JULY 11, 1971. THEODORE RILEY OF THE ONWARD BLUES BAND PLAYED TAPS ON THE FIRST HORN THAT ARMSTRONG OWNED. OPPOSITE: LOUIS ARMSTRONG'S FUNERAL, NEW YORK, JULY 8, 1971.

8
BESSIE SMITH AND ALBERTA HUNTER

AMERICA'S LOVE AFFAIR with the automobile began just after the First World War. In 1919 there were fewer than seven million passenger cars on the road. By 1929 the number had soared to over twenty-three million. In 1919 most of the cars were high, open, and started with a crank. By 1929 the closed sedan was in vogue. It had a self-starter and was available in a variety of colors. Henry Ford, who had already revolutionized the industry by making vehicles affordable to the average citizen, further transformed the workplace by introducing the five-dollar workday in his plants. In River Rouge, he also revolutionized hiring policies by employing a large number of black workers, migrants from the South. In 1910 fewer than 600 of the more than 100,000 automotive workers in America were black. By 1929 there were more than 25,000 black auto workers, and Ford employed approximately half of them. The African-American community was taken with the automobile and with Mr. Ford's offer of opportunity, however self-serving. Everyone who could, owned a car. Friends teased Alberta Hunter because, though she was well paid, she refused to buy one. "I knew I would either injure or kill somebody," she said.

IN FEBRUARY 1923 BESSIE SMITH ENTERED INTO A RECORDING CONTRACT WITH COLUMBIA RECORDS THAT LASTED NINE YEARS. BY 1925 SHE WAS THE HIGHEST PAID STAR OF "RACE RECORDS." IN 1931 COLUMBIA, NOW THE TOP RECORD COMPANY, DROPPED THEIR STAR BECAUSE OF HARD TIMES.

BESSIE SMITH HAD A "GRAVE voice of overpowering weight, and a superb grasp of the blue notes," music critic James Collier claimed. Langston Hughes said her blues were the essence of "sadness . . . not softened with tears but hardened with laughter; the absurd, incongruous laughter of a sadness without even a god to appeal to." Alberta Hunter said simply, "Bessie Smith was the greatest of them all."

Bessie Smith's blues were cultivated and nurtured in her southern roots. Although she went north and settled in Philadelphia, she never lost her attachment to down home. She performed mostly before black audiences, though she was occasionally booked into all-white southern theaters. Those audiences too knew the misery of which she sang. Indeed, a southern white music dealer told the *Pittsburgh Courier,* "that Bessie Smith's records actually outsell everything else in the catalog."

Alberta Hunter, on the other hand, sang the blues with a bold, sophisticated style. Her southern roots were a springboard to another life. She clearly preferred the North. "If I'm lucky enough to leave here," she wrote, "I sho ain't coming back no mo'." Alberta Hunter wrote and sang the blues for over forty years, stopped for twenty years, and then, at the age of eighty-one, sang the blues again. Bessie Smith always sang the blues.

Blues singers were the poets laureate of the Renaissance era. Poor, black, and illiterate, they grew up in the South at a time when blacks were more of an untouchable caste than a lower class and opportunities were few. Singers became successful by ignoring the conventions that defined and constrained most people's lives. As Alan Lomax explains, they were an atypical group: "With few exceptions, only women of questionable reputation, women who flaunted their loose living, publicly performed the blues." On the stage they were sometimes bawdy, sometimes rough, often outrageous, but by exploding old taboos and stereotypes they became powerful. Their lyrics struck a nerve. Women, in particular, even women from vastly different circumstances, identified with their tales of love and betrayal. "You can send me up the river or send me to that mean ole jail,/I killed my man and I don't need no bail," sang Bessie Smith in the popular "Sing Sing Prison Blues."

Women blues singers explored all the parts of their lives—poverty, exploitation, loneliness, and abuse—and found solace in the exercise. They did it mostly for themselves ("When we sing the blues, we are singing our hearts out," Alberta Hunter explained), but they were also offering advice and support to other women. "Bessie sang of mean mistreaters and two-timing husbands with tragicomic optimism, offered advice to the dejected, and made it quite clear that she herself was not immune to such problems," wrote Chris Albertson, her biographer. Langston Hughes recalled one party given by Carl Van Vechten where Nora Holt, whose beauty and notorious lifestyle were legendary in Harlem, sang a ribald song called "My Daddy Rocks Me with One Steady Roll." When she finished, a "well-known New York matron cried ecstatically, with tears in her eyes: 'My dear! Oh, my dear! How beautifully you sing Negro spirituals!'"

The blues became so popular in the early twenties that pamphlets were published by the record industry to explain the genre. Bob Ricketts and Bessie's good friend Porter Grainer wrote in one: "To render a 'Blues Song' effectively, it is necessary to possess a fair knowledge of the spirit and circumstances under which this publication was created. If one can temporarily play the role of the oppressed or the depressed, injecting into his or her rendition a spirit of hopeful prayer, the effect will be more natural and respectful." Enthusiasts needed no such instruction.

Bessie Smith and Alberta Hunter are among the best-known blues singers. Both were born in the South, came north at the time of the great migration, and were able to capitalize on the recording industry's discovery of the profits offered by what were called race records. The two women never met. "I don't think she disliked me," Alberta said. "She didn't have a chance to like or dislike me. She was a woman that just didn't bother." Each had a distinctive style, and each made a singular contribution— different approaches, different goals, different accomplishments—and yet somehow they arrived on the same train.

BESSIE SMITH WAS BORN in Chattanooga, Tennessee, on April 4, 1894, one of seven children. Her father, a part-time Baptist preacher, died soon after her birth. Her mother died when she was eight or nine. Cared for by members of her extended family, Bessie earned money by singing for nickels on a street corner. It is often claimed that "the Empress of the Blues" was discovered at the age of thirteen by Ma Rainey. The story is told that Rainey and her husband kidnapped young Bessie, forced her to tour with their show, and along the way, taught her to sing. Smith's biographer thinks it is just a story, pointing out that "the Raineys didn't have their own show until

ALTHOUGH FAMOUS FOR HER FOUL MOUTH AND DRINKING BINGES, SMITH WAS A WARM AND GENEROUS PROTECTOR OF HER FRIENDS.

1916, by which time Bessie had been on her own for several years."

Film actor Leigh Whipper remembers Smith performing in Atlanta in 1913, at the "81" theater. He said of that night: "She was just a teenager, and she obviously didn't know she was the artist she was. She didn't know how to dress—she just sang in her street clothes—but she was such a natural that she could wreck anybody's show." As she grew older, she began touring the South in local road shows. She was kicked out of one because she was too dark. Bessie married a man named Earl Love during those years. Little is known of him other than that he was from a "prominent" Mississippi family and died young.

Singer May Wright remembered Bessie performing in Atlanta in 1921. Bessie had her own show then and was the smallest woman in it. As the curtain went up on the opening number "there was the chorus dressed in close-fitting bloomers, bent over with their backs to the audience. The orchestra struck up 'Liberty Bell,' and there was that whole chorus shakin' every muscle in their bodies." May thought it was the funniest thing she had ever seen.

By 1922, after Smith had established a reputation in the South and along the Mid-Atlantic coast, she moved to Philadelphia and was featured in several clubs in Atlantic City. In February 1923, surprisingly long after the 1920 success of the first race record, she cut her first disc in New York City for Columbia Records. Bessie was an instant success. "Downhearted Blues," her first hit, sold two million copies in six months, establishing her as a star in the field. The song was written by Lovie Austin and Alberta Hunter. "Got the world in a jug; got the stopper in my hand,/ And if you want me, you must come under my command."

Also in 1923, Bessie met and fell in love with John Gee, a handsome, illiterate night watchman. Jack, as he was called, has often been portrayed as an opportunist who lived off Bessie's money, but her view of him was more charitable. Jack once pawned his uniform to buy her a dress for her first audition, and she never forgot it. He also figured out that she was being cheated in her first record contract by pianist Clarence Williams, who had arranged the session. Jack went with her to Williams's office and stood by her as Bessie—the "two-hundred-pound foul mouth presence"—jumped on the pianist and pounded his head on the floor, thus persuading him to honor his contractual obligations. "Nobody messed with Bessie."

Bessie recorded for Columbia Records from 1923 to 1931, accompanied by Fletcher Henderson. Their relationship was a smooth one—perhaps because the "prissy Henderson," as Ethel Waters called him, was willing to let Bessie, a woman of "enormous and barely controlled passions," call the shots. It was during this time that the "Saint Louis Blues" session with Louis Armstrong was done.

NEWLY MARRIED BESSIE SMITH AND HER HUSBAND, JACK GEE, JUNE 1923.

Shortly after her session with Armstrong, Bessie began a southern tour that netted more and more cash and acclaim as her records were simultaneously released. Her fee for a personal appearance started at $350 a week and was soon raised to $1,500. Bessie and Jack had more money than they had ever had in their lives.

Like Louis Armstrong, Smith gave away much of her newfound wealth, paying the hospital bills of friends, bailing them out of jail, buying expensive presents for members of her family and luxury items for herself. After her death, the *Amsterdam News* reported: "Bessie Smith, blues singer, who died last week at the peak of her career, was paid $2,500 weekly and once had $75,000 . . . [but she] spent it all in a few weeks." As Chris Albertson wrote, "The more she made, the more she doled out."

Smith was also a binge drinker, and her drinking was beginning to affect her work. She developed a reputation for walking out on engagements. This meant less money for Frank Walker, her manager, who handled much of her money, and for Jack, who spent large amounts of it. Because they wanted Smith to earn as much as possible, they kept her on an exhausting schedule.

The success of Smith's southern tour earned her invitations to Detroit and Chicago. Moving into center stage increased her earnings, her fame, and her drinking. When Jack was not around, Smith liked to party and to keep company with other men and with women. When

Jack *was* around, he beat her up, forced her to stop drinking, and saw to it that she kept her engagements. Clarinetist Sidney Bechet described Jack as a "mean man, a really mean man who she had a hard time with." The marriage was not a happy one. "Oh the blues had got me on the go," Smith sang. "They runs around the house, in and out my front door." Still, in 1924, Bessie Smith was the highest-paid black performer in the country.

Carl Van Vechten attended one of Smith's performances in 1925 recalling "a voice full of shouting and moaning and praying and suffering." He also described an almost all black audience that hung on every note, an experience for him nearly as novel as the concert itself. "Yo' brag to women. I was yo' fool. So den I got dose sobbin' h'ahted blues," Smith sang. The audience burst into "hysterical shrieks of sorrow and lament and amens rent the air," Van Vechten reported. "Dat's right, a girl cried out from under our box." Bessie and Carl became friends.

Langston Hughes recalled a Van Vechten party at which Margarita D'Alvarez of the Metropolitan Opera Company sang an aria. Bessie "did not know D'Alvarez," Hughes said, but, liking her voice, went up to her when she finished and cried, "Don't let nobody tell you you can't sing." Nobody messed with Bessie.

By 1926, however, Smith's popularity was beginning to wane, and though she still commanded high salaries because of her records, she now faced competition from Ethel Waters, Alberta Hunter, and Josephine Baker. In an attempt to bring order to her life, and perhaps save her marriage, Smith adopted Snooks, the six-year-old son of a friend, whom she and Jack renamed Jack junior. Bessie curtailed her performances during mid-1926 to take care of the child, who became an important and tragic part of her life.

"THERE AIN'T NOTHIN I CAN DO OR NOTHIN I CAN SAY THAT FOLKS DON'T CRITICIZE ME, BUT I'M GOING TO DO JUST AS I WANT TO ANYWAY, AIN'T NOBODY'S BUSINESS IF I DO."

Smith also began an affair with Lillian, a chorus girl—the first of many liaisons with other women. She and her close associates went to great lengths to keep these affairs a secret from Jack. But in 1927 he caught Bessie with another woman and claimed to have a nervous breakdown as a result. According to Bessie's family, Jack had numerous breakdowns, all calculated to elicit Bessie's sympathy and open her purse strings. The technique had always worked before and did in this case as well. "Bessie would do anything for him, so she'd give him all the money he wanted, and tell him to go and take a rest." There was no hint that Jack threatened to expose Bessie's affairs. To do so would probably have ended his main source of income. Bessie probably paid him off because of her love for him and because, a deeply religious woman, she felt some shame for her actions. Chris Albertson said that friends thought she was a candidate for turning from "debauchery to divinity," like Ma

Rainey and Ethel Waters. "I truly believe Bessie was getting ready to turn," said companion Maud Smith. "In every town we would get in, if we got in on a Sunday morning early enough, we'd all go to church." But Smith did not "turn."

Smith continued to perform: "Please listen to my pleading 'cause I can't stand these hard times long. They'll make an honest man do things you know is wrong." Smith's own hard times began in 1929. First, "talking features" signaled the demise of vaudeville, a major source of her revenue. Second, her own Broadway debut in *Pansy* received disastrous reviews from the New York press. Brooks Atkinson of the *Times* called it, "The worst show of all time." It closed after three performances. Third, Jack—using funds provided by Bessie—put money into a show starring Gertrude Saunders, Florence Mills's friend from *Shuffle Along*, and the show did well. Saunders and Jack were rumored to be involved, a claim that Saunders denied. Gertrude was light-skinned with long hair, traits Jack was said to admire. For her part, Gertrude insisted that "the ignorant darky" was only her manager. Smith was devastated by Jack's betrayal in using her money to advance the career of another woman. They fought publicly for months and it is not clear that Smith ever forgave him. The October stock market crash was a mere footnote by comparison. Smith continued to find work, recording songs and performing in southern

BESSIE SMITH PHOTOGRAPHED BY CARL VAN VECHTEN, FEBRUARY 3, 1936. SHE WAS "VERY AMICABLE AND COOPERATIVE," VAN VECHTEN SAID.

theaters in late 1929 and early 1930, but nothing like what Alberta Hunter, Paul Robeson, and Ethel Waters were experiencing. Appropriately, her best recording that year was "Nobody Knows You When You're Down and Out."

Jack responded to Bessie's public assaults by getting the authorities to take Jack junior away from her, suggesting she was an unfit mother. Bessie was devastated but did not fight back. Instead she threw herself into her work, trying to make a living in the heart of the Depression. Now she could command only $500 to $750 a week, out of which all of her expenses had to be paid. Worst of all, Columbia Records, facing bankruptcy, dropped her in late 1931.

What saved Bessie Smith during these years was her relationship with Richard Morgan, a bootlegger from Alabama who had known her before she was famous. They renewed their friendship when Bessie played in Chicago and became involved after Jack's treachery. Said Chris Albertson: "Bessie had a new lover." He suggests that Richard was amazingly faithful to Bessie during those last years and helped her to stage a comeback of sorts. Richard's nephew, Lionel Hampton, confirmed the attachment. Bessie appeared at the Apollo in New York in 1935 for a brief engagement and at Connie's Inn in 1936, as a last-minute replacement for an ailing Billie Holiday, the new kid on the block and the talk of the town, whom Duke Ellington called "the essence of cool."

Smith's career had always contained a lot of travel from city to city. Her comeback was the same, continuing with an engagement in Memphis in 1937. Wanting to get there ahead of the other performers, she prevailed upon Richard to take her. As they were driving along a dark Mississippi road, their car hit a truck, and her right arm was nearly severed. Stories of her death vary. Jack junior was told that even though she was bleeding profusely, she was refused admittance to three hospitals because she was black. Finally she was taken to a black hospital in Clarksdale, Mississippi, where she died. Reports from bystanders, recorded years later, suggest that she died because of the indifference that would have been shown to any black woman unknown to locals lying injured on a Mississippi road. Police and ambulance came but they took their time. As Sidney Bechet explained, "She was *too* far in the South. I was told the doctors, they hadn't too much concern for getting to her quick . . . she was just another that could wait. That's all, I guess; that was the end of it."

Her funeral in Philadelphia was not a high-profile affair. Celebrities like Ethel Waters, Duke Ellington, and Bill Robinson sent telegrams, but none attended. Professional pallbearers rather than friends carried the casket into the church. Ten thousand mourning fans did observe Jack Gee basking in the publicity while Richard Morgan stood silently by. The *Philadelphia Tribune* reported that Jack threw himself on the casket and wept. Smith's sister-in-law told Albertson: "Jack didn't throw himself over no casket but he was good for putting up a cry, he'd cry in two minutes, and I'd have to say 'Stop those crocodile tears, Jack,' because he was just putting on a show." The *Chicago Defender* reported that "Bessie scaled the heights and overcame almost insurmountable odds, and all of it can be traced to the ingenious management of her husband." While Jack and other members of her family fought over her estate, none purchased a headstone for her. For thirty-three years, her grave remained unmarked. "There ain't no place for a poor old girl to go," Smith moaned in her hit song "Back Water Blues." In 1970 a headstone was at last purchased by singer Janis Joplin and the wife of the head of the local NAACP chapter as the result of a story by a reporter for the *Philadelphia Inquirer.*

CARICATURE BY MIGUEL COVARRUBIAS, 1935.

ALBERTA HUNTER WAS BORN IN Memphis, Tennessee, in 1897. Her father, Charles Hunter, was a sleeping car porter, the most prestigious nonprofessional job available to black men. Alberta had a sister who was two years older. Laura, her mother, maintained their home until Charles abandoned them when Alberta was two or three. Thereafter her mother worked as a maid in a bordello. A very prudish woman, Laura shielded her daughters from the activities of her place of employment and passed her Victorian sensibilities on to her younger daughter. Laura was a strong woman, whom Alberta admired. "She wasn't a crybaby type. I guess that's the reason I'm so strong," Alberta recalled. "She'd say if something's gotta be done, let's get it done. Don't feel sorry for yourself or anybody else." In 1906 or 1907 her mother married a man whom Alberta hated. Leaving home became her fondest dream.

Like many of those who got the migration fever, Hunter traveled to Chicago in the teens with little more than the clothes on her back. At the train station, she asked a black porter to direct her to the black community. Her first job was as a cook in a South Side restaurant. From there she moved on to running errands and singing in "sporting houses." As her career advanced she proceeded from Dago Frank's club in Chicago to the Dreamland, "singing earthy, funny, sophisticated blues." One of her most famous songs

ALBERTA HUNTER AS A CHILD WITH SISTERS LA TOSCA, LEFT, AND JOSEPHINE, CENTER, CIRCA 1911.

was "A Good Man Is Hard to Find," which she introduced. Mezz Mezzrow, the musician, recalls seeing her at the De Luxe Cafe at Thirty-fifth and State in Chicago. "When Alberta Hunter hit the floor singing 'He may be your man but he comes to see me sometime,' the house came down. Alberta kept working her way around the floor, stopping to sing a chorus at each table, so that by the time she was through she'd gone over the one song ten or fifteen times, giving it a new twist every time."

Lil Hardin Armstrong claimed that Blossom Seeley, a local gangster, once tipped Alberta three hundred dollars to sing the blues. Hunter, a lesbian, was philosophical about her relations with men. "Bessie had trouble with her men. Not me. 'Cause I was evil. If I thought someone was trying to put something over on me, I'd laugh them off and go on about my business. Bessie would suffer."

Arriving in New York in the early twenties, she, like Josephine Baker, was considered too dark for *Shuffle Along*. Noble Sissle, she claimed, had a "color complex." But Hunter was ambitious and not one to accept rejection. She tried out for a number of other shows and performed both in Broadway revues and at A'Lelia Walker's famous Renaissance salons. What Hunter liked best about A'Lelia Walker, who was shunned by Harlem's mulatto elite, was that A'Lelia snubbed them right back. Hunter would sometimes take A'Lelia's

Alberta Hunter, London, 1934.

wealthy white guests for tours of Harlem nightspots, negotiating with doormen in her most cosmopolitan manner, for the privilege of bringing a mixed group into the all-white clubs. Alberta, thought of by some as the "most sophisticated woman in New York," was never refused.

While she was living in Harlem, Hunter began a relationship with Lottie Tyler, niece of Mrs. Bert Williams. While they lived together for quite some months, Hunter kept the affair private. Harry Watkins, one of the few associates to visit their home, said, "They were like two friends ordinarily would be in public. Lottie was very sedate. She was brought up that way." Hunter was disgusted by women performers who fought with their girlfriends in public. "What will people say?" she asked. Hunter decided to bring her mother, now ailing, to live with them in New York. She stayed only one day, shocked by her daughter's living arrangement. Hunter, now more than ever, kept her sexual preference a secret. Though she was very friendly with both Adelaide Hall and Marian Anderson, neither knew she was gay, and both expressed surprise upon learning it many years later. Friends of Anderson reported that the knowledge was repugnant to her, and she refused to talk about Alberta. Hall, on the other hand, recalling many fond memories, simply claimed she never knew Alberta was gay.

Like Ethel Waters, Hunter owed her suc-

ALBERTA HUNTER WITH MILDRED HUDGINS, WIFE OF JOHNNY HUDGINS, IN PARIS, 1920S.

cess to the recording industry, becoming a best-seller on the Gennett label. She also recorded on the Black Swan, Paramount, OKeh, and Bluebird labels. Because she was under contract to Gennett, she recorded for the others using the names Josephine Beaty and May Alix. With a group called the Red Onion Jazz Babies, featuring Louis Armstrong, Lil Hardin, and Sidney Bechet, she cut several records. Alberta had a distinctive style. Eubie Blake said of her, "You felt so sorry for her you wanted to kill the guy she was singing about."

She had little formal education, claiming simply to have picked up what she knew. However Alberta was constantly studying. When in New York, she never missed a poetry reading by her good friend Langston Hughes. Travel for Alberta was also an important substitute for a conventional education. In August 1927 she left for France with Lottie. Though she was actually looking for employment, she told friends she was on vacation, in case her job prospects fell through. She took notes on what she learned on her travels and wrote letters home, which were published in the *Amsterdam News*. In her October 23 letter from Paris, she wrote, "The shows here are most spectacular but lack the real punch and talent we have in America. They depend solely upon nudity, which has a tendency to get on one's nerves." But like many of the performers, Alberta fell in love with Paris. "I do not know

AT BRICKTOP'S IN PARIS IN THE 1920S, THREE AFRICAN-AMERICAN WOMEN STARS OF THE NIGHTCLUB SCENE: BRICKTOP, STANDING, MABEL MERCER AND ALBERTA HUNTER SEATED ON THE PIANO.

when I will be home. I am mad about the freedom of Paris. Color means nothing over here. If anything they treat the colored people better," she wrote.

Lottie did not share Hunter's attachment to Paris. She had fallen in love with the wife of her attorney and sailed to New York to be with her. "Alberta resented being rejected by Lottie and carried a chip on her shoulder toward women for the rest of her life," reported her biographer Frank Taylor. But she and Lottie remained close friends until Lottie's death.

Hunter quickly learned independence and, in her own words, "when to hang in there and not be pushed around and when to pack up and move on." She honed a persona of a tough woman who could take care of herself. She was a seasoned performer who could belt out the blues with the best of the blues singers and sing a ballad that pleased the nightclub and theater crowd. Though her most famous composition, "Down-hearted Blues," is associated with Bessie Smith, it is Hunter who we can hear sing "I ain't never loved but three men in my life/'Twas my father, my brother, and the man who wretched my life."

Hunter understood what showmanship was and put her utmost into every performance. When a show did not meet her standards, she left it. When she was not working, she attended concerts, went sight-seeing, and studied languages. When Paul Robeson opened in *Show Boat* in London in 1928, Hunter got a supporting role. "To think," she wrote, "that I—me—poor, little, humble me was walking out onto the stage at the Drury Lane Theater in London, the theater of the world." Hunter was fond of Paul Robeson, suggesting that he was "unassuming like people used to be to each other in the South." Many years later she told an interviewer: "When [Paul] sang 'Ol' Man River,' his voice was like a bell in the distance, and people would scream. The night King George and Queen Mary came to see us, Paul got off pitch, and he never got himself back on, and afterward he cried like a child."

It was not all work for Hunter. In December 1928, Paul Robeson gave a party for his dear friends Carl Van Vechten and Fania Marinoff. It was a very exclusive affair. The guests included Fred and Adele Astaire, Alfred

Knopf, writer Hugh Walpole, Lord Beaverbrook and Mrs. Patrick Campbell, and his costar Alberta Hunter.

But her job security did not last long. She received a note from Sir Alfred Butt, the show's producer: "I want to say to you I have no criticism whatsoever to make in regard to your performance in our show. I think it is an admirable one in every way, and the only reason that we are, with reluctance, dispensing with your services is that our expenses are so extremely heavy that we are obligated to keep them as low as possible."

Wealthy friends intervened, and Hunter was able to stay, but she realized that her time in London would be of short duration. Preparing herself for another move, she studied French at the Berlitz School.

From London, Hunter went to Paris, where she replaced Josephine Baker at the Folies-Bergère. She was well received in Paris, though no match for

HUNTER, 1938. IN 1937 SHE HAD BEGUN BROADCASTING HER OWN NBC RADIO SHOW.

Josephine. Arthur Briggs, a trumpet player from the Caribbean, commented on her lack of flamboyance: "Alberta? She never spent anything but an evening." Noël Coward seemed to capture an important part of Alberta's reserve when he wrote a song for her: "When the dream has ended and passion has flown, I travel alone."

Because of the uncertain political situation in Europe, she returned to the United States in the late twenties—with a slight British accent,

it was said—and was able to support herself with radio broadcasts and occasional recording sessions. "When I came home I was on WEAF and WJZ and on the 'Lower Basin Street' show, before Dinah Shore took over," she recalled. In 1939 she took a part in Ethel Waters's show, *Mamba's Daughters*, at the Empire. "She sure gave me a hard time," she later said. "I guess I outsang her, because she put everything but the kitchen stove on me." Alberta joined the USO in 1944. "I got a mind to ramble but I don't know where to go," she often sang.

Alberta Hunter, after tasting fame, had the courage to choose an ordinary life. After withdrawing from the spotlight to care for her ailing mother, she later, at age fifty-nine, enrolled in a practical nursing course, earned a certificate, and worked for the next twenty years in a New York City hospital. Though friends encouraged her to return to the stage, she demurred, saying she wanted to help people. It was not until she retired from nursing at age eighty-one that she resumed her career as a blues singer.

Her return to singing mirrored the other stages of her life. Alberta told Whitney Balliet in an interview in the *New Yorker* that at a party given by Bobby Short for Mabel Mercer she ran into Charles Bourgeois of the Newport Jazz Festival. According to Short, "Alberta came in one of her outfits. She didn't like to dress up," he said. (Hunter told the *New Yorker*:

"When I was entertaining, I spent a lot of money on clothes, but after my mother passed I gave them away.") Bourgeois, struck by her presence, asked her to sing. She said, "I did, real soft. He told me, 'You should be out working again, with that voice and all your experience,' and right away the next morning Mr. Barney Josephson [of the Cookery, a bistro in Greenwich Village] called and asked was I interested in singing for him, and I was so nervous I dropped the phone."

Alberta began working at the Cookery in 1977 and was an instant success. Frank Taylor, her biographer, remembered hearing her by chance in 1978. "Every part of her was in motion," he wrote, "from her eyebrows, which punctuated risqué lyrics, to her gold earrings, the size and shape of doughnuts, which dangled and swayed with her sassy beat." From then until her death in 1984, she enjoyed the acclaim that had before eluded her, singing at the Cookery, at engagements throughout the world, and at the White House, for "her" president, Jimmy Carter.

ALBERTA PERFORMING AT THE COOKERY, NEW YORK, 1979. PHOTOGRAPH BY DAVID REDFERN.

THOUGH BESSIE SMITH AND ALBERTA HUNTER were mirror opposites in style, with Bessie remembered for her art but not her life and Alberta for her life but not her art, their contributions were strikingly similar. In hearing their music, we sense the liberation they both experienced when they performed onstage. "If I should get the feelin', To dance upon the ceiling,/'Taint Nobody's Business If I Do," Bessie challenged. The blues, for them, were more than a vehicle for creative self-expression; they were a mechanism of defiance. Alberta Hunter always draped herself in stylish clothes, refusing to accept the idea that attractive black women had to appear tasteless. "They wouldn't accept us Negro girls in smart clothes," she once recalled. Alberta paid no attention. Bessie, however, "stormed stages, circling and courting her audience, dressed in outrageous getups: short horsehair wigs, sequined gowns, ostrich plumes, furs and jewels, and outlandish hats." Onstage, Bessie did as she pleased. And nobody messed with Bessie.

Their enormous capacity to reinvent themselves was also evident. When the blues faded, Bessie changed. Her stint on the stage as a replacement for the silver-tongued Billie Holiday did not send the audience howling for refunds but was instead a huge success. When Alberta Hunter did not find things to her liking, she made something better for herself. Against tremendous odds, these singers of the blues never gave in or gave up. Bessie sang their theme: "When I get home I'm gonna change my lock and key,/When you get home you'll find an awful change in me."

9

JESSIE FAUSET AND NELLA LARSEN

$\mathcal{I}$ N THE EARLY SPRING OF 1924, Richard Simon, who had just started a publishing house with his friend Lincoln Schuster, came up with the idea of putting out a crossword puzzle book, complete with pencil. Although the crossword puzzle had been invented in 1913 and published in newspapers ever since, this was the first time anyone had put it in book form. Booksellers were cool to the idea, suggesting that the public would not be interested. They were wrong. Within a month of its publication, one hundred thousand copies of the crossword puzzle book had been sold. The Baltimore and Ohio Railroad placed dictionaries in all the trains of its main line. By 1930, it was estimated, sales had reached over two million.

Howard University in Washington, D.C., was founded by General Oliver O. Howard of the Freedmen's Bureau in 1867 to educate newly emancipated slaves. It was one of the first historically black institutions of higher education in the United States. Departments of law, pharmacy, and medicine were opened in 1869. Others followed. Mordecai Johnson, one of the "bright skins of the race," was born in Columbus, Tennessee, in 1890, and went to Morehouse College in Atlanta, where he prepared for a career in the ministry. Possessing unusual oratorical skill, he gave a commencement address at Harvard University in 1923, upon

A PORTRAIT OF JESSIE FAUSET FROM 1939.

receiving a master's degree in theology. His address, "The Faith of the American Negro," attracted national attention. It took fifty-nine years, but in August 1926 the white board of trustees of Howard University appointed Mordecai Johnson its first black president.

JESSIE FAUSET WAS BORN INTO a black middle class that did not permit its women to breathe in public. As historian Stephanie Shaw explains, "Parents hoped that extremely upright behavior would ward off dangerous attention and counteract the negative stereotypes of African Americans that were common throughout White America." Believing them to be most vulnerable to unwanted sexual attentions, parents went to great lengths to guard their daughters. Strict rules regarding dress and makeup were common, as was the selection of companions. "Booker T. Washington went so far as to dispatch his daughter's escorts from Tuskegee whenever she had to attend a school event in Massachusetts that required one," Shaw wrote. While Jessie Fauset's father and stepmother were not as well off as the Washingtons, she was brought up in a similarly "choking" atmosphere. Fauset, who never quite shed the starch of her Victorian upbringing, remained overconcerned with respectability (declining to translate Haitian author René Maran's novel *Batouala* because she feared she would never be thought respectable again) and highly offended by bad language. Over the years her name became synonymous with conventionality. James Weldon Johnson suspected that the character Hester Albright in Van Vechten's novel *Nigger Heaven* was a somewhat cruel portrait of Jessie. Hester, a spinster of thirty-eight, was a thorough prig who was easily shocked. She "lived with her mother, a deaf, querulous, garrulous tiresome old lady." Yet Fauset's considerable contribution rests in large part in her ability to

rise, at times rather dramatically, above her Victorian roots that normally prevented freedom of expression. For this she was never properly recognized.

Nella Larsen, like her heroine Helga Crane of *Quicksand*, drifted onto the surface of the Harlem Renaissance and was slowly and painfully sucked under the surface of the quagmire by jealousy, hubris, and conceit. Called the "mystery woman of the Harlem Renaissance," at the height of the movement she published two critically acclaimed novels in less than two years. She was heralded as a rising star in ways that Jessie Fauset was not. In 1930 Larsen received additional acclaim as the first African-American woman to be awarded a Guggenheim Fellowship. But at precisely the moment of her greatest triumphs, her public life was rocked by a charge of plagiarism and her private life was shattered by marital infidelity. A lover of word games and puzzles, Larsen created so many artificial layers of self that even her closest friends thought her aloof and retiring. Her fall was swift, her infamy enduring. Like Helga Crane, Nella Larsen "had ruined her life." Two different women, two different stories, yet the fates of Fauset and Larsen were all too similar.

JESSIE FAUSET, BORN outside Camden, New Jersey, in 1882, was educated at Cornell University and received a master's degree in French literature from the University of Pennsylvania. In 1914 she studied at the Sorbonne for six

LEFT TO RIGHT: REGINA ANDREWS, ESTHER POPEL, HELEN LANNING, LOUELLA TUCKER, JESSIE FAUSET, MARIE JOHNSON, ETHEL RAY (CHARLES S. JOHNSON'S ASSISTANT AT THE JOURNAL *OPPORTUNITY*), CLARISSA SCOTT, AND PEARL FISHER AT A PARTY FOR LANGSTON HUGHES ON THE ROOF OF 580 ST. NICHOLAS AVENUE, HARLEM, IN 1924.

months and was there at the outbreak of World War I. "Picture to yourself some such concentration of misery and pain and suffering of *all* the people in France and you know something of the pall which hung over the nation last summer," she reported. "It was a veritable twilight of the gods." Like Zora Neale Hurston, she pretended to be younger than she was, variously claiming to have been born in 1886 and 1891. Poet Claude McKay wrote that she "belonged to that closed decorous circle of Negro society, which consists of persons who live proudly like the better class of conventional whites, except they do so on much less money."

Upon graduation from Cornell, she assumed the expected role of one of her class and gender: schoolteacher. She dutifully taught French at Washington's Dunbar High School for fourteen years. While not experiencing many overt acts of discrimination, she fought daily against what she called the "inhibition" of natural liberties. Was the waiter who was taking so long to serve her really so busy? Did that salesperson not realize she wished to make a purchase? She decided in 1919 to throw caution to the wind and move to New York City to become the assistant to W. E. B. Du Bois at the NAACP. Fauset was at that time single, thirty-seven, and among other things, a superb dancer. Du Bois was the director of publicity and research and editor of the association's journal, *The Crisis: A Record of the Darker Races.* For seven years their personal friendship, professional collaboration, and mutual respect combined to produce one of the finest literary journals published.

Jessie lived in New York with her older sister, Helen (perhaps Van Vechten's querulous, garrulous, tiresome old lady), in an apartment on Seventh Avenue. She was an active participant in Harlem social life. In 1921 she gave a surprise silver wedding anniversary party for

Du Bois and his wife for about one hundred guests. She was at Claude McKay's farewell party in 1922, held at the James Weldon Johnsons'. Langston Hughes explained, "At the Seventh Avenue apartment of Jessie Fauset, literary soirees with much poetry but little to drink were the order of the day. A good time was shared by talking literature and reading poetry aloud and perhaps enjoying conversations in French." (Guests at Hester Albright's parties, in Van Vechten's novel, also spoke French, using phrases like "J'aime l'arte beaucoup."). "White people were seldom present," Hughes continued, "unless they were very distinguished white people, because Jessie Fauset did not feel like opening her home to mere sightseers, or faddists momentarily in love with Negro life." Jessie Fauset was never fond of Carl Van Vechten.

In editing the *Crisis*, Du Bois had a dream of creating "a high class journal circulating among the intelligent Negroes and binding them together in pursuit of definite ideals." He at first wanted to place talented African-Americans at the center of American culture, creating what George Hutchinson called a "darkening of American culture." Jessie shared this vision. In the years that she worked for the journal, it achieved a level of cross-fertilization with the literati of the dominant society that had not been seen before or since. Everybody published in the *Crisis*: Sinclair Lewis, Carl Van Vechten, Sherwood Anderson, Langston Hughes, James Weldon Johnson. They all published in the *Nation*, the *Century*, and the *American Mercury* as well. Still, there was a difference. The *Crisis* had an established niche, publishing articles about race, with an intensity that was absent from the other journals. It was *the* record of the darker races.

Fauset, who had been contributing to the journal for some years, was given the title literary editor in 1919. Her salary was $100

a month. Records reveal the considerable input and authority she had in its day-to-day operations and "near full responsibility" for *Brownies' Book*, a children's magazine the association produced from 1920 to 1922. Fauset's stamp on the journal was unmistakable, with frequent bylines.

The subjects of articles in the *Crisis* ranged from politics to popular culture, including reviews of works written in the United States, Europe, Africa, and the Caribbean. Fauset's interests were broad and wide-ranging. Sensitive to their absence from other journals, Jessie showcased a number of women writers, both black and white. As editor of one of the few outlets for black writers, she was able to encourage young authors and in many ways to shape the content of their production. She is said to have discovered Jean Toomer (two of his poems were published in the *Crisis* in 1922), Langston Hughes, Countee Cullen, and Wallace Thurman, four of the major younger writers of the Renaissance.

In her 1926 review of Langston Hughes's *Weary Blues*, she recalled her discovery of him in 1921. "Then one day came 'The Negro Speaks of Rivers.' I took the beautiful dignified creation to Dr. Du Bois and said: 'What colored person is there, do you suppose, in the United States who writes like that and is yet unknown to us? And I wrote and found him to be a Cleveland high school graduate who had just gone to live in Mexico.'" When Hughes moved from Mexico to Harlem, it was Jessie who tracked him down by his change-of-address information. Hughes later wrote, "Jessie Fauset, the managing editor, invited me to lunch at the Civic Club. I was panic-stricken. I pictured the entire staff of the *Crisis* as very learned Negroes and very rich, in nose glasses and big cars." To protect himself, Hughes brought his mother along, "for I knew she would do the talking." Hughes need not have been nervous. He found "Jessie Fauset charming—a gracious tan-brown lady, a little plump, with a fine smile and gentle eyes."

FAUSET PUBLISHED FOUR NOVELS, making her one of the most prolific of the Renaissance writers. Hughes in fact claimed that she was "'mid-wife' to the Renaissance." The centrality of her employment and her ability to further the careers of major figures did not, however, afford her a prominent place in the historical record of the era. One of the most frequently published of the Renaissance writers was also, as critic Cheryl Wall observes, one of the least respected. "Miss Fauset is dainty as a primrose, and her novels are quite as fastidious and precious," said Claude McKay. Historian Nathan Huggins, who wrote one of the first major studies of the period, devotes barely one page to Fauset. He characterizes her as a writer who tried to project the Negro image only in very conventional terms. Historian David Levering Lewis, who has written the classic text on the movement, is kinder to Fauset, suggesting that her influence, though not as great as that of Charles Johnson, Alain Locke, or Walter White, was "for honesty and precocity, unequaled." Yet he too uses language of subordination to describe her, suggesting she was "active but hardly daring, proper, prim and unmarried."

Critics of her novels are particularly hard on her melodramatic plots, flat characterizations, and stilted prose. While her works are somewhat mechanistic—in the style of popular novels of the day—none attempt to downplay or ignore the oppression or discrimination that blacks faced. Introducing topics like promiscuity, interracial marriage, and incest, she strays frequently from her straitlaced label. Her work, she explained, focused on "those breathing-spells, in-between spaces where colored men and women love and work." Her characters constantly battle public wrongs and private wounds, attempting to convey to a white audience a sense of a middle-class sensibility trapped in a black body. It was a dilemma she thought would intrigue white America. She may have been right. Her novels, while never best-sellers, sold reasonably well.

Though her work was rarely panned, her friends were often critical of it. NAACP board member Mary White Ovington, in reviews sent to the black press, asked, "Is this colored world that Miss Fauset draws quite true?" After her fourth novel Fauset was attacked by Alain Locke—they never got along—who said it was "time to move beyond the Jane Austen phase of Renaissance literature."

Jessie Fauset's race consciousness mirrored that of Du Bois, Locke, and Walter White. A proponent of the notion that individual achievement must rise above the sea of racial stereotypes, she had a mission to produce, as a counterpoint to "coons, clowns and claptrap," an "undisguisedly beautiful presentation of Negro ability." She thought more than anything that middle-class black America was America. In her work *There Is Confusion* she has her black protagonist say, "In brief, there is nothing so indigenous, so completely 'made in America' as we."

Yet Fauset was aware of the problems of that sort of message. "We are constantly being confronted," she wrote in 1922, "[with] the tendency of the white world to judge us always at our worst and our own realization of that fact. The result is a stifled art and a lack of frank expression on our part." These are precisely the criticisms that are leveled at much of her own work.

Fauset appeared unable at times to separate her race consciousness from issues of skin color. For her, there seemed to be an unconscious

Jessie Redmona Fauset came from the slow but aristocratic town of Philadelphia. Strange to say, she did not receive very much infection from the atmosphere of her native town, as anyone who has seen her sprint down the hill after 12 o'clock will say. She has but one fault, her devotion to Horace. She believes that it is her mission to persuade benighted America that the 22nd ode should be sung to the tune of "Hail Columbia." In spite of her classic tendencies, she has a repertoire of rollicking rag-time, which is the envy of her friends.

Jessie R. Fauset

200

JESSIE'S CORNELL YEARBOOK PICTURE, 1905. SOME SUGGEST SHE WAS THE FIRST AFRICAN-AMERICAN WOMAN ELECTED TO PHI BETA KAPPA.

PARTY FOR LANGSTON HUGHES, HARLEM, 1924. "THE ATMOSPHERE WAS ALREADY HEADY BUT THE APPEARANCE OF LANGSTON HUGHES, WEARING A PLAID MACKINAW, SMILING SHYLY, GALVANIZED IT," REMEMBERED HUGHES'S GOOD FRIEND, WRITER ARNA BONTEMPS.

ABOVE LEFT: *THE CRISIS*, AUGUST 1926. RIGHT: JACKET DESIGN FOR FAUSET'S LAST NOVEL *COMEDY: AMERICAN STYLE* (1933), ABOUT A LIGHT-SKINNED MOTHER SO FILLED WITH RACIAL HATRED SHE CAUSES THE SUICIDE OF THE DARKER-SKINNED CHILD WHOM SHE LOATHES.

ADVERTISEMENT FOR FAUSET'S FIRST BOOK, *THERE IS CONFUSION* (1924). ITS PUBLICATION WAS OSTENSIBLY THE REASON FOR THE FIRST *OPPORTUNITY* DINNER IN 1925. JESSIE ALWAYS FELT THAT HER RECOGNITION WAS DOWNPLAYED WHEN HOST CHARLES S. JOHNSON CHOSE ALAIN LOCKE MASTER OF CEREMONIES. SHE GAVE A GRACIOUS SPEECH DESPITE HER ANGER.

JESSIE FAUSET WAS A FREQUENT LECTURER AT CONFERENCES IN ADDITION TO HER DUTIES AT THE NAACP OFFICES. LEFT TO RIGHT: MISS LAWLESS, MISS WILLIAMS, DR. BROWN, MRS. JACQUITH, MISS RIGGS, MRS. LANE, MISS MCCROREY, MISS HOLMES, MISS BRIGGS, MISS CAUTION, DR. BUCK, MISS SADDLER, MISS DERRICOTE, MISS FAUSET, MISS WYGAL, AND MR. TOBIAS. THIS PICTURE APPEARED IN *CRISIS*, SEPTEMBER 1923.

correlation between the "best blacks" and those who were light-skinned. In "Emmy," a short story published in the *Crisis* in 1912, long before she became literary editor, she described her heroine as "a pretty brown girl" engaged to Archie Ferrers, a young engineer, whose "Negro blood is just perceptible." The story revolves around the fact that Archie has not told his employer that he is black. He has advanced in the firm to the point of a significant promotion, when his employer finds out about his engagement to Emmy. Unable to bear the insults directed at her, he reveals that he too is black and is fired. But he and Emmy separate because she feels that he was wrong to hide his race. Archie, poor but honest, returns to Emmy, protesting his love, and miraculously gets his job back.

This "noble mulatto" plot line, fraught as it is with the problem of identity, is vintage Fauset. The difficulty, never quite surmounted in her work, is to convey this identity dilemma without implying that the darker-skinned character is wanting by comparison. Emmy, the "pretty brown girl," is not the subject of her own story.

Fauset's class consciousness is also complex. She had all of the middle-class trappings but less of the conventionality. The prim and proper Fauset, after all, published love poems in James Weldon Johnson's 1922 anthology, with lines like these: "there's a man whose lightest word / Can set my chilly blood afire; and / Better the choking sigh, the sobbing breath / Than passion's death!" In a poem published in the *Crisis* in 1917, she writes of "A swift response, an instant glad surrender / To kisses wild and burning."

Fauset's lifestyle matched her poetry. Her first contact with W. E. B. Du Bois occurred in 1903, when she wrote him to praise his book *The Souls of Black Folk*. Du Bois at that time was the only prominent challenge to the domi-

nance of Booker T. Washington, and Fauset appears to have been taking sides in this debate. "We have needed someone to voice the intricacies of the blind maze of thought and action along which the modern, educated colored man or woman struggles." David Levering Lewis suggests the possibility that her real motivation in taking on the NAACP assignment was an infatuation with Du Bois. Though that connection has not been confirmed by other historians, even the hint of it would have stepped beyond the bounds of respectability in the 1920s. Du Bois, after all, was a married man. Yet Jessie was often on the edge of that respectability. Ethel Ray Nance, Charles Johnson's assistant at *Opportunity*, describes in her memoirs being shocked "when she first saw Jessie Fauset sitting at a table in the Civic Club with Du Bois and smoking." Nance writes that "she was very graceful about it. . . . And as I sat there, I thought, when I write home to my father, I guess I just won't mention this part of it."

Fauset did not fear traveling alone, although for a black woman of her social class, it would have offended propriety. After publication of *There Is Confusion*, she took several months off from the *Crisis* and toured Europe and North Africa. "In an age when the idea of Africa enthralled the imaginations of many black American intellectuals," literary critic Cheryl Wall points out, "Jessie Fauset was one of a handful who actually saw the continent." This "active but hardly daring" woman also visited the Casbah in Algiers unaccompanied. After being told, upon her return, that such an activity was dangerous, she did not again go alone; she continued to travel to exotic places, which seems to belie her "prim and proper" label.

Still Fauset, like the other women writers of the Renaissance, was constrained by the black community's yoke on middle-class women. In a *Crisis* essay Radcliffe graduate Marita Bonner used words like "stifles," "chokes," and "stunts" to describe this condition. And it was Fauset who in 1925, with the publication of *The New Negro*, objected strenuously to artist Winold Reiss's depiction of two black teachers with dark skin and nappy hair. She said she did not find this a representative image, and she attempted to have her own contribution include a critical reference to the portrait. Locke, however, edited it out.

Unforgiving to some extent of her elitism, younger Renaissance figures were tolerant but not always respectful of her. Though she had discovered Hughes, he clearly did not trust her judgment, and he often ignored her advice. On the back of one of her letters, he wrote, "middle class people are so conventional. They would have me a 'nice boy' and a college graduate."

In 1926 the journal carried a series of questions asked of both black and white authors, editors, and publishers: "The Negro in Art: How Shall He Be Portrayed?" The series was probably inspired by Du Bois, although several scholars suggest the questions were actually written by Carl Van Vechten. Fauset contacted a number of people, including Sinclair Lewis, H. L. Mencken, Langston Hughes, Walter White, and the poet Georgia Douglas Johnson. Du Bois's primary concern was this question: "Can publishers be criticized for refusing to handle novels that portray negroes of education and accomplishment, on the ground that these characters are no different from white folk and therefore not interesting?" While the answers varied, Sherwood

JESSIE WITH HER PEARLS AND PHI BETA KAPPA KEY.

Anderson's response was typical: "I do not believe the negroes have much more to complain of than the whites in this matter of their treatment in the arts." Alfred Knopf was more direct: "This question seems to be senseless." Interestingly, many of the young black writers responded in a similar way, infuriating Du Bois and establishing a rift between him and them. As George Hutchinson points out, only Jessie got the answer right.

She was not rewarded for her effort. For Du Bois, at that time, was pondering the role of art in black community life. His concerns were first addressed in remarks made at an NAACP conference in May 1926: "How is it that an organization like this, a group of radicals trying to bring new things in the world, a fighting organization which had come out of the blood and dust of battle, struggling for the right of black men to be ordinary human beings —how is it that an organization of this kind can turn aside to talk about art? After all, what have we who are slaves and black to do with art?" Du Bois then expressed the fear that recognition of young black artists could become part of a conspiracy to keep blacks in their place. Whatever the merits of his fears of white cooptation in the arts, their expression clearly made the position of his literary editor more precarious.

Although the exact reason is not known, Fauset's employment at the *Crisis* soon ended. In 1923 Du Bois had borrowed twenty-five hundred dollars from her, which he later was unable to pay back. It is David Levering Lewis's view that "the embarrassment of a financial debt merely made Du Bois less chivalrous as he went about making his associate editor miserable enough to resign." Her biographer, Carolyn Sylander, is not so convinced, pointing out that Fauset continued to do research for Du Bois, supported him at testimonial dinners, and nominated him for a Harmon prize in 1928. Still, Sylander admits that their relationship cooled off after 1926.

At first, Jessie tried to get others to help Du Bois. She asked Joel Spingarn to advance by two years Du Bois's birthday gift, so that his "financial worries would be made less pressed and he thereby would have more time to devote to his real interests." Although it was perhaps simply a self-serving appeal on her part, Du Bois, who lost his house and his life insurance in 1930, had been experiencing financial troubles for some years.

Fauset's leaving the *Crisis* had serious repercussions for the journal. It was she who had organized the files, kept up with correspondence, and laid out the issues. Correspondence from leading writers reveals the extent of the loss. Poet Sterling Brown wrote Du Bois on March 28, 1927, that he had opened his latest issue to find a poem of his there. "I am properly thankful that you thought it worth publishing, but I am in the dark as to how it got in your hands." Du Bois, ever the diplomat, responded that Brown must have sent

WINOLD REISS'S PORTRAIT OF AFRICAN-AMERICAN SCHOOLTEACHERS, 1924, WHICH APPEARED IN THE *SURVEY GRAPHIC* SPECIAL EDITION, MARCH 1925. FAUSET COMPLAINED THAT THE TEACHERS WERE TOO DARK. THEY TOO WEAR PHI BETA KAPPA KEYS.

it. But Langston Hughes had written in apparent exasperation just a month before, "Some months ago I asked for my old manuscripts in your office, but they couldn't be found. I was hoping they were really lost, but lately some of the poems have been in the *Crisis*, and I don't think they are quite good enough to be there, so please throw them in your wastebasket if there are any more."

In 1927, obviously with no more attractive alternative, Jessie got a job at DeWitt Clinton High School and taught there until 1944. At the age of forty-seven, she married Herbert Harris—"dear little Herbie"—a successful insurance broker. The Harrises were married in Jessie's Seventh Avenue apartment before seventy-five witnesses. The bride wore white satin, and her four attendants wore rainbow-colored taffeta. Said guest Harold Jackman: "She made a beautiful bride, as the old folks say, and she looked very young." The couple lived in the apartment with her sister Helen, until Helen's death in 1936. The marriage was by all accounts a successful one. Jackman reported to Cullen that "Fauset took the marriage business very heavily, from fixing meals to wanting to write a book about sex." Jessie describes herself in her alumnae notes of the 1940s as "enjoying housework, meal-getting and occasionally turning out verse."

Fauset's last publication was a novel, *Comedy: American Style*, which received a favorable review in the *Nation* and a rather unfavorable one, by Alain Locke, in *Opportunity*. Hardly a comedy, it has been called by later critics an overly ambitious piece that was well beyond Fauset's literary talent. The story centers on a light-skinned antiheroine, who more than anything wants to be white. Having no better alternative, she marries a light-skinned doctor, and they have several children, one of whom is darker than the rest. His mother hates this child, banishes him from her house, and eventually causes his suicide. The protagonist's hatred for all things black permeates the novel and undermines the supposedly happy ending. The normally reticent Fauset took exception to the negative reviews. She wrote to Locke: "I have always disliked your attitude toward my work," then criticized his "stuffiness, pedantry, and poverty of thought," challenging him to point out one page where "my mid-Victorian style prevails." Yet in her personal life it was precisely to a mid-Victorian style that Jessie fled—teaching high school French, caring for "dear little Herbie" until his death, enjoying housework, and being all but banished from the literary world she had midwifed—a fate from which she has yet to be rescued.

⚜

NELLA LARSEN WAS BORN IN 1891 in Chicago. Her mother had immigrated from Denmark, her father from the Virgin Islands. The relationship (Larsen calls it marriage, but no such records exist) lasted only two years after Nella was born, according to information she provided for the dust jacket of her second novel, *Passing*. She remained with her mother, who then, by some accounts, married Peter Larsen, a bigoted white man. In a 1928 interview in the *Amsterdam News*, Larsen claimed her real father had died before she was old enough to know much about him. By other accounts, Peter Larsen was actually her father and was passing for white; he protected his darker-skinned daughter as much as he could but found it increasingly difficult to explain her presence in his otherwise white household. It has also been suggested that it was not her father but her mother with whom Nella had difficulty. For her part, Larsen never cared to set the record straight.

Whatever the circumstances, we may surmise that Larsen had a difficult childhood and that a significant part of it centered on rejection by her family. Biographer Thadious Davis speculates that early in her life she was placed in the Erring Woman's Refuge for Reform, "an institution from which she was later rescued." Cheryl Wall suggests the motive was "the inconvenient fact that she remained colored in a family that was passing for white." Larsen once wrote, "I don't see my family much now. It might make it awkward for them, particularly my half sister." Upon her death Nella left her entire estate of $36,000 to this sister, who said, "I did not know I had a sister."

In 1907, when she was sixteen, Larsen was sent to Nashville, where she attended Fisk as a high school student. Fisk's atmosphere was probably no more welcoming to Larsen, with her limited means, than her home life had been, however, and she remained there only one year. Like Zora Neale Hurston, Larsen preferred fictionalized versions of her life, and no one knows what she did from 1908 to 1912. In some accounts she claimed to have been in Denmark, but no records of that trip exist. We do know that she was in New York in 1912 and was trained as a nurse at Lincoln Hospital. This was a very acceptable career path for one aspiring to the middle class. But in the twenties Larsen would leave nursing because it would not have impressed her Renaissance

The "MYSTERY WOMAN" OF THE RENAISSANCE, 1928. SHE HAD MANY NAMES: NELLIE WALKER, NELLYE LARSON, NELLIE LARSEN, NELLA LARSEN, NELLA IMES, ALLEN SEMI (NELLA IMES SPELLED BACKWARD).

LINCOLN SCHOOL OF NURSES GRADUATING CLASS OF 1915. NELLA LARSEN IS SECOND FROM THE LEFT IN THE FRONT ROW.

friends, most of whom were college-educated.

In 1915 she left New York to work as an assistant superintendent of nurses at Tuskegee Institute in Alabama. She returned a year later, disillusioned by her experiences and critical of southern black churches and class systems. Ten years later she would write that "her dislike of the conditions there and the school authorities' dislike of her appearance and manner were so intense that after a year [we] parted with mutual disgust and relief." Back in New York she worked as a nurse for the Department of Health.

Through a service organization of visiting nurses, she met Elmer Imes, newly arrived in the city. Elmer, eight years her senior, was a research physicist with a Ph.D. from the University of Michigan who worked for Burrows Magnetic Equipment in New York City. On May 3, 1919, they were married in the chapel of the Union Theological Seminary in Manhattan by the groom's brother.

Marrying Dr. Imes conferred instant social status on Larsen. A brilliant scientist, Elmer had been initiated into a national honors society at Michigan and was later a member of several national physics and engineering societies as well. He was the son and brother of college-trained ministers and descended from a family of free, landowning blacks. Widely read in literature and with excellent taste in music, he was, in short, the perfect catch.

Nella was pretty, lively, and intelligent, sharing with him a love of reading and gracious living. She was also "only slightly brown, light enough in complexion to be considered one of the 'bright skins' of the race," explained Thadious Davis. "She represented an excellent mate for a man who was himself light brown skinned but darker than his brothers and his mother." He "liked white women," friends would later say.

For all of her wit and sophistication, and the voice on which she prided herself (she laughingly admitted it was "acquired"), Larsen was uncomfortable in Elmer's world, often standing in the shadow of her more outgoing husband. She alternated between feeling pleasure at his social prominence and resenting everything he stood for. In a later interview, for example, she would confess to "not believing in religion, churches and the like," the core of Elmer's family background. At the same time, though, she shared the contempt for darker-skinned people held by many Renaissance figures. She once wrote to her friend Dorothy Petersen: "Right now when I look out into the Harlem streets I feel just like Helga Crane in my novel. Furious at being connected with all these niggers." While she occasionally attended the parties of A'Lelia Walker, the "mahogany princess," she never sought her out. "Had Walker been the white daughter of a washerwoman, turned businesswoman and self-made millionaire," Davis suggested, "she would have been more greatly admired by Larsen, who did not discriminate class position as distinct from wealth so keenly among the whites she met."

Larsen threw herself into a writing career, in the hope of a promising result. Desperate to find something to be admired for, she worked hard at her craft. "I have gone back to my novel," she wrote Van Vechten in 1926. "Celebrated the return by destroying a good half of what was completed. It was awful."

Through writing, she found an outlet for feelings she may have otherwise been unable to express. Her written work was sensual and erotic, filled with sharp social commentary. Her life was not. She was often accused of being standoffish and aloof, there were hints that some frigidity on her part led to sexual dissatisfaction in the marriage, and numerous public statements made her appear foolish and flighty. Because of her writing, she avoided most of the prudish labels that Jessie Fauset acquired, but because of her personality she had many acquaintances and few friends.

In 1921 Larsen got a job in the Harlem branch of the New York Public Library, which gave her access to major Renaissance figures. Not surprisingly, her first publications appeared in Fauset's *Brownies' Book*. "Three Scandinavian Games" (June 1920) begins, "Dear Children: These are some games which I first learned long ago in Denmark, from little Danish children." Biographers, of course, have found no records to indicate that Larsen ever set foot in Denmark.

Nella's friendships with Jessie Fauset, Gladys White, "and other cultural or social leaders were tinged with envy and uncertainty, and were relatively short-lived," Thadious Davis wrote. She was rarely included in the salon hosted by Fauset's friends Regina Andrews (assistant librarian at the Harlem library branch), Ethel Ray Nance (secretary to *Opportunity* editor Charles Johnson), and Louella Tucker. When Dorothy Hunt Harris had a going-away party before a European trip, she did not invite Nella, though they had played bridge the week before. Ethel Waters, briefly a neighbor—as well as a rising star—accepted an invitation to tea but never appeared. "We sat about and waited and waited, got hungrier and hungrier," Larsen reported to Van Vechten. "All waited until 7:00 before eating the sandwiches and cakes. I was very disappointed because I felt sure it was going to be a success. Everything was just right."

Not having been born into the middle class preyed on Larsen, as if it were a cruel joke that class as well as skin color mattered. She had no network of relatives who could facilitate introductions, no sorority sisters to ease her way. Perhaps like her protagonist Helga Crane, she feared more than anything that her illegitimacy would be a barrier to middle-class acceptance. "Negro society," she had Helga explain, "was as complicated and as rigid in its ramifications as the highest strata of white society. If you couldn't prove your ancestry and connections, you were tolerated, but you didn't belong."

Two of Larsen's greatest supporters were Walter White and Carl Van Vechten. Nella's gravitation toward them and their wealth, power, and whiteness is not surprising. Correspondence suggests that not only were Nella and Elmer frequent guests at both their homes but the couple considered both men their friends. In the summer of 1926, when Walter White published his second novel, *Flight*, and received a devastating review in *Opportunity*, it was Larsen whom editor Charles Johnson asked to write a rebuttal. It is unclear whether Johnson knew what good friends they were. Larsen's piece praised the novel and attacked the reviewer. Her outrage was rewarded. By October of that year, White had already read a draft of her first novel and had given her comments. His secretary would type the final draft.

Larsen's friendship with Van Vechten was equally rewarding. She wrote him many letters, always praised his work, and over the years developed a real attachment to him. On receiving *Nigger Heaven*, with a mixture of schoolgirl awe and bourgeois materialism, she wrote:

> *I'm terribly excited. Too, almost inclined to forgo the ritual which the reading of particular books always demand [sic] from me, a Houbigant scented bath, the donning of my best green crepe de Chine pyjamas, fresh flowers on the bed side table, piles of freshly covered pillows and my nicest bed cover, —and set right down to it. But no, impatient as I am, I shall make it a ceremony. Not to do so would be blasphemous.*

In 1926 she also published two short stories, "The Wrong Man" and "Freedom," under the pseudonym Allen Semi (Nella Imes spelled backward). Choosing both a male identity

PORTRAIT OF NELLA INSCRIBED "FOR DEAR CARL AND LOVELY FANIA," 1927.

and a nonracial theme increased the chance of acceptance, at this point probably more important to Nella than recognition. The plots of both stories concern troubled marriages. That the Imes marriage at this time had a public face of felicity and a private one of discord may also account for the pseudonym.

Prior to 1927 Nella and Elmer had lived in Jersey City. In March of that year, at Nella's urging, they moved to a walk-up apartment at 236 West 135th Street. Her correspondence of those years mentions many parties—with the Van Vechtens, the Walter Whites, the Weldon Johnsons. "For the past month," she wrote, "it has seemed always to be tea time, as the immortal Alice remarked, with never time to wash the dishes between whiles."

LARSEN'S FIRST NOVEL, *Quicksand*, was published in 1928 by Knopf. Characteristic of both this work and her second novel, *Passing*, published in 1929, was a critique of the hypocrisy and materialism of the black bourgeoisie, a critique notably absent from Fauset's work. *Quicksand* protagonist Helga Crane's first job was a teaching position at Naxos (an anagram of Saxon), a Tuskegee-esque southern school where Negroes knew their place. "Enthusiasm, spontaneity, if not actually suppressed, were at least openly regretted as unladylike or ungentlemanly qualities," Larsen wrote. "The place was smug and fat with self-satisfaction."

Helga eventually arrives in Harlem and comes in touch with a passionate self, long denied. As the novel evolves, she tries to reconcile two opposing needs, one for sexual fulfillment, the other for social respectability. Her solution to the dilemma is to return to the South, marry a rural preacher, and suffer "emotional and physical collapse" from bearing too many children. (Not surprisingly, Nella's in-laws were outraged at her characterization of the black church.) As literary critic Deborah McDowell suggests, on the surface at least Larsen has "sacrificed a daring and unconventional heroine to the most conventional fates of narrative history—marriage and death." But below the surface Larsen had

COVER FOR *QUICKSAND* (1928), LARSEN'S ACCLAIMED FIRST NOVEL. INSCRIBED TO THE VAN VECHTENS.

produced an attack on the suffocating expectations placed on intelligent middle-class African-American women by the black community itself. Many men did not get it. Wallace Thurman, in a review of the book in his journal *Harlem*, stated: "The author of *Quicksand* no doubt pleases Dr. Du Bois. She stays in her own sphere and writes about the sort of people one can invite to one's home without losing one's social prestige."

The novel did please Du Bois, and he wrote a review of *Quicksand* for the *Crisis*. "It is," he observed, "the best piece of fiction that Negro America has produced since the heyday of Chestnutt" (the dean of black poets)—high praise indeed coming from Du Bois. The novel, he adds, "stands easily with Jessie Fauset's *There Is Confusion*, in its subtle comprehension of the curious crosscurrents that swirl about Black America."

Larsen is even more daring and modern in her second work. Again essentially autobiographical, or seemingly so, *Passing* is a psychological novel full of an "internal as opposed to an external reality." Moreover, her exploration of female sexuality strongly hints at "one female character's awakening sexual desire for another." This was not an acceptable subject for Sugar Hill drawing rooms, not "what a woman ought to be or do."

Passing was published barely thirteen months after *Quicksand*. Carl Van Vechten called it "a strangely provocative story, superbly told." Du Bois liked it even more than *Quicksand* but worried that "the success of the novel would be limited because the passing theme would be threatening to white readers because so many white people in America either know or fear that they have Negro blood." To black readers, he advised, "Buy the Book."

Du Bois failed to mention any of the sexual themes that are the centerpiece of the works but instead concentrated on the secondary issue of racial identity. Larsen's ability to hint at gender issues within the black middle class helped keep them unexamined by most of the male Renaissance figures and many of the females as well. An exception was the review written in *Opportunity* by Eda Lou Walton. "To tell the story of a cultivated and sensitive woman's defeat through her own sex-desire is a difficult task," she wrote. "When the woman is a mulatto and beset by hereditary, social and racial forces over which she has little control and into which she cannot fit, her character is so complex that any analysis takes a mature imagination. This, I believe, Miss Larsen is too young to have." Though she was critical, Walton did understand what Larsen was trying to do.

Larsen's success caused media attention. But like that of other successful black women writers, the coverage emphasized her appearance, possessions, background, and personal life rather than her work. The reviewer for the *Amsterdam News* began by saying that Nella Larsen had skin the "color of maple syrup." She was described as a modern woman who smoked, wore short dresses, and felt "that people of the artistic type have a definite chance to help solve the race problem." The article made no mention of her book.

For her part, Larsen played these images to the hilt, bragging in the article that she did her own housework. "There is much to do to keep a five-room apartment so clean." She "sews and plays bridge," she said, once again donning the bourgeois lifestyle of which she was so critical in her work.

Larsen's career troubles began in 1930, when *Forum* magazine published her story "Sanctuary." Set in the rural South, the story revolves around an old black woman who, out of a sense of race loyalty, hides a young fugitive who believes he has murdered a white man. With the arrival of the local sheriff, both the old woman and the fugitive learn that the man he killed was her son. Though the police are portrayed as sympathetic, the old woman still refuses to turn in the fugitive. Larsen argues that race loyalty has a stronger claim on the woman's emotions than revenge, and she allows the young man to escape. Several readers of the magazine noticed a "striking resemblance" between Larsen's story and that of a popular English writer who had published a work eight years before set in Ireland. Larsen was charged with plagiarism.

The similarities in plot, tension, and pacing are unmistakable. Writer Harold Jackman, delighting in her situation, wrote to his friend Countee Cullen, who was recovering in Europe from his ill-fated marriage to Yolanda Du Bois: "and as for the dialogue, little Nell, I'll call her this time, had just changed it to make it colored. The technique and method is identical—description, dialogue, denouement—are incontestably congruent." Had Larsen acknowledged the debt and called

NELLA LARSEN IMES, CIRCA 1930, AFTER WINNING A GUGGENHEIM FOR A YEAR OF TRAVEL AND STUDY. SHE WAS THE FIRST AFRICAN-AMERICAN WOMAN TO WIN SUCH AN AWARD.

it an appropriation, she might have salvaged her career. But her denials in the face of the evidence served only to isolate her further.

Acquaintances within the black literary community, perhaps out of envy, publicized the incident, and Larsen was humiliated. "All literary Harlem knows about it, and I hear that the *Forum* has gotten wind of it—and has written Nella about it," Jackman gleefully wrote to Cullen. "Nella's benefactor, Carl Van Vechten, is trying to justify his protegee but his arguments are so weak and in this case stupid."

After Larsen spent a difficult year producing drafts and other evidence of authorship, the magazine concluded that she was not culpable, but the artistic community never did. "No one who has heard about Nella Larsen's steal had quite gotten over it," Jackman wrote to Cullen. After she appeared at a party at her friend Dorothy Petersen's, Jackman recounted to Cullen, "you should have heard painful Nella Imes tell about a cocktail party on Park Avenue and a luncheon date here; she thinks she is so much hell—I could have strangled her that night." With her marriage also crumbling under her husband's infidelity, 1930 was not a good year for Larsen.

The announcement in March, in the midst of the controversy, that she was the first black woman to receive a Guggenheim did not help her. "Now that Nella has been awarded a Guggenheim fellowship, everyone is quite sorry," Jackman wrote to Cullen. "Especially when such people like Langston Hughes and Bud Fisher are on the horizon and are more deserving of the award." In a letter to Van Vechten in the summer of 1930, Larsen wrote, "It has been a rotten summer—from my point of view."

HARMON FOUNDATION AWARDS CEREMONY AT THE ZION CHURCH, FEBRUARY 12, 1929. LEFT TO RIGHT: MISS HARMON, DAUGHTER OF THE FOUNDER, CONGRATULATING THE WINNERS; NELLA LARSEN IMES AT THE MICROPHONE, WHO RECEIVED THE BRONZE FOR *QUICKSAND;* CHANNING H. TOBIAS; JAMES WELDON JOHNSON, ACCEPTING THE GOLD MEDAL FOR POET CLAUDE MCKAY; MALVIN GRAY JOHNSON; AND DR. GEORGE HAYNES, AWARDS ORGANIZER.

Elmer Imes, meanwhile, had been spending time away from home for some years, doing research in Ann Arbor and Toronto. His star had not been on the rise, as his wife's had been. "At forty-five, Imes was anxious about his own career," wrote Thadious Davis. Early in 1930 he accepted a professorship at Fisk University and moved to Nashville, leaving Nella in New York. "Please cheer Nella up if occasionally she seems to be a little blue about my leaving," he wrote to Van Vechten.

As a further embarrassment to both Nella and the university, Imes began an affair with Ethel Gilbert, director of publicity at Fisk, a white woman with liberal racial attitudes who was well loved on campus. Nella found out about it, and Elmer wrote to Van Vechten for assistance: "There can be not [sic] publicity—my job would be done in ten minutes and I wouldn't be able to do anything for anybody." With a modern attitude toward marriage, which his wife did not completely share, Elmer concluded, "I want to do all for her that I can and be everything to her that she will let me be. I am not denying that I am very much in love with the other girl—very much indeed, but she does not expect or wish me to forget to love Nella."

On September 19 Larsen sailed for Lisbon in connection with her fellowship, arriving on the last day of the month. From Lisbon she went on to Majorca and began her writing project. To Van Vechten she wrote: "I think my book, my white book [probably another work in which race is not the subject] is really good. Perhaps being a bit lonely is doing me good, or rather doing what I'm trying to do, good." By the next March, however, she had written to the Guggenheim Foundation asking for a three- to six-month extension, explaining that her writing was going a little slower than usual. Her request was denied.

In June, Larsen wrote to Van Vechten, giving the latest sorry chapter in her marriage:

"About Elmer: I heard from him the other day for the first time in four months. And then only to berate me for having spent as much money as I have."

She also sent a copy of her writing project to Knopf. Due to problems with the mails, it did not arrive until August. Knopf, probably at Van Vechten's urging, sent it out for review. According to a reviewer's notes—all that is left of the manuscript—it is the story of a woman in an unhappy marriage who discovers that her husband is still in love with his first wife.

Knopf rejected the novel in September 1931. Larsen's withdrawal from the literary scene began in 1932. Her correspondence with Carl Van Vechten and Walter White tapered off, and because she moved around a lot, her address was often unknown. She returned to Nashville in April 1932 because the president of Fisk, who had heard the rumors, thought it unseemly that she was away so much while still married to Imes. But in June she was back in New York in her "small, depressing place." Elmer wrote to Van Vechten: "I don't know how wise it is to have her here [in Nashville]. She has the most ungodly ability to keep me in an unpleasant stew."

Nella and Elmer were divorced in 1933. After a few fainthearted attempts to restore her position, she tried to disappear completely in 1937 by pretending to sail to South America. She returned instead to a career in nursing on Governor's Island. On March 30, 1964, she was found dead in her apartment on lower Second Avenue. The medical examiner ruled that she died of "acute congestive heart failure due to hypertensive and arteriosclerotic disease." Friends feared that she had actually been dead a week before she was found. It seems incredible that one of the most creative and inventive minds of the Renaissance would fall into such obscurity. But in death as in life, Nella Larsen was an enigma.

NELLA LARSEN, AUGUST 17, 1932, PRIOR TO HER DEPARTURE FOR
NASHVILLE. PHOTOGRAPHED BY CARL VAN VECHTEN.

WASHINGTON, D.C., CONNECTIONS

A BIOGRAPHER OF DUKE ELLINGTON WROTE, "FROM 1917 UNTIL HE WENT TO NEW YORK FIVE YEARS LATER DUKE RAN HIS MUSICAL AFFAIRS FROM HIS HOMETOWN, WASHINGTON, OFTEN SENDING OUT FIVE BANDS A NIGHT." JUST ONE YEAR BEFORE, ALAIN LOCKE, EDUCATED AT HARVARD, OXFORD, AND THE UNIVERSITY OF BERLIN, HAD JOINED THE FACULTY AT HOWARD UNIVERSITY, WHERE HE WOULD REMAIN UNTIL HIS DEATH IN THE 1940S. WASHINGTON, A SOUTHERN CITY WITH NORTHERN ASPIRATIONS, HELD SPECIAL PROMISE, AND MANY RENAISSANCE FIGURES WERE FREQUENT VISITORS.

DUKE ELLINGTON AT THE WHITE HOUSE AFTER A VISIT WITH PRESIDENT HERBERT HOOVER, OCTOBER 1, 1931.

FLORENCE MILLS,
IN A PORTRAIT BY
JAMES VANDERZEE,
1927.

10

FLORENCE MILLS

A WOMAN SUFFRAGE amendment to the Constitution was scheduled for a vote in the U.S. House of Representatives on January 10, 1918. The vote was expected to be close. "It was with real anguish that the women keeping their tallies up in the galleries saw the hair-line finish shaping up, and their supporters rounding up every possible vote," wrote historian Eleanor Flexner. Representative Thetus W. Sims from Tennessee had a broken arm and shoulder, which he refused to have set lest he miss influencing one more colleague. Republican House Leader James Mann of Illinois, who'd been hospitalized for six months, appeared on the floor pale and barely able to stand. Representative Henry Barnhart of Indiana was carried in on a stretcher. Representative Frederick Hicks of New York kept a deathbed promise to his ardent suffragist wife: he went to Washington for the roll call and then returned home for the funeral. The amendment passed 274 to 136, having gotten the exact number of votes it needed. Three roll calls and three recounts later the outcome was announced to a cheering throng of amendment supporters. Someone started to sing the familiar hymn "Old Hundred"—"All people that on earth do dwell, sing to the Lord with cheerful voice"—and many joined in. The amendment passed the Senate several months later and was ratified on August 26, 1920. Women had won the right to vote.

FLORENCE MILLS, CALLED THE Queen of Happiness, was one of the most successful entertainers of the 1920s. A delicate woman with a fragile constitution, she sang, danced, and developed a comedic style etched with melancholy. Captivating audiences with her "dainty wistfulness," poet Countee Cullen said, "she was all too slender and slight for the bright and vivacious flame of her being." Many spoke of her enchanting qualities. "Her control over an audience was so superb that at times it seemed almost supernatural," wrote the *Inter-State Tattler*. But it was her singing, most of all, that was spellbinding. "There are notes in her voice that come from far away and long ago with an infinite pathos and are an undercurrent to her gaiety and comedy," said the *New York Graphic*. "High silver notes like beams of light, floating into a dark auditorium" is how another reviewer described her voice. "And yet, after all, did she really sing?" asked James Weldon Johnson. Ethel Waters was more sure. "She had a small voice," Waters explained. "They had been using a choir around her to get volume, and then Florence would come in and sing the punch line." But Johnson's assessment was more typical: "The upper range of her voice was full of bubbling, bell-like, bird-like tones. It was a rather magical thing Florence Mills used to do with that small voice in her favorite song, 'I'm a Little Blackbird Looking for a Bluebird,' and she did it with such exquisite poignancy as always to raise a lump in your throat":

> *Never had no happiness*
> *Never felt no one's caress.*
> *I'm just a lonesome bit of humanity*
> *Born on a Friday, I guess.*

Florence Mills—a very small, very capable, very brave performer—elicited both admiration and devotion. "The masses love Miss Mills," the *Tattler* reported. "More, they adore her. It is not too much to say that some of us even worship her, for it is only a step from the pedestal of a heroine to the immortality of a goddess." At her untimely death, just six years after her rise to stardom in *Shuffle Along*, there was an outpouring of grief so intense that it stunned even the most blasé of Harlemites. "The funeral service of the Beloved Florence was the largest, the most impressive and tearful in the memory of Harlem," the *Tattler* wrote. Her body lay in state for four days and was viewed by over 100,000 people. Some 57,000 mourners mobbed the church where the funeral was held, pushing and shoving to get even a brief glance of the coffin. Fifty people fainted in the crowd and several were trampled. When the mourners reached Seventh Avenue and 133rd Street, Robert Brown, the cornet player in the band that marched with the procession, dropped dead in the street of heart failure.

Despite her sweetness of temperament and her fragility, Florence Mills was not a vacuous starlet. She was a lady of strong opinions who refused to accept the status quo for blacks. When a reporter for the British newspaper *Sketch* referring to Carl Van Vechten's bestseller, *Nigger Heaven*, asked if she had read "a certain famous American novel, in which Harlem was revealed in all its strangeness," Florence replied that she had read it and did not like it. "They are so weak, she said. All the colored people in that book crumple up when they're put to the test. They've no stamina—nothing. We're not like that." Feeling the need to put her statement in context, she continued, "Do you know what all this does for us? . . . It makes us fight—fight all the harder till we come out on top. That's what it does."

Coming from other performers, or said without Florence's charm, these words could have sounded brash or even militant. But there was no bitterness or resentment in her expressions, "only pluck and a smile in the face of tremendous odds," according to James Weldon Johnson, who saw this as a gift of grace. "She could be whimsical, she could be almost grotesque; but she had the good taste that never allowed her to be coarse." She also had "a naivete that was alchemic," he noted.

FLORENCE MILLS WAS BORN in Washington, D.C., in 1895. She first appeared onstage at the age of four at the Bijou Theater in Washington and, as James Weldon Johnson points out, was "on the stage practically all of her life." A child prodigy, she "appeared a number of times as a singing and dancing entertainer in the drawing rooms of the diplomatic set at the capital." She was presented with a gold bracelet at one point by the wife of the British ambassador. "The silliest, smallest thing I was," she explained in the *Sketch* article.

She moved with her mother and sisters to New York when she was nine or ten and continued her stage appearances. During one such performance authorities in Philadelphia ordered Florence to go to school. Thereafter, she is said to have attended private schools in New York. Years later when interviewed in London, she was asked what she liked to read. She replied Pushkin and Dumas, "who had colored blood in them." She also professed a love for the music of English composer Samuel Coleridge-Taylor "because he was black." Such preferences did not, however, reflect an anti-white bias but rather the sentiments of middle-class educators like Du Bois and Fauset. "It is ridiculous to think that we are different from white people," Florence explained, "because we are educated and brought up to think the same way as you. After all, it is white authors whose books we read and it is a white culture that surrounds us."

After attending school for an unknown length of time, she returned to the stage with her sisters Olivia and Maude, performing as the Mills Sisters. In 1914 she was joined by a girl named Kinky, a protégée of Buddy Gilmore. They traveled through the South and Midwest, on the vaudeville circuit. In Chicago, when Kinky married and left the act, Florence joined a group called Panama Trio, with Cora Green and Ada "Bricktop" Smith. Cora Green would later appear in *Hot Chocolates*. Bricktop was a light-skinned black woman who dyed her hair bright red. Unable to make it in the United States, she emigrated to Paris where she ran a hugely popular cabaret. It was for her that Cole Porter wrote "Miss Otis Regrets," a song about a woman who kills her lover:

Miss Otis regrets she is unable to lunch today.
She is sorry to be delayed.
When she woke up and found that her true
*   love was gone,*
She ran to the man who had led her so far
*   astray,*
And from under her velvet gown,
She drew a gun and shot her lover down.
Miss Otis regrets she is unable to lunch today.

Bricktop, one of the leading blues singers of the day, and a sometime lover of Josephine Baker, had a jaded view of men reminiscent of Bessie Smith's. "Those bums," she said, "sometimes you have to kill 'em. Kill 'em before they kill you, baby." But Bricktop, too, had only good things to say about Florence Mills.

For the time when black performers were not yet in vogue, the Mills Sisters did fairly well, but they broke up after a western tour. Florence next joined the Tennessee Ten, a standard Keith and Orpheum Circuit Act. There she met U. S. Thompson, a comedian and dancer whom she later married. Thompson was her constant companion and manager

THE PANAMA GIRLS,
AS PICTURED IN
THE *MESSENGER*.

throughout her engagements, and their marriage was one of the happiest and most successful in the profession.

She played from coast to coast in vaudeville and in road companies until she was twenty-five. She struggled "through that particularly hard sort of life, from a start of nine dollars a week up to four or five times that amount . . . gaining a sure grasp on her art," James Weldon Johnson observed. Years later her Broadway contract stipulated a weekly salary of $3,500, and at her death she was said to be worth over a quarter of a million dollars. But she never forgot her modest beginnings or her responsibility to those who would follow. Many who came after owe much to her, for she made "the path upward easier," the *New York Graphic* said.

Her big break came in 1921 when she was cast in Sissle and Blake's revue, *Shuffle Along*, a big hit that introduced such great songs as "I'm Just Wild about Harry," and "Love Will Find a Way." "Florence Mills skyrocketed to fame in the second act," Langston Hughes wrote. "Trixie Smith sang 'He May Be Your Man But He Comes To See Me Sometimes.' And Cate-

rina Jarboro, now a European prima donna, and the internationally celebrated Josephine Baker were merely in the chorus. Everybody was in the audience—including me."

Poet Claude McKay was equally impressed. "Never had I seen a colored actress whose artistry was as fetching as Florence Mills'," he wrote. He remembered going backstage after the opening and telling her she was the star. "No, she said the stars were Lottie Gee and [Gertrude Saunders, whose name McKay did not remember]. I said, 'You're the star for me and I'm going to say so in my review.' She laughed deliciously."

As a result of her success, Florence received an offer from the Ziegfeld Follies and one from Lew Leslie "to head a cast in an all-colored revue." Florence reasoned that Lew Leslie's proposition would "give her a chance to do something for her own people in breaking down the colored barriers on Broadway." She passed on the Follies contract—Ziegfeld, after all, had already featured the late Bert Williams—and agreed to lead Lew Leslie's company. The show opened at the Plantation, the first high-class black cabaret on Broadway. Leslie signed Florence to a three-year contract.

Leslie, a Broadway impresario whose fame rested on the "discovery and exploitation of black talent," was a driven man, according to Barry Singer, lyricist Andy Razaf's biographer. "An intemperate perfectionist, he began planning his shows at least six to eight months prior to rehearsals, virtually closeting himself with his creative teams, working out every element of a show in advance." His creative teams were for the most part white, establishing an unfortunate precedent, to the disadvantage of great black lyricists like Razaf and composers like Eubie Blake. Leslie insisted that white men "understand the colored man better than he does himself." Leslie's fame, however,

rested on the performances of Mills, Adelaide Hall, and Bill Robinson. When they left him, as each did in turn, his career was at an end.

Leslie engaged in an elaborate scheme to ensure the success of the Plantation show, recalled Jimmy Durante. With a heavily advertised opening night, the streets were filled with customers trying to enter. "They could hear a hot jazz band blazing away and Miss Mills singing and frantic applause. But they couldn't get in." Two uniformed ushers politely explained to the crowds that the club was full. This went on for two weeks, with the clamor to see the show building daily. "Finally Leslie began to accept reservations. He was fairly flooded with them. The club became a mint." For two weeks Leslie had Florence and the band perform before an empty house. Leslie understood fully, Durante

FLORENCE MILLS
WITH PERFORMERS
FREDI JOHNSON
AND HER HUSBAND,
U. S. THOMPSON,
1922.

THE PANAMA GIRLS IN THE 1920S: CORA GREEN,
FLORENCE MILLS, AND ADA "BRICKTOP" SMITH.
PHOTOGRAPHED BY GUSHINIERE.

FLORENCE MILLS
COVERED IN
THE *MESSENGER*.

"I'M JUST WILD ABOUT HARRY," A HIT SONG FROM
SHUFFLE ALONG.

PLAYBILL FROM THE 1922 HIT *SHUFFLE ALONG*
BY NOBLE SISSLE AND EUBIE BLAKE.

FLORENCE MILLS AND THE CHORUS LINE FROM THE SHOW *DIXIE TO BROADWAY*, 1924.

FLORENCE MILLS IN TUXEDO, 1925, ANTICIPATING THE ANDROGYNOUS LOOK THAT WOULD BECOME THE VOGUE A FEW YEARS LATER.

SIGNED PORTRAIT OF FLORENCE MILLS THAT GIVES CREDENCE TO HER NICKNAME, LITTLE TWINKS.

explained, "the New York manner of flocking only to places where it's hard to get in."

Mills was engaged as an added attraction in the Greenwich Village Follies at the Winter Garden in 1923. When advance advertising for the production placed Florence Mills's name above all the others, the white cast threatened to walk out. But her professionalism apparently saved the show. She received top billing, the cast remained, and the show was acclaimed. Reported the *New York Age*, "Miss Mills is as modest as she is gifted. Her rapid rise from a member of a vaudeville act to an international favorite has not turned her head. She is more concerned over her work before the footlights than any silly appeal to 'go big' off the stage and gain a lot of cheap notoriety."

Leslie next produced *Dixie to Broadway* at the Broadhurst, which played only a season but had great success. He added some white performers and in 1923 took *From Dover to Dixie* to London, playing at the Pavilion Theatre for C. B. Cochran, the English producer, for a long run. "The success acquired by Miss Florence Mills, the American coloured girl playing in *From Dover to Dixie*, is something unequaled by any American playing here in the last decade," the London *Times* reported. "She is by far the most artistic person London has had the good fortune to see." She returned to America in the fall of 1923 and went again into the Plantation.

In the summer of 1924, Mills went on tour and the Plantation sought a replacement. Producer Earl Dancer persuaded Ethel Waters to audition. Ethel hesitated because, in her words, "I felt that Broadway and all downtown belonged to Florence Mills." She got the part, though, and worked all through the hot summer. "But in late August or early September they closed me out," Ethel complained, "because Florence was coming back. And Florence Mills came in on my smoke. But, after

all, it was her show and it had been built around her. So I had no beef. The world loves a winner, but you have to be a hell of a good loser, too, in show business."

Duke Ellington was, at this time, beginning his career as a composer. Members of his band thought Duke was putting the arrangements down on paper incorrectly because he would give what they thought was the clarinet part to the saxophone. But a spate of novel pieces soon convinced them of his originality. One of the first musical portraits he wrote was called "Black Beauty." It was written for Florence Mills.

In 1926, Leslie produced his first *Blackbirds*, which ran in New York, then moved to Paris where it was held over for sixteen weeks. Josephine Baker was a star in Paris by this time, and comparisons between her and Florence were inevitable. "You take a coconut, with its fiber, its crust, its lumps," said one reviewer, "and then you take an ivory ball, with its paleness, its smoothness, its caress for the eyes. That's the difference between Josephine Baker and Florence Mills. One is a rat who kicks, with so much spirit! The other an island bird." Apparently Josephine, the rat, did not mind. "She loved Florence Mills," her biographer Jean-Claude Baker said, "even when reviews comparing them were not always favorable to her."

Besides, Florence soon left France and went to London for a year. "Miss Mills' popularity was unbounded. Her photographs were displayed everywhere, and her portrait was painted," the *Daily Express* reported. Playing at the Palladium, Florence stunned her British audiences by introducing the Charleston. "When the shimmy hit London in 1921, it was condemned as vulgar." The Charleston brought equally outraged responses from some quarters. The vicar of Saint Alden's in Bristol said, "Any lover of the beautiful will die rather than be associated with it. . . . It is neurotic! It is rotten! It stinks!" But Florence herself received no criticism.

In London she was given the affectionate name of Little Twinks. The Prince of Wales is said to have attended the show between thirteen and twenty times. Florence was interviewed frequently while she was in Europe, reporters often asking her about race relations in the United States. Her responses revealed her deep commitment to service. She told the *London Express* in 1927 that she dreamed "dreams of the future of her people." She told the reporter: "I want to help the colored people. I realize that, in my line of work, I am doing much to help them. The stage is the quickest way to get to the people. My own success will make people think better of other colored folk." Her response to the *Observer* was even more illuminating: "To return to my heart's one real and great ache, does personal popularity, enthusiasm and applause count for anything? I had hoped—and, in fact, I go on hoping—that for every friend I have made in this country, the colored people as a whole have also gained a friend."

MILLS'S VISION RESEMBLES critic Ann Douglas's Renaissance ingenue in *Terrible Honesty* attempting to "sing and dance her way out of oppression." And yet one senses a difference. "Because the great Creator made some of us different colors—be it black, brown, or yellow—is it in the power of anyone honestly and sincerely Christian at heart to look down upon us as something inferior?" Florence asked. She did not wear blinders. "Even today," she told the London press, "there are many colored boys in America who, after being trained as lawyers and doctors, have to become train attendants because they are black and there is no place for them."

Florence Mills's contribution may also be found in the juxtaposition of her professionalism and her humility. She worked hard at her craft and never allowed herself to indulge in the trappings of stardom. A reviewer once wrote, "Florence Mills is, within the limits of her field of theatrical enterprise, America's foremost feminine player. What Jolson is among the men she is among the women. There is not one of them who can sing a song so effectively as she can, though a hundred of them have voices far superior. There is not one of them who can dance as she does, try as they will to imitate her. And surely there is not one of them who can so quickly, so certainly, and so electrically get an audience into her grip and keep it there." And yet it was said, "success never changed her. When she was here she was always the same. She never wanted any special favor." Though wealthy, Mills never owned an automobile and was said to prefer the subway to taxis.

Tired from so many straight performances without a rest, she went to Germany for a needed vacation. Returning to America in September 1927, she received a royal welcome. Thousands greeted her at Pier 57 in New York as she stepped off the *Ile de France*. She was driven home to Harlem in a motorcade. Fifty guests greeted her at the Footlights Club on West 133rd Street several days later, including Alain Locke, Eubie Blake, Flourney Miller, and Gertrude Saunders. Miller, acting as toastmaster, said he was going to shoot any speaker who talked too long. His threat was apparently idle, as the program of speakers went on for five hours. Only Gertie Saunders heeded the warning, though, saying simply: "We are glad you are back, Miss Mills."

While she was in New York, Mills decided to have an appendectomy, which she had long postponed. The press would later report that "for a lengthy period prior to her last illness,

she had known that she needed a rest and the services of a surgeon. But there were friends who had invested heavily in her popularity and the security of those investments depended on her remaining at the post of duty." Wishing to avoid alarming her mother, she concealed from her the fact that she was sick. Finally, warned that delay could be fatal, she entered the hospital on October 24, 1927. The *Amsterdam News* reported: "Florence Mills, internationally known actress, was operated on for appendicitis at the Hospital for Joint Diseases, 124th Street and Madison Avenue yesterday morning, by Dr. Grossman. She was reported improving nicely last night." But on November 2, the press revealed that "Miss Mills died exactly one week from the day upon which she was operated on for appendicitis. She was rushed to the hospital very early last Monday morning, October 24, in a serious condition, and Dr. Grossman performed the operation the next morning. Very little hope was held for her recovery. 'She was, indeed, a very sick woman,' the physician said."

James Weldon Johnson wrote that "Harlem was stunned" at the news of her death and "at first refused to believe that it could be true. Then there followed vague rumors of foul play." The *New York News* suggested she may have been poisoned. The *Amsterdam News* attempted to reassure its readers by noting that she "was a private patient at the hospital and every available method known to medical science was employed to save her life. Dr. Grossman was constantly in attention upon Miss Mills, and she was surrounded by private nurses every moment of the day and night."

The inevitable was finally accepted. "The death of the Queen of Happiness," the *Amsterdam News* reported, "brought sorrow to the whole world." Said Johnson: "Her funeral was one such as Harlem, perhaps all New York, had never seen before." She lay in state at Howell's Funeral Home for four days and it was estimated that 100,000 filed into the chapel to view her body. Langston Hughes reported that the funeral was held on a Sunday afternoon. "It was a beautiful procession," he wrote, "with the chorus girls from her show marching all in gray." Eleven automobiles conveyed the flowers. Fire escapes, windows, and roofs were "crowded with onlookers along the line of march, and it is said that some people sold window space for a peep at the cortege of the most popular Negro woman in the world." Five thousand people were packed to suffocation in Mother Zion Church. Inside, a tower of roses four feet broad and eight feet high was displayed with the note "From a Friend." The friend was rumored to be the Prince of Wales. Fred Moore, editor of the *New York Age*, read a eulogy written by Bill "Bojangles" Robinson. The air quivered with emotion. "Hall Johnson's choir sang spirituals, and the whole throng wept and sobbed." Juanita Stinnette of the stage team of Chappelle and Stinnette rose at the end of the service to sing a song dedicated to the dead star. "She started, she faltered; she struggled on; her efforts ended in a frantic cry, 'Florence!' and she swayed and collapsed in a heap on the floor." As the heavy casket, weighing over 750 pounds and costing over $10,000, was taken to the cemetery, Florence's mother asked for one last look. "The great lid was raised, the rose blanket having been removed, and the weary mother peered through the heavy glass covering to see the body of her child for the last time," the *Amsterdam News* reported.

It was said by onlookers that just as the

FLORENCE MILLS IN LONDON, JANUARY 8, 1923. SHE WAS A STUNNING SUCCESS ON HER LONDON TOUR. PHOTOGRAPHED BY ALEXANDER BASSANO.

pallbearers were carrying the lifeless body into the church, a hundred blackbirds were released from an airplane, celebrating her theme song "I'm a Little Blackbird Looking for a Bluebird." At the burial site, stunt pilot Herbert Julian, the Black Eagle, dropped flowers from his plane. But it was also said that another, larger flock of blackbirds, not ordered, flew south over her grave.

One explanation for the adulation that Florence Mills received at her death was provided by the *Inter-State Tattler.* The explanation suggests that an untimely death of a young female icon produces something like a statue of a goddess frozen in time. The *Tattler* observed: "Her existence is no longer a succession of dates and events, but an imperishable memory. She is no longer subject to the laws of change and decline. The millions will remember her as they last saw her—a lovely girl with the fire of youth undimmed and a magic beauty in her voice." Shortly after her death, a fund was started by Earl Dancer to erect a fitting memorial to the star. The fund-raising campaign began with a benefit performance by Ethel Waters and Eddie Cantor, among others. The fund was still operational in 1931, when the *Tattler* announced the election of Jessie Shippe as president, Henry Parker as treasurer, and W. C. Handy as financial secretary. The committee planned to raise money for the Florence Mills Memorial Home for Disabled and Indigent Performers.

Beverly Nichols, interviewing Mills for the *Sketch* in February 1927, had observed: "There is, to me, a hidden rhythm in the art of all coloured people—a super-syncopation behind their melodies, a strange stirring life even in their gestures, a quality even in their broadest smiles, which seems to hint of a melancholy not yet forgotten. And especially do I feel this with Florence Mills."

In this interview, Mills had spoken of the American South in her usual forthright manner. "Down South is still terrible," she said. "There isn't slavery any more—not real slavery—but there's something very like it." She shut her eyes quietly, according to Nichols—"a line of black lashes over a delicate, coffee skin. Then she looked up again with that appealing smile of hers, and again, even through the smile, I had a sense of 'melancholy not quite forgotten.' But it's all going to be better, she said. It's all going to be much better." Less than eight months later she was dead.

11

DUKE ELLINGTON

*T*HE FIRST RADIO BROADCAST in America was heard in the fall of 1920. By 1922 sales of radio sets, parts, and accessories had amounted to over $60 million. The radio craze had struck. By 1925 radio sales had reached $430 million and by 1929 over $842 million. But not everyone was thrilled with the new medium. Groups such as the General Federation of Women's Clubs demanded "restrictions on the playing of recordings," particularly race records. Said the group's national music chairperson: "Jazz disorganizes all regular laws and order; it stimulates to extreme deeds, to a breaking away from all rules and conventions; it is harmful and dangerous, and its influence is wholly bad." At stake was the important question of "who should be allowed to exert cultural authority." Who would define performing art for the ladies of Peoria and Terre Haute? In one way, at least, their fears were prophetic. As Ann Douglas writes, "Black artists and the new sound media met in mutual enthusiasm." Duke Ellington was one of the first to broadcast to a national audience. Through radio, African-American jazz became part of American culture.

THE DUKE, 1933.

D
UKE ELLINGTON WAS AN American composer who wrote for the members of his own band. "Bach and myself both wrote with the individual performer in mind," Duke explained. One of "the most fascinating and original minds in American music," in the words of his longtime friend and associate, Billy Strayhorn, "Ellington plays the piano, but his real instrument is his band. Each member is to him a distinctive tone color and set of emotions, which he mixes with others equally distinctive to produce a third thing, which I like to call the "Ellington Effect.'"

By the strength of his personality and the generosity of his purse, Ellington kept his band together for nearly fifty years, a feat unprecedented in the field of music. He was a great showman. Observed jazz critic Hughes Parnassie, "Duke directed his orchestra in a lordly fashion. At the piano, with a quick, elegant gesture, he would lift an arm from time to time to indicate a nuance to his musicians." Ellington was a musical scholar. "I don't write jazz," he once noted. "I write Negro music. The tragedy is that so few records have been kept of the Negro music of the past. It has to be pieced together so slowly. But it pleases me to have a chance to work at it." He was also a compassionate man. When asked to state his artistic philosophy, he replied: "I like great big ole tears."

Critics often commented on Ellington's ability to remain unruffled in the face of controversy. Members of his band, thinking it metabolic, suggested: "His pulse is so low he can't get excited." But Duke maintained that the trait was acquired through practice. In the face of constant distractions and some detractors (Spike Hughes called him "a prophet without honor in his own country"), he always managed to "work and write." A deeply religious man and an immense talent, he never lost faith in himself.

FROM THE MOMENT OF HIS BIRTH in April 1899, Edward Kennedy Ellington was spoiled by a host of relatives, mainly women. James Edward, his father, was first a butler and later a blueprint maker for the U.S. Navy. The Ellingtons lived well in Washington. His father instilled in him the importance of good manners—"A gentleman never has any problem selecting the proper fork, spoon or knife," he told the child—and, according to his son, taught him how to "sweet-talk anyone." Duke's mother, Daisy, adored him. "When I was five years old," he said, "my mother put my age up to six so that I could get into first grade at school. She dressed me, and sent me off to school just a few blocks away. She didn't think I saw her, but I did, and every day she followed me, all the way to that school. After school, she was waiting for me at the front door of our home, if she wasn't waiting in front of the school door."

Ellington got his deep religious faith from his mother. She often told him he had nothing to worry about in life because he was blessed. He believed her. "She was very soft-spoken, and I knew that anything she told me was true. No matter where I was, or what the conditions, my subconscious seemed very much aware of it. So until this day I really don't have any fears, beyond what I might do to hurt or offend someone else." Ellington read the Bible from cover to cover four times before he was twenty. He was meticulous about saying grace before meals and in his later life performed as often in churches as in nightclubs.

Ellington got his love of music from his parents; his mother played the piano—"pretty things like 'Meditation,' so pretty they'd make you cry," he said—and his father was an opera fan. He was, at an early age, given piano lessons, and a high school teacher taught him harmony. But before long, Duke rebelled against his classical training.

Upon graduation from high school in Washington, he was given a scholarship to Pratt Institute in New York. But "music was his mistress," as he later titled his autobiography, so he stayed in Washington and played. "By booking bands for dances, I was making a lot of money," he wrote. Clarinetist Sidney Bechet remembered: "He was hanging around the stage door, coming in all the time when we were doing our rehearsals and asking to play the piano."

On July 2, 1918, he married Edna Thompson, who lived across the street and whom he had known most of her life. Their son, Mercer Kennedy Ellington, was born in 1919. A second son died in infancy. Said Edna, "We were very young, then. Kids, really. I think we both thought Mercer was a toy."

The marriage was not a happy one, although they were never divorced. Edna soon learned that music was Duke's real passion. Nothing was allowed to stand in its way. As he became more famous, she did not want to share him, she later claimed. Duke thought she should be more understanding. "I guess I should have been," she said. They permanently separated in 1923, but Duke always supported her. She lived in a spacious apartment in Washington, which contained a baby grand piano, and boasted that she had taught both Duke and Mercer how to read

DUKE, AN ADORED CHILD, AT AGE 4. WHEN HIS MOTHER DIED IN THE 1930S, ELLINGTON FELL INTO A DEEP DEPRESSION.

music. After their separation, Duke refused to talk about his wife, and many people did not know he had one. In 1959, when *Ebony* ran a feature article about her, Duke was furious. Unlike some of his fellow performers, he was a very private person.

Although Ellington never married again, he was, by all accounts, a great ladies' man. Wrote Richard Boyer in the *New Yorker* in 1944: "He is also fond of what he calls 'the chicks,' and when they follow him to the station, as they often do, he stands on the back platform and, as [the train] pulls out, throws them big, gusty, smacking kisses." His most steady girlfriends were drawn from the chorus line of the Cotton Club. First was Mildred Dixon, "a regular companion for several years," according to biographer Derek Jewell, and later Beatrice Ellis, another dancer, who came to be known as Evie Ellington and with whom Ellington spent much of the rest of his life. But there were others as well. Ralph Gleason, a critic, claimed that Duke once asked him to reserve a hotel room "for the young lady who is traveling parallel to me."

The call to New York came in 1922. Wilbur Sweatman, a bandleader whose gimmick was to play three clarinets simultaneously, offered drummer Sonny Greer, Duke's good friend, a job. Sonny agreed to come if he could bring two friends. The other friend was Otto Hardwick, who played the clarinet and alto sax.

"New York filled our imagination," Duke later observed. "We were awed by the never ending roll of great talents there, talents in so many fields, in society music and blues, in vaudeville and songwriting, in jazz and theatre, in dancing and comedy. We had to go there." Greer and Hardwick went ahead of Duke. By the time Duke arrived, they were out of money and opportunities. They went around to clubs looking for work, but they did not make much money and frequently dined on hot dogs.

But New York was a university education for Ellington. It was "the endless circuit of parties and barroom explosions where the piano professors, with pounding cross rhythms and striding right hands, could always be found," wrote Derek Jewell. In the early days, Duke befriended Willie "the Lion" Smith, who gave him pointers and occasionally lent him money, and Fats Waller, a friend of Louis Armstrong. Said Ellington of Willie Smith: "We were exposed to the luxury of his fire, his harmonic lavishes, his stride." Ellington listened and absorbed but found no job. He did find $15 in an envelope on the street one day, "and bought me a new pair of shoes and the fare back to Washington for the three of us." Not long after that, Waller came to town with a burlesque show and told them of a job in New York for all three and their friends Elmer Snowden and Arthur Whetsol as well. The others again went ahead of Duke. "On my way up, I travel in style, blowing all my money on the train (took a parlor car, ate a big expensive dinner in the diner, and got a cab at Pennsylvania Station to take me uptown). After all, I'm a big shot, I've got a job waiting for me in the big town." But when he got there, "everything had gone wrong." Once again, no job.

Their luck changed when in 1923 Bricktop, who knew Ellington from Washington, persuaded Barron Wilkins, who ran a popular nightclub at 134th Street and Seventh Avenue,

to hire them. "Mr. Barron Wilkins was a beautiful man. He had lots of money, but he never hustled a customer. Of course, that was the spirit of those times. People in that life did not so readily underestimate others, and for young kids like us, they had many suggestions for ways to get along in the world." The band called themselves the Washingtonians. "We were only five, but we had arrangements on everything," Ellington recalled. "It was what we've now named conversation music, kind of soft and gutbucket." Appearance was very important to the group. "If any one of us came in improperly dressed Whetsol would flick his cigarette ash in a certain way, or pull down the lower lid of his right eye with his forefinger and stare at the offending party. Whetsol was our first unofficial disciplinarian."

Barron Wilkins's club was "the place the top entertainers and gamblers and sports stars would come in, get change for a $100 and scatter coins on the floor for the musicians and the singers. In addition, the band was paid $50 a week. The tips could be as high as $1,000 a night." Once in the limelight, Ellington could always make money.

He also sold compositions to Broadway music publishers for $20 apiece. It was a cash deal, no royalties. "The procedure . . . was very simple," Duke explained, "no hassle. Just give him the lead sheet, sign the outright release, pick up the money, and go." Among the songs he sold were "Blind Man's Buff" and "Choo Choo (I Gotta Hurry Home)." He wrote the complete score for *Chocolate Kiddies* for $500, which he split with the producer. The show went to Berlin when Josephine Baker was there and made the producer, but not Ellington, rich.

In the fall of 1923 the band switched to the Kentucky, "a low-ceilinged, dank den of a nightclub" at Broadway and Forty-ninth Street—downtown. It was a good move, because in the spring of 1924 Barron Wilkins

Dudley Murphy, Duke Ellington, and Carl Van Vechten photographed at RKO studios in Hollywood with Fredi Washington, August 21, 1929.

NIGHTCLUB MAP OF HARLEM FROM 1932 BY E. SIMMS CAMPBELL.

"was bumped off by a gunman named Yellow Charleston, who tried to stick him for getaway money after killing Yum Yum Parker," or so Jimmy Durante remembered.

The Washingtonians were at the Kentucky for four years and their fame began to spread. Paul Whiteman, Bix Beiderbecke, Tommy Dorsey, Joe Venuti, and scores of others were regular visitors to the Kentucky after other clubs around town had closed for the night. Sidney Bechet joined the band for a while before going to Paris with Josephine Baker. Duke "was not writing much of his own music in the years 1925 and 1926; rather he was twisting the pop hits of the day to the band's coloring and capacities," his biographer wrote. By 1927, though, his early education was at an end.

Andy Preer was the leader of the Missourians, the band that played at the Cotton Club in 1927. But Andy Preer died that year, and the club was looking for new musicians. They scheduled many auditions. They wanted King Oliver, Louis Armstrong's mentor, but he asked for too much money. They also wanted an eleven-piece band, since the club could hold five hundred. Ellington heard about the vacancy late and had to rush around town rounding up musicians to augment his six-piece band. "The audition was set for noon, but by the time I had scraped up eleven men it was two or three," Ellington recalled. Fortunately, gangster Owen "Owney" Madden, the club's owner, was also late. There were six other bands, but Duke's was the only one Madden heard. They were hired. The Washingtonians already had an engagement at the Standard Theater in Philadelphia. The owner refused to release them until Madden's associates in Philadelphia brought the message, "Be big or you'll be dead." Big was better, they decided.

The ambience of the Cotton Club was always one of its draws. "Impeccable behavior was expected—demanded—of the guests, particularly while the show was going on. A loud talking customer would be touched on the shoulder by a waiter. If he persisted, he was thrown out," Ellington recounted. The staff—waiters, busboys—behaved with equal decorum. The waiters at some of the other clubs did the Charleston while balancing their trays; the waiters at the Cotton Club considered such displays in extremely bad taste. Everything, from menus to drinks to meals, was served with a flourish. Located in the heart of Harlem, catering to the beautiful people of the world, the club defined good taste.

Ellington's own appearance mirrored the elegance of the club. Over the years he acquired an extensive wardrobe, dress representing the one place where public and private images were fully aligned. He even attended rehearsals in cashmere sweaters. "He has a passion for color and clothes," wrote Richard Boyer. "He has forty-five suits and more than a thousand ties, the latter collected in forty-seven states of the Union and seven European countries, and his shoes, hats, shirts, and even his toilet water are all custom-made." Words frequently used to describe him included "aristocratic in demeanor, charming, well mannered and easy with people from all walks of life." Duke considered it bad form to lose his temper or to speak ill of anyone.

Many saw self-delusion in Duke's acceptance of the club rules. Racial mixing was not considered acceptable: the Cotton Club was famous for its segregated policy—black entertainers and white audiences. English composer and music columnist Spike Hughes noted, "It is a place where no Negroes are admitted, though as a special concession the more distinguished members of the race, like Paul Robeson and Ethel Waters, are allowed, rather apologetically, to sit away in the corner." Yet in the beginning, Duke was mostly silent on this point.

The club was also famous for its "high yellow" chorus line, in which the girls also had to be "at least five foot six, able to carry a tune, and not over 21 years old," Jim Haskins wrote.

The line became so famous in fact that white women sometimes pretended to be light-skinned Negroes to get a job. Race matters in America were nothing if not complicated.

Ellington opened at the Cotton Club on December 4, 1927, having arrived from Philadelphia minutes before the performance. The modest debut featured chorus girls, lead singers, and a revue extravaganza, with the band backing them all. Jimmy McHugh, who had written the show, was nervous. He had recommended Ellington and feared they would all be fired. McHugh had a new songwriting partner, Dorothy Fields, who was twenty-three and the daughter of Lew Fields of the vaudevillian team Weber and Fields. Fields was adamant about not letting any of his children get involved in the theater, but Dorothy was persistent. While writing songs and waiting for a break, she teamed up with McHugh without telling her father, who would have objected strongly to any association with the mob-run club. But somehow she convinced him. "The owners were very solicitous of me," she wrote, and Fields was there on opening night. He brought Walter Winchell with him.

Her only effort that evening was the lyrics of a song, performed by Edith Wilson. Wilson was celebrated for her rendition of "He May Be Your Man but He Comes to See Me Sometimes," introduced in a Florence Mills revue. Without consulting Fields, the singer spiced up the lyrics on that first night. "They were so dirty, I blushed," Dorothy Fields recalled. "I told Pop I was not the author. He went to the owner, who was a big gangster of the period, and told him that if he didn't announce that his daughter did not write those lyrics he would knock his block off." The announcement was made. It was not a good beginning.

Ellington claimed that what saved the band in those early days was the other black musi-

AN EARLY CARICATURE OF ELLINGTON BY AL HIRSHFELD.

THE COTTON CLUB, 1930, WITH A LOG CABIN EXTERIOR MEANT TO EVOKE THE SOUTH. ELLINGTON OPENED THERE IN 1927.

POSTER FOR THE 1929 FILM SHORT *BLACK AND TAN*, FEATURING FREDI WASHINGTON.

ELLINGTON IN HOLLYWOOD, 1934.

Duke Ellington at the London Palladium, June 1933.
He was overwhelmed by his London reception.

Cab Calloway, who would star at the Cotton Club
when Ellington was out of town with the cast of
Brown Sugar, 1938. Photographed by Morgan and
Marvin Smith.

Ivie Anderson performing with the Duke
Ellington Orchestra, Savoy Ballroom, 1936.
Photographed by Morgan and Marvin Smith.

DUKE ELLINGTON WITH HIS COTTON CLUB ORCHESTRA, NEW YORK, 1931. ELLINGTON WAS ABLE TO KEEP MOST OF HIS BAND WITH HIM THROUGHOUT HIS CAREER, AN UNPRECEDENTED FEAT. LEFT TO RIGHT: FREDDY "LITTLE POSEY" JENKINS, TRUMPET; COOTIE WILLIAMS; SONNY GREER, DRUMS; DUKE ELLINGTON, PIANO; ARTHUR WHETSOL, TRUMPET; JUAN TIZOL; WELLMAN BRAND, BASS; JOHNNY HODGES; HARRY CARNEY, BARITONE; JOE NANTON; FRED GUY; BENNEY BIGARD.

cians of Harlem, who "talked it up uptown" even though they were not allowed to attend the club. Curiosity led the patrons of other places to check out Ellington. "We came in with a new style. Our playing was stark and wild and tense," Duke explained. Drummer Sonny Greer added, "I had a fabulous set of drums made for me, with timpani, chimes, vibraphone, everything. Musicians used to come to the Cotton Club just to see it." With the drums, Greer could manufacture all manner of jungle sounds, which became the band's signature. But it was not only the drums. Every section of the band contributed to the sound. It was exciting, it was different, it was a hit. Some people said that "Paul Whiteman and his

arranger, Fred Gafe, visited the Cotton Club nightly for more than a week but finally admitted that they could not steal even two bars of the amazing music," according to Jim Haskins.

Press agent Ned Williams remembered being unimpressed the first time he heard the band at the Cotton Club. "It didn't have the form and polish that it acquired later," he said. But he went back on "the unforgettable night when Ethel Waters stood in the spotlight, with the Ellington band pulsating behind her, and sang for the first time in public the Harold Arlen [of 'Over the Rainbow' fame] song, 'Stormy Weather.'" Ned Williams was also there the night the entire brass section rose and delivered such an "intricate and unbelievably integrated chorus that the late Eddy Duchin, usually a poised and dignified musician, actually and literally rolled on the floor under his table in ecstasy."

Within weeks of its opening, the band had become known as Duke Ellington's Jungle Band. Cotton Club patrons loved the music, which was more accessible and, some said, less creative than that played at Smalls' Paradise and the Savoy Ballroom. Success was sweet to Ellington and it became sweeter when a local radio station, WHW, began to broadcast a nightly session of his music. Then the Columbia Broadcasting System decided to extend it to a large national audience. The Cotton Club became familiar to every American who owned a radio. Tourists in New York clamored for a trip to Harlem and the club.

Sunday was *the* night at the club. "All the big New York stars in town, no matter where they were playing, showed up at the Cotton Club to take bows," Ellington explained. "Somebody like Sophie Tucker would stand up, and we'd play her song 'Some of These Days' as she made her way up the floor for a bow. It was all done in pretty grand style."

Ellington became such a hot property for the club that he finally prevailed upon them to relax their whites-only policy. After all, he argued, the families and friends of the musicians should be admitted to the club. The management reluctantly agreed but scrutinized any blacks who were let in.

Money poured into the club, tips flowed, and even waiters did not complain about their one-dollar-a-night salaries. As for the entertainers, "It didn't really matter what the salary was," Duke recalled. "A big bookmaker like Meyer Boston would come in late and the first thing he'd do was change $20 into half dollars. Then he'd throw the whole thing at the feet of whoever was singing or playing or dancing."

The band also became fond of the owner.

Owen Madden rarely showed up at the club, but when he did, he arrived in a bulletproof Duesenberg with a bevy of bodyguards. Madden, called "wraith-like, bloodthirsty and ruthless," dominated Manhattan nightlife but also earned the respect of his employees. "I keep hearing how bad the gangsters were," Sonny Greer recalled. "All I can say is that I wish I was still working for them." Elllington agreed. Another gangster, Big French DeMange, loved Ellington's music. "Anything you want, Duke, you ask for it, and it's yours," he said. They often played cards together. Because of his associates, the New York City homicide squad regularly questioned Duke: "Hey, Duke, you didn't know so-and-so, did you?' they would ask. 'No,' I'd say. But I knew them all."

Some nights Ellington would go to Connie's Inn. Connie Immerman, a Harlem native who left the area when blacks started moving in, had more liberal employment practices than Madden: he hired Fats Waller and Andy Razaf, both black, rather than McHugh and Fields, to write his scores. He maintained a similar patron policy, however: few blacks were admitted. And Connie's was expensive, Jimmy Durante said, with the average check for an evening over twelve dollars. "Connie Immerman welcomed the black musicians in the early-morning hours after they finished their stints in other clubs." Dutch Schultz was a regular.

Another favorite spot was Mexico's, "the hottest gin mill" on 133rd Street. Mexico was a nickname; the owner was from South Carolina. "You were always seeing cats walking along the streets, tubas on their shoulders, making their way over to Mexico's cutting contests," according to Duke. "We used to hang out at his place, drinking up his booze. We called it a 'ninety-nine percent,' one more degree . . . would bust your top." Duke, Miles Davis once observed, "puts everybody on."

Durante also spoke of the Lenox Club,

where the weekly breakfast dance featured big-name acts. Said Durante: "All the kings and queens of Harlem are there—and they get out on the floor and do their stuff, cool Bill Robinson and Jazz Lips Richardson and Ethel Waters and the Bon Bon Buddies. Hey, boy! They're rarin' to go at six o'clock in the morning, and so is everybody else. It was a great party."

As Duke Ellington's popularity rose, his artistic license expanded and greater originality marked his compositions. At the same time he always argued for the simplicity and naturalness of what he was attempting. He once stated about his work: "The memory of things gone is important to a jazz musician. Things like the old folks singing in the moonlight in the back yard on a hot night, or something said long ago." Memories like these, he said, "may be more important to a musician than techniques." One of his early compositions was "Mood Indigo"—the story, Duke said, of "a boy and a girl who are in love, and visit each other every day and then one day he does not come and [the song] tells how she feels." Another was "Black Beauty," one of his first musical portraits. He wrote it in honor of Florence Mills, who had died a month before he came to the Cotton Club. Over the years he wrote many such portraits,

THE DUKE ELLINGTON ORCHESTRA ONSTAGE, CHICAGO, 1933, FEATURING SONNY GREER AND HIS "CHIMES, GONGS, TOM-TOMS, SNAREDRUMS, BASSDRUMS, TYMPANIES, CYMBALS."

including "Creole Love Call," a song for Bessie Smith.

Ellington did not work alone. "I can score with a lead pencil while riding on a train. But usually I gather the boys around me after a concert—say, about three in the morning—when most of the world is quiet. I have a central idea which I bring out on the piano. At one stage, Cootie Williams, the trumpeter, will suggest an interpolation, perhaps a riff or obbligato for that spot. We will try it and, probably, incorporate it. A little later on, Juan Tizol, the trombonist, will interrupt with another idea. . . . Thus, after three or four sessions, I will evolve an entirely new composition."

When the stock market crashed in 1929, someone forgot to tell the patrons of Connie's Inn and the Cotton Club. The Ellington band appeared simultaneously at the club and in Ziegfeld's Broadway production *Show Girl*, for which George Gershwin had written the music and which introduced "An American in Paris" and "Liza." In 1930 the band went to Hollywood and appeared in the movie *Check and Double Check* with Amos and Andy. When Ellington's band was out of town, Cab Calloway, who had the same agent as Duke, filled in.

McHugh and Fields left the Cotton Club in 1930. They had already been moonlighting, writing "I Can't Give You Anything but Love" for Lew Leslie's *Blackbirds* of 1928, and they were anxious to move on. By the end of 1930 Cotton Club life had also begun to fade for Duke. He was tired of playing show tunes. One did not, of course, leave the Cotton Club, not without permission, not if you were a hit. But Cab Calloway's novel fill-in appearances had been very successful. "He waved his arms, ran back and forth between orchestra and microphone and danced in a frenzy, with his hair going one way, his coattails another," Jim Haskins explained. The audiences loved it, so gangster Madden was willing to make the change.

The Cotton Club, like the Renaissance itself, did not last forever, however. Owney Madden left in 1933 to take up residence in Sing Sing. Others took over, but the Depression caught up to the club, and it finally closed its doors in 1936.

Unlike many other black jazzmen, both Duke and Cab enjoyed enormous success performing before mostly white audiences. That was where the money was, although they were sometimes accused of selling out. The success of the two men was viewed differently by the Harlem elite, however. Though both lived on Sugar Hill, an article in *Fortune* suggested that Cab Calloway "belonged to Harlem society—having been sponsored by a Harvard-bred doctor"; Duke Ellington, however, did not. Writer Jervis Anderson found the claim hard to believe: "This was odd, in view of Ellington's personal elegance, brilliant gifts, and outstanding contributions to American music. Odd,

indeed; unless it was a case of everyone, in an unusual example of consensus, agreeing that Ellington constituted an aristocracy in himself —'beyond category.'" Ellington may have been beyond category, but the special badge of Harlem's elite should not be forgotten. Duke did not attend college; Cab had been pre-law at Chicago's Crane College. And Cab was lighter.

Ellington maintained a grueling schedule after he left the Cotton Club. The band was booked in city after city, with few long-term engagements. In 1931 he and the band were playing at a theater in Chicago. Moving into Chicago usually prompted some gangs to ask for "contributions," but they soon discovered that Duke had a big protector in Al Capone, friend of Madden, who "warned everyone to lay off Ellington." Everybody did.

The band went to Europe for the first time in 1933. Duke's reputation preceded him. In England they played the Palladium and entertained at a private party at Lord Beaver-

AT THE WHITE HOUSE AFTER A VISIT WITH PRESIDENT HERBERT HOOVER, OCTOBER 1, 1931.

brook's. The guest list included the Prince of Wales and the Duke of Kent. The prince was particularly interested in drumming and stayed close to Sonny Greer all night, observing his technique. They were all drinking gin, and by the end of the evening the Prince of Wales was calling the drummer Sonny and "I was calling him the Wale," Sonny recalled. The prince introduced Ellington as "the Duke of Hot."

When they appeared at the Champs-Élysées Theatre in France, "all of Paris was there, including every American musician and performer," Bricktop recalled. At the concert, Josephine Baker's husband, Pepito, took Bricktop aside and asked her to introduce Josephine to Duke. Bricktop thought he had nerve since he had insisted Josephine give up their friendship, but decided that holding a grudge was of no use. Baker entertained Ellington at her house. "She heaped goodies on me as though I was really somebody," Duke explained. Bricktop also invited Duke and the band to her club. The party was well under way when Josephine walked in. She had not been there in years. Also present were several young Americans who were thrilled by the celebrities in their midst. One in particular, Franklin Roosevelt Jr., son of the president, asked for an introduction to Ellington. Said Bricktop: "I brought Franklin, Jr., to the Duke's table, and he sat with Josephine on one side and the President's son on the other, having the time of his life."

ELLINGTON RETURNED FROM EUROPE with the confidence to be more experimental in his work. His music became more sophisticated. The band traveled across America during the Depression and suffered less than other performers did because Duke paid them well and protected them when he could. "If the town was in the North, Ellington could occasionally get into a hotel, since his name was well and favorably known, but the other members of the band had to scurry around the Negro section, if there was one, and make their own arrangements of lodgings." Sometimes they all went hungry before a performance because no one in the vicinity of the theater would serve them. Tours through the Deep South and the Southwest were even more problematic. To overcome these difficulties, they hired two Pullman railway coaches for the band plus a van for the luggage. By living on the trains, they avoided the trouble caused by American racial policies.

Duke continued to compose during this period. He wrote some of his best-known songs: "It Don't Mean a Thing (If It Ain't Got That Swing)," "Solitude," and "Sophisticated Lady." In fact, "the train was his sanctuary," a favorite place to work. "He would listen to the chattering of trains at crossings, to the hissing and chuffing as they left stations, and above all the whistles," biographer Derek Jewell wrote. Duke said that "especially in the South . . . the firemen play blues on the engine whistle—big smeary things like a goddam woman singing in the night." The train was also a favorite place to sleep, something he did with a concentration so intense it was difficult to wake him. It was said to take "an hour of the most ingenious torture to put the slumbering band leader on his feet." Jack Boyd, his manager, remembered a night in San Francisco "when [Duke] got off the train so sleepy he got in a line of men that were being herded into a van. They were prisoners for San Quentin. When Ellington tried to get out, the guard wouldn't let him." Boyd had to rescue him.

Unlike many of his contemporaries, Ellington was not a wealthy man. He paid his men well and never saved a lot of money. He earned $160,000 in 1939, for example, and spent $80,000 on his payroll and $25,000 in travel. Said Richard Boyer: "Duke spends money lavishly, supports a good many hanger-ons, lends money freely, gets it back infrequently, and is usually broke when the weekly pay day rolls around."

It is always difficult to put into a few paragraphs a summary of any life, especially a musical genius like Duke Ellington. "His career cannot be described in a few sentences," English-born music critic Stanley Dance pointed out. "Where would one start?" He was a man of the present and of the future, not interested in yesterdays.

"The most fascinating piece of music for him was always the one he was writing at any given moment." Duke was unique, "a constant revelation." As music critic R. D. Darrell wrote in 1932, "[His work] was alien to all my notions of jazz. It had nothing of the sprightly gusto of Gershwin or Kern, nothing of the polite polish of the Whiteman school, nothing of the raucous exuberance of the Negro jazz I had known. Nor was it in the heavily worked 'spiritual' tradition, except in that it sounded an equal depth of poignance. For all its fluidity and rhapsodic freedom it was no improvisation, tossed off by a group of talented virtuosi who would never be able to play it twice in the same way. It bore the indelible stamp of one mind, resourcefully inventive, yet primarily occupied not with the projection of effects or syncopated rhythms, but concern of great music."

Ellington performed until a few months before his death. He died of lymphatic cancer in 1974 at the age of seventy-five. "He worked hard, did not spare himself, and virtually died in harness," Stanley Dance said in his eulogy. Ellington had a distaste for all biographical portraits. "Biographies are like tombstones," he said. "Who wants one?" When Langston Hughes died in May 1967, his friends and associates conducted the funeral that he had requested. It was a celebration of blues, poetry, and jazz and ended with Ellington's "Do Nothing Til You Hear from Me." The sentiments are vintage Duke: "Pay no attention to what's said. Why people tear the seam of anyone's dream is over my head. Do nothing til you hear from me. . . . And you never will." It was a fitting tribute to Ellington, who died seven years later.

PALLBEARERS CARRYING DUKE ELLINGTON'S CASKET INTO THE CATHEDRAL OF ST. JOHN THE DIVINE, MAY 27, 1974. HE WAS 75.

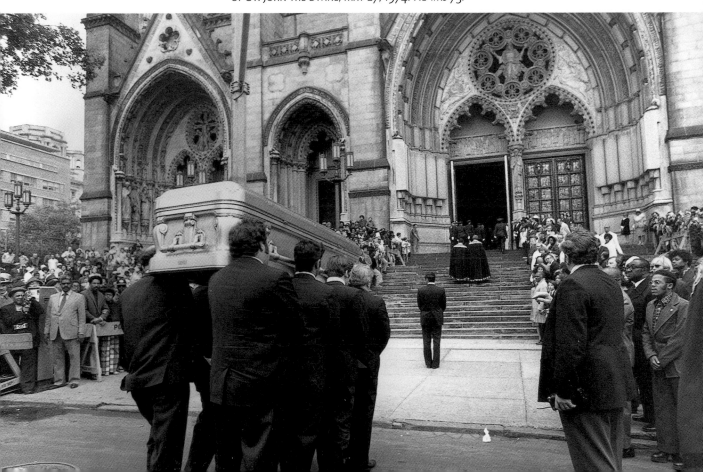

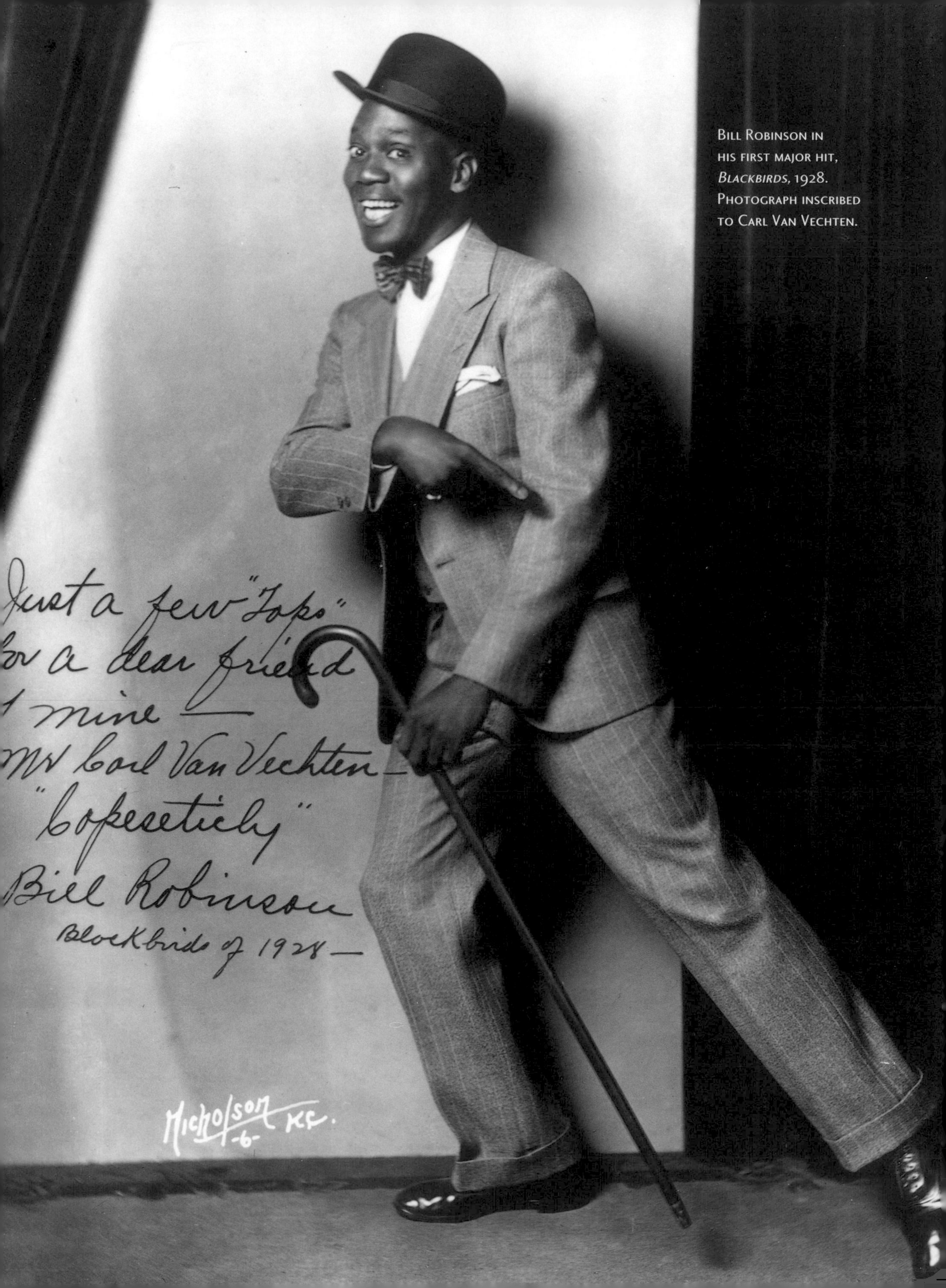

ust a few "Taps"
or a dear friend
f mine
Mr Carl Van Vechten—
"Copesetically"
Bill Robinson
Blackbirds of 1928—
Nicholson
-6-
K.C.

Bill Robinson in his first major hit, *Blackbirds*, 1928. Photograph inscribed to Carl Van Vechten.

12

BILL "BOJANGLES" ROBINSON

On December 26, 1908, Jack Johnson, a boxer born in Galveston, Texas, in 1878, defeated Tommy Burns, a Canadian, to become the first African-American heavyweight champion of the world. Johnson, a gambler, was a fancy dresser, a lover of fast cars, and a free spirit. His triumph was intolerable to many white Americans, and the search began for a "great white hope" to reclaim the title. Johnson continued victorious, however. In 1910 he fought Jim Jeffries, who had retired in 1904 never having been defeated or even knocked down and who was brought out of retirement "to remove the golden smile from Johnson's face." Jeffries was knocked down in the fifteenth round. It was the unkindest punch of all. Johnson, emboldened by victory, laughed and bragged about his powers, and there was rioting in several cities. Nineteen people were killed. Johnson's second wife, who was white, committed suicide soon after. He married again. Again his wife was white. Found guilty of violating the Mann Act, which forbade the transportation of women from one state to another for immoral purposes, he moved to Europe. At the start of World War I he left Europe for Argentina. Johnson held the title until 1915, when poor training habits and too much of the good life caused him to lose his crown to Jess Willard. At last, a great white hope had been found.

BILL ROBINSON, DECLARED Carl Van Vechten, "employed his entire body in his act. He tapped not only with his nimble feet, but also enlisted, with electrifying results, the aid of both hands, both expressive eyes, his mobile torso, and even his hat, which appeared to have a life of its own."

A hat with a life of its own is an appropriate image for a generation of black male performers who danced and whined and played the fool and made more money than most of the other black entertainers combined. Bert Williams, Johnny Hudgins, Stepin Fetchit, and most of all, Bill Robinson played powerless, slow-talking, slow-witted, fast-footed, loyal servants who were loved and tolerated like children by their employers.

Adopting a minstrel role begun after the Civil War by white actors, these black actors added to their version a bit of pathos, a dose of irony, and a heavy hand of slapstick. By the time talking pictures emerged at the end of the Renaissance era, these portrayals had been seen by a much wider audience than had the performances of Josephine Baker and Paul Robeson. Shirley Temple, the pint-sized heroine of countless epics, was ordering these black actors about and relying on their protection in almost every film she made. White audiences adored them and didn't seem to notice the odd combination of race and gender that was presented.

"Bill Robinson is a well-preserved Negro who had moved through the past fifty years to the hoarse pulsation of jungle drums," the *New York World Telegram* reported in a feature article in 1937. "The real Bill Robinson is a childish, lovable fellow who never forgets an injury or a favor." The paper's claim was strangely inconsistent with much of the detail the article provided. He was, they said, a disciplined athlete, built like a middleweight boxer, who got no more than four hours of sleep a night, jumped out of bed on many mornings to try out new steps, insisted on total silence when he performed, and ran productions he starred in like a czar, sometimes fining the sepia chorus girls for talking onstage. Somehow the professional performer never emerged from under the rhythmic taps and winsome coon songs of the performance. Bill Robinson was never a grown man; he was just a hat with a life of its own.

BILL "BOJANGLES" ROBINSON WAS BORN in Richmond, Virginia, in 1878, the grandson of an ex-slave. He never took a dancing lesson in his life. His father worked in a machine shop, and his mother was a choir singer. Both died when he was very young, and he was raised for a time by his grandmother. His only brother, Percy, became a drummer and worked as a redcap at Grand Central Station. Bill's first job was shelling peas for five cents a quart in Richmond. He ran away from home at the age of eight and earned his living by dancing on the streets for small change. When he grew older, he worked in restaurants, eventually rising to the job of waiter and "putting the tap on everything but the boss" until his obsession with dancing finally landed him employment in vaudeville, a venue he always preferred.

Over time, Bill Robinson became an accomplished tap dancer and a prominent vaudeville performer. According to Ethel Waters, "Harlem was crazy about Bojangles. They would yell 'Bo! Bo!' when they saw him." Robinson was a favorite of the common people, the "working men and women, the shoeshine boys, the cooks, the chambermaids, the elevator operators, the Pullman porters, the little shopkeepers," wrote St. Clair McKelway in an article in the *New Yorker* in October 1937. The people who, Langston Hughes argued, had never heard of the Harlem Renaissance.

Details of Robinson's educational background are sparse. The Richmond school system is said to have found him incorrigible at the age of six, when his schooling ended. He confirmed this in an interview with the *Daily News* but added that he could memorize the words and music of a song in fifteen minutes. McKelway reported that Robinson "reads only with difficulty and seldom writes anything longer than an inscription on a photograph. His conversation is largely anecdotal and his mode of verbal communication is mostly laconic." Education, however, was something Robinson valued. After becoming famous he donated a cash prize every year to the brightest student at Public School 119 in Harlem, where he gave a one-sentence graduation speech—"Boys and girls, go as high as you can"—followed by a brief dance. And he had one accomplishment that few academics could match: he added his own made-up word—"copacetic," meaning satisfactory—to the lexicon.

Bill was performing as the lower billed member of the team of Butler and Robinson in 1908 when Marty Forkins, a talent agent, agreed to handle their bookings. During one of the engagements, Robinson, who loved to gamble, got involved in a poolroom brawl in which a policeman was injured. Forkins got Robinson out of the difficulty, thereby earning his eternal gratitude. Butler and Robinson broke up, but four years later Robinson, earning $25 a week, asked Forkins to become his manager. Marty got him $75 and became his trusted adviser as well. Bill called him Boss and never made "a move in his business or personal life without consulting him." By the 1930s he was, with Forkins's help, earning $3,000 a week. Said Robinson: "I'd rather leave my wife than him. And she sure knows it too." He never left Marty.

The wife to whom he refers is Fannie, his second wife. Little is known of his first wife, Lena, whom he married in 1907 and was separated from by 1916. His biographers suggest

BILL ROBINSON ON THE DRUMS AND FATS WALLER AT THE KEYBOARD.

that his gambling, fighting, constant absences from home, and inability to save money "did not sit well with Lena." Fannie was working as a cashier in a Chicago drugstore and studying to be a pharmacist when they met in 1920. Robinson claimed it cost him a thousand dollars in sodas to court her. She was, like Lena, an educated woman, who would later help him with his reading and penmanship. Light-skinned and very attractive, she had never worked on the stage before their marriage, but afterward she traveled with him everywhere. Bill showered her with fur coats and diamonds; Harlem neighbors often saw him "out riding with his bejewelled, fur-coated spouse beside him and a chauffeur" at the wheel. They lived in a seven-room apartment and employed a maid who cooked and cleaned. Robinson never owned a car, preferring to take taxis or to be driven in the rented Duesenberg, with the license number BR6. His one regret was that he and Fannie had

BILL ROBINSON MAKING A TRANSATLANTIC PHONE CALL TO FRED ASTAIRE TO CONGRATULATE HIM ON THE BLACKFACE NUMBER FROM *SWING TIME,* ASTAIRE'S INTERPRETATION OF "BOJANGLES OF HARLEM." ROBINSON CALLED ASTAIRE THE GREATEST DANCER OF THEM ALL.

no children. "But he was," according to the *World Telegram,* "partial to them. They would cluster around him as he strutted through Harlem. Bojangles, dance! they scream and he usually does."

Robinson had a great sense of humor. Once he seated himself at a table in a Midtown restaurant in New York. A white patron complained, and the manager asked Robinson to leave. Instead he asked the manager for a ten-dollar bill. Surprised, the manager gave him one. Robinson then took six more tens from his own considerable bankroll, shuffled them, and asked the manager to close his eyes and pick the colored one. He was served.

In the mid-1920s Fred Astaire frequently visited Harlem and learned many of his dance movements from black entertainers, most notably Bill Robinson. A generous teacher, Robinson always paid tribute to Astaire, whom he called "the greatest dancer of all times." Curiously, Astaire give Robinson only passing mention in his autobiography "with no discussion of his dancing," according to Ann Douglas. His response was no different from that of a host of other white performers who borrowed steps, plots, themes, and songs from Harlem entertainers without giving them credit. What, after all, do you owe to a hat?

In 1928 Lew Leslie took a chance and used Robinson in the *Blackbirds* musical that he had planned for Florence Mills. With the show in some trouble, Leslie brought in Robinson three weeks after the opening as a featured dancer. It was a gamble that paid off handsomely and led to a run of five hundred performances. "Bojangles" became the dancing delight of Broadway. Unknown downtown at that time, Robinson "forgot the words to his big number on opening night only to win over the audience with his extraordinary dancing virtuosity," according to Andy Razaf. The most celebrated part of his act was his famous stair dance. Said James Weldon Johnson: "His stunt of dancing up and down a set of stair steps was acknowledged as a demonstration of the utmost perfection in tapping out intricate rhythms." Continuing his Broadway career, Robinson starred in *Brown Buddies* in 1930 and *Hot from Harlem* in 1931.

Robinson established a strong relationship with the local police in any city he lived or performed in, giving benefit performances and making large contributions to welfare funds. "When Bill visits another city, he invariably goes straight from the railroad station to the police headquarters, either to renew his acquaintance with the chief or to introduce himself by means of his array of documents and identification cards." He did this because of his prior difficulties with the police and his perpetual gambling problem.

Robinson also had a reputation for giving. He readily accepted almost any benefit he was asked to do. Said the *New Yorker:* "A benefit performance without him would be like a Milk Fund affair without Mrs. William Randolph Hearst." On one occasion in the midst of the Depression, he personally wrapped packages for the poor and destitute in Harlem. His generosity soon had to be halted because too many of the needy protested packages *not* wrapped by him, claiming they were given something of lesser value.

ARRIVING IN NEW YORK FROM HOLLYWOOD WITH HIS WIFE, FANNIE, AND DOG, 1935.

When in Harlem, the Robinsons resided at the Dunbar Apartments, where their neighbors were W. E. B. Du Bois, Paul and Essie Robeson, and Fletcher Henderson. The apartments, conceived and built as high-quality, low-priced housing for Harlem's working class, were financed by John D. Rockefeller Jr. Rents in Harlem were the highest in the nation, which was why there were rent parties and so much overcrowding. Rockefeller's housing complex was meant as a remedy. "By the time the great enclosed courts and gardens and playgrounds and nurseries had been constructed," however, "the rent schedule was not so low and the accommodations offered were the most luxurious in all Harlem," McKelway wrote. The Robinsons paid $100 a month for their apartment.

While the Robinsons attended benefits with the Renaissance crowd, there is very little evidence of their social intermingling. The *New Yorker* suggested that their intimates were "the spectacularly well-to-do—the dancers, the singers, the actors and actresses, the prizefighters, and the night-club proprietors." Ethel Waters recalled that when she was performing in Saint Louis, Bill came to see her and invited her to a party. "I promised to come. I forgot what happened, but at the last minute I couldn't go. I'm sorry to say that Bill never forgave me for what he took to be a slight. He always disliked me after that." But she admitted she had trouble talking to him. "They used a different language,

A CANDID SHOT OF ROBINSON WITHOUT COSTUME.

THE CAKEWALK, AS INTERPRETED BY MIGUEL COVARRUBIAS.

ON A DARE, ROBINSON RUNS BACKWARD AGAINST FRANK CUMMINGS AND JOHN RUMBO OF THE HARVARD TRACK TEAM. A. S. "POOCH" DONOVAN, HARVARD'S COACH, IS READY TO START THE RACE ON APRIL 15, 1927.

ROBINSON IN BLACKFACE WITH JOE E. BROWN, CIRCA 1936.

BILL "BOJANGLES" ROBINSON DANCING UP BROADWAY
ON HIS SIXTY-FIRST BIRTHDAY, MAY 25, 1939.
PHOTOGRAPHED BY MORGAN AND MARVIN SMITH.

BERT WILLIAMS
IN BLACKFACE.

ROBINSON WITH SHIRLEY TEMPLE IN
THE LITTLE COLONEL, 1935.

and I didn't understand it or know what to say to them," she said.

Robinson also enjoyed a career in motion pictures, benefiting from the NAACP's pressure on Hollywood to employ black actors. Prior to their push, black characters were played by whites in blackface. "Studio heads were well aware," Ann Douglas points out, "that most Americans, particularly in the South, did not want to watch Negroes on the screen." In 1919 *Birth of a Nation* was the first and most famous of these films, with an entire cast of blacks played by whites in blackface. The last, and some say the best, was Al Jolson's *The Jazz Singer*, released in 1927. *Hearts in Dixie*, made in 1929, was the first movie to feature a black actor. That actor was Stepin Fetchit, who played a "disoriented, baffled clown." Fetchit thus helped to create a niche. Others soon followed, creating slightly different versions of the bewildered menial. Robinson made four movies as the faithful, sometimes sassy, always dumb servant of Shirley Temple. In *The Littlest Rebel*, filmed in 1935, Robinson plays a slave who, because of the Civil War, is made guardian to Temple and must protect her from the Union soldiers and help her to convince President Abraham Lincoln to pardon her father, a Confederate soldier. In this oddly constructed Civil War movie, Robinson plays the faithful slave, Uncle Billy, who risks his life on numerous occasions to save the littlest daughter of the Confederacy. Explaining to her dying mother that there is nothing to fear, Temple reasons: "Uncle Billy can do anything. He can sing. He can dance. He can climb trees." Film critic Donald Bogle suggested that this was indeed the basis of the comfort. Audiences could relax knowing that the cool, confident, and contented slave would save the day, keep his head when others lost theirs, but never cease being a tree climber. The *New York Times* also seemed to recognize

this in its review: "As Uncle Billy, the faithful family butler, Bill Robinson is excellent and some of the best moments . . . are those in which he breaks into song and dances with Mistress Temple." The wooden Robinson, who walked through his part as if he were trapped in the wrong soundstage, was much more seen than heard—also appropriate slave behavior.

In *The Little Colonel*, made several months before, Robinson's servant is less stiff, flirting with the women domestics and undermining some of the authority of his employer, Temple's stubborn grandfather (Lionel Barrymore) whom Temple calls a "bad, mean, wicked, hateful old man." But Robinson's motives are always based on a deep love for the child, Temple, who is really in charge, after all, and who ends wars, saves marriages, and reunites families. Still, it is deft footwork that allows a society that lynches a black man for simply looking at white women to embrace Robinson as a child protector. An even more curious part is presented by the character Henry Clay, a black child, younger than the six-year-old Temple, pictured repeatedly eating watermelon, silent and at times looking into the camera as if he has no relationship whatsoever to the script.

Robinson met and fell in love with Elaine Plaines in 1939. A chorus girl at the Apollo Theater, she was forty years his junior. Fannie was aware of the friendship but did not think it serious. When they moved to California and Elaine moved too, however, Fannie realized her error and confronted him. She never thought Bill would leave her "for that little girl," Marty Forkins's wife claimed. Fannie and Bill had been married for over twenty years, and she had been devoted to him. But Bill was in his sixties and terrified of growing old. They divorced in 1943, and he married Elaine in 1944. The press constantly reported on public hostilities between the two women, which they both denied.

Bill Robinson was said to have earned over

three million dollars in his career. Most of it he spent, gambled, or gave away. Asked by McKelway to explain what accounted for his great success in life, Robinson, "with a faintly troubled expression, tried to sum it all up. 'I guess it's mostly my dancin', he said." Mary Austin, writing for the *Nation*, tried to analyze the aesthetics of his work for him because, she said, "Bill Robinson does not know *intellectually* that the capacity for rhythmic coordination is the fundament, not only of art but all human development." Perhaps he did know, after all.

· · · ·

BERT WILLIAMS, THE droll, comic black-in-blackface performer, was a predecessor to Bill Robinson. Williams was the first black actor to appear with an otherwise all-white cast in the Ziegfeld Follies. Writer Jim Haskins observed that Williams "was sitting on top of the entertainment world and treated like trash." He had to stay in segregated hotels, eat in segregated

BERT WILLIAMS WITHOUT MAKEUP.

restaurants, and use freight elevators while white cast members enjoyed significantly better accommodations. Williams was well aware of the hardships of being first. "We've got our foot in the door, we mustn't let it close again," he said. Williams paid a price. "Bert Williams was the funniest man I ever saw," said W. C. Fields, "the saddest man I ever knew." His sacrifice allowed those who followed to advance with more dignity.

Bert Williams was born in Antigua in 1875. "I was always a big boy for my age," he said. "No matter what age I was, I never seemed able to catch up in years with the strides that my hulk made. I had the conspicuous feeling of being overgrown in comparison to my playmates, what a Shepard dog puppy might feel in a neighborhood of pekes."

He was never fond of school. His father stated that Bert studied just enough so that he passed and his reports were good. "I am inclined to think," his father said, "that all the joy he got out of studying came from his own observations." When his father's health began to fail, the family moved to California. Bert spent his early teens there and graduated from high school with a newfound ambition to go to Stanford. Lacking the funds, he went on the stage instead. As with many of the Renaissance entertainers, his first stage was the streets. He played the banjo in San Francisco and sang simple melodies. Possessing the gift of mimicry, he perfected a southern dialect that was completely acquired—Williams had never lived in the South. To enhance his performance, Williams darkened his face with burned cork and became, according to the *New York Herald*, "a great black face comedian" by "imitating whites imitating blacks."

Bert Williams played, above all, the melancholy Negro. Luck was always against him. In "I'm a Jonah Man," a song he wrote and often performed, he sang: "When I was young, Mamma's friends to find a name they tried,/ They named me after Pappa—and de same day Pappa died." In 1889 he teamed up with George Walker, a man so different from him in temperament that they were said to form a complete whole. They were a good pair.

Walker was generous and honest; Williams loved harmony. Walker arranged the contracts; Williams had no head for business. Williams depicted the slovenly, lazy, stupid Negro; Walker was the sporty one. They called themselves Two Real Coons, because so many of the minstrels of that time were white. In 1895 they played in Chicago and were first seen by Carl Van Vechten, then a college student. Their debut on the New York stage came in 1896 in *The Gold Bug*, which starred Marie Cahill, Max Figman, and William Pruette. "*The Gold Bug* did not quite catch Broadway's fancy, but Williams and Walker did," reported James Weldon Johnson. The biggest applause went to "the Negro comedians." It was in this production that they popularized the cakewalk, which had originated in minstrel shows where white performers imitated slaves who dressed up in fancy clothes and imitated the dances of their masters. The turn-of-the-century version was blacks imitating whites imitating blacks imitating whites. In 1903 Williams and Walker introduced the cakewalk in London and taught it to the royal family. But in 1905 Walker's poor health forced him to drop out, and Bert had to go on alone. Williams never really recovered from the loss of his partner, and continued to give him the same share of the profits until Walker's death in 1907.

Williams performed by himself for a while, but in 1910 he signed with the Ziegfeld Follies. He remained loyal to the organization for over ten years. Some critics have suggested that the fame and acclaim that Williams received in the Follies masked the unfortunate waste of his talents. Writer Ring Lardner observed: "The people who wrote the Williams and Walker show knew how to write for Bert—the Follies people didn't." Bert himself said that "he was just out there to give the girls in the beautiful dancing chorus a chance to change."

Commenting on his performance at the Follies, Williams once expanded on this theme: "I often think of the old court jesters; how they used to make the guests weep before they would make them laugh, but I have to do the thing of the moment because time is too short." Columnist Heywood Broun summed it up best: "It did not seem to us that Williams was a great comedian and certainly he was not a great clown, but that was the role to which he was assigned, season after season. . . . Somehow or other laughing at Bert Williams came to be tied up in people's minds with liberalism, charity and the Thirteenth Amendment."

Bert Williams died in 1922. Harlem staged no massive ritual to mark his passing, though Langston Hughes did cut an important examination at Columbia University to attend his funeral. The editors of the *Messenger* published a somewhat bitter obituary. "Bert Williams," they said, "had the ignoble lot of dragging his people through the flotsam and jetsam of art to the derisive and vulgar hand-clapping of race prejudiced America." Bert Williams was another hat with a life of its own.

JOHNNY HUDGINS'S BLACKFACE pantomime performances were similar to those popularized by Bert Williams. "When the lights would shine on me, them folks would holler like hell," he once reminisced. The Wah-Wah man, as he was called, benefited as well from the path that Bert Williams had cleared. And he also danced—"a clever dance that stopped the show at each performance," one reviewer wrote. Born in Baltimore, where his father was an oyster shucker, he too earned money as a child dancing on the streets for small change.

"I'd never heard of Harlem," he said, but like many others, he soft-shoed his way to New York, where he performed in such productions as *Chocolate Dandies*, Sissle and Blake's 1924 follow-up to *Shuffle Along*. The *Inter-State Tattler* said that Hudgins "carries the burden of the comedy upon his shoulders, and this funny fellow surely makes a hit with the public. His clever dancing has stopped the show at each performance since the opening night and if the show has the long stay predicted, Hudgins will have a great share in its success." Unfortunately, *Chocolate Dandies* was a very expensive failure. *Variety* called it "white folks material and not good darky entertainment." That was a clarion call, and few others dared again to stray from the "minstrel-evocative stereotypes, solidly grounded in Dixie." But *Chocolate Dandies* did have one other thing, according to James Weldon Johnson: "a girl in the chorus who showed herself to be a comedienne of the first order." Her name was Josephine Baker.

Later, while playing in *Broadway Scandals*, Hudgins once fell ill with laryngitis before a performance and considered not going on. Instead he appeared as a deaf-mute and became an instant hit. Ever after, he sang and danced but never said a word. Unable to sustain his bookings in the United States, Hudgins and his wife, Mildred, went to Paris where they shared the spotlight with Josephine and Bricktop. They later traveled to South America.

STEPIN FETCHIT WITH ROBERT YOUNG
IN *CAROLINA*, 1934.

LINCOLN THEODORE MONROE ANDREW Perry was born in Key West, Florida, in 1902. He once aspired to the ministry, or so his press releases claimed. He found vaudeville instead. With another comic he had an act called "Step and Fetch It." In the late 1920s he found his way to Hollywood, and Fox signed him.

Stepin Fetchit played the lazy, slow-witted coon with such skill that he quickly became one of the best-known black American entertainers. Between 1929 and 1935 he appeared in twenty-six films. At times he worked in as many as four films at once. Directors often added parts for him in their comedies. In *Stand Up and Cheer*, for example, his character was "tricked into thinking that a talking penguin was actually a shrunken Jimmy Durante," according to film critic Donald Bogle.

Fetchit developed a character who was so stupid that he suffered few repercussions for his inactivity and inability to do as he was told. Always agreeable, he managed instead to do pretty much as he pleased. He played the jester role to its most demeaning level.

Like many of the Renaissance era entertainers, Fetchit had a private life very different from his public image. He owned six houses, employed sixteen Chinese servants, wore two-thousand-dollar cashmere suits imported from India, and had twelve automobiles. His champagne-pink Cadillac had his name on its side in neon lights. He always traveled in a caravan of three chauffeured limousines, two to carry his clothes. He gave lavish parties.

In the late 1930s civil rights groups began protesting his work and threatening to boycott the films. Even more devastating to his career, Fetchit began to seem disillusioned with the

role, and the quality of his work gradually declined. Like all of the court jesters, he struggled to give great performances in demeaning roles. The work paid well and was the only opportunity available, but it never satisfied. Fetchit eventually went bankrupt, with debts of over $4 million. Langston Hughes wrote in "Minstrel Man,"

> *Because my mouth*
> *Is wide with laughter,*
> *You do not hear*
> *My inner cry?*
> *Because my feet*
> *Are gay with dancing,*
> *You do not know*
> *I die?*

WHEN BILL ROBINSON DIED on November 25, 1949, Harlem staged its last great Renaissance funeral. It was said that 32,000 people passed by his coffin in tribute to the world's greatest tap dancer. The three thousand mourners inside the church included Jimmy Durante, Duke Ellington, Irving Berlin, Cole Porter, and Fannie, his second wife. Some 10,000 devoted fans waited outside. The "mayor of Harlem" died with an estate worth less than $25,000. His friends paid for his funeral, which was well attended because the "ordinary Negroes" of Harlem wanted to celebrate in death, as they had honored in life, one of their own. They did not seem to share the literati's concern that the court jesters like Robinson, Williams, Hudgins, and Fetchit were "content to make the world *laugh*, but not to *think*." As Langston Hughes suggested, "they hadn't heard of the Renaissance and if they had, it hadn't raised their wages any." But Mr. Bojangles, now all tapped out, had danced for them.

ABOVE AND OPPOSITE: THOUSANDS TURNED OUT TO PAY TRIBUTE TO BILL ROBINSON AS HIS FUNERAL PROCESSION MADE ITS WAY FROM HARLEM TO TIMES SQUARE FOR A MUSICAL TRIBUTE AND FAREWELL, NOVEMBER 28, 1949.

Paris: Société des Amis des Noirs

During the 1920s, Paris became home for a rather large and diverse community of American expatriates. Gertrude Stein once commented, "It was not what France gave you but what it did not take away from you that was important." Black expatriates in particular embraced Paris with the hunger of those long ignored, but perhaps they were overly generous toward a society that would as soon embrace master race theories as those of racial harmony. Tales of a brief respite in Paris are common among the Renaissance figures. Jessie Fauset, for example, told the Paris *Tribune* in 1925, "I have felt that my growth as a writer had been hampered in my own country. And so — but only temporarily — I have fled it."

In June 1932, Langston Hughes and associates left for the Soviet Union to make a movie about race relations in America. Langston Hughes is just right of center. Dorothy West, who also went, may be seated, legs crossed, in the right corner.

13

CARL VAN VECHTEN

$\mathcal{I}$N JULY 1925 JOHN THOMAS SCOPES, a twenty-four-year-old biology teacher at Central High School in Dayton, Tennessee, went on trial for teaching the theory of evolution in his high school classes, which was unlawful in the state of Tennessee. He was defended by Clarence Darrow, a champion of the underdog with a national reputation. On its side the prosecution had William Jennings Bryan, former secretary of state, three-time candidate for president of the United States, and acclaimed orator. The trial pitted "old-fashioned American idealism against twentieth-century modernism." Covering the trial were more than one hundred members of the press and several radio news services. During the trial, Darrow was accused of slurring the Bible. Bryan, after agreeing to testify as an expert on the Bible, was forced to try to defend literal interpretations of such stories as Jonah and the whale and the flood. Scopes was found guilty and fined one hundred dollars. "Old-fashioned American idealism" had been put through a humiliating ordeal and had won, at best, a Pyrrhic victory.

CARL VAN VECHTEN.

ARL VAN VECHTEN PUBLISHED his first novel, *Peter Whiffle: His Life and Works*, a biography of an imaginary person, in 1922 to much critical acclaim. His father, Charles, who read the novel and was not convinced of its excellence, wrote to his son asking for the meaning. "But there are so many," Carl replied. "To begin with, it may be taken as a picture of certain phases of a period, & a very faithful picture. The book is, of course, a moral document of the highest value, but fortunately for its prospective sales it is also amusing and may be (& has been) read by people who find it delightful. Indeed, up to date, you are the only one who has not been immensely pleased with it."

Charles Van Vechten at that time was eighty-two years old. He'd been raised in the Midwest and was uncomfortable with a modern book and, we must infer, with modernism in general. The elder Van Vechten complained: "I can't afford on nearly every page to be using the dictionary to look up words that my vocabulary doesn't contain."

In many ways, Carl Van Vechten, the wealthy white heavy-drinking author of *Nigger Heaven, was* the Renaissance. Without his constant lobbying on behalf of those he had "discovered," many of the poems, essays, short stories, and novels that constitute the rich tapestry of the period would not have been published. His close association with publisher

PORTRAIT OF A QUINTESSENTIAL VICTORIAN FAMILY, 1883.
LEFT TO RIGHT: EMMA, CHARLES, RALPH, ADA, AND
CARL VAN VECHTEN.

Alfred Knopf—"We have never had a quarrel or even a serious argument, or even a disagreement; one of us always gives in at once if the other wants something badly enough"—led to book contracts for James Weldon Johnson, Langston Hughes, and Nella Larsen.

His friendships were genuine and lifelong. At his death in 1964, the *New York Times* reported that he "received up to 25 letters a day from Negro friends." Zora Neale Hurston called him a "Negro-tarian," her word for whites who specialized in African-American uplift. The *Times*, reporting the vast array of occupations in which he excelled, described him as "critic, author, portrait photographer, collector, enthusiastic discoverer of young or overlooked talent, and lover of cats." He described himself as "unpredictable, undependable, and inefficient, an atheistic opportunist with a hankering for liquor and a variety of odd ideas about sex." His life included a fifty-year marriage to actress Fania Marinoff and a ten-year love affair with literary publicist Mark Lutz.

Van Vechten wrote seven novels—*Peter Whiffle, The Tattooed Countess, Spider Boy, The Blind Bow Boy, Firecrackers, Parties,* and *Nigger Heaven*—which were called documentary exposés of the "splendid drunken nineteen-twenties." All but *Nigger Heaven* were witty and clever and included thinly veiled portraits of the era's best-known bohemians, with the recurrent message "Let's keep this light opera." Jervis Anderson claims that Van Vechten was one of America's Sonnenkinder, a term applied to a generation of English upper-class dandies who became famous in literary circles after the First World War. They were said to be preoccupied with style, rebellious against tradition, and in love with ornament. Called by his friends "flippantly fastidious and a voyeur," Van Vechten probably would have happily pled guilty to all. Alfred Kazin suggested that he "thrived on his own affectations." He once appeared at a party dressed in "red and gold Oriental robes looking like the Dowager Empress of China, gone slightly berserk."

In 1913, long before he met Walter White and James Weldon Johnson, Van Vechten persuaded his friend Mabel Dodge Luhan "to allow two Negroes he had discovered to entertain at one of her parties." Mabel was detailed in her description: "While an appalling Negress danced before us in white stockings and black buttoned boots, the man strummed a banjo and sang an embarrassing song. They both leered and rolled their suggestive eyes and made me feel first hot and then cold, for I had never been so near this kind of thing before; but Carl rocked with laughter and little shrieks escaped him as he clapped his pretty hands."

Yet between parties, Van Vechten managed to leave a magnificent legacy. "No one in this

CARL AND HIS FATHER, CHARLES DUANE VAN VECHTEN, IN CEDAR RAPIDS, IN A POSE REMINISCENT OF AUGUST SANDER'S PORTRAITS OF GERMAN CITIZENS, 1892.

country," wrote James Weldon Johnson, "did more to forward the Harlem literary movement." His contribution to the Renaissance was twofold: he discovered the talent—"Sullenmouthed, silky haired author Van Vechten has been playing with Negroes lately, writing prefaces for their poems, having them around the house, going to Harlem," *Time* reported in 1925—and he kept the record, collecting letters, photographs, phonograph records, and manuscripts that became the foundation of the James Weldon Johnson Memorial Collection of Negro Arts and Letters at Yale University. "I became violently interested in Negroes," he explained in a 1960 interview, "violently because it was almost an addiction."

CARL VAN VECHTEN was born in Cedar Rapids, Iowa, in 1880. "I loathed it from the first," he would later write. Biographer Bruce Kellner called him "the late and last child of a financially comfortable family." His father failed at running a store on his wife's farm in Michigan and then went broke in Iowa, but he finally made money in insurance with the help of his wealthy brother. Charles Duane Van Vechten raised his son to address the blacks who worked for his family as "Mr." and "Mrs." rather than by their first names, which was the usual practice. He had helped found the Piney Woods School for Negro

Children in Mississippi, when a young black teacher in Iowa asked for his financial support. And when his son chose to call his sixth novel *Nigger Heaven*, Charles wrote to him in some distress, "I have never spoken of a colored man as a 'nigger.'" His mother, Ada Fitch Van Vechten, a college friend of activist Lucy Stone, supported the woman suffrage movement long before it was popular, and successfully lobbied the state legislature to fund the first Cedar Rapids Free Public Library.

Carl, whose siblings were much older than he was, grew up without the companionship of other children. He did grow up, however, with Grandmother Fitch, his mother's mother, who smoked a pipe and predicted that Carl would die on the gallows. She was fond of urinating on the front lawn, to the embarrassment of her daughter, who feared for the neighbors, and her son-in-law, who feared for the grass. Carl, on the other hand, "was enchanted, watching the great bell skirts billow out as she sank into position."

By the age of thirteen, Carl was six feet tall—an unusual height for the time, at least a head taller than most with whom he is pictured—awkward and uncoordinated. He also had two very large protruding front teeth, never straightened by the primitive and painful orthodontia of the 1890s. At their first meeting, many years later, actress Mae West pronounced him "blond, buck-toothed, bored and chi-chi."

Friends remembered that both his looks and his behavior were strange. "We thought him very odd, queer almost," one suggested. "Carl wasn't any good at ball—he wasn't any good at the things the rest of us did—but he did almost everything we couldn't do." Luckily for Carl, he was not entirely alone during those years. He had a girlfriend, Anna Elizabeth Snyder. A handsome girl nearly six feet tall, she was his "most constant companion through his teens."

Her eccentricity matched his. Anna was said to be "remote," to possess a "maddening serenity," and to project an aura of indifference. It was assumed that she and Carl would marry.

At the end of the century Anna left Iowa to go to Wellesley and Carl to attend the University of Chicago. "Chicago was actually not much better, but I did not know that yet," he recalled. Quickly bored with classes and college life, he began to investigate Chicago's theater district. He also discovered ragtime and black performers as a 1900 photograph, one of his earliest, of the famous black minstrels Bert Williams and George Walker suggests. After graduating from the university in 1903, Carl became a reporter for the *Chicago American*, a Hearst newspaper. His increasingly satirical pieces in the society column about Chicago matrons—"She has studied herself and decided she could wear all the colors at once!"—drew their ire, which Carl over the years would embellish, saying he "was discharged for lowering the tone of the Hearst newspapers."

Tiring of Chicago (properly read fired), Carl, who in the early years was constantly short of money, decided to go to New York. Already in debt to his father, he had to borrow from him once again to finance the trip. After doing some successful freelance work, he was hired as a cub reporter for the *New York Times*. New York's conservatism in the arts, particularly in regard to opera, bothered Carl, however, and he longed to go to Europe, a desire that was stimulated by Anna's vivid reports on opera in Europe during a postgraduation tour. Carl wrote to ask his father for additional funds. "How much money do you have on hand?" his father replied. "What particular advantage is there in listening to the opera in European cities that you don't have in New York?" Having failed in his first attempt to secure funds, Carl applied a second time, proposing to borrow on his life insurance. "You take my breath," his father wrote back, still providing no money. Finally Carl admitted that he also planned to marry Anna in Europe. This delighted his father: "Dearest boy, why didn't you tell me what you wanted on the very start & save me the humiliation I now feel. I should not have argued with you a moment." In 1907 Carl arranged for a leave of absence from the *New York Times*, and he and Anna were married in England.

Back in New York, Carl was promoted to assistant to music critic Richard Aldrich and was assigned to cover performances Aldrich felt were not worthy of his presence. Carl was the first to cover newcomers Anna Pavlova and Isadora Duncan. From his position at the *Times*, he was quickly absorbed into the New York musical and theatrical scene. As assistant critic, he was given passes to all of the performances, but passes were not provided for Anna. So Carl,

who was devoted to his work, spent more and more time away from home. The marriage, which had always been most strongly based on a mutual "desire to escape Cedar Rapids," crumbled under the neglect. In the spring of 1912 Anna sued for divorce, claiming that Carl was discovered in a dalliance—actually, it was a prearranged encounter mutually agreed upon, meant to satisfy the state's divorce laws. The court ordered Carl to pay Anna twenty-five dollars a week in alimony.

The divorce liberated Carl. He threw himself into his work and into a social life centered on the "thousand and one queer little places" he'd found in New York. His good friends included not only Mabel Dodge Luhan but also Gertrude Stein, H. L. Mencken, Theodore Dreiser, Sinclair Lewis, and Fannie Hurst. Two months after the divorce, he dined alone at Claridge's in New

THIS 1906 MARTHA BAKER PHOTOGRAPH OF VAN VECHTEN, NOW CLEARLY A TWENTIETH-CENTURY MAN, WAS ENTITLED BY MABEL DODGE LUHAN ABOUT 1913 "THE CONSCIOUS DESPAIR OF IRREVOCABLE DECADENCE."

York, a favorite restaurant of singers and actors. Seeing a friend across the room dining with an attractive young companion, he asked for an introduction. It was there he first met Fania Marinoff, an actress. A child of Russian-Jewish immigrants, Fania's early life had been as impoverished as Carl's was privileged. Seven years his junior, she had begun performing on the stage in minor parts at age twelve. By the time he met her, she was fairly well known in New York theatrical circles.

In 1913 Carl left the *Times* for the *New York Press*, where he turned his attention to the theater. He wrote to Fania in May: "I went to see the managing editor today and the dramatic position on that paper seems to be mine for the middle of August. Everything does seem to be working out." Unfortunately, this assessment was premature, as he was hired in September and fired in May because of disagreements with the publisher. He was given two weeks' severance salary and two weeks' vacation pay. Never one to let diminished circumstances interfere with his daily life, he married Fania Marinoff in October 1914. Anna sued him for back alimony several months later, believing his marriage meant that his financial situation had improved. When he refused to pay, she threatened him with jail. Carl wrote to his friend Edna Kenton, a Greenwich Village writer, "I have really been postponing writing to you because I expected to be in jail now." In characteristic fashion, he had made elaborate plans. "I am expecting jail daily, from the portals of which I shall send forth manifestoes about love, life, and liberty. I have been promised a Matisse, two Persian rugs, and a telephone. Perhaps you will send literature. If I stay there six months I shall have read everything." His stay was about four weeks, as it turned out. Press accounts varied. One suggested that he was carried off to jail, screaming. Another headline implied that he was happy in jail: "Resents the Intrusion of the Turbulent Outer World, Revels in Turgenieff; Recipient of Many Gifts." He was released in early April, having agreed to pay Anna $783 in cash, an obligation for which he went deeper into debt. Anna left for Europe.

Unemployed and without funds, Carl searched for new sources of revenue while living on Fania's income from the theater. At the suggestion of a friend, he gathered together and rewrote several essays he had done on music and the ballet. The volume, *Music After the Great War* was published by Schirmer, the music publishing company. Although it sold only moderately well, it received favorable reviews and began a new career for Van Vechten. His next effort—a series of essays on painters, writers, and musicians and some autobiography—was rejected by Schirmer and thirteen other publishers. Carl sent it to Alfred Knopf, who had just founded a publishing house. Knopf disliked the essays but liked Carl's work on music and suggested a new project, which was eventually published by Knopf as *Music and Bad Manners* in November 1916. With critical acclaim surrounding the second book, Carl's writing career was launched. In 1918 he wrote to Fania: "Dearest Baby, I'm afraid I have enough work now to last me for forty years. Freddo Knopf called me up yesterday and presented me with Underhill's emendations and suggestions for my Spanish book [*The Music of Spain*, 1918]. As a result the back room looks like a factory." By the 1920s, when Carl began writing novels, his financial fortunes were ensured. His first novel went through eight printings in the first year. *Nigger Heaven*, published in 1926, went through nine printings in four months. In 1928 his brother Ralph added to his coffers by leaving him a million dollars in trust.

Carl Van Vechten with Fania Marinoff, photographed by Nickolas Muray, 1922.

FANIA MARINOFF, ACTRESS, N.D. SHE SAID IN 1932 SHE "HAD TASTED ALL THE DRINKS IN ALL THE SPEAKEASIES, IT WAS ALL VERY HOLLOW."

VAN VECHTEN'S FAVORITE CARICATURE WAS THIS ONE BY COVARRUBIAS, INSCRIBED "A PREDICTION."

a prediction to Carl from COVARRUBIAS.

THE NEGRO

as author and   as subject

THE AUTOBIOGRAPHY OF AN EX-COLOURED MAN

By *James Weldon Johnson*

With an Introduction by *Carl Van Vechten*

A rare, much-sought source-book about Negro life in America, first published anonymously in 1912, and at length made really accessible. In its account of inter-racial contacts, especially in the South, it is still probably the wisest, most restrained, and most comprehensive thing on its subject. There are passages which, once read, can never be forgotten—notably, among others, that on a lynching in the South. In short, here is a novel which is not fiction—and which is, by any standard, literature. $3.00

AT ALL BOOKSHOPS OR FROM THE CRISIS

Alfred A. Knopf,

In Canada, from The Macmillan Company of

NIGGER HEAVEN
By
Carl Van Vechten

Recognized in every quarter, including the colored press, as *the* portrayal of contemporary life in Harlem.

Twelfth large printing. $2.50

THE WEARY BLUES

FINE CLOTHES TO THE JEW

By *Langston Hughes*

Two volumes of poems that belong most poignantly to the race. Others appreciate them as literature, and realize that they are good. But the Negro himself knows that their substance is his very birthright.

Each, $2.00

Publisher, New York

Canada, Ltd., St. Martin's House, Toronto

BORZOI BOOKS

ALFRED A. KNOPF'S ADVERTISEMENT IN *CRISIS* FOR *THE AUTOBIOGRAPHY OF AN EX-COLOURED MAN* AND *NIGGER HEAVEN. CRISIS* EDITOR W. E. B. DU BOIS GAVE *NIGGER HEAVEN* A STINGING REVIEW.

OPPOSITE: THE EVER-PRESENT VAN VECHTEN PHOTOGRAPHED
BY NICKOLAS MURAY IN FRONT OF THE ALGONQUIN,
THE WRITER'S MECCA, WITH THE LATEST CAMERA EQUIPMENT,
A LEICA, MAY 17, 1937.

POSTCARD OF FANIA MARINOFF AND
CARL VAN VECHTEN, MAY 1915.

"GO INSPECTIN WITH CARL VAN VECHTEN,"
WROTE ANDY RAZAF.

OPPOSITE: SELF-PORTRAIT,
MARCH 9, 1934,
CAPTURING VAN VECHTEN'S
CHARISMATIC GRACE.

A RARE MOMENT. CARL VAN VECHTEN AND MIGUEL COVARRUBIAS,
THE TWO MAIN CHRONICLERS OF THEIR ERA, PHOTOGRAPHED
TOGETHER, MAY 17, 1937, BY NICKOLAS MURAY.

IN ADDITION TO ESSAYS AND NOVELS, letter writing was something of an art form for Van Vechten. He wrote on distinctive stationery that was either buff, lavender, canary yellow, or raspberry with his name sometimes watermarked into the paper. His letters were almost always typed, filled with abbreviations of his own invention, and ending with affectionate closings like "poppies and cornflowers to you." As a record of the period, they are invaluable. "Almost everything is happening here, beside our going to war," he wrote to Gertrude Stein in April 1917. "Everything" included Sarah Bernhardt's successful kidney operation and a rousing performance by Isadora Duncan, who "comes out slightly covered by an American flag of filmy silk and awakens still more enthusiasm. I tell you she drives 'em mad." In 1921 he wrote to Fania, who was appearing out of town, about his evening with Mabel Dodge and her fourth husband, Tony Luhan. "We had a special seance of medicine songs, appeals to the gods of water, fire, etc. in Tony's room. Mabel and I sat on the bed, while Tony and John [Evans, Mabel Dodge Luhan's son] in their full Indian regalia, banged tom-toms, shook gourds, and sang."

There were also hundreds of letters about the legendary parties with George Gershwin, Tallulah Bankhead, Paul Robeson, Fannie Hurst, Salvador Dalí, and James Weldon Johnson. Always integrated after 1924, these parties were filled with brilliant talk and plentiful drink, and few guests were left standing at the end of the night. "They were so Negro," Langston Hughes reported, "they were written up as a matter of course in the colored society columns just as though they occurred in Harlem." Walter White referred to the Van Vechtens' apartment on West Fifty-fifth Street as the "midtown branch of the NAACP."

Walter White was the first of the Harlem crowd Van Vechten met. He had read and been fascinated by *The Fire in the Flint* and asked Knopf for an introduction. He wrote to Edna Kenton: "Walter White, the author of *The Fire in the Flint*, spent two hours with me the other day. He speaks French and talks about Debussy and Marcel Proust in an offhand way. An entirely new kind of Negro to me. I shall, I hope, see something of these cultured circles." To Mabel Dodge Luhan, he wrote: "I'm causing to have sent to you soon a novel, *The Fire in the Flint*, written by a Nigger. It is some document & I want you to talk about it & write intriguing letters around the world about it. I was thinking the other day if all your acquaintances read a book that it would sell out three large editions."

Walter White introduced Carl Van Vechten to James Weldon Johnson, and their friendship was lifelong. "We became intimate friends almost immediately," Van Vechten wrote. "It was not long before I heard him recite (this is certainly not the word; probably intone would be better) 'The Creation,' his first sermon in poetic form. This performance was repeated many times; one evening after dinner at HIS apartment before the enthusiasm of Clarence Darrow and Newman Levy; several times at my apartment; certainly on one occasion when Paul Robeson sang 'Let My People Go.'" Near the end of 1925 Carl wrote, "Dear Grace and James, Thank you—and bless you. Perhaps the most important thing to me of the past year has been the growth of our intimacy."

Through Johnson, Van Vechten met Langston Hughes and Countee Cullen. He arranged, soon after, for their poems to be published in 1925 issues of *Vanity Fair*. Hughes's first volume of poems, *The Weary Blues*, was published by Alfred Knopf at Van Vechten's instigation. He also wrote the preface. It began, "At the moment I cannot recall the name of any other person whatever who, at the age of twenty-three, has enjoyed so pic-

A birthday party for Carl Van Vechten, James Weldon Johnson, and Alfred Knopf Jr. Standing, left to right: Ettie Stetheimer, Van Vechten, Johnson, Witter Bynner, poet, and Grace Nail Johnson. Seated: Blanche Knopf, Pat and Alfred Knopf at a party at the Knopfs' Connecticut retreat, June 17, 1931.

turesque and rambling an existence as Langston Hughes." It would also be difficult to think of the number of twenty-three-year-olds, white or black, who had a published book of poetry. Over the course of their forty-year friendship, they exchanged over six hundred letters. In one of the earliest, Van Vechten wrote to Hughes: "Your letters are so very charming, dear Langston, that I look forward every morning to finding one under the door." In March 1927, when yet another negative review of *Nigger Heaven* appeared in the black press, Hughes wrote to commiserate. Van Vechten replied: "Thanks a lot for what you say about *me*. Thanks a lot for your paper which I think is superb. The situation is easy to explain. You and I are the only colored people who really love *niggers*."

Langston was a regular at the Van Vechtens' parties. He remembered with great fondness one where "Chief Long Lance of the cinema did an Indian war dance, while Adelaide Hall of *Blackbirds* played the drums, and an international assemblage crowded around to cheer." At

a gossip party held on George Washington's Birthday, "everybody was at liberty to go around the room repeating the worst things they could make up or recall about each other to their friends on the opposite sides of the room." Hughes met Somerset Maugham, Hugh Walpole, Fannie Hurst, and Salvador Dalí at the Van Vechtens' parties. Carl wrote to Hughes about a cocktail party at the home of Dorothy Petersen, Nella Larsen's friend, followed by an *Opportunity* dinner where "the principal excitement was our late arrival, slightly soused, about which there was much unfavorable comment." Van Vechten loved Petersen and based the heroine of *Nigger Heaven* on her.

Van Vechten's friendship with Countee Cullen was less warm, although in 1925 he wrote to Fania that Countee was giving him his first Charleston lesson. After accepting his initial assistance, Cullen rejected further offers. As Bruce Kellner points out, though, Cullen's promising career did not last much beyond the decade of the twenties. This is testament perhaps to Van Vechten's ability to get people published. Still, their lack of close association did not diminish Van Vechten's respect for Cullen's work. In 1942, when he was gathering materials for the James Weldon Johnson Memorial Collection, he called the two boxes of Cullen manuscripts "the gems in the Crown of the Collection." It may be that Cullen shared with his friend Jessie Fauset a suspicion of Van Vechten. Fauset thought that Van Vechten's influence had corrupted Hughes. Also, Cullen's "sometime lover, perhaps" Harold Jackman was also Van Vechten's friend (no dalliance was ever confirmed), a situation that might have caused strain in their relationship.

It was not only the literati whom the Van Vechtens befriended. Carl was fascinated by Bessie Smith. He collected "boxes and boxes of [her records] which I played and played in the early Twenties and everybody who came to my apartment was invited to hear them." He saw her in performance for the first time on Thanksgiving Day, 1925, at the Orpheum Theater in Newark, New Jersey. "Forced to rise from the dinner table shortly after eight o'clock," Carl and two friends made their way to Newark, where the audience was "a vast sea of happy dark faces." Van Vechten pointed out that "there was not a mulatto or a high yellow visible among these people." The performance and the performer were mesmerizing:

JAMES WELDON JOHNSON AND CARL VAN VECHTEN AT FIVE ACRES, PHOTOGRAPHED BY FANIA, OCTOBER 2, 1926. "I WAS INTRODUCED TO JAMES WELDON JOHNSON IN 1924 AND WE BECAME INTIMATE FRIENDS ALMOST IMMEDIATELY," VAN VECHTEN RECALLED.

Walking slowly to the footlights, to the accompaniment of the wailing, muted brasses, the monotonous African pounding of the drum, the dromedary glide of the pianist's fingers over the responsive keys, she began her strange, rhythmic rites in a voice full of shouting, and moaning and praying and suffering, a wild, rough Ethiopian voice, harsh and volcanic, but seductive and sensuous too, released between rouged lips and the whitest of teeth, the singer swaying slightly to the beat, as is the Negro custom.

Bessie Smith also came to the Van Vechten home in 1928. Carl recalled the visit. "Fania Marinoff and I were throwing a party. George Gershwin was there and Marguerite D'Alvarez and Constance Collier, possibly Adele Astaire. The drawing room was well filled with sophisticated listeners." Bessie wanted a drink before she would sing. She asked for whiskey, but was, to her annoyance, given straight gin, and with one gulp she downed a glass holding nearly a pint. Then, with a burning cigarette in her mouth, she got down to the blues. "I am quite certain that anybody who was present that night will never forget it. This was no actress; no imitator of a woman's woes; there was no pretense. It was the real thing: a woman cutting her heart open with a knife until it was exposed for us all to see, so that we suffered as she suffered, exposed with a rhythmic ferocity, indeed, which could hardly be borne." It was, Van Vechten concluded, "her greatest performance."

Everybody in New York remembered this as the night that Bessie, reeling from drink, knocked Fania Marinoff to the floor for trying to kiss her good night. "Get the fuck away from me. I ain't never heard of such shit," Bessie is said to have shouted. According to Ann Douglas, "Bessie herself loved to tell the tale, complete with wicked imitations of the distressed and dicty [Porter] Grainger [her accompanist] and the oh-so-polite Van Vechtens and their guests. 'Shit,' she exclaimed, 'you should have seen them ofays lookin' at me like I was some kind of singin' monkey!'"

Apparently her behavior toward Fania did not affect their acquaintance. In fact, in 1936 Bessie came to their apartment to be photographed by Van Vechten, who later wrote, "She was making one of her final appearances (although we were not aware of this fact) at a downtown nightclub and she came to see me between shows, cold sober and in a quiet reflective mood." He believed that the photographs he took that day were perhaps "the only adequate record of her true appearance and manner that exist."

While Van Vechten admired Bessie Smith, he thought Ethel Waters was "superior to any other woman stage singer of her race." He knew Ethel when she sang in Harlem dives such songs as "You Can't Do What My Last Man Did" and was condemned by upper-class Harlem. He first heard her perform "Georgia Blues" at the Lafayette Theater, where he was taken by James Weldon Johnson. It took several attempts for him to finally meet her because she mistrusted white people and had never heard of Carl Van Vechten. With the intervention of intermediaries, a meeting was finally arranged. "At any rate," Van Vechten wrote, "it was not too long before we became great friends; I broke down part of her prejudice against pink people and I broke down part of social Harlem's prejudice against her." But he never claimed to have discovered her. "I am probably the only person in America, pink or brown, connected with her early life in any way, who doesn't claim that he discovered her." He did say that after their initial meeting, whenever she appeared on Broadway or in Harlem, he was there, cheering. "Occasionally she came to our apartment for dinner or a party." And in 1934 he began to photograph her. Over the years, he collected a "nearly complete set of her recordings." On April 30, 1931, he wrote to Johnson, "the enormous Majestic Theatre in Brooklyn has dusted up the SRO sign and is using it for the first time in weeks. The GREAT Ethel Waters had at last come into her Kingdom."

CARL VAN VECHTEN WITH BILL ROBINSON. VAN VECHTEN MAINTAINED FRIENDLY RELATIONS WITH MOST OF THE RENAISSANCE FIGURES REPRESENTED HERE.

VAN VECHTEN'S ATTITUDES toward race changed over time. Like many whites of his age and class, he saw at first an appealing primitivism in blacks. He shared with Charlotte Mason the view that primitives, by a return to nature, would save a rotting civilization—or at least save him from a life of boredom. In 1925 he wrote to Gertrude Stein: "I shall start my Negro novel. I have passed practically my whole year in company with Negroes and have succeeded in getting into most of the important sets."

He moved from there to a rather astute assessment of the commercial value of the Renaissance, serving as "agent, PR man, banker, and confidant to a host of talented Harlemites" and called by the *Herald Tribune* "the beneficent godfather of all of sophisticated Harlem." For a *Crisis* symposium, he asked, "Are Negro writers going to write about this exotic material (the special gift in the arts that black folk gave to America) while it is still fresh or will they continue to make a free gift of it to white authors who will exploit it until not a drop of vitality remains?" But over time his friendships with James Weldon Johnson and Langston Hughes, among others, caused him to once again revise some of his ideas. He particularly loved his correspondence with Hughes and through it began to get an understanding, if not of the race problem, at least of Hughes's point of view. In *Nigger Heaven*, through the character of Hester Albright—probably based on Jessie Fauset—he expresses all of the frustration that the younger members of the movement experienced. "[Hester] particularly assumed an aggressive and antagonistic attitude toward the new literary group which was springing up in Harlem," he wrote. "This antagonism was inspired by the fact that this younger group was more inclined to write about the squalor and vice of Harlem life than about the respectable elegance of Washington

society." Hughes often said the very same thing. But on a more profound level, Van Vechten has Byron Kasson complain: "Nigger Heaven! That's what Harlem is. We sit in our places in the gallery of this New York theatre and watch the white world sitting down below in the good seats in the orchestra. Occasionally they turn their faces up toward us, their hard, cruel faces to laugh or sneer, but they never beckon." This is a view of Harlem in which Jessie Fauset would concur.

One of the more enlightening assessments of Van Vechten came from Claude McKay. They met in Paris after the publication of *Nigger Heaven* and McKay's even rawer *Home to Harlem*. It was to be a grand meeting of the outcasts of the talented tenth. McKay had been warned by other friends that Van Vechten "patronized Negroes in a subtle way, to which the Harlem elite were blind because they were just learning sophistication." McKay did not find this to be the case, pronouncing Carl "quite all right." Still McKay's reaction was negative because Van Vechten, drunk, lapsed into silence upon learning that McKay was not drinking, then excused himself to go to the men's room and stiffed him with the bill. They became friendly but were never friends.

Van Vechten's empathy for the Harlem community also served a purpose. As journalist George Schuyler, who wrote the satiric novel *Black No More*, explained:

Most of the white people of Van Vechten's circle knew Negroes only as domestics and had never had them as associates. It was extremely daring for a white person to dine publicly with a Negro, and certainly to dance with one: but if those of the upper crust could be weaned over to such social acceptance, it was likely that a trend would be started which would eventually embrace the majority of those whites who shaped public opinion and set the social pace.

To this laudable endeavor Carl Van Vechten and his famous actress wife Fania Marinoff, devoted themselves as assiduously as any sincere revolutionists could. Once the idea took hold it spread in geometric progression.

Van Vechten faced his severest critics within the black community over the publication of *Nigger Heaven*. Du Bois called it "A blow in the face, an affront to the hospitality of the black-fold and to the intelligence of the white." Smalls', one of Van Vechten's favorite cabarets in Harlem, banned him from the premises. The *Pittsburgh Courier* refused to run ads for the book until persuaded to do so by Walter White. Like White, Hughes and James Weldon Johnson supported their friend and the work. Hughes claimed that most of those who opposed the novel had not read it. Johnson in a review published in the Urban League journal *Opportunity* wrote: "Mr. Van Vechten is the only white novelist I can think of who had not viewed the Negro as a type, who had not treated the race as a unit, either good or bad." Present at the signing of the contract for the book, Johnson later wrote a prophetic epitaph for his friend:

Here lies the tallow-headed late
Idol of the sophisticate:
He kneads his dough with a dingy leaven;
He rolls his own and shouts "Come seven!"
He's got wings in Nigger Heaven.

As Bruce Kellner has observed, "in 1932 Van Vechten took up the hobby of photography and for the next thirty years faithfully, like a 'messianic missionary,' preserved for posterity the images of black artists and writers."

NICKOLAS MURAY'S PORTRAIT OF VAN VECHTEN, 1922. "YOU HAVE HAD SUCH A TREMENDOUS INFLUENCE ON THE ARTS OF THE LAST TWENTY-FIVE YEARS, THAT I THINK IT OUGHT TO BE PRECIPITATED OUT OF THE MASS OF LIES THAT ARE NOW GROWING UP," WROTE ZORA NEALE HURSTON IN 1948 SHORTLY BEFORE HER DISAPPEARANCE.

14

LANGSTON HUGHES

*T*HE FIRST MASS EXODUS of African-Americans from the South began in 1916. The migration started slowly. Job seekers, hearing of fabulous opportunities in Pittsburgh, Detroit, and, most of all, Chicago, could not rest in their beds for wanting to take off for the promised land. Labor agents combed the cities of the South, searching for workers and offering free railroad passes. The numbers of migrants began to swell. James Weldon Johnson witnessed more than twenty-five hundred people leaving in one day from a southern rail station "on a train run in three sections, packed in day coaches, with all their baggage and all their impedimenta." They came "from the docks of Norfolk, Savannah, Jacksonville, and New Orleans, from the cotton-fields of Mississippi, and the coal mines and steel mills of Alabama and Tennessee," Johnson wrote. By 1918 more than one-tenth of the African-American population had moved from South to North. The Great Migration was under way.

PORTRAIT OF LANGSTON HUGHES BY NICKOLAS MURAY, 1924.

Langston Hughes wandered throughout his life. He wandered in and out of Harlem, across the Americas, up and down the west coast of Africa, and through France and Italy and Russia. It was a journey of discovery, of his race, his roots, himself. All who knew him loved the awe and wonderment of this child-innocent. Some grew to hate that, over time, he never seemed to age.

"My theory," Langston Hughes wrote, "is that children should be born without parents —if born they must be." These thoughts of an old poet, written not long before his death, reveal much of what propelled the shy, handsome young man into the heart of the Harlem Renaissance. Hughes, the blessed "child that's got his own," paid, in the words of biographer Arnold Rampersad, "in years of nomadic loneliness and a furtive sexuality; he would die without ever having married, and without a known lover or a child." Langston Hughes was the bard of the Renaissance, who, like the bard of James Weldon Johnson's poem, "sang far better than he knew."

Early in his life, Langston Hughes laughed a lot, "loud laughter in the hands of fate." It was armor he never removed. Ignored by his father, whom he hated, and abandoned countless times by a mother he loved, he "learned to play a wild free tune upon his flute," but not to find solace in the exercise.

No other figure quite captured the spirit of the era as clearly as Langston Hughes did. No other figure produced so many volumes of poems, plays, fiction, humor, autobiography, and letters. No other figure has been so widely read. Yet none is harder to know or understand. Langston Hughes represents all the constituent parts of this book: the poetry, the blues, the jazz, the scholarship. He represents all the parts and something more. In the poem "Beggar Boy," the poet asks, "What is in this

beggar lad,/That I can neither know nor understand,/And still it calls to me?"

Langston Hughes was born on February 1, 1902, in Joplin, Missouri. His father, James Nathaniel Hughes, was a stenographer for a mining company; his mother, Carrie Mercer Langston, "light olive in complexion, stylish and popular," was the belle of the black community. The ambitious James, who hated blacks and being black, soon went to Cuba and then to Mexico to make his fortune. Carrie and Langston stayed behind at the home of her mother, where they lived in poverty.

Frequently in search of employment, Carrie often placed Langston in the care of her mother, who was "past seventy and rarely left her home." In 1908 Carrie moved to Topeka, Kansas, sent for Langston, and put him in school. But in 1909 she sent him back to his grandmother. Somewhere along the way Carrie married Homer Clark, a cook and steel mill worker. When Carrie's mother died in 1915, Langston moved to Lincoln, Illinois, to live with his mother, his stepfather, and his stepbrother. A lonely child but a good student, Langston was named class poet of the eighth grade. Said Hughes: "In America most white people think, of course, that *all* Negroes can sing and dance, and have a sense of rhythm. So my classmates, knowing that a poem had to have rhythm, elected me unanimously—thinking, no doubt, that I had some, being a Negro."

The one and only thing that Hughes believed in at that time was books. "In nothing but books and the wonderful world in books—where if people suffered, they suffered in beautiful language, not in monosyllables as we did in Kansas, " he wrote in his autobiography, *The Big Sea*.

The family moved to Cleveland in 1916,

where he attended high school. "Rents were very high for colored people in Cleveland," he observed, "and the Negro district was extremely crowded, because of the great migration. It was difficult to find a place to live." The school had a majority of students of foreign-born parents when Hughes was there. There was an almost fifty-fifty split between Catholics and Jews. "That was perhaps why I held many class and club offices in high school, because often when there was a religious deadlock, a Negro student would win the election." It was in high school in Cleveland that he published his first stories and verse in the student newspaper.

In 1919, at the age of seventeen, he received a letter from his father, the first communication in eleven years, instructing him to board a train in Cleveland for the purpose of spending the summer in Mexico. His mother was furious, but Langston wanted to see Mexico and to see a father who in his absence had become larger than life. When the family moved from the address where his father had contacted him, Langston made elaborate plans to have any message forwarded. But as luck would have it, he failed to receive until the next day the one telegram that was sent. Fearing that his father had gone on to Mexico without him, Langston called several Cleveland hotels in the hope of finding him. He did. James had stayed and Langston rushed to find him. When they met, his father demanded to know why he was not on the train.

BABY PICTURE OF HUGHES WITH HIS MOTHER, CARRIE.

When he was told they had moved, his response was: "Just like niggers. Always moving!" He then instructed his son to meet him in half an hour for the trip. "He never said a word about being glad to see me," Hughes wrote. Hastily, he said good-bye to his mother, who was still angry. "Sure, go on!" she told him. "Hard as I've worked and as little as you care about me." He went with his father to Mexico and had a miserable summer. "I did not hear from my mother for several weeks. I did not like my father. And I did not know what to do about either of them."

Hughes returned to Cleveland in the fall and to his senior year in high school. He was again elected class poet and now became editor of the yearbook as well. Langston's father again told him to come to Mexico to discuss his future. His father hinted at a promise of college tuition. "I didn't want to return to Mexico, but I had the feeling I'd never get any further education if I didn't, since my mother wanted me to go to work and be, as she put it, 'of some use to her.'" Rationalizing that he could be more use to her with more education, he returned to Mexico. His mother reacted much as she had before.

"I felt guilty for the next three or four years, to tell the truth," he wrote, "and those were the years when I wrote most of my poetry. (For my best poems were all written when I felt the worst. When I was happy, I didn't write anything.)" While on the train traveling to Mexico, he composed the poem that first caught the attention of Jessie Fauset at the *Crisis*. "I've known rivers ancient as the world and older than the flow of human blood in human veins," he wrote. "My soul has grown deep like the rivers."

When Langston got to Mexico, his father laid out the plan. He wanted his son to study mining engineering. He wanted him to go to Switzerland to college, where one could learn three languages at once. Then he wanted him to go to a German engineering school. Langston protested, saying he had no interest in engineering and that he wanted to be a writer. "A writer?" his father asked. "Do they make any money?" When Langston responded, "Some," his father assured him that black writers did not earn any at all. As a compromise, Langston proposed Columbia University because it was in Harlem. "More than Paris, or Shakespeare country, or Berlin, or the Alps, I wanted to see Harlem, the greatest Negro city in the world." It was 1921 and *Shuffle Along* had burst on the scene and more than anything, he wanted to hear Florence Mills sing. His father said no.

Remaining in Mexico, Hughes began to write and have his work published. "The Negro Speaks Rivers" was published in June 1921 and a short story appeared in *Brownies' Book*. When he showed them to his father, he asked only, "Did they pay you?" Tiring of

HUGHES IN 1928. "JUST FINISHED CLAUDE'S *HOME TO HARLEM* AND AM WILD ABOUT IT. IT OUGHT TO BE NAMED *NIGGER HELL*, BUT I GUESS THE COLORED PAPER WILL HAVE EVEN GREATER SPASMS THAN BEFORE," HE WROTE TO ALAIN LOCKE, MARCH 1, 1928.

Langston's stubbornness, however, he gave in and consented to pay for Columbia. Langston applied and was admitted in the fall of 1921.

Upon arriving in New York in September, Langston went uptown immediately. "I had never been in a subway before and it fascinated me—the noise, the speed, the green lights ahead. At every station I kept watching for the sign: 135th Street. When I saw it, I held my breath. I came out onto the platform with two heavy bags and looked around. It was still early morning and people were going to work. Hundreds of colored people! I wanted to shake hands with them, speak to them."

Langston did not like Columbia, though. He thought it was too big, too impersonal, too racist. He did not want to be in college anyway. His father had underestimated the expense of living in New York and began to ask for an accounting from Langston, who was rapidly spending money and thought "All gone" was sufficient explanation. Langston loved New York. He went to shows, read books, attended lectures, and skipped an important exam to witness the funeral of Bert Williams. It was spring of 1922 and, having finished his first year, he did not intend to go back to Columbia. He wrote his father and told him he was quitting school to go to work and not to send any more money. "He didn't. He didn't even write again," Hughes complained.

He worked at "dull jobs for low wages" until he secured a position on a rusty ship that kept a skeletal crew to keep it oiled but went nowhere. Hughes worked on the ship all winter. One day he got a note from Alain Locke, a Harvard-trained Rhodes scholar and Howard University professor who had read his poems in the *Crisis* and was eager to meet him. "It was written in a very small hand," Langston said. "I wrote back. 'No.' I didn't want to see him, anyway, being afraid of learned people in those days." He had already met Jessie Fauset and Du Bois with no ill results and had his first fillet of sole for lunch. But as he explained, "the *Crisis* people did everything they could to put me at ease; still I was afraid to see any more like them."

Locke had gotten his address from Countee Cullen, whom Hughes had met at the 135th Street library. Cullen was Hughes's closest friend in those early days. Cullen, the adopted son of a pastor of a large and influential church in Harlem, was deeply religious. Their attraction was that of opposites: Hughes was handsome; Cullen was not. Cullen was religious; Hughes was not. Hughes was Afrocentric and race conscious; Cullen was not. But as students with a love of learning—Cullen attended New York University—they liked each other and went to plays, movies, and lectures together. Cullen, seeing Hughes's lack of interest in women, assumed he was gay. Cullen's own sexual preference was for men, but he fully expected to marry and did so twice, believing strongly in the sanctity of that institution. Cullen's subtle advances toward Hughes were not reciprocated, and he withdrew them, concluding that Hughes's lack of interest was a result of his innocence. He thought, however, that his friend Alain Locke might succeed where he had failed. "Write to him," Cullen wrote to Locke, "and arrange to meet him. You will like him; I love him; his is such a charming childishness that I feel years older in his presence."

Locke, who had a vindictive nature, was annoyed by Hughes's refusal to meet him but soon recanted when he received a charming note from him: "I do want your help, and friendship, and criticism, and how good you are to offer them to me. . . . Of course, I'm stupid and only a young 'kid' fascinated by his first glimpse of life." Locke proposed a trip to Europe in the summer to get to know each other. Cullen suggested one for the three of them. Hughes declined all offers, stating that he had to work all summer, but writing of "how delightful it would be to come surprisingly upon one another in some old world street! Delightful and too romantic! But, maybe, who knows?" Hughes's teasing notes, born of innocence or artifice, eventually exasperated Locke, who wrote, "See Paris and die. Meet Langston Hughes and be damned."

Hughes finally got to sea in the spring of 1923, sailing on a steamship trading up and down the west coast of Africa. Seeing Africa had been a long cherished dream for him, but his first glimpses were a disappointment. "You should see the clothes they wear," he wrote his mother, "everything from overcoats to nothing. I have laughed until I can't." He returned to New York in October, looking like a "virile brown god," Cullen reported to Locke.

Back in Harlem, Hughes participated in the evening poetry readings and lectures at the 135th Street library hosted by Jessie Fauset and Ethel Ray Nance of the Urban League. It was Fauset most of all who encouraged a small group of writers to meet and talk about their work. That group also included Countee Cullen; Regina Andrews, a librarian at the branch and Ethel Nance's roommate; Harold Jackman, a teacher and great friend of Cullen's; Eric Walrond, a writer from British Guiana; and Gwendolyn Bennett, an artist and writer from Texas. "In this circle, Hughes was welcomed back from Africa as a hero."

In 1924 he set sail once again, this time as a messboy on a ship bound for Rotterdam. He liked everything about the city. "The canals, and the kids in wooden shoes, and the low, quaint houses of the town were picturesque and beautiful," he wrote. But when the ship sailed for home, he was aboard.

Hughes was weighing the decision to continue to travel or return to school—not Columbia but perhaps a black school. Locke, when in hot pursuit, had invited him to Howard University on several occasions, so Hughes wired him: "May I come now please. Let me know tonight by wire." Locke, beginning perhaps to tire of the coyness, responded by letter rather than wire. His response was ardent: "At increasing cost, for pride is my master sin, I have opened my arms three times to you, closed my eyes in confidence, and waited. And three times, I have embraced thin air and blinked and then stared at disillusionment. . . . I do not recognize myself in the broken figure that says 'come, come when you can, come soon.'" But Locke's invitation arrived too late. Failing to hear from him immediately, Langston sent a note apologizing for the "sudden and unexpected message," expressing a desire to come to Washington in the future, but announcing that he was leaving for Holland again the next day.

Hughes jumped ship on this trip and went to Paris. After changing what little money he had into francs, he boarded a bus and ended up in Montmartre. With the help of Rayford Logan, a former student of Jessie Fauset's who received the *Crisis* and had read Hughes's poem, he got a job as a dishwasher at Le Grand Duc nightclub.

The star attraction of the club was Florence Embry Jones, who "was very pretty and brown, and could wear the gowns of the great Paris couturiers as few other women could." When Jones left to open the famous Chez Florence, she was replaced by Ada "Bricktop" Smith, Josephine Baker's confidante. As Bricktop told it, "Years later Carl Van Vechten was in my place and he said, 'Bricky, you know who Langston Hughes is, don't you?' And I said, 'No, only by reading about him.' He said, 'Langston Hughes was that colored boy that was working here when you came.'" Bricktop was stunned. Nobody knew who he was, she claimed.

LEFT TO RIGHT:
LANGSTON HUGHES, CHARLES S. JOHNSON
(EDITOR OF *OPPORTUNITY*), FRANKLIN FRAZIER,
RUDOLPH FISHER, AND HUBERT DELANY.

Early in the morning of July 31, 1924, Hughes awoke to a rap at his attic door. It was his first meeting with "a little brown man with spats and a cultured accent, and a degree from Oxford." It was Alain Locke, who had come to Paris in search of his prize. "I cannot describe what I have been going through," he had written in the ill-fated letter. "It has felt like death—but out of this death and burial of pride and self there has suddenly come a resurrection of hope and love." Locke steered Hughes into a sidewalk café near the Place de Clichy. The two made plans for Hughes to contribute a selection to Locke's anthology, *The New Negro*, which would launch the Renaissance writers. They also discussed plans for Hughes to attend Howard University in the fall and to live in Locke's house.

Hughes soon left Paris to visit friends in northern Italy. Locke wrote him there proposing a rendezvous in Venice. Hughes agreed. "Dr. Locke knew Venice like a book," he wrote. "He knew who had painted all the pictures, and who had built all the old buildings, and where Wagner had died." But before the week was over, Langston grew tired of the sights and wandered off to the poorer sections. Locke apparently had also grown tired of his prey, because when Langston was robbed of all his money and his passport, Locke left him without offering to cover his loss. "Perhaps his ardor, either satisfied or frustrated, had cooled," biographer Rampersad speculated. "Certainly he made no further attempt to help Hughes." Langston, penniless, did odd jobs for weeks until he found a job on a ship that would take him back to America.

Langston Hughes was pursued, without success, by many Renaissance figures, male and female: Locke, Cullen, Dorothy West, Louise

"I WROTE THE HARMON AWARD LADY THAT THE *WEARY BLACKS* WOULD NOW GO GET THEIR *FINE CLOTHES FROM THE JEWS* AND THE WORLD WOULD BE *NOT WITHOUT LAUGHTER*—BUT TO PLEASE EXCUSE ME FROM THE NEW YORK CEREMONY ON THE 8TH," WROTE LANGSTON HUGHES TO CARLO (VAN VECHTEN), JANUARY 28, 1931.

Thompson, Wallace Thurman, and perhaps Zora Neale Hurston. The subject of his sexuality has both puzzled and fascinated scholars and friends. Van Vechten told his biographer that "he knew two men who seemed to thrive without having sex in their lives. Of the two, never had he any indication that either was homosexual or heterosexual. One of them was Langston Hughes." Rampersad was even more direct: "If certain of his responses to Locke seemed like teasing (a habit Hughes would never quite lose with women or, perhaps, men) they were not therefore necessarily signs of sexual desire; more likely, they showed the lack of it." Langston's friend Roy Blackburn supported this interpretation: "Even then, it seemed to me odd, this lack of interest. We were both young men, and young men usually talk about women. There were times when I wondered whether he had any sexual feeling at all. I'm really not sure he had any."

On the night of his return to New York, Langston attended an NAACP benefit at "Happy" Rhone's Club on Lenox Avenue. The attendees were lavish in their praise of the nomadic poet. It was a marvelous evening. Almost everybody was there. Alberta Hunter sang, "Everybody loves my baby but my baby don't love nobody but me." Florence Mills sang. Bill Robinson danced to the music of Fletcher Henderson and his band,

House at 514 Downer Street, Westfield, New Jersey, where Hughes, Zora Neale Hurston, and Louise Thompson worked on *Mule Bone* in 1928.

Consuela Kanaga's portrait of Hughes taken in Carmel, California, 1933.

Charlotte Mason, the "Godmother."

Langston Hughes and friends.

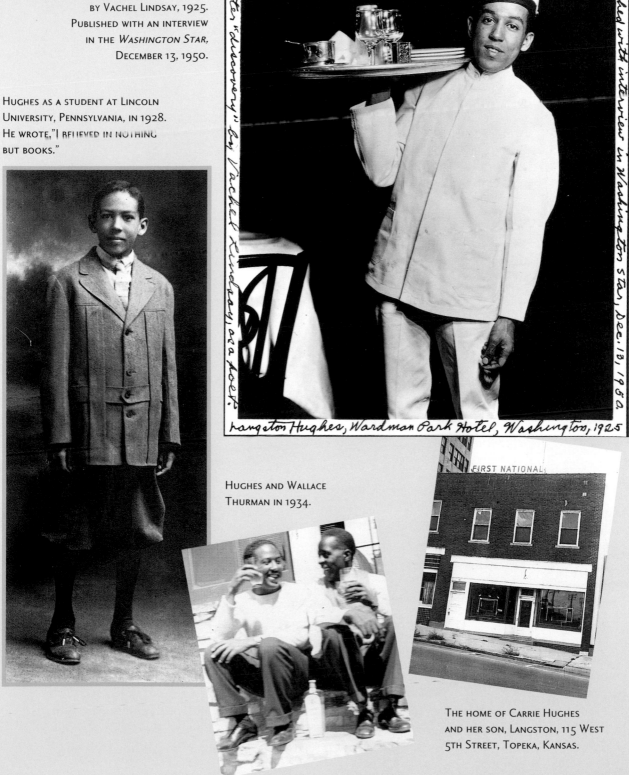

Hughes as a busboy at the Wardman Park Hotel, Washington, the day after his "discovery" by Vachel Lindsay, 1925. Published with an interview in the *Washington Star*, December 13, 1950.

Hughes as a student at Lincoln University, Pennsylvania, in 1928. He wrote, "I believed in nothing but books."

First newspaper photograph, U. & U. Syndicate *Day after "discovery" by Vachel Lindsay) as a host.* *Published with interview in Washington Star, Dec. 13, 1950.* *Langston Hughes, Wardman Park Hotel, Washington, 1925*

FIRST NATIONAL

Hughes and Wallace Thurman in 1934.

The home of Carrie Hughes and her son, Langston, 115 West 5th Street, Topeka, Kansas.

ON THE SHIP FOR THE VOYAGE TO THE SOVIET UNION. ALSO ONBOARD WAS LOUISE THOMPSON, CALLED VILE BY ZORA NEALE HURSTON. SHE MAY BE SEATED IN THE DECK CHAIR AT LEFT. HISTORIAN NATHAN HUGGINS SAID, "THOMPSON WAS SOMETIMES WHITE, SOMETIMES MEXICAN, AND SOMETIMES IT DID NOT MATTER."

of which Louis Armstrong was a member. Said Langston: "I sat at a table with Walter White's charming and very beautiful wife, and I was properly dazed. She looked like a Moorish princess." Langston was introduced for the first time to Carl Van Vechten, who wrote in his diary that he had met "Kingston Hughes" and was very impressed. James Weldon Johnson and W. E. B. Du Bois were also on hand. Only Jessie Fauset was missing. She had gone to Paris.

On the night of the NAACP event, Hughes had received a letter from his mother telling him that she and his stepbrother were living in Washington with prominent relatives who had read about him in the black press. She invited him, at their suggestion, to join them. "It all sounded risky to me, but I decided to try it," he wrote. In 1925 he finally arrived in Washington. When his cousins introduced him to their friends as just back from Europe, he knew he had made a mistake. He had no money.

He worked at various menial jobs, including a stint as a busboy in a Washington hotel. He met poet Vachel Lindsay, showed him some of his poems, and was written up in the Washington press: "Vachel Lindsay Discovers a Negro Bus Boy Poet." It was, said Hughes, "my first publicity break." Unfortunately, the publicity meant that "often the head waiter would call me to come and stand before some table whose curious guests wished to see what a Negro bus boy poet looked like." Langston quit his job.

Everyone he met in "cultured colored Washington" was impressed with his poetry and his family background—a distant relative, John Langston, had served in Congress during Reconstruction. All had "souls deep like the rivers," or so they told him. But none had a job for him. The people at Howard University, including Locke, were also impressed. But no one had a scholarship for him. Jessie Fauset sent him addresses of educational foundations but begged him to apply to Harvard instead. Langston, who rarely followed Fauset's advice, continued to work at menial jobs. This did not impress the cousins, so he and his mother and stepbrother moved out on their own.

Opportunity magazine, edited by Charles Johnson, held its first literary contest in early 1925. Langston sent in several entries, including "The Weary Blues." It won first prize. A banquet was held in New York and Langston was given forty dollars. The literary world, both black and white, was there in force, including Alfred Knopf, Fannie Hurst, Zona Gale, Van Wyck Brooks, and several Van Dorens. James Weldon Johnson awarded the prize and read the poem aloud. "Droning a drowsy syncopated tune,/Rocking back and forth to a mellow croon,/I heard a Negro play." Langston met there for the first time Zora Neale Hurston, who had won second prize for her short story. "She is a clever girl isn't she?" he later wrote to Van Vechten. "I would like to know her." Van Vechten later arranged to have his poems published by Alfred Knopf.

Langston returned to Washington, to more menial jobs and the literary salon of Georgia Douglas Johnson. Johnson had attended Atlanta University and studied music at Oberlin and at the Cleveland College of Music. In 1903 she had met and married Henry Lincoln Johnson, a lawyer who had graduated from the University of Michigan Law School. The Johnsons moved to Washington, D.C., some

years later. Georgia began writing poetry at that time, publishing her first poems in the *Crisis* in 1916, and was called the foremost black woman poet of her time. In 1922, well before the Civic Club dinner and the publication of Jessie Fauset's *There Is Confusion*, she published a second volume of poems. Her fame now rests almost entirely with her salon, however, a more familiar role for women of the Renaissance. According to Hughes, she was "a charming woman poet [who] turned her house into a salon for us on Saturday nights. Marita Bonner, Richard Bruce Nugent and others used to come there to eat Mrs. Johnson's cake and drink her wine and talk poetry and books and plays. Sometimes Alain Locke would drop in, too." Georgia's salon brought her no special favors. After she died, in 1962, most of her papers were destroyed. Poet-playwright Owen Dodson remarked, "as the car stopped in front of her house returning from her funeral the men were cleaning out the cellar, and I clearly saw manuscripts thrown into the garbage. I said, 'A lifetime to the sanitation department.'"

But Langston's tale was not so grim. In early 1926 a collection of poems entitled *The Weary Blues* was published by Alfred Knopf and received wonderful reviews. *Vanity Fair*—again thanks to Van Vechten—bought several poems in the same year, the first he had sold. The *Crisis*, not to be outdone by *Opportunity*, offered an Amy Spingarn literary prize. Amy Spingarn was the daughter of a very rich mill owner and landlord in New Jersey and the wife of Joel, of the NAACP. Langston again won a prize. Amy was impressed with him, invited him to tea at her studio on West Seventy-third Street, and made sketches of him, which she later turned into an oil portrait. "As she sketched, the maid brought tea and cinnamon toast, and Mrs. Spingarn recited Wordsworth and Shelley in a deep voice," Langston recalled. Later she financed his studies at Lincoln University in Pennsylvania, the first black school he attended.

During this period Hughes also met Wallace Thurman, whom he called "a strange kind of fellow, who liked to drink gin, but didn't like to drink gin, who liked being a Negro, but felt it a great handicap; who adored bohemianism, but thought it wrong to be a bohemian." Thurman thought himself an "incarnation of a cosmic clown." Born in Salt Lake City in 1902, he was raised there and educated at UCLA. He came to Harlem in 1925. Homosexual and alcoholic, he was darker-skinned than any of the other Renaissance writers. His color was frequently noted. "He was black in a way that it's hard for us to recognize that people ever had to be black," wrote writer Richard Bruce Nugent. Langston called him a "brilliant black boy, who had read everything, and whose critical mind could find something wrong with everything he read."

Thurman worked as the managing editor of the *Messenger*, a radical journal run by A. Philip Randolph, later of the Brotherhood of Sleeping Car Porters. The *Messenger* bought Langston's first stories, paying ten dollars a story. "Wallace Thurman wrote me that they were very bad stories, but better than any other they could find, so he published them." Thurman and Hughes became friends.

Wishing to break out of the mold of "the old, dead conventional Negro-white ideas of the past," Hughes, along with Thurman, Zora Neale Hurston, Richard Bruce Nugent, Dorothy West, and others of the younger crowd, seven in all, decided to publish a journal they called *Fire*. Each was to contribute fifty dollars for the publication. Only three did, but Thurman, the editor, went ahead with it. With the exception of Locke, none of the other Harlem intellectuals supported the journal. Du Bois wrote a critical review of it in the *Crisis*. The reviewer for the *Baltimore Afro-American* began

his comments with "I have just tossed the first issue of *Fire* into the fire." Of Hughes he said, "Langston Hughes displays his usual ability to say nothing in many words." What had offended the talented tenth most was a homoerotic tale by Nugent. But Hurston's story of a black farmer killed by a snake with which he had intended to kill his wife also brought them no comfort. *Fire* was ignored by the white press. No second issue appeared. Thurman and Hughes had their income attached for the expenses of the first one. "Finally, irony of ironies, several hundred copies of *Fire* were stored in the basement of an apartment where an actual fire occurred and the bulk of the whole issue was burned up," Langston wrote.

Alain Locke introduced Hughes to Charlotte Mason in 1927. Locke had first met her a few months before when she came up to him after a lecture he had given on African art. She was excited by his ideas and felt a rapport with him. At a concert at Carnegie Hall, sponsored by the Urban League and attended by Hughes in the company of the Van Vechtens, Locke introduced them. The next day, Locke arranged for Hughes to visit her at her Park Avenue apartment. Mason was already committed to elevating African art to the place of honor she felt it deserved. She was committed as well to the creation of a museum of African art in New York, where "little Negro children [would run] in and out learning to respect themselves through the realization of those treasures." Mason saw Hughes as "the innocent and noble young savage." Langston wrote: "I found her instantly one of the most delightful women I had ever met." When he left, she gave him fifty dollars, "a gift for a young poet."

After a second meeting, Mason arranged to pay Hughes's expenses for the summer so that he could write a novel. He was, she wrote, "my winged poet Child who, as he flies through my mind, is a noble silent Indian Chief." She asked

"IN SHARP CONTRAST TO HIS FELLOW NEW NEGROES, HUGHES' OUTPUT NEVER SLACKENED,"
STEVEN WATSON WROTE. PHOTOGRAPHED HERE BY MORGAN AND MARVIN SMITH.

him to address her as "Godmother." That summer he wrote a draft of *Not Without Laughter*. He also toured the South—"The lazy, laughing South,/With blood on its mouth"— with Zora Neale Hurston, collecting folk material. Hurston was a wonderful guide, sharing with him a love of the common folk. Zora knew much about the culture of the South. "Of all the niggerati," he wrote "she was the most amusing."

In the fall of 1927 he returned to Lincoln University. He was given a "generous monthly allowance by my patron [Hughes never named her], who had read both drafts of the book, had helped me with it, and found it good." The stipend was $150 a month or so, details to be

worked out later "with advice from Locke." It was Hughes's idea to introduce Hurston to Charlotte Mason. They met finally in October and talked of producing a black folk opera. A month later, Hurston also entered into an agreement with Mason. Zora was given $200 a month, a car, and a movie camera, but Mason "held contractual power over Hurston's material." Locke served as an intermediary between the two women.

Langston spent a wonderful year of economic independence, traveling and writing little. He escorted Mason to concerts, plays, and lectures whenever he was in New York. He saw little of his friends Bruce Nugent and Wallace Thurman. Godmother, who was getting her information from Locke, thought them a bad influence. While not writing, Langston was on the lecture circuit and, while speaking at Hampton Institute, renewed his acquaintance with Louise Thompson, the woman Dorothy West called "an itty-bitty thing with a great big Momma." Louise was pretty and light-skinned and, like Hughes, had grown up in alienating white communities. A graduate of the University of California, she was teaching at Hampton, a prestigious traditionally black school in Virginia, when Langston passed through. She was also a rebel of sorts, having written a letter to Du Bois about the conditions at Hampton. Du Bois published the letter, and as a result, she was about to be fired. Kindred spirits, she and Langston became close friends. There was always speculation about their relationship, speculation she always denied. Louise was married for a short time to Wallace Thurman.

It was no stranger a union than that of Langston's other close friend. April 1928 brought the social event of the Harlem season: the wedding of Countee Cullen to Yolanda Du Bois, daughter of W. E. B. Du Bois. Three thousand guests were crammed into the Salem Methodist Church. Du Bois saw the union as a joining of the muse of poetry and great intellect (hers inherited from him). He planned to "crown the exchange of vows with the release of one thousand doves" but was dissuaded at the last minute. Cullen, who loved pageantry, insisted that guests wear formal attire and sent a special reminder ("pardon the impertinence") to Langston, toward whom he had grown very cool. The marriage lasted a bit longer than the ceremony, but not much. In May, Du Bois wrote Cullen apologizing for his pampered daughter but reminding him of a husband's duties. On June 30 Cullen left for Europe with Harold Jackman. "Groom Sails with Best Man," read the headline.

Langston graduated from Lincoln in the spring of 1929 and continued his relationship with Godmother, who was becoming increasingly disappointed with his work. To help him along, Louise Thompson was hired in September as his secretary. He was also settled in a house in Westfield, New Jersey, close to New York but without the distractions. In the early spring of 1930 Hurston returned after two years of study in the South and moved into the Westfield house as well. She, too, was to share the secretarial services of Thompson. The three spent an amusing time together until Locke complained to Mason of too much playing in Westfield. Hurston and Hughes then settled down to write a play together, but the collaboration did not last. Langston's version was that Hurston departed in May out of boredom when the project was near completion but still in need of work.

More devastating to Hughes was his break with Godmother, which he said arose from philosophical differences and a matter of honor. In his autobiography he speaks of a clean but devastating break, but his correspondence reveals numerous attempts at reconciliation. "I am not wise, Godmother. . . . The inner soul is simple as a fool, sensitive as a shattered child, at odds too often with the reasons of the mind." But Mason was through with him.

Langston's version of the break with Zora is also very different from hers. Amateur players in Cleveland were preparing to present *Mule Bone*, a play by Zora Neale Hurston. Langston was enraged and demanded recognition. Zora at first did not respond but then arrived at his mother's house in Cleveland. As he wrote to Van Vechten: "she pushed her hat back, bucked her eyes, ground her teeth, and shook manuscripts in my face, particularly the third act which she claims she wrote alone by herself while Miss Thompson and I were off doing Spanish together (and the way she said *Spanish* meant something else). She admitted that we had worked jointly, and that characteri-zations were mine, but she dared and defied me to put my finger on a line that was my own." I guess this is the end of *Mule Bone*, he said to Van Vechten. "But nine-tenths of Zora's talk here was not about the play at all, but Madame Thurman [Louise Thompson]—the very thought of whom seemed to infuriate Zora. Do you think she is crazy?" he asked.

It had been a difficult two years for Hughes, and for all of his literary success, he was at the bottom, not the top. A'Lelia Walker died in the spring of 1931, and it is perhaps not surprising that with her death, Hughes proclaimed the Renaissance at an end. "We were no longer in vogue, anyway, we Negroes. Sophisticated New Yorkers turned to Noel Coward. Colored actors began to go hungry, publishers politely rejected manuscripts, and patrons found other uses for their money. The cycle that had Charlestoned into being on the dancing heels of *Shuffle Along* now ended in *Green Pastures* with De Lawd." Langston Hughes had come of age.

Hughes was the only writer included in this volume to make the transition to the more hard-hitting social realism of the 1930s. Steven Watson wrote that Hughes spent the decade "lecturing throughout America, and addressing international congresses of radicals." He settled in Harlem, and his politics would soften a little in the 1940s and 1950s though his writing career continued as strong as ever. Hughes produced poems, song lyrics, anthologies, newspaper columns, and numerous books, working up until his death. In May 1967, "not wanting to trouble friends about acute abdominal pains, he taxied himself to the hospital." He died of complications following prostate surgery.

"I'VE DONE NOTHING ALL WEEK BUT PLAY A MARVELOUS OLD RECORD BY ETHEL WATERS CALLED *AFTER ALL THESE YEARS* AND GIVEN AWAY HALF MY CLOTHES TO THE VILLAGE BOYS BECAUSE I'M TOO LAZY TO START PACKING THEM," HUGHES WROTE TO WALLACE THURMAN, JULY 1929.

15

DOROTHY WEST

$\mathcal{I}$N THE 1890S most Americans followed a winter diet and a summer diet. The winter diet was strictly meat and potatoes, with no thought of fresh fruit or green vegetables. "In those days the first beans and tomatoes began to be shipped from the South in May. Then came local gardens. But with the October frosts, green things disappeared." The orange, given at Christmas in the children's stockings, was considered a delicacy. But over time, refrigeration, cold storage, and rapid transportation significantly altered the typical diet. Then, just before World War I, vitamins A and B were discovered and C and D soon afterward. Fruits and vegetables "gained prestige in a country that followed the new discoveries avidly." Fannie Hurst, in her best-seller *No Food with My Meals*, said that "restaurateurs became familiar with Melba toast, spinach, and saccharine." President Wilson established a Food Administration that used "schools, the pulpit, motion pictures, posters, and the press to familiarize people with calories, vitamins, proteins, and carbohydrates, and the value of fruits and vegetables." Today, wrote the authors of *Middletown* in 1929, "more and more Middletown housewives are buying fresh vegetables and fruits through the winter." It was a good time to be in perishables.

Rachel Benson West, one of twenty-two children, mother of Dorothy West.

DOROTHY WEST, THE YOUNGEST and longest surviving member of the Harlem Renaissance, died on August 16, 1998. She was the foremost chronicler of the manners and mores of the black bourgeoisie. Plucked from the ashes of oblivion in 1993 by Doubleday editor Jacqueline Kennedy Onassis, West's Jane Austen sensibility, complete with ironic humor, has found a more appreciative audience at the end of the twentieth century than at its beginning. She published her first story in 1926 and her first novel in 1948, and she watched her first television miniseries based on her work in 1998.

More than anything, young Dorothy had wanted to be a writer. "When I was seven, I said to my mother, may I close my door? And she said yes, but why do you want to close your door? And I said because I want to think. And when I was eleven, I said to my mother, may I lock my door? And she said yes, but why do you want to lock your door? And I said because I want to write." She once further explained, "I have no ability nor desire to be other than a writer, though the fact is I whistle beautifully." Her novels closely parallel the autobiographical details of her life that she shared with intimates like Nella Larsen but their accuracy remains uncertain.

West also shared with Larsen the community's obsession with skin color. While the importance of white ancestry had diminished over time as consciousness of class position gained greater ascendancy in her world, it did not disappear. In the 1920s an intricate and interconnected division along class and color lines was maintained within black elites. Light skin carried privilege in the schools (dark-skinned students were not encouraged to apply to the professional schools at Howard University), in social life (black fraternities had "color tax parties," where members with darker-skinned dates paid a higher

tax to get in), and in the selection of mates (children were urged to "lighten the line"). While color preferences were strongest among the upper classes, they did not reside there exclusively. Writer Konrad Bercovici recalled in his memoirs that "when [Paul and Essie] Robeson first came to dinner the colored maid shed her apron, declaring that she wouldn't serve no Niggers and left." Explained activist Nannie Burroughs, "Many Negroes have colorphobia as badly as the white folk have Negrophobia."

The color palette within the black community was extensive and nuanced, ranging, it was said, from "high noon to midnight." Zora Neale Hurston, a student of the social sciences, constructed a typical scale: high yaller, yaller, high brown, Vaseline brown, seal brown, low brown, dark brown, low black, lamp black, and damn black. ("Why, lightning bugs follows him at twelve o'clock in the day, thinking it's midnight.")

But dark skin, too, had its subtleties. As West explained in her first novel, *The Living Is Easy*, "they were not too dismayed by a darkish skin if it were counterbalanced by a straight nose and straight hair that established an Indian origin. There was nothing that disturbed them more than knowing that no one would take them for anything but colored."

Dorothy West was struck with a particularly virulent form of this mark of oppression. But she also possessed a keen insight that exposed the hypocrisies of both race and class snobberies. "West writes about the black middle class from the viewpoint of the marginalized insider," literary critic Mary Helen Washington explained, "both a fierce critic of the bourgeois life and a loyal daughter upholding the values of family and class." Said critic Elizabeth Benedict: "She can be wickedly eloquent about the costs of living in a world where the shadings in the color of

DOROTHY WEST, AGE ONE.

one's skin are more important than the bonds between blood relatives." The tortured persona was not a deceived observer.

DOROTHY WEST WAS, by all accounts save race, a Boston Brahmin. Born in 1907 to Isaac and Rachel Benson West, she attended the prestigious Girls Latin School, Boston University, and the Columbia School of Journalism. She was especially proud of her old school ties. Girls Latin was a magnet school, which Dorothy attended by virtue of her high grade-point average. It was there that she developed her love of writing, trained and encouraged by teachers who, forced by state law to remain unmarried, devoted their lives to their students. Dorothy was proud of her Girls Latin badge. "So I went to the Latin School on opening day," she wrote, "holding my head erect, hearing myself formally addressed by my teachers, and not for a moment feeling that the title crowned my head unbecomingly."

Her father, "ambitious and industrious," was born in Virginia, a house slave, the child of a cook. At slavery's end, his mother worked in a boardinghouse, and Isaac made money by shining shoes and running errands. He saved his money, except for what he used to "pay an indigent townsman to teach him to read and write and figure sums."

By the age of ten, he had a dream to own a business of his own. He persuaded his mother to pool their savings and buy a boardinghouse. This she did, and together they made a success of it. Isaac wanted more, so he moved to Springfield, Massachusetts, where he apprenticed himself to a wholesale buyer of fruits and vegetables. When he learned the trade, he opened two stores. But he was still not finished. "My father's dream was to be a wholesale merchant of fruits and vegetables in the venerable Boston Market," Dorothy wrote. "And so he was." He was called the "Black Banana King."

By Dorothy's published account, her mother, light-skinned and beautiful, one of twenty-two children, had been sent north for protection against the lecherous designs of certain southern white men. She met and married Isaac, and the union was a happy one. Said

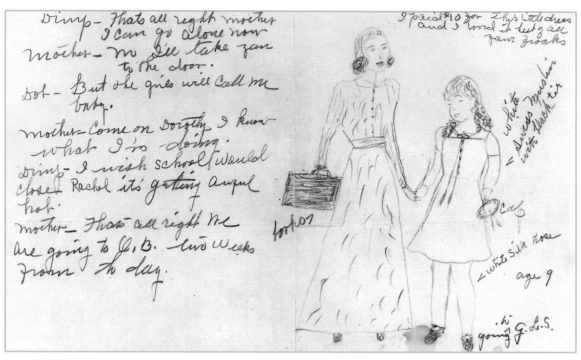

Dorothy: "My father was a generation older than my mother. Yet I cannot imagine either one married to anyone else." In private conversations, however, she suggested that her mother hated the dark-skinned man, whom she had married for his money (the white wife of the dark-skinned man in *The Wedding* says that "he was good and kind, and I cannot bear the sight of him") and that she resented the dark-skinned child as well. Perhaps in explanation, a child in *The Wedding* says, "Brown mothers hugged you a lot and made you laugh a lot. White mothers made you feel sorry and sad." Dorothy later told friends that she had a difficult relationship with her mother and that her mother made her take care of her lighter-skinned cousins, who lived nearby. "I helped raise my grandmother's nineteen children," she said. But friends also reported that West adored her mother, creating a fantasy life about her when the reality was too harsh. Like

her mother, Dorothy herself did not care for dark-skinned people.

Isaac West's business was so prosperous that his family summered in Oak Bluffs on Martha's Vineyard, part of a small black middle-class enclave of privilege and prosperity. "By the time I was ten," she said in an interview in 1995, "my father was listed in Dun and Bradstreet." Her childhood summers at Oak Bluffs were idyllic. "The days were full. There were berries to pick, a morning's adventure. There were band concerts for an evening's stroll. There were invitations to lemonade and cookies and whist." There was much security and self-assurance in her protected world, and she was, by all accounts, a very happy child.

Dorothy West wrote a great deal about her childhood. Her family lived year-round in the Back Bay section of Boston, the original center of the old city that "had always had a small African-American presence." They were part of an elite living among whites but keeping their distance. "We were always stared at," she remembered. "Whenever we went outside the neighborhood that knew us, we were inspected like specimens under glass. My mother prepared us. As she marched us down our front stairs, she would say what our smiles were on tiptoe to hear, 'Come on, children, let's go out and drive the white folks crazy.'" Her mother meant no bitterness; she was merely voicing a familiar black middle-class survival strategy for a world that "outranked us and outnumbered us," West wrote.

In 1926 Dorothy left Boston for New York with her cousin, the poet Helene Johnson, to attend *Opportunity* magazine's awards dinner, at the invitation of editor Charles Johnson. Dorothy was not yet twenty, and it was probably a minor miracle that her parents had let her go at all. She and Helene stayed at the Harlem branch of the YWCA. West received a second-place award for her short story "The Typewriter." She later recalled: "God allowed me to share a second prize with the now legendary Zora Neale Hurston. At first [Zora] had mixed feelings about sharing a prize with an unknown teenager. But in time I became her little sister, and my affection for her has never diminished."

West went back home and finished her education at Boston University. She later returned to New York, where she rented an apartment previously leased to Zora. She befriended all the younger Renaissance crowd—Zora, Langston Hughes, Arna Bontemps, and Louise Thompson—and joined in all their antics. "We thought we were going to be the greatest writers in the world. We were all young, and we fell in love with each other. We all had the same ambitions: writers and painters and so forth. We were free. We had an innocence that nobody can have now." Through Zora she met and befriended Fannie Hurst, Carl Van Vechten ("I learned from Carl"), and Elisabeth Marbury, a wealthy literary agent and patron of the arts. West was especially fond of her. Sir Osbert Sitwell, who wrote sketches of 1920s literary figures for the *Atlantic Monthly*, explained some of Marbury's appeal: "To write that she was large is an understatement. She was of such enormous size that it was always difficult for her to get in or out of an automobile, but this disability in no way discouraged her from going about and usually caused her to laugh uproariously." Both West and Sitwell were clients of Marbury's.

West was shy but well liked. "I went to the Harlem Renaissance and never said a word," she told literary critic Mary Helen Washington in a 1980 interview. "I was young and a girl so they never asked me to say anything." Her professed shyness, however, may have been overdone. Friends would later talk of her "mile-a-minute patter," her great storytelling ability and her quick mind—traits she had probably always possessed. She made an impression on a number of people. Langston Hughes gave her the nickname "the Kid." Harold Jackman often asked for her, several times referring to her as "little black Dorothy" to Nella Larsen. It was a term of endearment, or so he thought. Countee Cullen proposed marriage; Dorothy turned him down. "If I had married him, I would have had to go south, where he was going to teach," she explained. "I didn't want to be one of these women who sat around and drank tea. I was not that person at all."

Her favorite friend was Wallace Thurman, an incredibly intense young man, educated at UCLA, a "brilliant black boy, who had read everything," according to Langston Hughes. Thurman first came to New York in 1925, where he knew no one. He wandered around for a while without money or employment until he was hired to work at the *Messenger*, a radical black journal edited by A. Philip Randolph. Thurman's intensity—"he wanted to be a very great writer, like Gorki or Thomas Mann"—befit the title of his own journal, *Fire*, which he published later in the decade. It was a publication of only a single issue, highly critical of older writers and too avant-garde for the general public. The unsold issues burned in a basement, where they were being stored.

But West's attraction to Thurman had another source as well. "Thurman was a slight man, nearly black," she wrote in a tribute to him published in 1970, "with the most agreeable smile in Harlem and a rich, infectious laugh." Wallie, she explained, "had come into the world the unwanted shade of black. He was not his mother's pride and joy, and this undesirability was made apparent to him." His childhood trauma struck a resonant chord with Dorothy, as did his hesitancy to talk about it.

Thurman, who was so black that Richard Bruce Nugent said he wanted to throw up when he met him ("he was more black than anyone had a right to be"), articulated his racial humiliations only in his literature. Observed West, "In *The Blacker the Berry*, the dark-skinned heroine suffered many of the humiliations he would not have admitted having suffered himself." The book was supposed to be a satire, she explained, but "because of the angry overemphasis, it becomes a diatribe." In her own work on the subject, West said simply,

ARNA BONTEMPS AND LANGSTON HUGHES. "I HAVE BECOME SO AWARE OF YOUR NEED OF A WOMAN. LET ME BE THAT WOMAN. I AM NOT ASHAMED TO ASK YOU. LET ME GIVE YOU THE REST OF MY LIFE. LET ME MAKE IT RICH," WEST WROTE TO HUGHES, MAY 26, 1933.

"Dark skins have never been the fashion among Negro upper classes." It was an understatement that masked a lot of pain.

Wallie, never known for his charity, produced a kind portrait of Dorothy and her cousin in his satirical novel, *Infants of Spring*, describing "two young girls, recently emigrated from Boston. They were the latest to be hailed as incipient immortals. Their names were Doris Westmore and Hazel Jamison. Doris wrote stories, Hazel wrote poetry. Both had become known through a literary contest fostered by one of the leading Negro magazines. Raymond liked them more than he did most of the young recruits of the movement. For one thing, they were characterized by a freshness and naivete which he and his cronies lost. And, surprisingly enough for Negro prodigies, they actually gave promise of possessing literary talent." This was high praise indeed from one who was said to have found something wrong with everything he read.

From his position on the editorial staff at the *Messenger*, Thurman gained prominence, particularly among the younger crowd. He was rumored to be able to simultaneously read eleven lines of print, a valuable editorial skill. From his post at the journal, he was instrumental in publishing their writing, including Dorothy's first story, in 1926, and a poem by Helene Johnson as well. "We used to call Wallie our leader," Dorothy observed.

Thurman, whose lifestyle Arnold Rampersad has described as "a whirlwind of activity, of laughter and carousing but also of intense, rebellious creativity," was alcoholic, homosexual, and tubercular. He possessed a restless, frenetic energy that caused people to collect about him like insects to a night-light. He was also frequently in debt. "He began to surround himself with a queer assortment of blacks and whites of the lost generation. They clung to him like leeches," Dorothy reported in her 1970 tribute. Thurman, however, found sustenance in that company. "Unless buttressed by stimulating personalities I am lost," he explained, "no matter how despicable or foolish these personalities may appear in retrospect. They are the life of me." For Dorothy, Thurman with his thirst for knowledge and his quest for perfection *was* the Renaissance. He was "more typical of the epoch than the one or two more enduring names that survived the period," she remarked.

WEST'S FRIEND WALLACE THURMAN. "THURMAN HAD COME INTO THE WORLD THE UNWANTED SHADE OF BLACK. HE WAS NOT HIS MOTHER'S PRIDE AND JOY, AND THIS UNDESIRABILITY WAS MADE APPARENT TO HIM," SHE WROTE.

He passed across the Harlem stage in so many disguises that in the end they may have consumed him. From his deathbed he wrote to Langston Hughes, "Whodathought when I was in Carmel, that I would soon end up in the tubercular ward of the very hospital I damned and God-damned when I wrote *The Interne* [a novelized play published in 1932]. Ironic, I calls it. Or is nature finally avenging art?"

On August 22, 1928, Thurman married Louise Thompson. Louise, newly arrived in the city, had looked after Wallie that summer when he fell ill and had helped him type his manuscript. This was the very same Louise Thompson who would later serve as secretary to Langston Hughes and Zora Neale Hurston and would be intimately involved in their feud. This was the very same Louise Thompson who—according to Alain Locke, by then the jilted lover—was romantically involved with Langston Hughes and who had turned Langston into a "red," as Locke told Godmother.

Thurman's friends were skeptical about the union, which had been quick to form and was based on little of mutual interest. Nugent believed that "Thurman was interested primarily in the idea of the so-called companionate marriage which was coming into vogue." Companionate marriages consisted, among other things, of open sex and birth control. Dorothy said that Thurman "had an oft-repeated philosophy of doing everything once before he died." He himself offered several descriptions of the match. He wrote Claude McKay a few weeks after the marriage: "It's just one of those inexplicable things that happens even to the best of us. My only point of extenuation is that I happen to have married a very intelligent woman who has her own career and who also does not believe in marriage and who is as anxious as I am to avoid the conventional pitfalls into which most marriages throw one."

Dorothy had a different opinion. Wallie, she said, wanted a child and, fearing that his lifestyle precluded it, went in search of a mate, most likely one with the right credentials. Thompson, like Thurman, had attended UCLA before coming to New York, had a brief teaching career at Hampton Institute, and was so light-skinned she was "sometimes white, sometimes Mexican and sometimes it did not matter." Louise, Dorothy said, was a "little bitty woman who arrived in New York accompanied by a great big mother who was anxious to see her daughter married to somebody who was in the arts." The great big mother lived with the couple after the marriage. The arrangement was less than ideal for Wallie, and he complained to a number of friends. Zora had a suggestion, which she passed on to Dorothy: "Wallie should perk up. I know that it is annoying for his mother-in-law to keep on living and pestering him, but then there are gunmen on the East Side who hire out for as low as $25.00."

GROUP OF FRIENDS AT GAY HEAD, ON MARTHA'S VINEYARD, AUGUST 21, 1938.

Dorothy said that both Wallie and Louise confided in her. "I was in the middle, I don't know why, because Wallie used to come to me and tell me his story . . . [and] Louise would come on her lunch hour into my little apartment. . . . She was a chain smoker. . . . Louise liked me better than I liked her. . . . She was totally outside the Renaissance. Well, you know what I mean, she was married to Wallie, and

nobody liked her." At the end of November, Wallie fled Harlem on the pretext of caring for his ailing mother. He wrote Hughes: "I just had to flee. I was fed up on New York, on the magazine, and on married life (yes it's all over, but I dare you to mention that either)."

Thurman's play *Harlem* went into production, and in January 1929 he was somehow back with Thompson—"Woe is me," he wrote Hughes. The couple had a party on January 19, attended by Harold Jackman. "Yes, he is with his wife again," Jackman reported to Cullen, "but for how long I don't know." The play opened in February 1929. According to West, Louise left Wallie on the night before the opening, something Dorothy could neither understand nor forgive. "The fact that she could desert him at a crucial hour [made her] as much a failure as a writer's wife as he was as a conventional husband," West concluded, revealing the same Victorian ideals of marriage that muddled the thinking of most of the Renaissance crowd.

When it suited her, Dorothy used her youth as a protective shield, hiding behind her older, wiser friends. "I was just a little girl from Boston, a place of dull people with funny accents," she told Mary Helen Washington. Countee Cullen, another of her special friends, would often write to her as "Dear Little Dorothy" or "Darling Dot," and give her advice about her work, her life, even about guest lists for her parties. Others served as her protectors as well. On one occasion she wrote that Claude McKay was helping her to buy a dress for a party for James Weldon Johnson. A neighbor on Oak Bluffs suggested that Dorothy had never lost this quality, describing her as someone who "never grew up, the little girl of the Renaissance."

Yet her youth (supported by her slight, less-than-five-feet figure) gave her a unique perspective. "The Harlem Renaissance can never be repeated," she wrote. "It was an age of innocence, when we who were its hopeful members believed that our poems, our plays, our paintings, our sculptures, indeed any facet of our talents would be recognized and rewarded." Unfortunately, she was all but ignored by the major Renaissance chroniclers—Huggins, Lewis, and Rampersad —and more often than not relegated to lists of guests. Yet she appeared in the most unlikely settings, with friendships that were wide-ranging. In October 1929, days before the stock market crash, Cullen wrote to her, for example, complaining that she had not yet come to Paris. "Augusta Savage is here and Eric Walrond," he wrote, "and a few other people who might be worthy inmates. But since you and I were to be the guiding spirits of the venture, all must hang in abeyance until you come. Do come soon."

In 1931, in response to a letter about a

WEST IN HER NEW YORK APARTMENT ON 110TH STREET, 1930S.

party West was arranging, Cullen mentions another of her intimates, Alberta Hunter. "And by all means invite Alberta!" he advised her. Hunter was by education and background definitely not of their class—a turnoff in normal circumstances for both Dorothy and Harvard-educated Countee. But Hunter was really beyond category. Their friendship was based on a shared love of learning, elegance, and reserve. Alberta, whom Dorothy described as "giving the appearance of being a very simple woman and not much fun," was actually both talented and intriguing. ("Her presence and style marked you forever," the dancer John Scott remembered.) Dorothy met Alberta at one of A'Lelia Walker's parties. Hunter did not smoke or drink, as Dorothy complained. Yet the pair took on the role of native guides to downtown folks' safaris into Harlem. "Harlem," Dorothy wrote, "had a taste of white patronage and found it sweet to the palate. There was no party given which did not have its quota of white guests." Once they escorted two carloads of "Park Avenue people" in search of exciting nightlife. More often, though, their tour groups were smaller.

They remained friends throughout the 1930s, when Harlem was no longer in vogue. Alberta wrote her from Egypt: "Dot! Darling. Egypt is very picturesque, but . . . after seeing conditions in Egypt I realize that America is the best place for *poor* blacks."

In 1932 Dorothy went to the Soviet Union with a group of black intellectuals, including Louise Thompson and Langston Hughes. The group was going to produce a movie called *Black and White*, about black life in Alabama. The movie was never made, but Dorothy spent over a year in the Soviet Union. It was a thrilling time for her. "It was so good to hear from you, and especially to receive such an infectiously happy letter," Cullen wrote in response to a letter from her. "I wish I could be in Moscow with you." West expressed similar sentiments to her mother, who replied: "Mr. West [Dorothy's father] said he is so glad you are in Russia and he wants you to stay there as long as you can be treated like a human." Explained Dorothy: "Prejudice is quite unknown here."

Sylvia Chinn, a dancer ("one of the better known here"), was one of the people she met in the Soviet Union. She went to meet her with Langston. Dorothy, revealing her color preferences, described her as "half Chinese and half West Indian Negro. Her features are somewhat negroid, but her hair is beautiful and slightly curly. She has nothing of the American Negro in her." Dorothy added—admiringly, it seemed—that Chinn "talked with a very English accent." Apparently West had brought her color complex to Moscow with her.

Langston the wanderer soon left the Soviet Union and returned to the United States, but

PROBABLY ZORA NEALE HURSTON, FROM BOSTON UNIVERSITY'S DOROTHY WEST COLLECTION.

Dorothy stayed behind. Wishing to continue their friendship, she wrote a long letter to him, revealing her deep attraction. More than getting married (marriage, West believed, turned men into children and women into their mothers), she wanted a child. Hughes was a logical candidate, although skepticism has been expressed about their relationship. As she grew older, West frequently dropped hints but provided few details about the attachment. Though Hughes never destroyed West's letter, donating it eventually to the James Weldon Johnson Collection at Yale, there is no record of his response.

Hughes's life was, as we know, filled with these unsolicited declarations of love. Rampersad dismissed this liaison by suggesting that Hughes and West "were involved in some way, though probably not sexual." Hughes, after his falling out with Charlotte Mason, gained Mary McLeod Bethune as his matron-patron. "Bigboned, black-skinned, and dynamic, at once both commanding and maternal, Mrs. Bethune seemed to personify for Langston, in this pivotal moment of life, what their race might be—and what he himself might be in his relationship to it," Rampersad wrote. Hughes may well have developed a preference for darker-skinned people. "Don't stay in the United States, where you have to live like a nigger with niggers," his father had once said. "But I like Negroes," Langston responded. His father's hatred for dark skins and the man's own brown skin, combined with Hughes's hatred of his father and Dorothy's love of hers, all converged at this moment and could have fueled the unlikely alliance.

But the union between West and Hughes did not last long. While in the Soviet Union Dorothy learned that her father had died. "Dot, I have some news that I want to tell you only I know—how modern and how wonderful and brave you are—the best friend you and I ever had went to sleep the other night and passed into Glory," her mother wrote. Dorothy was philosophical about her loss. "My father's death is not hard for me. Perhaps because I am so far away, and it does not quite seem real."

She explained to her mother that she had known what was going to happen from a reading she had gotten from a fortune-teller. "All I want in life is to work hard for a few comforts for you, and marry within a year and start to make a baby. That is my fortune that was told in the cards long ago for me by that woman who saw everything that has happened, my coming here, my father's death and my knowing of it through a letter." Dorothy's usually keen perception seemed to fail her here.

If she was unhappy in love, she was certainly not bitter about her journey to the Soviet Union. "Don't think I mind coming back to work hard for the first time in my life," she wrote to her mother. "Because I've had enough joy and fun this past year to last me the rest of my life." Upon her return, Dorothy lived for a time across the street from Zora and shared meals with her. "She is a better cook than Lloyd [probably Lloyd Thomas, a friend of Carl Van Vechten's, who was active in the crowd and lived in Harlem with his wife, black actress Edna Lewis] . . . for with Zora and me it is fifty-fifty, of course," she wrote. Dorothy had purchased a fur coat in Russia and stored it in Zora's apartment. Like many things of Zora's, the coat disappeared under mysterious circumstances.

Using her own funds, Dorothy founded a journal called *Challenge*, which she hoped would recapture the spirit of the Harlem Renaissance, now dormant. It was published from 1934 to 1937. The associate editor was Harold Jackman. The journal attempted to combine art and politics, but its product was too moderate for the politicos ("It does not seem to challenge anything," Arthur Schomburg wrote to Nancy Cunard) and not arty enough for the critics ("high schoolish and pink tea," Thurman suggested). In 1937 West edited a new journal called *New Challenge*, with Richard Wright as associate editor. Among its claims to fame was the publication of Ralph Ellison's first article, "Creative and Cultural Lag." Harder-hitting than *Challenge*, it did not survive its second issue.

After the journals folded, West became an actress and a welfare investigator in Harlem, then joined the Federal Writers Project of the Works Progress Administration. She was also a regular contributor to the *New York Daily News*, writing two short stories a month for them at fifty dollars.

In 1945 West went to live on Martha's Vineyard year-round. She took on odd jobs, even working as a waitress, to make ends meet. The owner of the *Vineyard Gazette* discovered that the waitress was "the Dorothy West" and invited her to work as a reporter. She wrote a column commenting on teas and weddings, and on local flora and fauna. To some of her neighbors, who included Isabel Powell, former wife of Adam Clayton Powell Jr., and sister of Fredi Washington, this resurrection was not sufficient to lift her out of anonymity. "What has she written? What has she done?" some asked. West, who never married, did live with a woman for a number of years. Their relationship was not discussed in Oak Bluffs.

West's first novel, *The Living Is Easy*, was published in 1948 and was dedicated "To Ike," her father. It features a family unit strikingly similar to her own. Southern-born, light-skinned, beautiful Cleo, married to dark-skinned Bart, the "black banana king of Boston," ultimately destroys her own family and that of her sisters because of her perverted racial values. In the end West, again embracing Victorian marriage ideals, implied that tragedies could be avoided if women would remain beside their struggling mates. The novel also had a more positive message. Cleo and Bart have a child, Judy, who is darker than her mother would have liked: "She was dark. She had Papa's cocoa-brown skin, his soft dark eyes, and his generous nose in miniature. Cleo worked hard on her nose." Judy loves her father and ultimately breaks free of her mother's influence. Critic Mary Helen Washington wrote that Judy "is the fountainhead of the search for truth, allowing us to feel that the hope of the future will be this good little girl who usurps the power of the bad mother and replaces her as the head of a little flock." From underneath the melodrama West's deeply ingrained beliefs in the futility of color prejudice emerged. ("Color was a false distinction, love was not," Selby says at the end of *The Wedding*.)

Jacqueline Onassis, who spent time on Martha's Vineyard in the late 1970s, recognized the talent of the woman who wrote "local color" columns for the newspaper and published West's novel *The Wedding* in 1995. The two women became friends. "She came to see me every Monday to assess my progress," Dorothy told the *Vineyard Gazette*. "She drove herself in her blue jeep, losing her way fairly regularly in the Highlands." But Onassis died before the novel's publication. "Though there was never such a mismatched pair in appearance, we were perfect partners," Dorothy wrote in her dedication.

On August 29, 1997, Dorothy celebrated her ninetieth birthday on Martha's Vineyard. The huge tribute included President and Mrs. Clinton, Jessye Norman, Anita Hill, and Henry Louis Gates Jr. Oprah Winfrey, whose production company had filmed *The Wedding* for a television miniseries, sent a telegram.

In her 1970 article on Thurman, Dorothy belatedly assessed the Harlem Renaissance. The young writers, she said, were for the most part not ready for publication. She cited Thur-

WEST AND A
FRIEND.

DOROTHY WEST
WITH HILLARY CLINTON
ON MARTHA'S VINEYARD
ON DOROTHY'S
NINETIETH BIRTHDAY
IN 1997.

man's two novels as prime examples of "immaturity and incomplete experience." Dorothy was most critical of his lack of a guiding philosophy. "Wallace Thurman had no personal theory which he could substitute for those which he rejected," she explained. It was a perceptive critique of the period and the main reason why West thought Thurman *was* the Renaissance. Thurman had died in 1934 at the age of thirty-two. Tubercular and alcoholic, he had been warned by doctors to rest. Instead he went on a drinking binge, several times threatening suicide. He died on Welfare Island in New York, "with none of his dreams of greatness fulfilled."

"His death," Dorothy wrote, "caused the first break in the ranks of the 'New Negro.' Assembled at the funeral in solemn silence, older, hardly wiser, they were reminded for the first time of their lack of immortality." Aaron and Alta Douglas, Countee Cullen, Richard Bruce Nugent, Harold Jackman, Dorothy Petersen, Walter White, and Dorothy West were in at-

tendance. Louise Thompson was there as well, Dorothy reported. She wore a red coat.

James Weldon Johnson, then at Fisk, wrote his condolences to Dorothy, remarking on the loss for the literary community. "So suddenly I am serious and entirely grownup," she replied to him. It was an all-too-familiar Renaissance theme. The voices that had stirred a nation, that had emerged with so much passion and promise and fire, were one by one drifting into obscurity. "The younger Negroes are all about on their last legs," Alain Locke wrote to Charlotte Mason in 1932, adding somewhat cynically, "but do let us hold together the silent hope of the future." Locke's death knell was premature. The Renaissance was to become, despite its critics and detractors, one of the most studied periods in American literary history. Langston Hughes, "the darker brother sent to the kitchen," had predicted that "tomorrow, I'll be at the table when company comes." And so he was. One by one the others followed. Dorothy West was among the last to take her seat.

NOTES

INTRODUCTION

Page 10
"For generations" Alain Locke, *The New Negro* (New York: Atheneum, 1977), p. 5.
"to arouse the troubling" Ralph Ellison, in Cornel West, *Race Matters* (New York: Vintage, 1994), p. 3.

Page 11
"My only sin" Barry Singer, *Black and Blue: The Life and Lyrics of Andy Razaf* (New York: Schirmer, 1992), p. 218.
"Lightly, slightly and politely" Steven Watson, *The Harlem Renaissance* (New York: Pantheon, 1995), p. 22.
"It was characteristic of the Jazz Age" Fitzgerald, in Ann Douglas, *Terrible Honesty: Mongrel Manhattan in the 1920s* (New York: Farrar, Straus & Giroux, 1995), p. 18.
"It was a period" Langston Hughes, *The Big Sea* (New York: Hill and Wang, 1942), p. 228.
"It was a *decision*" Amiri Baraka, *Blues People* (New York: William Morrow, 1963), p. 96.
"What American literature" Van Doren, in George Hutchinson, *The Harlem Renaissance in Black and White* (Cambridge: Harvard University Press, 1995), pp. 216–17.
"a country settled" Brooks, ibid., p. 96.
"hegemonic Puritan and pioneer" Brooks, ibid., p. 99.
"Do you suppose" Edith Wharton, *The Age of Innocence* (New York: New American Library, 1920), p. 193.

Page 12
"This generation was the first" Douglas, *Terrible Honesty*, p. 53.
"The only way" James Baldwin, *The Fire Next Time* (New York: Dial Press, 1963), p. 110.
"art and letters" Nathan Huggins, *The Harlem Renaissance* (New York: Oxford University Press, 1971), p. 5.
"suddenly stars started falling" Arna Bontemps, *The Harlem Renaissance Remembered* (New York: Dodd, Mead & Co., 1972), p. 2.
"half in shadow" Cheryl Wall, *Women of the Harlem Renaissance* (Bloomington: Indiana University Press, 1995), p. xiii.

Page 13
"There's two things" Smith, in Chris Albertson, *Bessie* (New York: Stein and Day, 1985), p. 125.
"is confronted by both" Wall, *Women of the Harlem Renaissance*, p. 12.
"no theme" Wright, in Henry Louis Gates and Anthony Appiah, eds., *Zora Neale Hurston: Critical Perspectives Past and Present* (New York: Amistad, 1993), p. 17.
"Men had a better" Jessie Fauset, *Plum Bun: A Novel Without a Moral* (New York: Frederick A. Stokes, 1929), p. 8.
"a dazzling array of black talent" Douglas, *Terrible Honesty*, p. 5.

Page 14
"to be not afraid of anything" Johnson, in Douglas, *Terrible Honesty*, p. 93.
"the secret of life" W. E. B. Du Bois, *The Autobiography*
of W. E. B. Du Bois* (New York: International Publishers, 1968), p. 75.
"They came because" Frederick Douglass, *Narrative Life of Frederick Douglass, An American Slave, Written by Himself* (New York: Norton, 1997), p. 55.
"a whole race trying" Washington, in Carole Marks, *Farewell, We're Good and Gone* (Bloomington: Indiana University Press, 1989), p. 75.

Page 15
In 1705 in colonial Virginia Joel Williamson, *New People* (Baton Rouge: Louisiana State University Press, 1995), pp. 13, 19.
"refused to relegate" ibid., pp. 17–18.
"the pervasiveness of" Blassingame, ibid., p. 23.
"My love for my children" James Weldon Johnson, *The Autobiography of an Ex-Colored Man* (New York: Hill and Wang, 1960), p. 211.
"to all Caucasians" George Schuyler, dedication to *Black No More* (Boston: Northeastern University Press, 1994).
"Throughout the twentieth century" Kathy Russell, Midge Wilson, and Ronald Hall, *The Color Complex: The Politics of Skin Color among African Americans* (New York: Anchor Books, 1992), p. 33.

Page 16
"Wouldn't they be surprised" Angelou, ibid., p. 41.
Negro schools and colleges ibid., p. 24.
"little black Dorothy" Thadious Davis, *Nella Larsen: Novelist of the Harlem Renaissance* (Baton Rouge: Louisiana State University, 1994), p. 141.
"was the one he" Derek Jewell, *Duke: A Portrait of Duke Ellington* (New York: Norton, 1977), p. 17.
"undisguisedly beautiful" Wall, *Women of the Harlem Renaissance*, p. 53.
"intend to express" Hughes, in Douglas, *Terrible Honesty*, p. 83.
"the only plain one" and **"Pride relates more"** Jane Austen, *Pride and Prejudice* (New York: Houghton Mifflin, 1963), p. 14.
"Up you mighty race" David Cronen, *Black Moses: The Story of Marcus Garvey* (Madison: University of Wisconsin Press, 1969), p. 73.
"It is a rare" and **"But to presume"** Huggins, *Harlem Renaissance*, p. 3.

Page 17
"to enjoy that anarchy" W. E. B. Du Bois, *Dust of Dawn* (New York: Schocken, 1968), p. 134.
"a conscious, organized" Douglas, *Terrible Honesty*, pp. 4–5.
"Flaming, burning, searing" Wallace Thurman, foreword to *Fire* (Westport, CT: Negro Universities Press, 1970).
"The New Negro" Brown, in Amritjit Singh, William S. Shiver, and Stanley Brodwin, eds., *The Harlem Renaissance: Revaluations* (New York: Garland, 1989), p. 76.
"derivative, polished" David Levering Lewis, *When*

Harlem Was in Vogue (New York: Oxford University Press, 1981), p. 171.

1. JOSEPHINE BAKER

Page 21
In May 1927 Frederick Lewis Allen, *Only Yesterday: An Informal History of the 1920s* (New York: Harper & Brothers, 1931), p. 169.

Page 22
"Untermensch": in Lynn Haney, *Naked at the Feast* (New York: Dodd, Mead & Co., 1981), p. 89.
an Aryan lovely and an African beast Jean-Claude Baker, *Josephine: The Hungry Heart* (New York: Random House, 1993), p. 161.
"They denounced me as the black devil" ibid., p. 155.
"She had a very elegant" ibid., p. 161.
"He was a real" Josephine Baker and Joseph Bouillon, *Josephine* (New York: Paragon House, 1977), p. 72.
"western civilization," "aviation one of those," and **"sensate superiority"** Wayne Cole, *Charles A. Lindbergh and the Battle Against American Intervention in World War II* (New York: Harcourt Brace Jovanovich, 1974), p. 83.
"Everyone who came too close" Baker, *Josephine*, p. xvii.
"How can I convey the spontaneity" quoted in Phyllis Rose, *Jazz Cleopatra* (New York: Doubleday, 1989), p. 154.
"I had no talent" Baker, *Josephine*, p. 154.
"I don't lie" Haney, *Naked at the Feast*, p. 206.

Page 23
"coal black, pretty, tall" Baker, *Josephine*, p. 15; Haney, *Naked at the Feast*, p. 4.
"He had black skin" and **"light brown, the color"** Baker, *Josephine*, p. 18.
"Josephine's brown skin" ibid., p. 31.
"wanted at any price" ibid., p. 137.
"She hated the color" ibid., p. 245.

Page 24
"Josephine cut his head" ibid., p. 37.
"could hardly write" Bricktop with Jim Haskins, *Bricktop* (New York: Atheneum, 1983), p. 108.
"mirth, music" Baker, *Josephine*, p. 26.
"tears the blood" ibid., p. 38.

Page 25
"Very black" Baker and Bouillon, *Josephine*, p. 21.
"She has chosen" Carrie McDonald, in Baker, *Josephine*, p. 41.
"I'm sorry" Josephine Baker, in Stephen Papich, *Remembering Josephine* (New York: Bobbs-Merrill, 1976), p. 31.
"a pretty boy" Billy Baker, in Baker, *Josephine*, p. 46.
"too young, too small" Sissle, in Rose, *Jazz Cleopatra*, p. 53.
"All those girls" Fredi Washington, in Haney, *Naked at the Feast*, p. 37.
"She'd wear big picture hats" Mildred Hudgins, in Baker, *Josephine*, p. 69.
"doing fine" Adelaide Hall, ibid., p. 65.

Page 26
"Josephine was a mugger" Ethel Waters, *His Eye Is on the Sparrow* (Garden City, NY: Doubleday, 1951), p. 185.
"one of a trio" Haney, *Naked at the Feast*, p. 45.
"My dear, don't ever" and **"Why, those people"** Papich, *Remembering Josephine*, p. 50.

"the little one" ibid., p. 52.
"hips swaying" Rose, *Jazz Cleopatra*, p. 19.

Page 27
"swung and lowered" and **"like a hummingbird"** William Wiser, *The Great Good Place* (New York: Norton, 1991), p. 271.
"The 'Danse de Sauvage'" Essie Robeson, in Baker, *Josephine*, p. 165.
"Her magnificent dark" Haney, *Naked at the Feast*, p. 61.

Page 30
"I was given" Josephine Baker, in Baker, *Josephine*, p. 124.
"I'm not immoral" ibid., p. 175.
"She said she" Papich, *Remembering Josephine*, p. 51.
"I had to succeed" Baker and Bouillon, *Josephine*, p. 58.
"cracked ice" Papich, *Remembering Josephine*, p. 56.
"When he spoke" ibid., p. 57.

Page 31
"like a fabulous" ibid., p. 61.
gowns from the couturiers Wiser, *Great Good Place*, p. 284.
"her reputation" Bricktop, *Bricktop*, p. 108.
"Just as the show" Langston Hughes, *New York Post*, March 27, 1964, p. 26.

Page 32
Hemingway remembered Haney, *Naked at the Feast*, p. 114.
Bubu, a gorilla Baker, *Josephine*, p. 324.
"Thin bodies" Anne Holland, "Women and Fashion," in Kenneth W. Wheeler and Virginia Lussier, eds., *Women, the Arts and the 1920s in Paris and New York* (New Brunswick: Transaction, 1982), p. 116.
"a naughty schoolboy" ibid., p. 121.

Page 33
"We had to hold" Baker, *Josephine*, p. 139.
"small, pale" Haney, *Naked at the Feast*, p. 76.
in love—again Rose, *Jazz Cleopatra*, p. 111.
"He practically put" and **"Josephine was a smart kid"** Bricktop, *Bricktop*, p. 110.
"in Josephine's scheme" Baker, *Josephine*, p. 63.

Page 34
"manipulated her" Wiser, *Great Good Place*, p. 296.
"I want people" Baker, *Josephine*, p. 144.
"admitted that she had made" ibid., p. 147.
"I've heard a lot" Rose, *Jazz Cleopatra*, pp. 118–19.
"That book?" Baker, *Josephine*, p. 149.
two dogs, 196 pairs ibid., p. 154.
"ban Josephine's" Haney, *Naked at the Feast*, p. 147.
"in atonement for outrages" Rose, *Jazz Cleopatra*, p. 129.
"they tore my dress" Baker, *Josephine*, p. 157.

Page 35
"The citizens of Dresden" ibid., p. 161.
"It would have been disagreeable" Wiser, *Great Good Place*, p. 298.
"The sax was going" Rose, *Jazz Cleopatra*, p. 133.
"I don't want to live" Baker, in Rose, *Jazz Cleopatra*, p. 140.
"a dapper vaudevillian" and **"a former music"** Haney, *Naked at the Feast*, p. 159.
Martinique, Algeria Baker, *Josephine*, p. 174.
was not a native Rose, *Jazz Cleopatra*, p. 148.
"In *Chocolate Dandies*" ibid., p. 100.

Page 36

"At home she dressed" ibid., p. 153.
"She left us" Baker, *Josephine*, p. 171.
"She wanted" Langston Hughes, *New York Post*, March 27, 1964, p. 26.
"Josephine Baker is a Saint Louis" Haney, *Naked at the Feast*, p. 202.
"She'll need it" ibid., p. 203.
"One of four years" Baker, *Josephine*, p. 429.

2. WALTER WHITE

Page 39

"In the flickering light" Walter White, *A Man Called White* (New York: Arno Press and the *New York Times*, 1969), p. 11.

Page 40

"White could be one" W. E. B. Du Bois, *Autobiography of W. E. B. Du Bois* (New York: International Publishers, 1968), p. 293.
"I was never completely" Bruce Kellner, *Keep A Inchin' Along* (Westport, CT: Greenwood Press, 1979), p. 7.
"His mother was" E. J. Kahn, Jr., "The Frontal Attacks," part 2, *New Yorker*, September 11, 1948, p. 43.
"It seems altogether fantastic" Claude McKay, *A Long Way from Home* (New York: Arno Press and the *New York Times*, 1969), p. 111.
"I decided that" White, *A Man*, p. 5.
"No matter how low" and **"The South has so dehumanized"** Edward Waldron, *Walter White and the Harlem Renaissance* (Port Washington, NY: Kennikat Press, 1978), p. 53.

Page 41

"so many of the students" David Levering Lewis, *W. E. B. Du Bois: Biography of a Race, 1868–1919* (New York: Henry Holt, 1993), p. 214.
"Every year approximately" White, *A Man*, p. 3.
"impassioned, rabble rousing" ibid., p. 34.
"We never knew" and **"the only independent man"** ibid., p. 35.
"It is your duty" ibid., p. 37.

Page 42

"white man interested" ibid., p. 34.
"whispering about them" "The White House," *Ebony*, April 1946, p. 7.
"Walter White and his glamorous" Zora Neale Hurston, *Dust Tracks on a Road* (Urbana: University of Illinois Press, 1942), p. 313.
"never saw anything" Martin Duberman, *Paul Robeson* (New York: Alfred A. Knopf, 1989), p. 74.
"More vividly" Poppy Cannon, *A Gentle Knight* (New York: Rinehart, 1956), p. 17.
"Hanging like a cloud" and **"Along with these fears"** Walter White to Poppy Cannon, January 11, 1948, Carl Van Vechten Collection, Beinecke Library, Yale University.

Page 43

"After a highly emotional" Cannon, *A Gentle Knight*, p. 10.
"About almost every" ibid., p. 11.
"Newspapers rose" ibid., p. 12.
"a large white woman" ibid., p. 11.
"We lived in a wonderful apartment" Jane White, in

Jervis Anderson, *This Was Harlem* (New York: Farrar, Straus & Giroux, 1982), p. 343.
"Indisputably, the most splendid" ibid., p. 344.
"Since that time" Gladys White, *Ebony*, April 1946, p. 7.
"The Whites belong" ibid., p. 6.
"In all my married life" Gladys White to Walter White, February 5, 1949, Carl Van Vechten Collection.
"a heel" Walter White to Poppy Cannon, February 20, 1949, Carl Van Vechten Collection.
"Why don't you" and **"feverishly and incessantly"** Waldron, *Walter White*, p. 42.
"By the time" ibid., p. 43.

Page 44

"the Negro characters" ibid., p. 47.
"the verdict," "would only result," and **"Is it not about time"** ibid., p. 49.
"I have no quarrel" ibid., p. 51.
"thus giving the publishers" ibid., p. 54.
"I am sorry" ibid., p. 55.
"to see if he" ibid., pp. 59–60.
"yokels, hillbillies and peasants" Mencken, in Frederick Lewis Allen, *Only Yesterday: An Informal History of the 1920s* (New York: Harper & Brothers, 1931), p. 192.
"I can't imagine," "Aren't there some," and **"If not, wouldn't it"** Waldron, *Walter White*, p. 58.

Page 46

"colored people know" and **"You wrote me"** ibid., p. 59.
"that I know" and **"I realize my story"** ibid, p. 60.
"was often absolutely" Du Bois, *Autobiography*, p. 293.
"a bitter and sensational arraignment" Waldron, *Walter White*, p. 64.
"I shall not feel" ibid., p. 73.

Page 47

"Knopf tells me" ibid., p. 76.
"It is a pleasure" Kellner, *Keep A Inchin'*, p. 138.
"a novel must" Wallace Thurman, review of *Flight*, by Walter White, *Messenger*, May 1926, p. 154.
"Mr. White's style" Frank Horne, in Waldron, *Walter White*, p. 102.
"solely for private" and **"Mr. Horne's strictures"** Charles Johnson, ibid.
"surprise, anger and pity" Nella Larsen, ibid., p. 104.
"Horne fails to realize" ibid.
"I have followed" and **"I hasten to extend"** ibid., p. 131.
"ingratiating as Y.M.C.A." McKay, *A Long Way*, p. 110.
"Claude had sent" Waldron, *Walter White*, p. 146.

Page 48

"I hardly think" ibid., p. 149.
"Dr. Henry Grady" and **"Have we put"** White, *A Man*, p. 135.
"dilapidated building" David Levering Lewis, *When Harlem Was in Vogue* (New York: Alfred A. Knopf, 1981), p. 277.
"Dinginess, misery" and **"the pattern of nocturnal"** in White, *A Man*, p. 136.
"screeching hymns" ibid., p. 137.
"I suspect my own" ibid.
breakup of his marriage: Lewis, *When Harlem*, p. 273.
"White's assumption of office" Du Bois, *Autobiography*, p. 294.
"In 35 years" ibid., p. 298.

Page 49
"You have no idea" Cannon, *A Gentle Knight*, pp. 32–33.
"He was a gregarious" Lerone Bennett, *Confrontations: Black and White* (Baltimore: Penguin, 1966), p. 155.
"Walter White forced" Bruce Kellner, ibid.

3. ZORA NEALE HURSTON

Page 51
Leonard "Kip" Rhinelander *Inter-State Tattler*, November 27, 1925.

Page 52
"to the top of" Zora Neale Hurston, *Dust Tracks on a Road* (Urbana; University of Illinois Press, 1942), p. 36.
"the kind of life" Mary Helen Washington, "Zora Neale Hurston: Half a Shadow," in Alice Walker, ed., *I Love Myself When I Am Laughing* (New York: Feminist Press, 1979), p. 20.
"bossman" Zora Neale Hurston, *Their Eyes Were Watching God* (London: J. M. Dent, 1938), p. 1.
"with no white folks" Hurston, *Dust Tracks*, p. 10.
"tongueless, earless" and **"They became lords"** Hurston, *Their Eyes Were Watching God*, p. 1
"She was full" Langston Hughes, *The Big Sea* (New York: Hill and Wang, 1942), p. 239.
"I shall wrassle" Hurston, in Cheryl Wall, *Women of the Harlem Renaissance* (Bloomington: Indiana University Press, 1995), p. 187.
"There is something" and **"Dead leaves"** Hurston, *Dust Tracks*, p. 116.
"There were plenty" ibid., p. 18.
"exhorted all" ibid., pp. 20–21.

Page 53
"the heart and spring" ibid., p. 61.
"there were no" ibid., p. 62.
"That hour began" ibid., p. 89.
"sham and tinsel" ibid., p. 347.
"Although Locke rarely" Steven Watson, *The Harlem Renaissance* (New York: Pantheon, 1995), p. 70.
"No jobs, no friends" Hurston, *Dust Tracks*, p. 168.

Page 54
"not humbled" Walker, dedication to *I Love Myself*, p. 1.
"She walked into my study" in Fannie Hurst, "Zora Neale Hurston: A Personality Sketch," *Yale University Literary Gazette*, vol. 35 (July 1960), p. 17.
"no lurid tales," "a sacred black cow," and **"I found out about forks"** Hurston, *Dust Tracks*, p. 169.
"You made all" Carl Van Vechten to Fannie Hurst, in Bruce Kellner, *The Letters of Carl Van Vechten* (New Haven, CT: Yale University Press, 1987), p. 236.
"As a matter of fact" ibid., p. 276.
"When Zora was" Sterling Brown, in Watson, *Harlem Renaissance*, p. 21.

Page 55
"appeared attired" Bruce Kellner, *Keep A Inchin' Along* (Westport, CT: Greenwood Press, 1979), p. 148.
"tossed a huge" Kellner, *Letters of Carl Van Vechten*, p. 276; Walker, dedication to *I Love Myself*, p. 1.
"dressed up as an Asiatic" Hurston, *Dust Tracks*, p. 310.
"naive, childlike" and **"Miss Hurston was"** Hughes, *Big Sea*, p. 239.
"a highly" Washington, "Zora Neale Hurston," p. 7.
"We have trampled" Watson, *Harlem Renaissance*, p. 143.

"Negro protégés" Charlotte Mason, in Ann Douglas, *Terrible Honesty: Mongrel Manhattan in the 1920s* (New York: Farrar, Straus & Giroux, 1995), p. 282.
"a golden star" Watson, *Harlem Renaissance*, p. 147.
"playing the obsequious" Washington, "Zora Neale Hurston," p. 9.
"a distinguished" Hughes, *Big Sea*, p. 312.

Page 56
"sometimes I would feel" Hurston, *Dust Tracks*, p. 126.
"faithfully to" Charlotte Mason, in Wall, *Women of the Harlem Renaissance*, p. 154.
"guard mother who sits" Hurston, in Watson, *Harlem Renaissance*, p. 148.
"I went to see" quoted in Arnold Rampersad, *The Life of Langston Hughes* (New York: Oxford University Press, 1986), p. 154.
"a little bitty thing" West, in Eleonore van Notten, *Wallace Thurman's Harlem Renaissance* (Amsterdam: Rodopi, 1994), p. 172.
"in village-like Westfield" Hughes, *Big Sea*, p. 320.
"precious brown boy" Alain Locke, in David Levering Lewis, *When Harlem Was in Vogue* (New York: Alfred A. Knopf, 1981), p. 152.
"a malicious" Jervis Anderson, *This Was Harlem* (New York: Farrar, Straus & Giroux, 1982), p. 201.
"too much horseplay" Watson, *Harlem Renaissance*, p. 161.
"vile Louise Thompson" Lewis, *When Harlem Was in Vogue*, p. 261.
"I just went off" quoted in Watson, *Harlem Renaissance*, p. 161.
"except for a few" and **"litigation is the"** Lewis, *When Harlem Was in Vogue*, p. 260.
"had a tantrum" Carl Van Vechten, in Kellner, *Letters of Carl Van Vechten*, p. 186.

Page 58
"Langston and I" Hurston to Carl Van Vechten, 1931, Carl Van Vechten Collection, Beinecke Library, Yale University.
"in his mother's living room" Langston Hughes to Carl Van Vechten, 1931, Carl Van Vechten Collection.
"never heard" Hughes, *Big Sea*, p. 384.
"I really need" Mary Helen Washington, "Zora Neale Hurston," p. 13.
"little mother" ibid., p. 12.
"Your pickaninny, Zora" Douglas, *Terrible Honesty*, p. 283.
"winning and appalling" Alice Walker, dedication to *I Love Myself*, p. 2.
"she was quite capable" ibid., p. 1.
"Born so widely apart" Hurston, *Dust Tracks*, p. 309.
"broke with the tradition in which" Foreword by Mary Helen Washington in Zora Neale Hurston, *Their Eyes Were Watching God* (New York: Harper Perennial, 1999), p. vii.
"I am not tragically" Hurston, "How It Feels," in Walker, *I Love Myself*, p. 153.

Page 59
"pseudo-primitives" Alain Locke, in *Zora Neale Hurston: Critical Perspectives Past and Present*, ed. Henry Louis Gates Jr. and Kwame Anthony Appiah (New York: Amistad, 1993), p. 18.
"What I wanted to tell" Hurston, *Dust Tracks*, p. 206.
"groan when they" ibid., p. 215.

Page 60
"There was a white" ibid., p. 221.
"only an imposing line" and **"Our lives are so diversified"** ibid., p. 218.
"It was sad" Walker, *I Love Myself*, p. 153.
"Ah was born back due in slavery so it wasn't" Hurston, *Their Eyes Were Watching God*, p. 15.
"determined to write" Washington, "Zora Neale Hurston," p. 17.
"their own things" Wall, *Women of the Harlem Renaissance*, p. 141.

Page 61
"the status of earliest" "A Critic at Large," *New Yorker*, February 17, 1997, p. 86.
"dynamics of dissemblance" Darlene Clark Hine, *Hine Sight: Black Women and the Re-Construction of American History* (Brooklyn, NY: Carlson, 1994), p. 37.
"an inside and an outside" Hurston, *Their Eyes Were Watching God*, p. 68.
"pulled [the horizon]" ibid., p. 184.
"no theme" Richard Wright review of *Their Eyes Were Watching God*, *New Masses*, October 5, 1937, in Gates and Appiah, *Zora Neale Hurston*, p. 17.
"That Hurston held" Walker, *I Love Myself*, p. 4.
"I have loved unselfishly" Hurston, *Dust Tracks*, p. 348.

4. A'LELIA WALKER

Page 66
"joy-goddess of Harlem's" Langston Hughes, *The Big Sea* (New York: Hill and Wang, 1942), p. 245.
"no judge of character" Bruce Kellner, *Keep A Inchin' Along* (Westport, CT: Greenwood Press, 1979), p. 154.
"A'Lelia comes in" *Inter-State Tattler*, September 10, 1931, p. 3.
"She was tall" Kellner, *Keep A Inchin' Along*, p. 154.
"princess de-kink" and **"mahogany millionairess"** David Levering Lewis, *When Harlem Was in Vogue* (New York: Alfred A. Knopf, 1981), p. 166.
She also lived ibid., p. 106.
"parasites, jesters" ibid., p. 166.
"looked like a queen" Kellner, *Keep A Inchin' Along*, p. 154.

Page 67
"gorgeous dark Amazon" and **"light-skinned ladies in waiting"** in Jervis Anderson, *This Was Harlem* (New York: Farrar, Straus & Giroux, 1982), p. 340; Kellner, *Keep A Inchin' Along*, p. 154; Hughes, *Big Sea*, p. 245.
"gaslights brightened city nights" A'Lelia Bundles, in "Madam C. J. Walker," *American Heritage* (July/August 1996), p. 45.
"As I bent over the washboard" ibid.; Anderson, *This Was Harlem*, p. 97.
"A big black man" and **"Some of the remedy"** Anderson, *This Was Harlem*, p. 98.
Adopting the title "Madam" a common practice Bundles, "Madam," p. 46.

Page 68
the key to success ibid., p. 45.

Page 69
never use the word "straightener" ibid., p. 46.
"I want to say to every Negro," **"Get up and make them,"** and **A'Lelia did not cross the country** ibid., p. 1212.

A'Lelia married John Robinson *Inter-State Tattler*, September 3, 1931, p. 2.

Page 70
"Once at one" Hughes, *Big Sea*, p. 245.
After getting to know her Bundles, "Madam," p. 1212.
covered in both the black and white press *New York Age*, December 1, 1923.
"the most elaborate social function" Anderson, *This Was Harlem*, p. 225.
"There was an entire absence" *New York Age*, December 1, 1923.

Page 71
"She was too spoiled" Kellner, *Keep A Inchin' Along*, p. 154.
"Quite often" Anderson, *This Was Harlem*, p. 223.
"She made no pretense" Hughes, *Big Sea*, p. 244.
She subscribed *Inter-State Tattler*, August 27, 1931.
"After seven minutes" Lewis, *When Harlem Was in Vogue*, p. 166.
"She wore" Anderson, *This Was Harlem*, p. 226.
"to the intellectuals" Lewis, *When Harlem Was in Vogue*, p. 167.
"the ultimate expression" Annette Tapert and Diana Edkins, *The Power of Style* (New York: Crown, 1994), p. 10.

Page 74
"You should have" Van Vechten, in Kellner, *Keep A Inchin' Along*, p. 282.
"was so spectacular" ibid., p. 154.
"skin was almost black" Anderson, *This Was Harlem*, p. 217.
"but she was nicer" Kellner, *Keep A Inchin' Along*, p. 282.
"It is not for me; it is for my people" Anderson, *This Was Harlem*, p. 96.
"One couldn't help" and **"Literature, politics, painting and music"** Bruce Kellner, *Carl Van Vechten and the Irreverent Decades* (Norman: University of Oklahoma Press, 1968), p. 202.
"She made no effort" Kellner, *Keep A Inchin' Along*, p. 15.
"were attended" Lewis, *When Harlem Was in Vogue*, p. 166.

Page 75
"artists could meet" ibid., p. 168.
Douglas and Nugent ibid., pp. 168–69.
"breed of chiselers" ibid., p. 169.
Frankel papered it ibid., p. 169.
"We dedicate this tower" A'Lelia Bundles, private collection.
"The great room" Nugent, quoted in Lewis, *When Harlem Was in Vogue*, p. 169.
"Dear Members and Friends" Stanley Nelson, *Two Dollars and a Dream*, New York Filmmakers, 1987.
"I have been holding" Anderson, *This Was Harlem*, p. 229.

Page 76
"White Buyers Strip" Stanley Nelson, *Two Dollars*.
"many of which had never," **"The Flemish oak,"** and **"A few of us"** Anderson, *This Was Harlem*, p. 229.
"Mme. Lelia Walker" Lewis, *When Harlem Was in Vogue*, p. 263.
"a gown of beige" Anderson, *This Was Harlem*, p. 230.
"waving their white," **"great deep voice,"** and **A nightclub quartet** Hughes, *Big Sea*, p. 246.
Later at the grave site Ann Douglas, *Terrible Honesty: Mongrel Manhattan in the 1920s* (New York: Farrar, Straus & Giroux, 1995), p. 469.
"That was really the end" Hughes, *Big Sea*, p. 247.

5. JAMES WELDON JOHNSON

Page 79
On August 3, 1914 Barbara Tuchman, *The Guns of August* (New York: Macmillan, 1962), pp. 139–41.
"find all Gods dead" F. Scott Fitzgerald, *This Side of Paradise* (New York: Charles Scribner, 1920).

Page 80
"Not one marcher" David Levering Lewis, *When Harlem Was in Vogue* (New York: Alfred A. Knopf, 1981), p. 10.
"a war to make the world" James Weldon Johnson, *Along This Way* (New York: Viking, 1933), p. 319.
"Why not make America" Lewis, *When Harlem Was in Vogue*, p. 10.
"The ideal constantly" Johnson, *Along This Way*, p. 122.
"monarch material" Zora Neale Hurston, *Dust Tracks on a Road* (Urbana: University of Illinois Press, 1942), p. 296.
"In a land of black mammies" Johnson, *Along This Way*, p. 9.
"when the congregation" ibid., p. 11.

Page 81
"Que dice?" ibid., p. 65.
"in such situations" ibid., pp. 65, 89.

Page 82
"Every bus" ibid., p. 213.
Charles W. Anderson ibid., pp. 218–19; Lewis, *When Harlem Was in Vogue*, p. 145.
"pleasant two years" Johnson, *Along This Way*, p. 250; Lewis, *When Harlem Was in Vogue*, p. 146.
A Hungarian count Johnson, *Along This Way*, p. 379.
"wrote a novel" Lewis, *When Harlem Was in Vogue*, p. 146.
"Grace was heartbroken" Johnson, *Along This Way*, p. 274.

Page 83
"Bookerite" Mary White Ovington, in Lewis, *When Harlem Was in Vogue*, p. 147.
"The central purpose" Johnson, *Along This Way*, p. 309.
"In America . . . it is" Claude McKay, in Steven Watson, *The Harlem Renaissance* (New York: Pantheon, 1995), p. 39.
"the shame of America" Dorothy Sterling and Benjamin Quarles, *Lift Every Voice* (New York: Doubleday, 1965), p. 105.
"saw and talked" Johnson, *Along This Way*, p. 363.

Page 86
"We arranged ourselves" Alice Dunbar-Nelson, *Give Us Each Day: The Diary of Alice Dunbar-Nelson* (New York: Norton, 1984), p. 84.
"other things might" ibid., p. 85.
"We all had" and **"Funny how"** ibid., p. 87.
"So warm was" Carl Van Vechten, in Bruce Kellner, *Keep A Inchin' Along* (Westport, CT: Greenwood Press, 1979), p. 114.
"on the Van Vechten table" Langston Hughes, *The Big Sea* (New York: Hill and Wang, 1942), p. 254.
"all theologians" Frederick Lewis Allen, *Only Yesterday: An Informal History of the 1920s* (New York: Harper & Brothers, 1931), p. 193.
"big magazines threw" and **"Negro writers"** Johnson, *Along This Way*, p. 305.

Page 87
"He is not afraid" Johnson, in Ann Douglas, *Terrible Honesty: Mongrel Manhattan in the 1920s* (New York: Farrar, Straus & Giroux, 1995), p. 18.
"[I] struggled" ibid., p. 374.
"The final measure" James Weldon Johnson, *The Book of American Negro Poetry* (New York: Harcourt, Brace & World, 1959), p. 9; Lewis, *When Harlem Was in Vogue*, p. 149.
"a center for literary and theater people" Johnson, *Along This Way*, p. 378.
"There were present" ibid., p. 376.
"Clarence Darrow" ibid., p. 379.
"never in better" Van Vechten, in Kellner, *Keep A Inchin' Along*, p. 118.
"smart New York" and **"Everybody was wildly"** Essie Robeson, in Martin Duberman, *Paul Robeson* (New York: Alfred A. Knopf, 1989), p. 536.

Page 88
"She would as soon" Lewis, *When Harlem Was in Vogue*, p. 166.
"he was a close friend" quoted in Jervis Anderson, *This Was Harlem* (New York: Farrar, Straus & Giroux, 1982), p. 345.
"If you are in town" and **"Love to both from us"** Bruce Kellner, *The Letters of Carl Van Vechten* (New Haven, CT: Yale University Press, 1987), p. 116.
"complete with inscription" Heywood Hale Broun, *Whose Little Boy Are You?* (New York: St. Martin's, 1983), pp. 44–45.
"Supreme Court Justice" Johnson, *Along This Way*, p. 405.

Page 89
"It was a grateful relief" ibid., p. 408.
"The funeral was beautiful" Kellner, *Keep A Inchin' Along*, p. 263.
"the foremost black man" and **"literary dilettante, scribbling prose or verse"** Eugene Levy, *James Weldon Johnson: Black Leader, Black Voice* (Chicago: University of Chicago Press, 1973), p. 348.
"I don't know anybody" Van Vechten, in Kellner, *Keep A Inchin' Along*, p. 119.

6. ETHEL WATERS

Page 91
Hot Chocolates Barry Singer, *Black and Blue: The Life and Lyrics of Andy Razaf* (New York: Schirmer Books, 1992), pp. 212–22.

Page 92
"I was always" Ethel Waters, *His Eye Is on the Sparrow* (Garden City, NY: Doubleday, 1951), p. 1.
"dark brown in color" ibid., p. 3.
"She lived—after" ibid., p. 4.
"she took me" ibid., p. 67.
"She had very good reasons" Van Vechten, in Bruce Kellner, *Keep A Inchin' Along* (Westport, CT: Greenwood Press, 1979), p. 167.
"I've always thought" Waters, *His Eye Is on the Sparrow*, p. 65.

Page 93
"The boys in the band" ibid., p. 146.
"You don't become" Susannah McCorkle, "The Mother of Us All," *American Heritage*, vol. 95 (February–March 1994), pp. 60–73.

"Her world was really" Waters, *His Eye Is on the Sparrow*, p. 8.
"education in life" ibid., p. 49.
"With Mom and Ching" ibid., p. 60.
"If you dare" ibid., p. 64.
"to replace me" ibid., p. 73.

Page 95
"ran up and down" ibid., p. 74.
"It fell like rain" ibid., p. 73.
"direct from St. Louis" ibid., p. 75.
"I still had" and **"clean surroundings"** ibid., p. 87.

Page 98
"heavy-set, dark" ibid., p. 91.
"You ain't so bad" ibid., p. 92.
"In those days" ibid., p. 123.
"For entertainers" ibid., p. 124.

Page 99
"white society folks" ibid., p. 131.
"wanting to get away" ibid., p. 137.
"sitting behind a desk" ibid., p. 141.
A college chemistry major and **"He wasn't sure"** ibid., p. 142.
"he egg[ed] me into" ibid., p. 176.
"No white audience" ibid., p. 173.

Page 101
"stepped out of the line" ibid., p. 185.
"I didn't see" and **"White people"** ibid., p. 194.
"Cold borsch!" and **"the caviar"** ibid., p. 195.
"The rich, white historian" and **"informal way of living"** ibid., p. 196.
"who appeared out of nowhere" ibid., p. 197.
"Being a mother" ibid., p. 201.
"much lighter than I," **"almost white and very beautiful,"** **"couldn't figure,"** and **"I guess they suspected"** ibid., p. 203.
"I didn't like it" ibid., p. 211.
"the talent man" ibid., p. 198.

Page 102
"black jester" Donald Bogle, *Toms, Coons, Mulattoes, Mammies, and Bucks* (New York: Continuum, 1996), p. 19.
"the fleas outdrew us at every performance" Waters, *His Eye Is on the Sparrow*, p. 213.
"I was singing" ibid., p. 220.
"Ethel Waters" *New Yorker*, December 23, 1933, p. 11.
"Her features," **"iridescent,"** and **"sophisticated"** Bogle, *Toms, Coons*, p. 68.

Page 103
"I wish I was" *Chicago World*, February 28, 1935.
"the portrait" Bogle, *Toms, Coons*, pp. 59, 63, 82.
"blues singing" *Cleveland Press*, November 2, 1939.
"They were blessed" Langston Hughes, *The Ways of White Folks* (New York: Vintage, 1962), p. 20.

7. LOUIS ARMSTRONG

Page 107
Eighteenth Amendment Frederick Lewis Allen, *Only Yesterday: An Informal History of the 1920s* (New York: Harper & Brothers, 1931), pp. 82–83.

Page 108
no written record James Lincoln Collier, *Louis Armstrong: An American Genius* (New York: Oxford University Press, 1983), p. 4.
"all but invented jazz" Duke Ellington, *Music Is My Mistress* (Garden City, NY: Doubleday, 1973), p. 236.
"amazing virtuosity" Bruce Kellner, *The Harlem Renaissance* (Westport, CT: Greenwood Press, 1979), p. 15.
"a city of ancient wealth" Collier, *Louis Armstrong*, p. 9.
"I was touring," **"a real sharp man,"** and **"My father"** ibid., p. 19.

Page 109
"I sure had a ball" Armstrong, in Mike Pinfold, *Louis Armstrong: His Life and Times* (New York: Universe Books, 1987), p. 20.
"the old sisters of my neighborhood" Louis Armstrong, *Satchmo: My Life in New Orleans* (New York: Prentice-Hall, 1954), p. 7.
"chilling in the pulpit" and **"One of my father's"** James Baldwin, *Notes of a Native Son* (Boston: Beacon Press, 1955), p. 72.
"I used to take Mama" Collier, *Louis Armstrong*, p. 95.
"to carry on" Armstrong, *Satchmo*, p. 137.
"Mother, sister and I" and **"I did not stay"** ibid., p. 25.

Page 110
early instruction Pinfold, *Louis Armstrong*, p. 26.
"cute and cheerful" Collier, *Louis Armstrong*, p. 62.
"He was the one" Pinfold, *Louis Armstrong*, p. 26.

Page 111
"What a thrill that was!" Armstrong, *Satchmo*, p. 137.
"I had no idea" ibid., p. 189.
"I felt pretty bad" ibid., p. 158.
"a small, thin" Collier, *Louis Armstrong*, p. 81.

Page 114
"She never acknowledged" ibid., p. 82.
"She had a big basket" Armstrong, *Satchmo*, p. 229.
"There was no place" ibid., pp. 229–30.
"He wore" Robert Hoskins, *Louis Armstrong: Biography of a Musician* (Los Angeles: Holloway House, 1979), p. 114.

Page 115
"hearing from all" ibid., p. 118.
"Everything he had" Collier, *Louis Armstrong*, p. 94.
"The guys who called me Henpeck" Hoskins, *Louis Armstrong*, p. 94.
"One of the most" John Hammond, in Collier, *Louis Armstrong*, p. 223.
"I wasn't up" Pinfold, *Louis Armstrong*, p. 39.
"blackness" and **"blue vein society"** Collier, *Louis Armstrong*, p. 117.

Page 116
"He was big and fat" ibid., p. 125.
"We were going" Pinfold, *Louis Armstrong*, p. 41.
"I remember" ibid., p. 45.
"When them cats" Hoskins, *Louis Armstrong*, p. 130.
"O'Banion's head" Pinfold, *Louis Armstrong*, p. 46.
"Al always showed up" ibid., p. 47.
"Many stories have" Collier, *Louis Armstrong*, p. 152.

Page 117
"would run to the wagon" Earl Hines, in Pinfold, *Louis Armstrong*, p. 47.
"Danger was dancing" Armstrong, ibid.
"His salary" Collier, *Louis Armstrong*, p. 154.
"Louis was wild" Hines, in Pinfold, *Louis Armstrong*, p. 52.
"Long before time" Collier, *Louis Armstrong*, p. 205.

"Louis's habit" Mezz Mezzrow, quoted in Pinfold, *Louis Armstrong*, p. 56.
"When I saw Pops" Buck Clayton, quoted ibid.
"Don't know when" Lil of Alpha, quoted in Hoskins, *Louis Armstrong*, p. 133.

Page 119
"It reached the point" and **"Them characters"** Collier, *Louis Armstrong*, p. 31.
"There is a debt" *Inter-State Tattler*, November 11, 1927.
"Way back" Pinfold, *Louis Armstrong*, p. 103.

8. BESSIE SMITH AND ALBERTA HUNTER

Page 121
America's love affair Frederick Lewis Allen, *Only Yesterday: An Informal History of the 1920s* (New York: Harper & Brothers, 1931), pp. 5, 6, 134.
"I knew I would" Frank Taylor with Gerald Cook, *Alberta Hunter: A Celebration in Blues* (New York: McGraw-Hill, 1987).

Page 122
"grave voice of overpowering" James Lincoln Collier, *Louis Armstrong: An American Genius* (New York: Oxford University Press, 1983), p. 137.
"sadness . . . not softened" Daphne Duval Harrison, *Black Pearls: Blues Queens of the 1920s* (New Brunswick: Rutgers University Press, 1988), p. 53.
"Bessie Smith was the greatest" Nat Shapiro and Nat Hentoff, *Hear Me Talkin' to Ya* (New York: Dover Publications, 1955), p. 247.
"that Bessie Smith's" Chris Albertson, *Bessie* (New York: Stein and Day, 1972), p. 66.
"If I'm lucky enough" Alberta Hunter, in Harrison, *Black Pearls*, p. 201.
"With few exceptions" Alan Lomax, *The Land Where Blues Began* (New York: Dell, 1945), p. 360.
"You can send me" Harrison, *Black Pearls*, p. 53.
"When we sing" Hunter, in Shapiro and Hentoff, *Hear Me Talkin' to Ya'*, pp. 246–47.
"Bessie sang of mean" Albertson, *Bessie*, p. 50.
"well-known New York" Langston Hughes, *The Big Sea* (New York: Hill and Wang, 1942), p. 254.
"To render a 'Blues Song'" Barry Singer, *Black and Blue: The Life and Lyrics of Andy Razaf* (New York: Schirmer Books, 1992), p. 68.

Page 123
"I don't think" Hunter, in Taylor, *Alberta Hunter*, p. 64.
"the Raineys didn't have" and **"She was just a teenager"** Albertson, *Bessie*, p. 27.
"there was the chorus" Shapiro and Hentoff, *Hear Me Talkin' to Ya*, p. 242.

Page 124
"Got the world" Albertson, *Bessie*, p. 27.
"two-hundred-pound" and **"Nobody messed with Bessie"** Steven Watson, *The Harlem Renaissance* (New York: Pantheon, 1995), p. 120.
"prissy Henderson" Ethel Waters, *His Eye Is on the Sparrow* (Garden City, NY: Doubleday, 1951), p. 141.
"enormous and barely" Collier, *Louis Armstrong*, p. 137.
"Bessie Smith, blues singer" *Amsterdam News*, September 1937.
"The more she made" Albertson, *Bessie*, p. 59.

Page 125
"a mean man" Sidney Bechet, *Treat It Gentle* (London: Cassell & Co., Ltd., 1960), p. 137.
"Oh the blues had got me" Smith, in Harrison, *Black Pearls*, p. 79.
"a voice full of shouting" and **"Yo' brag to"** Carl Van Vechten, in Bruce Kellner, *Keep A Inchin' Along* (Westport, CT: Greenwood Press, 1979), p. 162.
"hysterical shrieks of" ibid., p. 163.
"Don't let nobody" Smith, in Watson, *The Harlem Renaissance*, p. 101.
"Bessie would do" Albertson, *Bessie*, p. 128.

Page 126
"I truly believe Bessie was getting ready" Albertson, *Bessie*, p. 131.
"Please listen" Harrison, *Black Pearls*, p. 71.
"The worst show" Albertson, *Bessie*, p. 156.
"the ignorant darky" ibid., p. 160.
"Bessie had a new lover" ibid., p. 177.

Page 127
"She was *too* far" Bechet, *Treat It Gentle*, p. 138.
"Jack didn't throw" Albertson, *Bessie*, p. 21.
"Bessie scaled" *Chicago Defender*, April 1937.
"There ain't no place" Albertson, *Bessie*, p. 127.
a headstone was purchased ibid., p. 234.

Page 128
"She wasn't a crybaby" Taylor, *Alberta Hunter*, p. 4.
"singing earthy" Harrison, *Black Pearls*, p. 200.
"He may be your man" ibid., p. 161.
"Bessie had trouble" Taylor, *Alberta Hunter*, p. 64.
"color complex" ibid., p. 51.

Page 130
"most sophisticated woman" ibid., p. 82.
"They were like" and **"What will people say?"** ibid., p. 72.
"You felt so sorry" Eubie Blake, in Donald Bogle, *Brown Sugar* (New York: Harmony Books, 1980), p. 27.
"The shows here" Taylor, *Alberta Hunter*, p. 91.

Page 131
"I do not know" ibid.
"Alberta resented" ibid., p. 94.
"when to hang" Harrison, *Black Pearls*, p. 207.
"Down-hearted Blues" ibid., p. 208.
"To think that I—me—poor" Taylor, *Alberta Hunter*, p. 102.
"unassuming like" "Let It Be Classy," *New Yorker*, October 31, 1977.
"When [Paul] sang" ibid., p. 102.

Page 132
"I want to say" Taylor, *Alberta Hunter*, p. 105.
"Alberta? She never spent" Jean-Claude Baker, *Josephine: The Hungry Heart* (New York: Random House, 1993), p. 165.
"When the dream" Taylor, *Alberta Hunter*, p. 126.
"When I came home" and **"She sure gave me a hard time"** ibid., p. 104.
"I got a mind to ramble" Harrison, *Black Pearls*, p. 199.
"Alberta came in one of her outfits" Taylor, *Alberta Hunter*, p. 232.

Page 133
"I did, real soft" and **"Every part of her"** ibid., p. 104.
"If I should get" Albertson, *Bessie*, p. 136.
"They wouldn't accept us" Taylor, *Alberta Hunter*, p. 68.

"stormed stages" Bogle, *Brown Sugar*, p. 31.
"When I get home" Bessie Smith, "Lock and Key" c. 1927.

9. JESSIE FAUSET AND NELLA LARSEN

Page 135
Richard Simon Frederick Lewis Allen, *Only Yesterday* (New York: Harper & Brothers, 1931), p. 159.
Howard University *Afro-American Encyclopedia*, s.v. "Howard University."

Page 136
"Parents hoped that" Stephanie Shaw, *What a Woman Ought to Be and Do* (Chicago: University of Chicago Press, 1996), p. 24.
"Booker T. Washington" ibid., p. 25.
novel *Batouala* Fauset admired *Batouala* and twice reviewed it in the *Crisis*. It contained, however, discussions of topics like polygamy and rituals like the "Dance of Love." Bonner, in Cheryl Wall, *Women of the Harlem Renaissance* (Bloomington: Indiana University Press, 1995), p. 4.
James Weldon Johnson Bruce Kellner, *Keep A Inchin' Along* (Westport, CT: Greenwood Press, 1979), p. 73.
"lived with her" Carl Van Vechten, *Nigger Heaven* (New York: Knopf, 1926), p. 66.
"mystery woman" Wall, *Women of the Harlem Renaissance*, p. 88.
"had ruined her life" Charles R. Larson, *Invisible Darkness: Jean Toomer and Nella Larsen* (Iowa City: University of Iowa Press, 1993), p. 72.

Page 137
"Picture to yourself" *Crisis*, September 1915, p. 249.
"belonged to that closed" Claude McKay, *A Long Way from Home* (New York: Arno Press and the *New York Times*, 1969), p. 122.
"inhibition" Fauset, in Wall, *Women of the Harlem Renaissance*, p. 39.
director of publicity and research W. E. B. Du Bois, *The Autobiography of W. E. B. Du Bois* (New York: International Publishers, 1968), p. 255.

Page 138
"At the Seventh Avenue" Langston Hughes, *The Big Sea* (New York: Hill and Wang, 1942), p. 247.
"a high class journal" George Hutchinson, *The Harlem Renaissance in Black and White* (Cambridge: Harvard University Press, 1995), pp. 143–44.
"near full responsibility" Carolyn Sylvander, *Jessie Redmon Fauset: Black American Writer* (Troy, NY: Whitston, 1981), p. 59.
"Then one day" Fauset, in Wall, *Women of the Harlem Renaissance*, p. 63.
"Jessie Fauset, the managing editor" Hughes, *Big Sea*, p. 93.
"for I knew" ibid., p. 94.

Page 139
"'mid-wife' to the Renaissance" ibid., p. 218.
"one of the least" Wall, *Women of the Harlem Renaissance*, p. 36.
"Miss Fauset is dainty" McKay, *Long Way from Home*, p. 112.
"for honesty" and **"active but hardly"** David Levering Lewis, *When Harlem Was in Vogue* (New York: Alfred A. Knopf, 1981), p. 121.

"those breathing-spells" Wall, *Women of the Harlem Renaissance*, p. 38.
"Is this colored" Ovington, in Lewis, *When Harlem Was in Vogue*, p. 124.
"time to move beyond" Locke, ibid., p. 274.
"undisguisedly beautiful" Wall, *Women of the Harlem Renaissance*, p. 53.
"In brief, there is nothing" Fauset, *There Is Confusion* (Boston: Northeastern University Press, 1989), p. 232.
"We are constantly" Sylvander, *Jessie Redmon Fauset*, p. 69.

Page 141
"a pretty brown girl" "Emmy," *Crisis*, May 1913.
"there's a man" James Weldon Johnson, *The Book of American Negro Poetry* (New York: Harcourt, Brace & World, 1959), pp. 206–7.
"A swift response, an instant glad surrender" Fauset, in Sylvander, *Jessie Redmon Fauset*, p. 102.
"I am glad" Fauset, in Sylvander, *Jessie Redmon Fauset*, p. 38.
"when she first" Ethel Ray Nance, in Gloria Hull, *Color, Sex, and Poetry* (Bloomington: Indiana University Press, 1987), p. 12.
"In an age" Wall, *Women of the Harlem Renaissance*, p. 32.
"stifles," "chokes" Bonner, in Wall, *Women of the Harlem Renaissance*, p. 4.

Page 142
"middle class" Hughes, in Hutchinson, *Harlem Renaissance*, p. 156.
"Can publishers," "I do not believe," and **"This question seems to be senseless"** "The Negro in Art," *Crisis*, vol. 31, 1926, pp. 214–20, 278–80.
As George Hutchinson points out Hutchinson, *Harlem Renaissance*, p. 156.
"How is it" Du Bois, in Lewis, *When Harlem Was in Vogue*, p. 177.

Page 143
"the embarrassment" and **"financial worries"** ibid., p. 177.
"I am properly" Sterling Brown, in Sylvander, *Jessie Redmon Fauset*, p. 113.
"Some months ago" Langston Hughes, ibid.
"She made a beautiful" Harold Jackman, in Thadious Davis, *Nella Larsen: Novelist of the Harlem Renaissance* (Baton Rouge: Louisiana State University Press, 1994), p. 306.
"Fauset took the marriage" ibid.
"enjoying housework" Sylvander, *Jessie Redmon Fauset*, p. 81.

Page 144
"I have always" Fauset, in Lewis, *When Harlem Was in Vogue*, p. 274.
Erring Woman's Refuge for Reform Davis, *Nella Larsen*, p. 29; Wall, *Women of the Harlem Renaissance*, p. 91.
"I don't see my family" Wall, *Women of the Harlem Renaissance*, p. 91.
"I did not know I had a sister" Davis, *Nella Larsen*, p. 454.

Page 146
"her dislike" Larsen, in Wall, *Women of the Harlem Renaissance*, p. 92.
"only slightly brown" Davis, *Nella Larsen*, p. 129.
"She represented" ibid., p. 30.

Page 147
"liked white women" ibid., p. 362.
"not believing in religion" Larsen, in Wall, *Women of the Harlem Renaissance*, p. 97.
"Right now when" Davis, *Nella Larsen*, p. 228.
"Had Walker been" ibid., p. 227.
"I have gone" Larsen, ibid., p. 212.
"and other cultural" ibid., p. 14.
"We sat about" ibid., p. 234.

Page 148
"Negro society" Nella Larsen, *Quicksand and Passing* (New Brunswick, NJ: Rutgers University Press, 1993), p. 8.
"I'm terribly excited" Davis, *Nella Larsen*, p. 209.
"For the past month" ibid., pp. 199–200.

Page 149
"Enthusiasm, spontaneity" Larsen, *Quicksand*, p. 4.
"sacrificed" Deborah McDowell, in Larsen, *Quicksand*, p. xi.
"The author of *Quicksand*" Wallace Thurman, in Eleonore van Notten, *Wallace Thurman's Harlem Renaissance* (Amsterdam: Rodopi, 1994), p. 165.
"It is . . . the best" Du Bois, in Davis, *Nella Larsen*, p. 280.
"one female character's" McDowell, in Larsen, *Quicksand*, p. xxvi.
"a strangely" Carl Van Vechten, in Larson, *Invisible Darkness*, p. 87.
"the success of the novel" Du Bois, ibid.

Page 150
"To tell" Eda Lou Walton, in Davis, *Nella Larsen*, p. 229.
"color of maple syrup" and **"that people"** Wall, *Women of the Harlem Renaissance*, p. 119.
"There is much" Larson, *Invisible Darkness*, p. 68.
"striking resemblance" ibid., p. 96.
"and as for" Harold Jackman, ibid.

Page 151
"All literary Harlem" ibid.
"No one who" Davis, *Nella Larsen*, p. 349.
"you should have heard" ibid., p. 354.
"Now that Nella" Jackman, ibid., p. 357.
"It has been a rotten" Larson, *Invisible Darkness*, p. 99.

Page 152
"At forty-five" Davis, *Nella Larsen*, p. 333.
"Please cheer Nella" ibid., p. 353.
"There can" Larson, *Invisible Darkness*, p. 102; Davis, *Nella Larsen*, p. 362.
"I want to do all" Larson, *Invisible Darkness*, p. 102.
"I think my book" ibid., p. 103.
"About Elmer" ibid., p. 106.
"small, depressing place" ibid., p. 109.
"I don't know how wise it is" ibid., pp. 109–10.
"acute congestive" ibid., p. 115.

10. FLORENCE MILLS

Page 158
"dainty wistfulness" Bruce Kellner, *The Harlem Renaissance* (Westport, CT: Greenwood Press, 1979), p. 246.
"she was all too" Countee Cullen, in Jervis Anderson, *This Was Harlem* (New York: Farrar, Straus & Giroux, 1982), p. 181.
"Her control over" *Inter-State Tattler*, November 11, 1927, p. 3.
"There are notes" *Sunday New York Graphic*, 1927.

"High silver" Beverly Nichols, in *Sketch*, February 16, 1927, p. 304.
"And yet" James Weldon Johnson, *Black Manhattan* (New York: Atheneum, 1975), p. 199.
"She had a small" Ethel Waters, *His Eye Is on the Sparrow* (New York: Doubleday, 1951), p. 183.
"The upper range" and **"I'm a Little Blackbird"** Johnson, *Black Manhattan*, p. 199.
"and she did it" ibid., p. 200.
"The masses love Miss Mills" and **"More, they adore her"** *Inter-State Tattler*, November 11, 1927, p. 2.
"The funeral service of the Beloved Florence" ibid., p. 3.
"a certain famous" and **"They are so weak"** Nichols, in *Sketch*, February 16, 1927, p. 304.

Page 159
"only pluck" and **"She could be whimsical"** Johnson, *Black Manhattan*, p. 199.
"on the stage practically all her life" and **"appeared a number"** ibid., p. 197.
"The silliest, smallest" Nichols, in *Sketch*, February 16, 1927, p. 304.
"who had colored," **"because he was black,"** and **"It is ridiculous"** Hammer Swafter, in *Daily Express*, September 1927, p. 229.
"Miss Otis regrets" and **"Those bums"** Bricktop, in Jim Haskins, *Bricktop* (New York: Atheneum, 1983), p. 166.

Page 160
"through that particularly hard" Johnson, *Black Manhattan*, p. 198.
"Florence Mills skyrocketed" Langston Hughes, *The Big Sea* (New York: Hill and Wang, 1942), p. 223.
"Never had I" Claude McKay, *A Long Way from Home* (New York: Arno Press and the *New York Times*, 1969), p. 141.
"to head a cast in an all-colored revue" and **"give her a chance"** *New York Graphic*, September 1927.

Page 161
"discovery and exploitation" and **"An intemperate perfectionist"** Barry Singer, *Black and Blue: The Life and Lyrics of Andy Razaf* (New York: Schirmer Books, 1992), p. 243.
"understand the colored man" Lew Leslie, ibid., p. 209.
"They could hear" and **"Finally Leslie"** Jimmy Durante, *Night Clubs* (New York: Alfred A. Knopf, 1931), p. 176.

Page 164
"the New York manner" ibid.
"Miss Mills is as modest" *New York Age*, October 27, 1927.
"The success acquired" *Times* (London), 1927.
"I felt that Broadway" Waters, *His Eye Is on the Sparrow*, p. 183.
"catchy lyrical passages" Derek Jewell, *Duke: A Portrait of Duke Ellington* (New York: Norton, 1977), p. 45.
"You can take" comparison to Josephine Baker, in Jean-Claude Baker, *Josephine: The Hungry Heart* (New York: Random House, 1993), p. 139.
"She loved Florence Mills" ibid.
"Miss Mills' popularity was unbounded" *Daily Express*, 1927.
"When the shimmy" Haney, *Naked at the Feast*, p. 188.

Page 165
"Any lover of the beautiful" Vicar of St. Alden's, in Ann

Douglas, *Terrible Honesty: Mongrel Manhattan in the 1920s* (New York: Farrar, Straus & Giroux, 1995), p. 216.
"dreams of the future of her people" *London Express,* September 1927.
"I want to help the colored" ibid.
"To return to my heart's one real and great ache" *Observer,* September 1927.
"sing and dance" Douglas, *Terrible Honesty,* p. 18.
"Because the great" *Inter-State Tattler,* September 23, 1927.
"Florence Mills is" Anderson, *This Was Harlem,* p. 181.
"success never changed her" *Amsterdam News,* November 2, 1927.
"We are glad" *Inter-State Tattler,* October 7, 1927.

Page 167
"for a lengthy period prior to her last illness" *Inter-State Tattler,* November 11, 1927.
"Florence Mills" and **"Miss Mills"** *Amsterdam News,* November 2, 1927.
"Harlem was stunned" Johnson, *Black Manhattan,* p. 206.
"was a private patient" *Amsterdam News,* November 2, 1927.
"The death of the Queen of Happiness" *Amsterdam News,* November 9, 1927.
"Her funeral was" Johnson, *Black Manhattan,* p. 200.
"It was a beautiful" Hughes, *Big Sea,* p. 274.
"crowded with onlookers" *Amsterdam News,* November 9, 1927.
"Hall Johnson's choir" and **"She started"** Johnson, *Black Manhattan,* p. 200.
"The great lid" *Amsterdam News,* November 9, 1927.

Page 168
"Her existence" *Inter-State Tattler,* November 11, 1927, p. 4.
"There is, to me" Nichols, in *Sketch,* February 16, 1927, p. 304.

Page 169
"Down South is still terrible" ibid.

11. DUKE ELLINGTON

Page 171
first radio broadcast Michele Hilmes, *Radio Voices: American Broadcasting, 1922–1952* (Minneapolis: University of Minnesota Press, 1997), p. 93.

Page 172
"Bach and myself" Richard Boyer, "Hot Bach," in Mike Tucker, ed., *The Duke Ellington Reader* (New York: Oxford University Press, 1993), p. 216.
"the most fascinating" Billy Strayhorn, ibid., p. 269.
"Ellington plays the piano" ibid., p. 220.
"Duke directed his orchestra" "Duke Ellington at the Salle Pleyel," in Tucker, *Duke Ellington Reader,* p. 84.
"I don't write jazz" ibid., p. 218.
"I like great" ibid., p. 230.
"His pulse is so low" Boyer, ibid., p. 225.
"a prophet" Spike Hughes, ibid., p. 69.
"A gentleman never" Duke Ellington, *Music Is My Mistress* (Garden City, NY: Doubleday, 1973), p. 12.
"When I was five" ibid., p. 9.
"She was very soft-spoken" ibid., p. 15.
"pretty things like" ibid., p. 20.

Page 173
"By booking bands" ibid., p. 32.
"He was hanging" Bechet, *Treat It Gentle* (London: Cassell & Co., 1960), p. 140.
"We were very young" Edna Ellington, in Derek Jewell, *Duke: A Portrait of Duke Ellington* (New York: Norton, 1977), p. 38.
"I guess I should" Edna Ellington, ibid., p. 31.
"He is also" Richard Boyer, in Tucker, *Duke Ellington Reader,* p. 217.
"a regular companion" Mildred Dixon, in Jewell, *Duke,* p. 49.
"for the young lady" Ralph Gleason, in Jewell, *Duke,* p. 49.

Page 174
"New York filled our imagination" Ellington, *Music Is My Mistress,* p. 35.
"the endless circuit" Jewell, *Duke,* p. 33.
"We were exposed" Ellington, *Music Is My Mistress,* p. 92.
"On my way up" ibid., p. 69.
"Mr. Barron Wilkins" and **"We were only five"** ibid., p. 64.
"It was what" ibid., p. 28.
"If any one of us" ibid., p. 70.
"the place the top entertainers and gamblers" Jewell, *Duke,* p. 34.
"The procedure . . . was very simple" Ellington, *Music Is My Mistress,* p. 72.
"a low-ceilinged" Barry Singer, *Black and Blue: The Life and Lyrics of Andy Razaf* (New York: Schirmer Books, 1992), p. 144.

Page 176
"was bumped off" Jimmy Durante, *Night Clubs* (New York: Knopf, 1931), p. 116.
"The audition was set" Ellington, *Music Is My Mistress,* p. 76.
"Be big" Jim Haskins, *The Cotton Club* (New York: Random House, 1977), p. 44.
"Impeccable behavior" Ellington, *Music Is My Mistreess,* p. 80.

Page 177
"He has a passion" Boyer, in Tucker, *Duke Ellington Reader,* p. 267.
"He has forty-five suits" ibid., p. 217.
"aristocratic in demeanor" John Husse, *Beyond Category* (New York: da Capo, 1993), p. 59.
"It is a place" Hughes, in Tucker, *Duke Ellington Reader,* p. 70.
"at least five foot six" Haskins, *Cotton Club,* p. 23.
white women often pretended to be light-skinned Negroes" ibid., p. 57.
"The owners were very solicitous" ibid., p. 48.
"They were so dirty" Lew Fields, ibid., p. 49.

Page 180
"We came in" Jewell, *Duke,* p. 46.
"I had a fabulous" Sonny Greer, in Haskins, *Cotton Club,* p. 52.
"Paul Whiteman" ibid., p. 58.
"It didn't have" Ned Williams, in Tucker, *Duke Ellington Reader,* p. 271.
"the unforgettable night" Tucker, ibid., p. 272.
"intricate and unbelievably" Haskins, *Cotton Club,* p. 53.

Page 181

"Before long, nearly every American who had a radio" Haskins, *Cotton Club*, p. 57.

"All the big" Ellington, *Music Is My Mistress*, p. 80.

"It didn't really matter" Haskins, *Cotton Club*, p. 58.

"A big bookmaker" ibid., p. 56.

"wraith-like" Singer, *Black and Blue*, p. 100.

"I keep hearing" Greer, in Haskins, *Cotton Club*, p. 58.

"Anything you want" ibid., p. 59.

"'Hey, Duke" Ellington, *Music Is My Mistress*, p. 82.

"Connie Immerman welcomed" Haskins, *Cotton Club*, p. 59.

"You were always" Durante, *Night Clubs*, p. 114.

"We used to hang out at this place" Ellington, *Music Is My Mistress*, p. 93.

Page 182

"puts everybody on" Davis, in Jewell, *Duke*, p. 16.

"All the kings and queens" Durante, *Night Clubs*, p. 114.

"The memory of" and **"may be more important"** Boyer, in Tucker, *Duke Ellington Reader*, p. 218.

"a boy and a girl" ibid., p. 230.

"I can score with a lead pencil" ibid., p. 219.

Page 183

"He waved his arms" Haskins, *Cotton Club*, p. 64.

"While Cab Calloway" and **"This was odd"** Jervis Anderson, *This Was Harlem* (New York: Farrar, Straus & Giroux, 1982), p. 336.

"warned everyone" Ellington, *Music Is My Mistress*, p. 135.

"Sonny, I was calling him the Wale" and **"the Duke of Hot"** ibid., p. 84.

"all of Paris" Bricktop with Jim Haskins, *Bricktop* (New York: Atheneum, 1983), p. 186.

Page 184

"She heaped goodies" Ellington, *Music Is My Mistress*, p. 196.

"I brought Franklin, Jr." Bricktop, *Bricktop*, p. 187.

"If the town" Boyer, in Tucker, *Duke Ellington Reader*, p. 221.

"the train" ibid., p. 218.

"He would listen" Jewell, *Duke*, p. 64.

"especially in the South" Boyer, in Tucker, *Duke Ellington Reader*, p. 218.

"when [Duke] got off" Jewell, *Duke*, p. 99.

"Duke spends money" Boyer, in Tucker, *Duke Ellington Reader*, p. 245.

"His career" Stanley Dance, ibid., p. 383.

Page 185

"The most fascinating" Jewell, *Duke*, pp. 16–17.

"a constant revelation" Tucker, *Duke Ellington Reader*, p. 367.

"He worked hard" Dance, ibid., p. 383.

"Biographies are like tombstones" Jewell, *Duke*, p. 21.

"Do Nothing Til" Steven Watson, *The Harlem Renaissance* (New York: Pantheon, 1995), p. 180.

12. BILL "BOJANGLES" ROBINSON

Page 187

Jack Johnson, *Jack Johnson in the Ring and Out* (Chicago: National Sports Publishing Company, 1927), pp. 7, 9, 70–88, 257.

Page 188

"employed his entire body" quoted in Bruce Kellner, *Keep A Inchin' Along* (Westport, CT: Greenwood Press, 1979), p. 188.

"Bill Robinson is a well-preserved" and **"The real Bill Robinson"** Walter Stewart, *New York World Telegram*, February 6, 1937.

"putting the tap" ibid., February 24, 1932.

"Harlem was crazy" Ethel Waters, *His Eye Is on the Sparrow* (Garden City, NY: Doubleday, 1951), p. 157.

"working men" St. Clair McKelway, "Bojangles," *New Yorker Profiles*, October 6–13, 1937, p. 32.

Page 189

"reads only with difficulty" ibid., p. 28.

"Boys and girls" ibid., p. 26.

"copacetic" and **"I'd rather leave"** *New York Daily News*, December 22, 1931.

Page 190

"did not sit well" Jim Haskins and N. R. Mitgang, *Mr. Bojangles: The Biography of Bill Robinson* (New York: Morrow, 1988), p. 97.

"out riding" McKelway, "Bojangles," part 2, p. 32.

"But he was . . . partial" *New York World Telegram*, February 6, 1937.

"with no discussion" Ann Douglas, *Terrible Honesty: Mongrel Manhattan in the 1920s* (New York: Farrar, Straus & Giroux, 1995), p. 360.

"forgot the words" Barry Singer, *Black and Blue: The Life and Lyrics of Andy Razaf* (New York: Schirmer Books, 1992), p. 208.

Page 191

"His stunt of dancing" James Weldon Johnson, *Black Manhattan* (New York: Atheneum, 1978), p. 214.

"When Bill visits" McKelway, "Bojangles," part 1, p. 27.

"A benefit performance" and **"By the time"** McKelway, "Bojangles," part 2, p. 33.

"the spectacularly well-to-do" ibid, p. 32.

"I promised to come" Waters, *His Eye Is on the Sparrow*, p. 157.

Page 194

"Studio heads" Douglas, *Terrible Honesty*, p. 420.

"disoriented, baffled clown" Donald Bogle, *Toms, Coons, Mulattoes, Mammies, and Bucks* (New York: Continuum, 1994), p. 28.

"Uncle Billy" Shirley Temple, in *The Littlest Rebel*, 1935.

"As Uncle Billy" Bogle, *Toms, Coons*, p. 50.

"bad, mean" Shirley Temple, in *The Little Colonel*, 1935.

"for that little girl" Haskins and Mitgang, *Mr. Bojangles*, p. 283.

Page 195

"with a faintly" McKelway, "Bojangles," part 2, p. 34.

"Bill Robinson" Johnson, *Black Manhattan*, p. 214.

"was sitting on top" Haskins and Mitgang, *Mr. Bojangles*, p. 133.

"Bert Williams was the funniest man" Mabel Rowland, *Bert Williams: Son of Laughter* (New York: Negro Universities Press, 1969), p. 128.

"I was always" Bert Williams, in Rowland, *Bert Williams*, p. 2.

"I am inclined" ibid., p. 9.

"a great black face" *New York Herald*, February 21, 1906.

"I'm a Jonah Man" in Rowland, *Bert Williams*, p. 41.

Page 196

"*The Gold Bug*" Johnson, *Black Manhattan*, p. 104.
the cakewalk Rowland, *Bert Williams*, pp. 60–62.
"The people who wrote" Ring Lardner, in Rowland, *Bert Williams*, p. 63.
"I often think of the old court jesters" Rowland, *Bert Williams*, p. 195.
"It did not seem" Heywood Hale Broun, in Rowland, *Bert Williams*, p. 97.
"Bert Williams" "Bert Williams," *Messenger*, April 1922, p. 394.

Page 197

"When the lights" and **"I'd never heard of Harlem"** Johnny Hudgins, in *Daily News Magazine*, February 21, 1988, p. 18.
"carries the burden" *Inter-State Tattler*, October 1924.
"white folks" and **"minstrel-evocative"** Singer, *Black and Blue*, p. 209.
"a girl in the chorus" Johnson, *Black Manhattan*, p. 190.
Stepin Fetchit and **"tricked into thinking"** Bogle, *Toms, Coons*, p. 41.

Page 198

civil rights groups began protesting ibid., p. 43.
"Minstrel Man" Langston Hughes, in Arnold Rampersad, ed., *Collected Poems of Langston Hughes* (New York: Vintage, 1995), p. 61.
debts Bogle, *Toms, Coons*, p. 49.
"content to make the world" "Who's Who," *Messenger*, April 22, 1922.
"they hadn't heard" Langston Hughes, *The Big Sea* (New York: Hill and Wang, 1942), p. 228.

13. CARL VAN VECHTEN

Page 203

"old-fashioned American idealism" Frederick Lewis Allen, *Only Yesterday: An Informal History of the 1920s* (New York: Harper & Brothers, 1931), p. 168.

Page 204

"But there are" Bruce Kellner, ed., *The Letters of Carl Van Vechten* (New Haven: Yale University Press, 1987), p. 44.
"I can't afford" Van Vechten, in Bruce Kellner, *Carl Van Vechten and the Irreverent Decades* (Norman: University of Oklahoma Press, 1968), p. 137.
"We have never had a quarrel" ibid., p. 57.
"received up to 25" obituary, *New York Times*, December 22, 1964.
"Negrotarian" Hurston, in David Levering Lewis, *When Harlem Was in Vogue* (New York: Alfred A. Knopf, 1981), p. 98. · ·
"unpredictable, undependable" Hurston, in Bruce Kellner, ed., *Keep A Inchin' Along* (Westport, CT: Greenwood Press, 1979), p. 114.
"splendid" Kellner, *Irreverent Decades*, p. 149.

Page 205

"Let's keep this" Jervis Anderson, *This Was Harlem* (New York: Farrar, Straus & Giroux, 1982), p. 142.
"flippantly fastidious" Ann Douglas, *Terrible Honesty: Mongrel Manhattan in the 1920s* (New York: Farrar, Straus & Giroux, 1995), p. 288.
"thrived on his" Anderson, *This Was Harlem*, p. 214.

"red and gold" Kellner, *Irreverent Decades*, p. 133; Douglas, *Terrible Honesty*, p. 285.
"to allow two" and **"While an"** Nathan Huggins, *Harlem Renaissance* (New York: Oxford University Press, 1971), p. 99.
"No one" James Weldon Johnson, in Anderson, *This Was Harlem*, p. 215.
"Sullen-mouthed" Lewis, *When Harlem Was in Vogue*, p. 182.
"I became violently" Carl Van Vechten, in Huggins, *Harlem Renaissance*, p. 99.
"I loathed it" obituary, Carl Van Vechten, *New York Times*, December 22, 1964.
"the late and last" Kellner, *Irreverent Decades*, p. 7.

Page 206

"I have never" ibid., p. 210.
"was enchanted" ibid., p. 8.
"blond, buck-toothed" ibid., p. 243.
"We thought" ibid., p. 17.
"Carl wasn't any good" ibid., p. 16.
"most constant" and **"maddening serenity"** ibid., p. 18.
"Chicago was actually" ibid., p. 20.
"She has studied" and **"was discharged"** ibid., p. 33.
"How much money" and **"What particular advantage"** ibid., p. 39.

Page 207

"You take my breath" ibid.
"Dearest boy" ibid., p. 40.
alimony ibid., p. 57.

Page 208

"I went to see" Kellner, *Letters of Carl Van Vechten*, p. 4.
"I have really been postponing" ibid., p. 14.
"I am expecting" ibid., p. 15.
"Resents" Kellner, *Irreverent Decades*, p. 88.
$783 Kellner, *Letters of Carl Van Vechten*, p. 15.
"Dearest Baby" ibid., p. 25.

Page 212

buff, lavender Kellner, private correspondence.
"Almost everything" Kellner, *Letters of Carl Van Vechten*, p. 23.
"We had a special seance" ibid., p. 33.
"They were so Negro" Langston Hughes, *The Big Sea* (New York: Hill and Wang, 1940), p. 251.
"the midtown branch" Bruce Kellner, *Keep A Inchin' Along* (Westport, CT: Greenwood Press, 1979), p. 135.
"Walter White" Kellner, *Letters of Carl Van Vechten*, p. 69.
"I'm causing" ibid., p. 70.
"We became intimate" Kellner, *Keep A Inchin'*, p. 117.
"At the moment" ibid., p. 141.

Page 213

"Your letters" Kellner, *Letters of Carl Van Vechten*, p. 79.
"Thanks a lot" ibid., p. 93.
"Chief Long Lance" Hughes, *The Big Sea*, p. 251.
"everybody was at liberty" ibid., p. 253.
"the principal excitement" Thadious Davis, *Nella Larsen: Novelist of the Harlem Renaissance* (Baton Rouge: Louisiana State University Press, 1994), p. 224.

Page 214

"the gems in the Crown" Kellner, *Letters of Carl Van Vechten*, p. 190.
"sometime lover, perhaps" Kellner, private correspondence.

Harold Jackman was also Van Vechten's friend Douglas, *Terrible Honesty.*
"boxes and boxes" Kellner, *Keep A Inchin'*, p. 131.
"Walking slowly" in Kellner, *Keep A Inchin'*, p. 162.
"Fania Marinoff and I" ibid., p. 164.
"I am quite certain" ibid.

Page 215
"her greatest performance" ibid.
"Get the fuck" Chris Albertson, *Bessie* (New York: Stein and Day, 1972), p. 143.
"Bessie herself" ibid., p. 145; Douglas, *Terrible Honesty*, p. 413.
"She was making" and "the only adequate" Kellner, *Keep A Inchin'*, p. 164.
"superior to any" ibid., p. 165.
"At any rate," "I am," and "Occasionally" ibid., p. 167.
"the enormous Majestic Theatre" Kellner, *Letters of Carl Van Vechten*, p. 92.

Page 216
appealing primitivism Douglas, *Terrible Honesty*, p. 288; Lewis, *When Harlem Was in Vogue*, p. 188. Kellner disputes.
"I shall" Kellner, *Letters of Carl Van Vechten*, p. 80.
"agent, PR man, banker" Douglas, *Terrible Honesty*, p. 288.
"the beneficent godfather of all" Anderson, *This Was Harlem*, p. 215.
"Are Negro writers" Lewis, *When Harlem Was in Vogue*, p. 177.
"[Hester] particularly assumed an aggressive" Carl Van Vechten, *Nigger Heaven* (New York: Alfred A. Knopf, 1926), p. 18.
"Nigger Heaven!" Anderson, *This Was Harlem*, p. 218.
"patronized Negroes" and "quite all right" Claude McKay, *A Long Way from Home* (New York: Arno Press and the *New York Times*, 1969), p. 319.
"Most of the white people" Anderson, *This Was Harlem*, p. 216.

Page 217
"A blow" and "Mr. Van Vechten" ibid., p. 219.
"Here lies" Kellner, *Irreverent Decades*, p. 218.
"in 1932 Van Vechten took up the hobby" obituary, *New York Times*, December 22, 1964.

14. LANGSTON HUGHES

Page 219
In 1916 the first mass exodus Carole Marks, *Farewell, We're Good and Gone* (Bloomington: Indiana University Press, 1989), p. 19.
"on a train" James Weldon Johnson, *Black Manhattan* (New York: Atheneum, 1975), p. 151.

Page 220
"My theory" quoted in Arnold Rampersad, *The Life of Langston Hughes* (New York: Oxford University Press, 1986), p. 4, Langston Hughes Papers, Yale University.
"in years of nomadic" ibid.
"sang far better" Johnson, *Black Manhattan*, p. 123.
"loud laughter," "learned to play," and "What is in" Langston Hughes, "Beggar Boy," in Arnold Rampersad, ed., *The Collected Poems of Langston Hughes* (New York: Vintage, 1995), p. 29.
"light olive in complexion" Langston Hughes, *The Big Sea* (New York: Hill and Wang, 1942), p. 11.

"past seventy" ibid., p. 17.
"In America" ibid., p. 24.
"In nothing but books" ibid., p. 16.

Page 221
"Rents were very high" ibid., p. 27.
"Just like niggers" ibid., p. 37.
"Sure, go on!" ibid., p. 38.
"I did not hear" ibid., p. 39.
"I didn't want" ibid., p. 53.
"I felt guilty" ibid., p. 54.

Page 222
"I've known rivers" ibid., pp. 55–56.
"A writer?" ibid., p. 61.
"More than Paris" ibid., p. 62.
"I had never" in ibid, p. 81.
"All gone" ibid., p. 84.
"He didn't" ibid., p. 85.
"dull jobs for low wages" ibid., p. 89.

Page 223
"It was written" ibid., p. 92.
"the *Crisis* people" ibid., p. 94.
liked each other Rampersad, *Life of Langston Hughes*, p. 63.
"Write to him" ibid., p. 67, Alain Locke Papers, Howard University.
"I do want" ibid., p. 68, Alain Locke Papers, Howard University.
"how delightful" ibid., p. 70, Alain Locke Papers, Howard University.
"See Paris and die" Steven Watson, *The Harlem Renaissance* (New York: Pantheon, 1995), p. 59.
"You should see" Rampersad, *Life of Langston Hughes*, pp. 73–74.
"virile brown god" ibid., p. 81, Alain Locke Papers, Howard University.
"In this circle" ibid., p. 82.

Page 224
"The canals, and the kids" Hughes, *Big Sea*, p. 140.
"May I come now please" David Levering Lewis, *When Harlem Was in Vogue* (New York: Alfred A. Knopf, 1981), p. 83.
"At increasing cost" Alain Locke to Langston Hughes, Langston Hughes Papers, Yale University.
"sudden and unexpected" Rampersad, *Life of Langston Hughes*, p. 83, Alain Locke Papers, Howard University.
Rayford Logan Hughes, *Big Sea*, p. 157.
"was very pretty" ibid., p. 160.
"Years later" Bricktop with Jim Haskins, *Bricktop* (New York: Atheneum, 1983), p. 86.
"I cannot describe" Langston Hughes to Alain Locke, July 31, 1924, Langston Hughes Papers, Yale University.

Page 225
"Dr. Locke knew Venice" Hughes, *Big Sea*, p. 189.
"Perhaps his ardor" Rampersad, *Life of Langston Hughes*, p. 94.
"he knew two men" ibid., p. 133.
"If certain of his responses" ibid.
"Even then" ibid., p. 289.
"I sat at a table" Hughes, *Big Sea*, p. 202.
"Kingston Hughes" Rampersad, *Life of Langston Hughes*, p. 97.

Page 228
"It all sounded" Hughes, *Big Sea*, p. 202.

"Vachel Lindsay" and "my first publicity break" ibid., p. 212.
"often the head waiter" ibid., p. 214.
"cultured colored" ibid., p. 204.

Page 229
"Droning a drowsy" Watson, *Harlem Renaissance*, p. 73.
"She is a clever girl" Rampersad, *Life of Langston Hughes*, p. 107, Carl Van Vechten Papers, Yale University.
"a charming woman poet" Hughes, *Big Sea*, p. 216.
"as the car stopped" Gloria Hull, *Color, Sex, and Poetry* (Bloomington: Indiana University Press, 1987), p. 210.
"As she sketched" Hughes, *Big Sea*, p. 218.
"a strange kind of fellow" ibid., p. 238.

Page 230
"incarnation" Watson, *Harlem Renaissance*, p. 86.
"He was black" ibid., p. 87.
"brilliant black boy" and "Wallace Thurman wrote" Hughes, *Big Sea*, p. 234.
"the old, dead conventional" ibid., p. 235.
"I have just tossed," "Langston Hughes displays," and "Finally, irony of ironies" ibid., p. 237.
The next day ibid., p. 238.
"little Negro children" Rampersad, *Life of Langston Hughes*, p. 147.
"the innocent and noble" ibid., p. 148.
"I found her" Hughes, *Big Sea*, p. 312.
"a gift for a young poet" ibid., p. 313.
"my winged poet Child who as he flies" Rampersad, *Life of Langston Hughes*, p. 149.
"The lazy, laughing South" Langston Hughes, "The South," in Rampersad, *Collected Poems of Langston Hughes*, p. 26.

Page 231
"Of all the niggerati" Hughes, *Big Sea*, p. 238.
"generous monthly allowance" ibid., p. 319.
"with advice from Locke" Rampersad, *Life of Langston Hughes*, p. 155.
"held contractual" Watson, *Harlem Renaissance*, p. 157.

Page 232
"an itty-bitty" Eleonore van Notten, *Wallace Thurman's Harlem Renaissance* (Amsterdam: Rodopi, 1994), p. 205.
"crown the exchange," "pardon the impertinence," and "Groom Sails" Watson, *Harlem Renaissance*, p. 162.
"I am not wise" Rampersad, *Life of Langston Hughes*, p. 188.
"she pushed her hat" Langston Hughes to Carl Van Vechten, February 4, 1931, Carl Van Vechten Papers, Yale University.

Page 233
"But nine-tenths" ibid.
"We were no longer" Langston Hughes, *Big Sea*, p. 334.
"lecturing throughout America" Watson, *Harlem Renaissance*, p. 176.
"not wanting to trouble" ibid., p. 179.

15. DOROTHY WEST

Page 235
"In those days" Robert S. Lynch and Helen Merrill Lynch, *Middletown* (New York: Harcourt, Brace & World, 1929), p. 157.
"gained prestige" Frederick Lewis Allen, *Only Yesterday:*

An Informal History of the 1920s (New York: Harper & Brothers, 1931), p. 133.
"restaurateurs became familiar" Fannie Hurst, *No Food with My Meals* (New York: Harper, 1935), p. 8.
"schools, the pulpit" Richard Hooker, *Food and Drink in America: A History* (Indianapolis: Bobbs-Merrill, 1981), p. 300.
"more and more" Lynch and Lynch, *Middletown*, p. 157.

Page 236
"When I was" Dorothy West, in *Vineyard Gazette*, August 21, 1990, p. 14.
"I have no ability" Dorothy West, *The Richer, the Poorer* (New York: Doubleday, 1995), p. 167.
"when [Paul and Essie] Robeson" Robeson, in Martin Duberman, *Paul Robeson* (New York: Alfred A. Knopf, 1989), p. 592 n. 20.
"Many Negroes have colorphobia" Nannie Burroughs, "Not Color But Character," *Voice of the Negro*, vol. 1, no. 7, July 1904, p. 277.
"Why, lightning bugs" Zora Neale Hurston, *Harlem Language*, University of Florida Collection.
"they were not too dismayed" Dorothy West, *The Living Is Easy* (Boston: Houghton Mifflin, 1948), p. 105.
"West writes" Mary Helen Washington, preface to West, *Richer, Poorer*, p. xiii.
"She can be wickedly eloquent" "Dorothy West, a Harlem Renaissance Writer Dies at 93," *New York Times*, August 19, 1998, p. A29.

Page 237
"So I went" West, *Richer, Poorer*, p. 177.
"ambitious and industrious," "pay an indigent townsman," "My father's dream," and "Black Banana King" ibid., p. 179.

Page 238
"My father was a generation older" ibid.
"he was good" Dorothy West, *The Wedding* (New York: Doubleday, 1995), p. 24.
"Brown mothers" ibid., p. 239.
"I helped raise my grandmother's" and "By the time" Dorothy West, *New York Times Book Review*, February 12, 1995, p. 11.
"The days were full" West, *Richer, Poorer*, p. 173.

Page 239
"We were always" and "outranked and" ibid., p. 171.
"God allowed" introduction to West, *Richer, Poorer*, p. 2.
"We thought" "Dorothy West," *New York Times*, August 19, 1998.
"To write that she" Eleonore van Notten, *Wallace Thurman's Harlem Renaissance* (Amsterdam: Rodopi, 1994), p. 250.
"I went to the Harlem Renaissance" Mary Helen Washington, "I Sign My Mother's Name," in Ruth Perry and Martine Watson Brownley, eds., *Mothering the Mind* (New York: Holmes and Meier, 1984), p. 150.
"mile-a-minute patter" obituary, *Vineyard Gazette*, August 21, 1998.
"If I had married him" Interview with Dorothy West, May 6, 1978, Black Women's Oral History Project, Radcliffe College.
"brilliant black boy" Langston Hughes, *The Big Sea* (New York: Hill and Wang, 1942), p. 234.
"he wanted to be" ibid., p. 235.

Page 240
"Thurman was a slight man" West, *Richer, Poorer,*
pp. 215, 216.
"he was more black" Nugent, in Steven Watson, *The
Harlem Renaissance* (New York: Pantheon, 1995), p. 87.
"In *The Blacker,*" and **"Dark skins"** West, *Richer, Poorer,*
p. 219.
"two young girls" in van Notten, *Wallace Thurman's
Harlem Renaissance,* pp. 283–84.
"We used to call Wallie" in Watson, *Harlem Renaissance,*
p. 88.
"a whirlwind of activity" Arnold Rampersad, *The Life of
Langston Hughes* (New York: Oxford University Press,
1986), pp. 118–19.

Page 241
"He began to surround" West, "Elephants Dance,"
Richer, Poorer, p. 220.
"Unless buttressed" ibid., p. 221.
"more typical of the epoch" ibid., p. 215.
"Whodathought" Thurman, in van Notten, *Wallace
Thurman's Harlem Renaissance,* p. 301.
"Thurman was" ibid., p. 103.
"had an oft-repeated" ibid., p. 203.
"It's just" ibid., p. 204.

Page 242
"sometimes white" Nathan Huggins, *Harlem Renaissance*
(New York: Oxford University Press, 1971), p. 23.
"little bitty" West, in van Notten, *Wallace Thurman's
Harlem Renaissance,* p. 203.
"Wallie should perk" ibid., p. 206.
"I was in the middle" ibid., p. 205.
"Woe is me" ibid., p. 207.
"The fact that she" West, *Richer, Poorer,* p. 272.
"I was just a little girl" Washington, "I Sign My
Mother's Name," p. 150.

Page 243
"The Harlem Renaissance" West, *Richer, Poorer,* p. 3.
"Augusta Savage is here" Countee Cullen to Dorothy
West, October 10, 1929, Dorothy West Correspondence,
Schlesinger Library, Radcliffe College.
"And by all means" Countee Cullen to Dorothy West,
July 19, 1931, Dorothy West Correspondence, Schlesinger
Library, Radcliffe College.
"giving the appearance" Frank Taylor, with Gerald
Cook, *Alberta Hunter: A Celebration in Blues* (New York:
McGraw-Hill, 1987), p. 80.
"Harlem . . . had a taste" West, *Richer, Poorer,* p. 220.
"Dot! Darling" Taylor, *Alberta Hunter,* p. 131.

Page 244
"It was so good" Countee Cullen to Dorothy West,
Dorothy West Correspondence, Schlesinger Library, Radcliffe College.
"Mr. West [Dorothy's father] said" Rachel Benson West
to Dorothy West, December 3, 1932, Dorothy West Correspondence, Folder 12, Schlesinger Library, Radcliffe College.
"half Chinese," March 5, 1933, p. 5, Dorothy West Correspondence, Schlesinger Library, Radcliffe College.
"were involved" Arnold Rampersad, *The Life of Langston
Hughes* (New York: Oxford University Press, 1986), p. 268.
"Big-boned" ibid., p. 211.
"Don't stay" Hughes, *Big Sea,* p. 62.

Page 245
"Dot, I have some news" Rachel Benson West to Doro-
thy West, February 10, 1933, Dorothy West Correspon-
dence, Folder 2, Schlesinger Library, Radcliffe College.
"My father's death" and **"All I want in life"** Dorothy
West to Rachel Benson West, March 5, 1933, May 26,
1933, Dorothy West Correspondence, Folder L, Schle-
singer Library, Radcliffe College.
"Don't think" Dorothy West to Rachel Benson West,
March 5, 1933, p. 6, Dorothy West Correspondence,
Schlesinger Library, Radcliffe College.
"She is a better cook" Dorothy West to Rachel Benson
West, Thursday, no year, Dorothy West Correspondence,
Folder 1, Schlesinger Library, Radcliffe College.
"It does not seem to challenge anything" and **"high
schoolish and pink tea"** van Notten, *Wallace Thurman's
Harlem Renaissance,* p. 302.

Page 246
"She was dark" West, *Living Is Easy,* p. 39.
"is the fountainhead" Washington, "I Sign My Mother's
Name," p. 153.
"She came to see" obituary, *Vineyard Gazette,* August 21,
1998.
"Though there was never" West, preface to *The Wed-
ding.*

Page 247
"immaturity and incomplete" and **"Wallace Thurman"**
West, *Richer, Poorer,* p. 227.
"with none of his" and **"His death . . . caused"** ibid.,
p. 215.
"So suddenly" West, in David Levering Lewis, *When
Harlem Was in Vogue* (New York: Oxford University Press,
1981), p. 304.
"The younger Negroes" Watson, *Harlem Renaissance,*
p. 163.
"the darker brother" Langston Hughes, in Arnold Rampersad, *The Collected Poems of Langston Hughes* (New York:
Vintage, 1995), p. 46.

PERMISSIONS

ILLUSTRATION CREDITS

ABBREVIATIONS

Beinecke: Courtesy of Yale Collection of American Literature, Beinecke Rare Book and Manuscript Library, Yale University, Estate of Carl Van Vechten and the James Weldon Johnson Papers

The Crisis, the official magazine of the NAACP, magazine of the National Association for the Advancement of Colored People.

Schomburg: Courtesy of Schomburg Center for Research in Black Culture, Photographs and Prints Division, the New York Public Library, Astor, Lenox, and Tilden Foundations

Endpapers: Courtesy Elizabeth Campbell Rollins.

I. OUT OF THE SOUTH

Page 18: Courtesy of the Hogan Jazz Archive, Tulane University, New Orleans.

1. JOSEPHINE BAKER

Pages 20, 23: Frank Driggs. **24:** Agence France Presse. **27:** The Image Works. **28:** *Tatler*, October 17, 1928, the Illustrated London News Library. **29:** Schomburg (top left), UPI/Corbis-Bettmann (top right), the *Inter-State Tattler* Collection, Schomburg (middle right), Courtesy of the Département des Photographies, Bibliothèque de Nationale de la Ville de Paris (middle left), Sygma, New York/Keystone, Paris (bottom). **31:** Courtesy of the Département des Photographies, Bibliothèque de Nationale de la Ville de Paris. **32** Sygma, New York/Keystone, Paris. **33:** Photograph by Harlingue-Viollet, Courtesy Roger-Viollet, Paris. **35:** Hulton Getty, Liaison Agency Inc., New York. **37:** Sipa Photos, New York.

2. WALTER WHITE

Pages 38, 41, 42, 45 (bottom left), **49:** Courtesy of Beinecke. **45:** Photograph by Morgan and Marvin Smith, Courtesy of Monica Smith and Schomburg, © Monica Smith (top left), Courtesy of the Library of Congress, Prints and Photographs Division, © Leigh Lewis and Nicholas Langen (top and bottom right). **46:** *The Crisis*, Courtesy the NAACP.

3. ZORA NEALE HURSTON

Page 50: Photograph by Carl Van Vechten, Beinecke. **52:** Photograph by Howard Sheen, Courtesy the Sheenway School. **55:** Courtesy the Amistad Research Center, Tulane University. **57, 60:** Courtesy of the Zora Neale Hurston Papers, George A. Smathers Libraries, University of Florida (top left, top right, bottom left and middle), Moorland Spingarn Research Center, Howard University (top middle), Beinecke (center), Photograph by Carl Van Vechten, Courtesy of the Library of Congress, Prints and Photographs Divi-

sion, **58:** Photograph by Alan Lomax, Courtesy of Library of Congress, Prints and Photographs. **61:** *The New York World Telegraph & Sun*, October 15, 1937, Courtesy of Library of Congress, Prints and Photographs.

II. HOME TO HARLEM

Page 62: Schomburg.

4. A'LELIA WALKER

Page 64: Schomburg. **67:** Beinecke. **68, 69:** Photographs by James VanDerZee, © Donna M. VanDerZee. **70:** The New York Age (top and bottom). **72:** *The Messenger* (left and top right), Courtesy of A'Lelia Bundles (middle and bottom right). **73:** *The Messenger* (top left and right), Courtesy of A'Lelia Bundles (bottom left and right). **77:** Courtesy the Countee Cullen/Harold Jackman Collection, Special Collections, Robert W. Woodruff Library, Atlanta University.

5. JAMES WELDON JOHNSON

Pages 78, 81, 89: Beinecke. **84:** Beinecke (top right and left, bottom left), Schomburg, Manuscripts Division (middle and bottom right). **85:** Beinecke (top left and right), *The Crisis* (middle), *The Messenger* (bottom left and right). **88:** Carl Van Vechten Memorial Papers, Manuscript Division, New York Public Library.

6. ETHEL WATERS

Pages 90, 95: Beinecke. **94:** Frank Driggs. **96:** Beinecke (top), Courtesy the Amistad Research Center, Tulane University (middle), Photograph by Morgan and Marvin Smith, Courtesy Monica Smith and Schomburg, © Monica Smith (bottom). **97:** Courtesy of the Theatre Stills Division, Schomburg, Photograph by Alfredo Valente, Courtesy of Keith deLellis (middle), Courtesy Private Collection (bottom right). **100:** Photograph by Rudolf H. Hoffman, Courtesy Private Collection. **103:** Photograph by Carl Van Vechten, Courtesy the Countee Cullen/Harold Jackman Collection, Special Collections, Robert W. Woodruff Library, Atlanta University.

III. GOING TO CHICAGO

Page 104: Courtesy Michael Ochs Archive.

7. LOUIS ARMSTRONG

Pages 106, 115, 117: Frank Driggs. **111:** Michael Ochs Archive. **112:** Courtesy Hogan Jazz Archive, Tulane University (top), Frank Driggs (bottom left), Courtesy *Vanity Fair* and Maria Elena Rico Covarrubias (bottom right). **113:** Schomburg (top left), the *Inter-State Tattler* Collection, Schomburg (top right), Hogan Jazz Archive, Tulane University, New Orleans (bottom). **114:** Institute of Jazz Studies, Rutgers University. **118:** Corbis-Bettmann. **119:** Wide World Photos, New York.

8. BESSIE SMITH AND ALBERTA HUNTER

Pages 120, 125, 129: Frank Driggs. **123:** Corbis-Bettmann. **124:** *The Chicago Defender.* **126:** Photograph by Carl Van Vechten, Beinecke. **127:** Courtesy of Maria Elena Rico Covarrubias. **128:** Schomburg. **130:** Beinecke. **131:** Courtesy of Jim Haskins. **132:** Photograph by Morgan and Marvin Smith, Courtesy of Monica Smith and Schomburg, © Monica Smith. **133:** Photograph by David Redfern, Courtesy of Retna Ltd.

9. JESSIE FAUSET AND NELLA LARSEN

Page 134: Courtesy of the Library of Congress, Prints and Photographs Division. **137:** Regina Andrews Collection, Schomburg. **140:** Courtesy Division of Rare and Manuscript Collections, Carl A. Kroch Library, Cornell University (top left), Schomburg (top right), *The Crisis* (middle and bottom left), Beinecke (middle right), *The Messenger* (bottom right). **142:** Moorland Spingarn Research Center, Howard University. **143:** Courtesy W. Tjark and Renate Reiss and Fisk University Art Galleries, Nashville, Tennessee. **145:** Courtesy of Library of Congress, Manuscripts Division, Harmon Foundation Records. **146:** Schomburg. **148, 149, 150:** Beinecke. **151:** Corbis-Bettmann. **153:** Photograph by Carl Van Vechten, Beinecke.

IV. WASHINGTON, D.C., CONNECTIONS

Page 154: Corbis-Bettmann.

10. FLORENCE MILLS

Page 158: Photograph by James VanDerZee, © Donna M. VanDerZee. **160:** *The Messenger.* **161:** Schomburg. **162:** Photograph by Gushiniere, Schomburg (top left), *The Messenger* (top right), Schomburg, Manuscripts Division (bottom left), New York Public Library Picture Collection (bottom right). **163:** Frank Driggs (top, middle), Culver Pictures Inc. (bottom left). **166:** Photograph by Alexander Bassano, Courtesy National Portrait Gallery, London. **168–169:** Corbis-Bettmann.

11. DUKE ELLINGTON

Pages 170, 180, 182: Frank Driggs. **173:** Courtesy of the Smithsonian Institution. **175:** Carl Van Vechten Papers, Manuscripts and Archives Division, the New York Public

Library. **176:** Courtesy Elizabeth Campbell Rollins. **178:** Schomburg (top left), © Al Hirschfeld (top right). Art reproduced by special arrangement with Hirschfeld's exclusive representative, the Margo Feiden Galleries Ltd., New York. Courtesy of Ole Brask (middle), Schomburg Manuscripts Division (bottom left). **179:** Corbis-Bettmann (top), Photographs by Morgan and Marvin Smith, Courtesy Monica Smith and Schomburg, © Monica Smith (bottom left and right). **183, 185:** Corbis-Bettmann.

12. BILL "BOJANGLES" ROBINSON

Page 186: Beinecke. **189, 198, 199:** Moorland Spingarn Research Center, Howard University. **190, 191, 192** (top left and bottom right), **193** (bottom right), **197:** The Museum of Modern Art, Film Stills Department. **192:** Courtesy of Maria Elena Rico Covarrubias (top right), Corbis-Bettmann (bottom left). **193:** Photograph by Morgan and Marvin Smith, Courtesy Monica Smith and Schomburg, © Monica Smith (top), Beinecke (middle), the Amistad Research Center, Tulane University (bottom left). **195:** The Amistad Research Center, Tulane University.

V. PARIS: SOCIÉTÉ DES AMIS DES NOIRS

Page 200: Beinecke.

13. CARL VAN VECHTEN

Pages 202, 204, 205, 207, 210 (top left and right, middle and bottom right), **211** (top left and bottom), **213:** Carl Van Vechten Papers, Manuscripts and Archives Division, the New York Public Library. **209, 217:** Photograph by Nickolas Muray, Courtesy of the International Museum of Photography at the George Eastman House, Rochester, New York. **210:** *The Messenger* (bottom left). **211:** Courtesy Maria Elena Rico Covarrubias (top right). **214, 215:** Special Collections Library, Millersville University, Pennsylvania.

14. LANGSTON HUGHES

Page 218: Photograph by Nickolas Muray, Courtesy of the International Museum of Photography at the George Eastman House, Rochester, New York. **221, 225, 226** (bottom), **227** (far left), **228, 233:** Beinecke. **222, 224, 226** (middle left), **227** (bottom right): Schomburg. **226:** Courtesy of the Westfield Historical Society (top right), the Moorland Spingarn Research Center, Tulane University (middle right). **227:** Photograph by Underwood and Underwood, Beinecke (top right), Atlanta (middle bottom). **231:** Photograph by Morgan and Marvin Smith, Courtesy of Monica Smith and Schomburg, © Monica Smith.

15. DOROTHY WEST

Pages 234, 237, 238, 242, 243: The Dorothy West Collection, Special Collections, the Arthur and Elizabeth Schlesinger Library on the History of Women in America, Radcliffe College. **240, 244:** Courtesy of the Mugar Collection, Department of Special Collections, Boston University. **241:** Schomburg. **246, 247:** Photographs by Betsy Corsiglia, courtesy of the photographer.